WATERFRONT

A JOURNEY AROUND MANHATTAN

Harlem
Morrisania
Buchanan I.
Hell
Montresor I.
Bloomingdale
Advanced Posts
Horn's Hook
NORTH or HU
NEW YORK ISLAND
Kepps Bay
Turtle Bay
Roebuck
Newtown Creek
Stuyvesants Cove
Bushwick
NEW YORK
EAST RIVER
Paulus Hook
British Army on the 3rd of Septr.
Head of Bushwick Cree where the Six Transpo on Voluntary Service too a Number of Troops for supporting the first Division
British Brigade on the 15th of Septr.
Wallabout Bay
Brookland or Brooklyn
Governors I. occupy'd by the Hessians after the Battle

WATERFRONT

A JOURNEY AROUND MANHATTAN

PHILLIP LOPATE

CROWN PUBLISHERS

NEW YORK

The following pieces have been previously published, usually in altered form, in these publications: Parts of the "Introduction" and "The Dilemma of Waterfront Development" appeared in *Toward the Livable City*, Milkweed Editions, 2003; parts of "Battery Park City" appeared in "The Planner's Dilemma: Battery Park City," *7 days*, 1989; "The Harbor and the Old Port" appeared in *The Common Review*, 2002; "Washington Heights and Inwood," in *Hotel Amerika*, 2002; "Fish Story" (Fulton Fish Market), in *The New York Times*, 2001; parts of "On the Aesthetics of Urban Walking and Writing" appeared in "The Pen On Foot: The Literature of Walking Around," *Parnassus*, 1993, and in "Manhattan, Floating City," *The Place Within*, W. W. Norton, 1996; "The Brooklyn Bridge," in *Bridge of Dreams*, Hudson Hills Press, 1999; "Under the Bridges," in *The Saint Ann's Review*, 2003; and "Robert Moses," in *Metropolis*, 2002.

PUBLISHED BY CROWN PUBLISHERS

NEW YORK, NEW YORK.

Member of the Crown Publishing Group,
a division of Random House, Inc.
www.randomhouse.com

CROWN is a trademark and the Crown colophon is a
registered trademark of Random House, Inc.

Printed in the United States of America

Design by Marysarah Quinn

Library of Congress Cataloging-in-Publication Data
Lopate, Phillip, 1943–
Waterfront: a journey around Manhattan / Phillip Lopate.—
1st ed. 1. Manhattan (New York, N.Y.)—Description and travel. 2. New York (N.Y.)—Description and travel. 3. Waterfronts—New York (State)—New York. 4. Walking—New York (State)—New York. 5. Lopate, Phillip, 1943—Travel—New York (State)—New York. 6. Manhattan (New York, N.Y.)—Tours. 7. New York (N.Y.)—Tours. I. Title.
F128.55.L67 2004
917.47'10444.dc22   2003015056

ISBN 0-609-60505-4

10 9 8 7 6 5 4 3 2 1

FIRST EDITION

"If there is magic on the planet, it is contained in water."

—LOREN EISELEY

"Islands—I don't get them. Surrounded by water, poor things."

—PATRIZIA, in Antonioni's *L'Avventura*

CONTENTS

INTRODUCTION

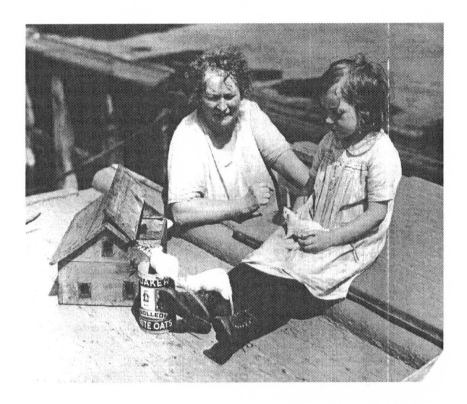

THIS BOOK BEGAN AS AN ATTEMPT TO WRITE A SHORT, LIGHTHEARTED BOOK ABOUT WANDERING THE WATERY PERIMETER OF MANHATTAN. I HAVE LONG BEEN FASCInated with walking-around literature, and everything about New York City. I thought I would write down whatever I was thinking and seeing in the course of my walk, including any encounters or adventures I might have. It was a quaint, likable idea, a sort of modern-day version of Robert Louis Stevenson's walks through France and England. But the first problem I encountered was that I could not pretend to be a tourist in my native city, discovering it with fresh wonder; I utterly lacked what the anthropologists call "culture shock." Moreover, I was no longer a young man, for whom any city walk could release buckets of lyrical verbiage; I had exhausted those sorts of poems and urban sketches earlier, for the most part. If I were to write about New York City now, it would have to be with the more reserved, critical perspective of a lifetime's accumulated uncertainties.

And I could not simply "meditate" (that last refuge of lazy belletrists such as myself) on what I saw, I would actually have to *know* something about the waterfront: its past, its economic importance, its ecological concerns and development constraints. Which raised the second problem, my ignorance. I've always had a generalist's smattering of background information, but that's a far cry from true understanding. So I started to read as well as walk. The more I researched, the more I saw that the evolving waterfront was the key to New York's destiny, as it is to many former port cities globally.

The advent of containerized shipping, with its demands for acres and acres of backspace to load, unload, store, and truck the containers, has meant that, over the last forty years, in city after city around the world, the port functions have had to be moved, sometimes seaward, inland, or upstream, to rural or suburban areas where there was more available cheap land. This severing of the age-old connection between city and port is having profound cultural and economic effects, which we may not fully grasp for some time. At the moment, all we know is that cities all over the map are faced with empty harbors, and lots of underutilized waterfront property.

Today, in my native New York City, the waterfront has become the great contested space. Newspapers regularly carry announcements of some plan for a stadium, recycling plant, sound stage, wetland, park, marina, ferry, electrical generator, or museum, that is then fought over by the local community board, developers, and municipal and state governments. Over the last few decades, New York, like Washington Irving's Rip van Winkle, always seems to be reawakening from long slumber to discover it possesses . . . a shoreline! "The new urban frontier" is what a 1980s Parks Council report called the city's waterfront, inviting, it would seem, the brash, gold-rush behavior often associated with American frontiers.

Why is it, then, that developing the waterfront continues to have a forced, reluctant quality, as if New Yorkers were trying to talk themselves into root canal? Are there unconscious resistances at work, which may need to be examined?

There is, first of all, this particular city's historic habit of turning inland. It has often been remarked that, unlike most great cities on water, which tease and flirt with their liquid edges in a thousand subtle, sensuous ways, New York has failed to maximize its aqueous setting. This underutilization of the waterfront is mentioned as a curious negligence, as if it just happened to have slipped the locals' minds. Actually, the main reason why this shoreline resource remained so long "untapped" is that it had been already allocated for maritime and industrial uses. These functions may not have provided the best urban design, public space, or environmental protection, but they were a huge economic motor driving the region's economy. So the present opportunity, bear in mind, stems from a vacuum left by the port's demise and relocation elsewhere.

Shabby and makeshift though much of the old working port may have been, its vitality issued from the way that purpose had dictated its construction. As more boats came in, as more docks were needed, they got built; warehouses were erected to hold the goods loaded off the ships; customs offices, shipping agents, chandlers and ropemakers, retailers of barrels and packing cases, brothels and seamen's churches, taverns and boardinghouses and union halls, all sprang up around the docks. Nothing can replace the beautiful, urgent logic of felt need. When it is met in an ad-hoc, accreted manner, urbanists speak glowingly of "organic" city growth. I put "organic" in quotation marks because I don't believe any large human endeavor such as constructing a metropolis can ever be spontaneous or unplanned—the term "organic" tends to cloak a good deal of maneuvering by powerful special interests, such as the shipping lobby; so let us say, then, "additive" or "incremental" instead of "organic," to connote the lot-by-lot assemblage of a classic New York streetscape.

Now that the old port is gone, and the river's edge sits dormant, waterfront recycling makes a certain sense ("We've got all this valuable riverview property close to the center of town, we got a populace starved for public access to water, we might as well do something about it"). But that reasoning still has a slightly abstract air, lacking as it does the keen urgency that commandeered the old port's growth. And that lack produces an ache—call it the ache of the arbitrary: we wish we could feel driven to redevelop the waterfront because the city's very life depended on it. Instead we are faced with more tepid drives: the profit motive of real-estate developers (but they can make money elsewhere), and the altruistic motive of community advocates for parks and a cleaner, greener environment. Yes, each of those interest groups may be passionately committed to their agendas; but there is not the same imperative to act promptly as in the past.

Some of the resistance is historical: Broadway and Central Park together had helped establish Midtown as the city's fashionable center, while its waterfront districts were associated with bad smells and low rents. All recent efforts to draw maximally upscale residential development to the water's edge have had to overcome that history, and the hierarchical superiority of the center to the periphery. In other words, however desirable a river view may be, for the wealthiest clientele it can never replace proximity to Central Park or Bergdorf's.

The sense of urgency is further vitiated by the incredibly long time that waterfront development projects seem to require, from inception to completion. Manhattan is now entering its fifth decade of waterfront "rebirth" (the original plans for Battery Park City were drawn up in 1961.) While New Yorkers might self-pityingly blame local corruption, the truth is it is a slow process everywhere. Waterfront projects are typically delayed five to ten years just by the complexities of achieving political consensus and government approvals; then there are the problems of site assembly, site clearance, environmental remediation, new infrastructure, and often millions in cost overruns. Hence, we who are living through the great leap forward of waterfront revitalization should cultivate patience, perspective, and reincarnation skills, because we may not see the changes in our lifetime.

There is also a clash between the waterfront zone—a separate corridor with redevelopment issues unto itself—and the neighborhoods it traverses. Traditionally the working waterfront has had a separate visual character, a more rough-hewn quality than the inland areas. The riverside highways that have come to rim the island compound the problem of getting to the Manhattan waterfront. These perimeter highways ignore the grid, or, rather, intentionally oppose a powerful counter to them, a moat between the everyday city and the water. They have also introduced disjunctions in scale, which can never be more than awkwardly reconciled, between highways meant for thousands of speeding cars and the buildings abutting them. In theological terms, the West Side Highway and the

Franklin D. Roosevelt Drive constitute the Original Sin of Manhattan planning. We may repent, we may patch, but—short of burying or lidding these highways, which would be very, very costly—we can never regain our wholeness.

NEW YORK'S WATERFRONT has undergone a three-stage revaluation, from a working port, to an abandoned, seedy no-man's-land, to a highly desirable zone of parks plus upscale retail/residential, each new metamorphosis only incompletely shedding the earlier associations. We may think of Manhattan's shoreline as a golden opportunity, a tabula rasa for leisure and luxury development, but the ghosts of stevedores, street urchins, and shanghaied sailors still haunt the milieu. Physically, no area of New York City has changed as dramatically as the shoreline, thanks to natural processes, landfill, dredging, and other interventions. Only by considering the waterfront's past can we account for New York's current, perplexing relationship to its future.

I WOULD HAVE BEEN HAPPY to write a traditional history of New York's waterfront, had I a historian's training, twenty years' leisure, and an independent income, but this book is not it. It is, however, saturated with history. Everywhere I walked on the waterfront, I saw the present as a layered accumulation of older narratives. I tried to read the city like a text. One textual layer was the past, going back to, well, the Ice Age; another layer was the present—whatever or whoever was popping up in my view at the moment; another layer contained the built environment, that is to say the architecture or piers or parks currently along the shore; another layer still was my personal history, the memories thrown up by visiting this or that spot; yet another layer consisted of the cultural record—the literature or films or other artwork that threw a reflecting light on the matter at hand; and finally there was the invisible or imagined layer—what I thought *should* be on the waterfront but wasn't. At any one point I would give myself the freedom to be drawn to this or that layer, in combination or alone.

Throughout, I walked the waterfront. The notion of one marathon circumambulation quickly gave way to a multitude of smaller walks in all seasons: when my legs got tired, or my head grew dizzy from absorbing impressions, I stopped for the day. In the end, I not only explored by foot the island's perimeter (including several stretches that seemed dicey or were closed to the public), I often revisited an area, reconnoitering the same ground until it spoke to me. Sometimes I brought along friends, who lightened my quest for the waterfront's soul. I made long-overdue pilgrimages to the Statue of Liberty, Ellis Island, the United Nations, and Gracie Mansion, all of which, as a native New Yorker, I had previously ignored. I also interviewed experts, and sampled the mixed pleasures of community board meetings and public hearings.

All along, I kept coming up against certain underlying questions: What is our capacity for city-making at this historical juncture? How did we formerly build cities with such casual conviction, and can we still come up with bold, integrated visions and ambitious works? What is the changing meaning of public space? How to resolve the antiurban bias in our national character with the need to sustain a vital city environment? Or reconcile New York's past as a port/manufacturing center, with the new model of a postindustrial city given over to information processing and consumerism?

No one book can tackle all such questions fully, much less respond to every inch of the waterfront, past and present. Gaps are unavoidable. I have had to restrict my scope to Manhattan, instead of covering all five boroughs and the extended New York harbor. Even so, I have had to be selective: what I've done is to look for representative stories or themes— to take soundings along the edge. In Part One, I make my way geographically up the West Side, from the bottom of the island to the top; in Part Two, I return to the island's southern tip, this time proceeding northward along the East Side's coast. The structure is as follows: I alternate accounts of my walks with digressions, which I call "excursuses," on individual topics that seemed to me characteristic of a larger pattern. These excursuses have been corralled into separate essays because they seemed to me too complex to deal with as throwaway insights along a walk.

The result is a mixture of history, guidebook, architectural critique, reportage, personal memoir, literary criticism, nature writing, reverie, and who knows what else. Consider it a catchment of my waterfront thoughts.

Writing about the Manhattan waterfront is like writing on water.

You've only to characterize some physical part of the cityscape or deliver an opinion on a current situation, for the reality to change next week. I am well aware that in years to come, much of what I have written in this book will sound dated, superseded as it will inevitably be by unforeseen circumstances. What can you do? I have described the waterfront I saw before me.*

The very fact that the waterfront remains so elusive and mutable has ultimately ensured its fascination for me: it has become the ever-enigmatic, alien fusion of presence and absence. Its meanings have needed to be excavated, its poetry unpacked. I hesitate to use that word "obsession," but, in my own limited way, I have become obsessed with the waterfront. I think about it when I drop off to sleep, and when I wake up; it forms a wavy limit hovering over my subconscious; I am quick to pick up any reference to it in periodicals, films, or overheard conversations. I have acquired the cultist's touchiness.

---

*Futurists predict big changes for the Manhattan waterfront. Global warming may further melt the ice cap, causing respiratory ailments and power brownouts. Starting in 2080, the raised sea levels may bring on huge storms that batter the New York coastline every three or four years. By that time I will seriously have to consider doing a revised edition of this book.

Map to come

A QUICK START-UP
OF MANNAHATTA

MANHATTAN IS SHAPED LIKE AN OCEAN LINER OR LIKE A LOZENGE OR LIKE A PARAMECIUM (WHAT REMAIN OF ITS PROTRUDING PIERS, ITS CILIA) OR LIKE A GOURD or like some sort of fish, a striped bass, say, but most of all like a luxury liner, permanently docked, going nowhere.

The Japanese of the early eighteenth century had a word, *ukiyo*, for the "floating world" of courtesans, actors, and rich merchants and their spoiled progeny who made up the town's most visible element. Manhattan is a floating world, too: buoyant as balsa, heavy as granite. The reason skyscrapers developed so readily on this spit of earth is that its bedrock, composed of Fordham schist, Inwood marble and White Mountain gneiss, was strong enough to withstand any amount of drilling. You can still bruise your ego against Manhattan's rough cheek. Like other island or aqueous cities—Istanbul, Venice, Hong Kong—it has a brash, arrogant energy far disproportionate to its size, and an uneasiness about domination by larger forces which it always tries to conceal.

The island of Manhattan extends about thirteen miles in length, and two miles across at its widest point. It rests in the arms of the Hudson (whose lower branch, alongside Manhattan, used to be called the North River) and the East River. Properly speaking, the East River is not a river but a saltwater estuary or strait, a leg of the sea. It connects with the Harlem River (also a tidal strait), which flows between the Bronx and the northern tip of Manhattan.

Seventy-five thousand years ago the glaciers began descending into the New York area, crushing the land, scooping out valleys and depositing boulders. The Ice Age was a period that, we know of a certainty, was extremely cold. Twenty thousand years later it was still rather cold; twenty thousand years after that, not quite so cold; twenty thousand years from that point, fairly chilly but approaching a tolerable coolness, suitable for human habitation. A mere eleven thousand years ago, as the glaciers were retreating and the seas rising, the first inhabitants arrived. In the final centuries of the Ice Age, these Paleoindians, as archaeologists call them, hunted mastodons with spears. Then they disappeared. In the Early Archaic period (10,000–8,000 B.P.), the Hudson River was still a fjord, the city's harbor had yet to be formed; in the Middle Archaic (8,000–6,000 B.P.), Native Americans began settling in, making tools and harvesting oysters; this was followed by the Late Archaic (6,000–3,700 B.P.), by which time the harbor had been formed and the sea levels were close to their current position. Following hard on the Late Archaic was the transitional period (3,700–2,700 B.P.), during which nothing very exciting happened, and then the Early and Middle Woodland (2,700–1,000 B.P.), a period of considerable pottery-making, hunting, fishing, and trading by the Munsees (a branch of the Lenape), but not much agriculture, surprisingly. This brings us to the arrival of the first Europeans.

The name "Manhattan," a Munsee tribe word, has been variously ascribed by linguists to mean "island," "place of general inebriation," or "place where timber is procured for bows and arrows." Washington Irving gave a more partial, tongue-in-cheek explanation in his *A History of New York:* "MANNA-HATA—that is to say, the island of Manna; or in other words—'a land flowing with milk and honey.'"

When Henry Hudson first sailed into the Upper Bay in 1609, searching for a westerly passage to China, he and the crew of the *Half Moon*, a Dutch ship, found a fair approximation to an isle of milk and honey. The natives met them in canoes with oysters the size of trays. (Later he was murdered by hostile Indians, but that's another story.) In 1624 the Dutch established an outpost at the southeastern tip of the island. Adriaen van der Donck, an early settler, described a place of streams and waterfalls and running brooks; copious wild turkeys that slept in the trees; a multitude of trout, striped bass, shellfish, and weakfish; natives "all properly formed and well-proportioned," who, despite their "particular aversion" to "heavy slavish labor," managed to grow maize, squash, and watermelon; an air "so dry, sweet and healthy that we need not wish that it were otherwise"; and, most important of all, beavers.

New York was founded on animal skins and oysters.*

The Dutch West India Company, granted a monopoly by the Netherlands government, ran New Amsterdam as a trading post, pure and simple. Almost immediately it attracted a polyglot, continental population, with forty languages spoken, and blacks, Jews, Portuguese, and Samoans intermingling. The Dutch found it a somewhat disappointing investment—less profitable, from their perspective, than Curaçao. When the British threatened in 1664, pointing cannons at Wall Street, the Dutch surrendered without a fight. Peter Stuyvesant, the Dutch governor, had

---

*One can never say enough about oysters. "The statistics on oysters alone were staggering. The area that includes New York Harbor and parts of the lower Hudson estuary had 350 square miles of oyster beds. Some biologists have argued that these beds alone produced more than half the world's supply of oysters," write Anne-Marie Cantwell and Diana diZerega Wall, the authors of *Unearthing Gotham*, a fine book about the archaeology of New York City. They wonder, however, how important oysters were to the Native Americans in the Archaic periods, since "a pound of shelled oyster meat adds up to only 475 calories. If that is the case, and if oysters did play a major role in the Archaic diet, then an average adult would have had to eat a staggering number of oysters, about 250 a day, to maintain daily caloric requirements." More likely, they speculate, oysters were eaten as a delicacy, or as a fallback food in starvation times.

wanted to defend it, but cooler, more mercantile heads prevailed. The next day they were doing business with the enemy.

Once upon a time, New York and New Jersey were part of the same British colony; then the Duke of York severed them—to pay off a gambling debt, according to legend. (Since then, politicians in Trenton and Albany have each tried to pretend that the Hudson River's problems affected only their own state lines). Both the Dutch and the British did not hesitate to tinker with Manhattan's shoreline, extending the waterfront streets outward through landfill, and giving love handles to its arrowhead profile at the island's southern tip. Swamps were filled in, piers built along the East River.

Very quickly the geographical advantages of New York's port were grasped: that it had a deep channel, sheltered from the ocean's rages, that it had a choice of two river routes leading to the sea (along either shore of Long Island), that it had a fairly mild climate and was rarely ice-choked in winter, compared with the more northern Boston or Halifax, that it had potentially good access to the western territories. In spite of this superiority to other American ports, it started slowly: in 1770 it ranked fourth, behind Philadelphia, Boston, and Charleston, in total tonnage. Yet its strategic importance seemed so manifest even then that, during the American Revolution, the British sent the largest naval force ever amassed to secure it.

They secured it. Washington's troops were forced to flee under cover of night, silently rowing across the East River, then the Hudson. New York spent most of the war as a Tory port. The British army stationed itself comfortably in Manhattan, drilling on Bowling Green, holding balls and wenching, a situation that may have contributed to the lingering mistrust of New York by patriotic Americans.

An extensive fire—either from sabotage or accident; we may never know—left much to rebuild after independence.

The look of Manhattan, its aesthetic destiny, so to speak, was sealed in 1811 with the approval of the commissioners' grid plan. This arrangement laid out a pattern of crisscrossed parallel bars for all the city's future thoroughfares, from above Houston Street to just below Washington Heights, disregarding any topographical impediments that might get in the way. The prevailing wisdom among today's planners is that it is important to honor the land's contours, which only goes to show how visionary the city fathers were: they created a New York as eccentrically "intentional" as St. Petersburg, a madly rational scheme imposed on nature. Nor did they have any use for the circles, ovals, and other geometric interventions so loved by Europeans. The commissioners loved the ninety-degree angle, the forthright, egalitarian plod of rectangle after rectangle, extended indefinitely: they would have gridded the sea and stars if given the chance.

One reason the city fathers liked the grid was that it facilitated the orderly sale and development of property. While one hears the Manhattan grid disparaged today as merely a capitalist device for real-estate speculation, to me it is a mighty form, existential metaphor, generator of modernity, Procrustean bed, call it what you will, a thing impossible to overpraise. The architect Rem Koolhaas called it "the most courageous act of prediction in Western civilization." It inspired Mondrian, Sol Lewitt, Agnes Martin, and that's good enough for me. Those who maintain it makes for monotony are at a loss to account for the vitality of Manhattan street life. They overlook this *particular* grid's power to invoke clarity, resonance, and pleasure through its very repetitions; they ignore the role of Broadway as a diagonal "rogue" street creating dramas of triangulation wherever it intersects an avenue (think, say, of 168th Street, 72nd Street, 59th Street, 42nd Street, 34th Street, 23rd Street . . .); and they forget variations in block length within the grid, which differentiate the petite, elegant poodle walks of the Upper East Side, say, from the long, punishing treks between avenue corners on the Upper West Side.

The grid pulls you ever forward, along those avenues that are the only true "streams" recognized by the New York pedestrian. Interestingly, the 1811 plan had rationalized its failure to provide for parks and other recreational breathers by stating that the island's river waterfronts would yield sufficient relief.

(The creation of Central Park, which opened in 1859, compensated in part for the 1811 grid plan's failure to provide for recreational spaces. Planted in the midst of the inland crowded streets to which New Yorkers were ever drawn, Central Park was the stroke of genius needed to complete the grid, by offering a counterpoint of man-made Nature: the largest and greenest of rectangles, superimposed on the checkerboard, immeasurably boosting land values; it drew like a magnet to its edges the most prestigious mansions and apartment buildings. "With the implantation of Central Park," wrote the historian Richard Plunz, "the morphology of modern Manhattan was firmly established: that of a luxurious center and of a marginal periphery in terms of residential real estate, and quite the opposite in terms of commercial and industrial property. In the Manhattan psyche, Central Park became the 'waterfront': a kind of 'green' sea. Bourgeois aspirations placed Manhattan in a park, rather than in the sea. Water was its lifeblood, but not its soul.")

To return to our chronological summary: the opening of the Erie Canal in 1825 secured the triumph of New York as a great port, by connecting the Atlantic seaport with the interior, all the way to Lake Erie. While the Erie Canal undoubtedly magnified the port's commercial importance, by bringing flour, wheat, lumber and other commodities from the frontier to the city, and transporting to the hinterlands those niceties of civilization Westerners wanted, other factors besides the canal, argued Robert Greenhalgh Albion in his classic study, *The Rise of New York Port* (*1815–1860*), may have contributed as significantly to the port's ascendance. First, there was the innovation of regularly scheduled ocean liners, such as the Black Ball Line, which contracted to leave at a certain date from New York and arrive at Liverpool on schedule, instead of dawdling from port to port, picking up a full complement of cargo. (Already the city was turning its temperamental impatience, the "New York minute," to commercial advantage.) Improvements in boat design made for faster ships, such as the famous China clippers. The East River Yards of Manhattan became a major center of quality shipbuilding. The city's banking institutions tied the hinterlands to New York as firmly as had the Erie Canal. Finally, the fact that the steamship was financed and perfected in New York gave the region a head start in that mode of traffic.

By 1860 the port of New York was handling 52 percent of the nation's combined imports and exports. The New York Custom House was the principal source of revenue of the federal government. An army of custom inspectors, including Herman Melville, collected duties there that, according to Albion, "were enough to pay the whole running expenses of the national Government, except the interest on the debt."

Part of this lucrative trade involved the Cotton Triangle, by which southern-grown cotton (in the first half of the nineteenth century,

America's most important export) passed through New York on its way to England and France. Though, geographically speaking, it made little sense to tack on several hundred miles' sea voyage by sending the cotton up north first, instead of shipping it directly from Charleston or New Orleans to Europe, New York's merchants and bankers were able to control the trade by financing the plantation owners' debts between crop payments. Some irate growers estimated that, when interest, commissions, insurance and shipping were factored in, the northerners had skimmed forty cents of every dollar paid for southern cotton. New York's deep commercial connections with the South led elements of its mercantile class to feel less than enthusiastic about the Union cause; that, plus the Draft Riots, gave the city a slightly Copperhead (pro-Confederate) reputation. As during the American Revolution, the rest of the country mistrusted New York's patriotism. No matter: after 1865, the city profited by the defeat of the South, just as it had by the war.

In the peacetime era that followed, the most important change affecting the city's form was the construction of the Brooklyn Bridge. Opening in 1883, this East River span, the "eighth wonder of the world," lost Brooklyn its status as an independent city and led to its incorporation, in 1898, with Queens, Staten Island, and the Bronx, into modern New York, all subordinated to Manhattan, the nerve center. In short order, a cat's cradle of the Manhattan Bridge, the Williamsburg Bridge, and many equally workaday bridges and tunnels (no longer wonders of the world) connected Manhattan to the other boroughs and New Jersey.

In northern Manhattan, Hell Gate, a section of the East River from 90th to 100th Streets that proved notoriously difficult to navigate (a thousand ships ran aground there in an average year) was tamed by the dynamiting and removal of its most treacherous rocks, in a complicated demolition project that stretched from 1851 to the mid-1880s. At the northern tip, in an area bounded by the Spuyten Duyvil Creek and the Harlem River, the Harlem River Ship Canal was dug, splitting the Marble Hill neighborhood from Manhattan and joining it to the Bronx.

Although the increasing use of steamships had shifted some maritime traffic from the East River to the Hudson in the mid-1850s, the piers along the East River in Lower Manhattan remained the center of the city's shipping until the start of the twentieth century. After that, the action moved to the Hudson River side, since ocean liners and tankers required a deeper channel and longer berths. In 1900, New York's shippers were still handling two-thirds of the nation's imports and one-third of its exports, a percentage that held throughout the massive increase in trade that occurred during World War I and into the early 1920s. Though the port began to lose market share by the mid-1930s, New York dock workers in 1950 were still unloading and dispatching nearly a third of all foreign cargo. They could still look back to the vital role the port of New York had played during World War II.

Twenty years later, Mannahatta's port, the one Walt Whitman had witnessed and sung ("hemm'd thick all around with sailships and steamships"), was dead. Supertankers and containerization required considerably more backspace (fifty acres per berth), such as could no longer be found in a dense metropolis. New York's maritime trade got shifted to New Jersey. With the concomitant loss of manufacturing, sweat-labor, for the most part, disappeared from the island.

Manhattan remained the world's financial capital, the nexus of global headquarters, a skyscraper magnet, and an endlessly self-celebrating concentration of media, culture, tourism, retail shopping, and restaurants. Still desirable, Manhattan retooled itself; its specialty became self-cannibalism, real estate. It now sold the image of itself. But Manhattan as solitary symbol has been overstressed, masking its interdependence on the larger region to which it belongs. The island is part of a 780-mile New York waterfront. To the north, Westchester, the suburbs, Albany; to the west, Newark, Arizona and so on, as Saul Steinberg would have said (or drawn).

PART ONE

THE WEST SIDE

Stand up, tall masts of Mannahatta! stand up,
  beautiful hills of Brooklyn!
Throb, baffled and curious brain! throw out
  questions and answers!
—WALT WHITMAN, "Crossing Brooklyn Ferry"

1

THE BATTERY

MY CLOSEST ESTIMATION OF THE BULBOUS V-POINT, THE MAGNETIC SOUTHERN TIP OF MANHATTAN ISLAND, IS THE STATEN ISLAND FERRY TERMINAL. It's a sunny winter day and, fortified by two cups of coffee and a poppy-seed bagel, I head to the terminal where one catches the boat to Staten Island.

For as long as I can remember, the scuzzy-looking terminal that was here until recently, abounding in pizza outlets, couldn't have been less impressive if it tried. It was to have been replaced long ago, first by a sober office tower designed by Kohn Pederson Fox, then by Venturi, Scott-Brown and Associates' playful terminal with a giant, iconic clock. But Staten Island politician Guy Molinari objected to having to stare at this whimsical timepiece, which he found insufficiently respectful of his oft-late-to-work commuters, and it was scrapped. Then architect Frederick Schwartz got the assignment, and has remade the terminal into an attractive, if very modest, corrugated steel box with waterfront views from an elevated public deck wrapped in blue and aquamarine glass.

I enter Battery Park, or, as it is historically known, the Battery (so named because of its cannons, which originally protected the harbor). It remains one of the most congenial parts of New York, its tree-filled grounds decompressing you from the financial district. Along the promenade, with its new, ergonomically correct walnut benches and pink marble backrests, you have the luxury to gaze out at the bay, then back to the parade of foreign tourists, locals, teenage girls arm-in-arm. "My imagination is incapable of conceiving any thing of the kind more beautiful than the harbour of New York," the visiting Frances Trollope wrote in 1832; "I doubt if ever the pencil of Turner could do it justice, bright and glorious as it rose before us . . . upon waves of liquid gold." The unhurried, ceremonial pace of meanderers along the promenade suggests a Spanish *paseo*—in any case, not what one usually associates with New York. The fact that the Battery has functioned in this way for so long adds to its appeal.

"In the year of our Lord one thousand eight hundred and four," wrote Washington Irving, "on a fine afternoon in the glowing month of September, I took my customary walk upon the Battery . . . where the gay apprentice sported his Sunday coat, and the laborious mechanic, relieved from his dirt and drudgery of the week, poured his weekly tale of love into the half averted ear of the sentimental chambermaid." During the day the park seems always popular, partly because the Statue of Liberty and Ellis Island ferries leave from it, partly because it has such juicy vistas. A well-worn recreation space, not even aspiring to the bucolic, the Battery works as a city park should, circulating people from the nearby skyscraper-thick streets to the water's edge.

Performers work the tourist crowds who are waiting for the next ferry. A West Indian with dreadlocks is playing "Santa Claus Is Coming to Town" on steel drums to one bunch, while an African contortionist in black shirt and red pants entertains another by twisting his legs around his neck and walking on his rump. Not an entirely appetizing sight, to my mind, though he releases his body-knot and comes up cheerfully for air, declaring, "Okay, folks, one dollar. Japanese—two dollars." A paterfamilias tells his children looking through coin-operated binoculars: "That's where Vito Corleone came over on a boat."

I wander over to the circular Castle Garden, historically the site of a fort, summer tea garden, concert hall, immigrant process center, and aquarium, and now the place to buy tickets to the Statue of Liberty/Ellis Island ferry. This moldy cinnamon donut, a spiffed-up ruin, has been rebuilt and remodeled so many times you would be hard pressed to feel any aura of the authentic emanating from its stones. But the gesture of retaining it is appreciated.

Originally built between 1808 and 1811, it was constructed about two hundred feet offshore in thirty feet of water, like a stable boat. This engineering feat was largely the achievement of Lieutenant Colonel Jonathan Williams, who covered the fort in stone thick enough to withstand hostile naval bombardment, and added iron filings to the mortar that held the façade together, which made the walls more durable and adaptable to a watery environment. Williams, one of the first professional military engineers in America, also designed Castle Williams on nearby Governors Island. In all, four batteries were installed to defend the harbor, and may have in fact helped dissuade the British from attacking the city during the War of 1812. A wooden bridge connected Castle Clinton to the Battery in Manhattan; ultimately it was made redundant by landfill.

In 1824 the federal government gave the fort to the city, which turned it into Castle Garden, a celebrated entertainment hall, where "the Swedish Nightingale," Jenny Lind, first sang on her American tour. In 1850, after the premiere of *La Sonnambula*, New York's indefatigable diarist, George Templeton Strong, wrote: "Everybody goes, and nob and snob, Fifth Avenue and Chatham Street, sit side by side fraternally on the hard benches. Perhaps there is hardly so attractive a summer theatre in the world as Castle Garden when so good a company is performing as we have here now. Ample room; cool sea breeze on the balcony, where one can sit and smoke and listen and look out at the bay studded with the lights of anchored vessels, and white sails gleaming. . . ."

In 1855, during a peak immigration period (more than 319,000 immigrants reached the New York port in 1854 alone), Castle Garden was converted into a reception hall for the entering masses. Before this innovation, those who came over in steerage had been routinely fleeced by runners at the docks, who stole their luggage or steered the newcomers to outrageously overpriced boardinghouses. These runners and touts often spoke the same language as their confused countrymen, the better to exploit their trust. Entering at Castle Garden, however, the immigrant could take stock, receive honest advice, and make further transportation arrangements at normal rates. In William Dean Howells's fine novel *A Hazard of New Fortunes,* the Marches approve of "the excellent management of Castle Garden, which they penetrated for a moment's glimpse of the huge rotunda, where the emigrants first set foot on our continent. . . . No one appeared troubled or anxious; the officials had a conscientious civility; the government seemed to manage their welcome as well as a private company or corporation could have done."

It is interesting to contrast this rosy picture with the testimony of one who actually went through the processing line, Abraham Cahan (in his classic immigrant novel, *The Rise of David Levinsky*): "We were ferried over to Castle Garden. . . . The harsh manner of the immigration officers was a grievous surprise to me. As contrasted with the officials of my despotic country, those of a republic had been portrayed in my mind as paragons of refinement and cordiality. My anticipations were rudely belied. 'They are not a bit better than Cossacks,' I remarked to Gitelson. . . . These unfriendly voices flavored all America with a spirit of icy inhospitality that sent a chill through my very soul."

The immigrant station at Castle Garden was closed in 1890; two years later the much more famous one at Ellis Island opened. In 1900 Castle Garden reinvented itself as the city's aquarium, around which time the journalist John C. Van Dyke compared it to "a half-sunken gas tank." Now Ellis Island beckons as the revered national landmark of immigration, while the rotunda-less, roofless Castle Garden operates as a sort of glorified tickets booth to that attraction.

THIS AREA NEAR THE TIP of the island was once thick with piers and docks. There used to be some seventy-five piers between the Battery and 59th Street. Now there are only thirteen left. The New York system of narrow, perpendicular "finger" piers that jutted out one after another, each holding a ship at a time, came about because the merchants could pack more vessels in that way, on an island with a fairly limited shoreline, than by having each boat tie up parallel to the land. The very advantage of New York's port, its sheltered harbors and deep waters, where any wooden pier would do to tie up at, deterred the city fathers from the large capital investments made by less geographically fortunate ports, such as Liverpool, which built majestic, palatial stone piers to hold off the fierce, crashing ocean waves. A slapdash setup ("the miserable wharves, and slipshod, shambling piers of New York," Herman Melville wrote in his 1849 novel, *Redburn*) was also justified at the time by the argument that ships kept getting wider and longer; thus it made little sense to "commit" to an expensive, heavy pier that would only have to be changed again in several years.

Besides pragmatic reasons, there almost seems something in the character of New Yorkers that prefers the rough-and-ready, provisional solution to the perfected, built-for-the-ages approach, just as there is a tolerance for dirt and clutter that far exceeds the standards of tidiness in many metropolises. The New Yorker gets a thing off and running and says, "Good enough." Perhaps it has something to do with the city's polyglot immigrant population, which never developed a culturally homogeneous, bourgeois communal standard, as in Holland or Japan, or perhaps it stems from the fact that, unlike other colonies in the New World, New York was not founded to serve some religious or civic utopian ideal, but solely to make money. Whatever the reasons, by 1872 an editorial writer in *Scribner's Monthly* was already commenting: "It must be a matter of serenest satisfaction and the most complacent pride that we, who have the reputation of being a city of money-getters and worshipers of the useful and the material, can point to our docks as the dirtiest, most insufficient, and the least substantial of any possessed by any first-class city on the face of the globe. To the strangers who visit us from abroad we can proudly say: You have accused us of supreme devotion to the material grandeur of our city and our land. Look at our rotten and reeking docks, and see how little we care for even the decencies of commercial equipment. . . ."

The waterfront was especially notorious for its muck. Edith Wharton, recalling that era in her memoir *A Backward Glance,* wrote: "I remember once asking an old New Yorker why he never went abroad, and his answering: 'Because I can't bear to cross Murray Street.' It was indeed an unsavoury experience, and the shameless squalor of the purlieus of the New York docks in the 'seventies dismayed my childish eyes. . . ."

ON THE NORTHERN END of the Battery sits Pier A, another eternally promised restoration job. No one can pass by that elegant, dilapidated Victorian structure (formerly the Fireboat House) without admiring its Beaux Arts shell, and fantasizing some amazing use for it. A visitors' center with retail or restaurant is proposed, you learn with a thud. The developer who was most recently brought in to revive it, a loyal Republican appointed by Governor George Pataki, claims to have gone bankrupt, and now there is much finger-pointing all around.

Pier A was originally one of two piers (the other, Pier 1, is now buried under landfill) to be constructed out of granite and ornamented with tinplate. In 1870, Peter Cooper, the millionaire manufacturer, urged the city to build all-stone piers, but his advice was not taken, except for these two, whose construction proved so costly that the rest were made of timber, and are now, appropriately, in various stages of rotting. Pier A is one of the only tangible signs left of that heroic and ingenious, if now mostly forgotten, effort—the greatest public-works project of its period—to improve the New York waterfront, which dragged on for six decades, from 1870 to 1930. (So important was it that George McClellan, the former Civil War general and 1864 presidential candidate, was appointed as its first engineer-in-chief, to lead New York City's Department of Docks and oversee its challenges). As ambitious, in its way, as the Brooklyn Bridge, employing more than a thousand workers, the Department of Docks' project erected a continuous concrete bulkhead or riverwall below sea level to "hold in" Manhattan Island and protect it from ramming boat hulls; transformed the island's geography by landfill; removed underwater reefs and shoals; constructed dozens of piers; dredged where necessary; and in every other way helped promote the Port of New York as a thriving commercial enterprise.

"The netting of the whale—in this case, the enclosing of its outline by the construction of bulkheads following the shape of the island—was a military action against a natural landscape, initially led by a Civil War general who was determined to triumph. The whale was to be molded or cast into a tight corset," wrote architect John Hejduk. It seems a paradox that, on the one hand, so much engineering effort was expended on recasting the waterfront's infrastructure, and, on the other, so little of the civic and cultural pride that had been lavished on other municipal projects percolated through sufficiently to elevate it above the makeshift. Le Corbusier, visiting New York in the early 1940s, wrote: "Along the avenue which skirts the river, the docks and ships form the teeth of a comb as far as you can see. The arrangement is clear, logical, perfect: nevertheless, it is hideous, badly done, and incongruous; the eye and the spirit are saddened. Ah! If the docks could be done over again!"

The docks will never be done over again, for shipping, but Le Corbusier may get his wish in the form of new recreational piers proposed for Hudson River Park. When the day arrives and they are all in place, surfboards and skates agleam, a part of us may long for the old, slipshod comb. Speaking of which, after September 11th, with the sudden need for increased ferry service, a temporary, tentlike ferry dock has been constructed of vinyl and steel rods, and run perpendicular to the midsection of Pier A, into the Hudson River. A vendor has installed a wagon inside the tent to sell hot dogs and pretzels to the waiting travelers. It is pleasing to see the ad-hoc, provisional genius of the New York docks surfacing again.

Before leaving the Battery, I note the rather morbid monument to the Merchant Marines, an academic-realist statue by ex-Pop artist Marisol, which depicts a seemingly fruitless attempt to rescue drowning seamen, who disappear between the incoming tide and emerge from its ebb.

2
BATTERY PARK CITY

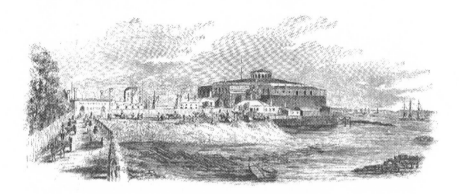

WHERE THE BATTERY IS POROUS, GRUNGY, DEMOCRA-TIC, BATTERY PARK CITY IS CONTROLLED, SELEC-TIVE, AND POLITE. BATTERY PARK CITY'S SOUTHERN end has an imposing iron gate, with a security guard's sentinel hut, and signs that say do not enter. Curiously enough, the gates have been left open in one area, a test of your sense of entitlement: if you feel sufficiently privileged (i.e., some combination of white/middle class/educated/solvent), you may pass through them into Battery Park City without announcing your presence to the guard, who is there, it would seem, to keep away only people with self-doubts.

After 11:00 P.M., however, the gates are closed to all except Battery Park City residents, who in any case tend to regard the waterfront parks next to their apartment buildings as their exclusive preserve. This tension between public space and private enclave pursues you throughout your perusal of the complex's extensive grounds.

By global standards, Battery Park City is a huge success. Delegations from cities around the world constantly consult it as a model of waterfront redevelopment—as much for its financing mechanisms as for its built environment. Certainly, you have to give the Battery Park City Authority credit for the creation from scratch of a middle-to-upper-middle-class neighborhood that operates in the black, adds to the municipal tax coffers, contributes mightily to Lower Manhattan's public spaces and waterfront access, and is reasonably pleasant to look at—if not architecturally vibrant, then by no means hideously ugly. Many cities would drool at the chance to replicate those results.

A native New Yorker like myself, on the other hand, may still regard it as something of a transplanted organ that has never quite taken hold. It still feels like landfill, or an insular theme park, City World. It seems to have everything you would need for a good Manhattan neighborhood, except a pulse. It's a cyborg, a clone, a replicant. One time, wandering around Battery Park City, I realized I was going to be late for my next appointment across town, and had started scheming how many blocks east I would have to walk before I met a cab, when an unoccupied taxi pulled into the cul-de-sac alongside me. I had not imagined that ordinary yellow cabs could penetrate the theoretical shield that surrounds Battery Park City and cruise its pretend boulevards.

BATTERY PARK CITY occupies a narrow strip of landfill, ninety-two acres long, extending from just north of Pier A, near the southern tip of Manhattan, to Chambers Street. It was built at a cost of $4 billion (a late-1980s figure). There are three zones, for purposes of discussion, into which Battery Park City should be divided: the residential blocks, the commercial/office high-rises that constitute the World Financial Center, and the parks and squares that form its public spaces. I will begin with the residential area, because there is where the grand experiment of urban design took place. But to explain what I mean, I will need to provide some historical background.

The idea for the complex first surfaced in the early sixties, under Governor Nelson Rockefeller's administration. The language of his February 1, 1966, message suggests that the project was sold as one that would avoid the brutalities of previous urban renewals: "Because space is at a premium in Manhattan, replacement usually requires displacement. To make room for progress, people's lives are uprooted and beauty is often bulldozed. . . . Now the opportunity exists to add to Manhattan's distinctive locales without making any such sacrifices. The development of Battery Park City adjoining the new World Trade Center presents an opportunity unique for Manhattan: the creation, literally from the ground up, of a large-scale, imaginatively planned community comprising residential, business, light industry, and recreational facilities." The light industry component quickly got scrapped, and the promised inclusion of low-income or "affordable housing" was put indefinitely on hold, but the landfill began.

For thirteen years the project remained nothing but a sandy white beach (some may remember sunbathing there or visiting the annual "Art on the Beach" exhibitions), stalled by complexities of planning, bureaucratic rivalries, and New York's fiscal crisis in the 1970s. "It sat like the Sahara off lower Manhattan," remarked Robert Wagner Jr., then a city councilman. Meanwhile, many noted architects, from Philip Johnson on down, took their crack at proposing futurist, space-station plans, Corbusian in their disdain for the typical New York streetscape. The original plan called for superblocks (those seemingly unending sidewalks) punctuated by apartment towers, our very own Brasilia. The first of these bland edifices, Gateway Towers, did go up. The rest of the complex remained in limbo.

Faced with bankruptcy in the dire bond-market days of 1979, the Battery Park City Authority decided to alter its course and, in their words, "look at the site afresh." The BPCA's then-chairman, Richard Kahan, turned to the design firm of Cooper, Eckstut Associates to come up with a new master plan. At the time, Alexander Cooper and Stanton Eckstut were unusual in the field of urban design (then riddled with garden-city utopians hostile to Gotham), because these two partners loved New York's density, diversity, and sidewalk vitality. Their notion was to create an area that would feel recognizably New York, by employing familiar materials and street patterns. The Cooper, Eckstut master plan rested on two premises: first, to avoid the usual antiurban design mistakes which had plagued large postwar projects (the superblock, the isolated, monotonously repetitive buildings that stood around like lunar objects, the lack of contextual relationship to the city nearby); and second, to learn from, even copy, the most successful high-rise neighborhoods in New York City, such as West End Avenue, Riverside Drive, Central Park West, Gramercy Park, Tudor City, Sutton Place.

Key to the plan was street layout. Stanton Eckstut put it this way: "The real design control comes not even from the buildings, it comes from the street plan. The city is set in motion there. Where are the avenues and the squares and esplanades? If I stopped right there, I could influence the shape of the city forever."

Eckstut is a thin, proud man with a full head of curly, graying hair, a trim Vandyke beard and mustache, warm, restless eyes, and, like many architects, a self-conscious manner of dress, given to red bow ties and matching striped shirts. His idea was first to create a pro-pedestrian environment in Battery Park City and then have the buildings respond to it. So the master plan laid out a traditional Manhattan grid, extending the east-west grid of the city's existing streets wherever possible, to knit the project more to its surroundings, and provided one slightly curved boulevard for visual interest. The promenade along the Hudson River would bring the project gracefully onto the water, and provide a place for the public to stroll; the recreational green spaces designed into the plan also would be urbane, rather than trying for an isolated Shangri-la.

The developers and architects who wished to build in Battery Park City would have to follow Cooper, Eckstut's strict guidelines, which were partly intended to connect the separate buildings visually through shared cues, and partly to reverberate with associations of their dignified forebears. These rules included using stone at the building's base, to give importance and human scale to the street level; brick above the stone base; and an articulated roof of some sort, for a varied skyline effect: in short, the familiar tripartite apartment building of base, shaft, and shaped roof that one sees, for instance, all along West End Avenue. Buildings would have to begin at the street wall and connect to each other in a continuous, unbroken line; cornices, changes in window, corner details, and other ornamental "expression lines" were encouraged, to break up the façades, particularly in taller buildings. No narcissistic, free-standing glass boxes. The emphasis would be on the totality of the ensemble.

Though the project has been criticized for its retro aesthetic, as its guidelines seemed to play into the hands of the postmodernists' historical eclecticism, Eckstut insisted the point was rather to offer the sort of comfortable apartment-house model that had been proven to work in the past, and that would put New Yorkers at ease. The guidelines, he argues, might just as easily have stimulated originality as inhibited it. As it happened, the participating architects chose to produce safe buildings that seemed like knockoffs of the past. "I wasn't really seeking great architecture," Eckstut admitted to me. "I like doing background buildings." The case for the background building, which doesn't show off or demand attention but fits in, in a neighborly fashion, with the rest of the street, springs from the valid notion that great cities are not necessarily the product of sublime architecture, but of certain basic, anonymously repeated building types. Still, a city with nothing but background buildings would be sad, missing out on a chance to shine.

The final guideline the BPC master plan had up its sleeve was that no one architect could impose his vision on the whole; each would get only one building to design, thereby ensuring a parti-textured diversity that would suggest, albeit in speeded-up form, the incremental way New York streets had traditionally gotten built.

The state legislature approved the master plan. It was familiar, people could picture it, and at the same time it was a very sophisticated urban design—architect-proof, in a sense. Even an ugly building would function adequately as part of the overall pattern. One of the side effects of Battery Park City was the momentary ascension of the once-lowly urban designer over the architect. A new star was born.

Shortly after, a collision of egos led to the Cooper, Eckstut design firm splitting up, and in the "divorce settlement," Cooper was given the northern sector of Battery Park City to oversee, and Eckstut the southern, residential end.

More than twenty years later, with most of that residential complex built, it is striking to see how much of Cooper, Eckstut's guidelines have been translated into reality without significant dilution. For instance, the buildings closest to the water had been drawn in at a lower scale, to avoid blocking out the sunlight of the buildings behind them, and so they stand today. Sunlight and river views—some of the most spectacular in the city—have been maximized for each structure. The goal of having a variety of building types, five-story townhouses and thirty-story apartment buildings, dovetail smoothly, has been realized without fuss.

Rector Place, the ensemble of grand apartment buildings around a civilized park rectangle, works, up to a point. The architecture won't make anyone's heart skip—today's bricks look so much blander and flatter, the effect is cartoonlike in comparison to the old apartment houses—but Charles Moore's extravaganza, River Rose, rises above the average, with its playfully chromatic art deco touches, and Parc Place, by Gruzen Samton Steinglass, holds its corner with a soberly majestic Upper West Side assurance.

Ironically, while these buildings may strike a nostalgic New York chord, they have very little to do with their immediate context, the Wall Street financial district. The stately proportions of buildings on West End Avenue and Sutton Place developed much later than the narrow, corkscrew Dutch lanes of downtown Manhattan. The master plan's intention to "extend the grid" evades the fact that lower Manhattan does not really operate according to the same orthogonal street grid that prevails above 14th Street.

A second irony is that the façades of these luxury apartment houses in Battery Park City deceptively suggest, by their historical references, the same roomy, high-ceilinged interiors one finds in pre–World War II apartment buildings. In actuality, most of the apartments' rooms are smaller, their halls narrower, their ceilings lower and walls thinner. "By putting more money into the skins of buildings," one architect complained in the magazine *Progressive Architecture*, "the developers cut corners on the interiors."

The final, most telling irony is that Rector Place still feels like a stage set. It incorporates all the most up-to-date urbanistic wisdom, but it's not fully alive. Like so much of Battery Park City, there's no street life, no random pedestrian flow. Rector Park, with its herringbone paving bricks and ornamental fence, may not be padlocked the way Gramercy Park, its obvious model, is, but it gives off the same signals. As the *AIA Guide to New York City* maliciously puts it: "Rector Park is veddy, veddy propuh, using the finest materials very carefully detailed. Meant to be looked at, not played in."

Battery Park City's residents have often had to trek many blocks for basic necessities; yet the shops along the South End Avenue arcade haven't done especially well, languishing from paucity of foot traffic. Some blame the design of the arcade, a concrete "colonnade," dark and uninviting to walk under; but the real problem is the incomplete grafting of a city spirit onto this sedate landfill community. Shopping is an appetite stimulated by complex environmental cues; you can lay down a street and designate it "retail" and it still won't necessarily hop to that beat.

Battery Park City—like Roosevelt Island, if to a lesser degree—feels cut off from the rhythms of New York. Its very aloofness could be an asset:

there aren't many places so detached from the hurly-burly. When I walk about it at night, especially by the water, I sense the wonderful, moody self-containment of the place, its dignified composure, its idealistic optimism, and I am tempted to live there. But then I remember: I would miss the city too much.

The greatest obstacle standing between Battery Park City and the rest of Manhattan is West Street. Hardly just a street, this eight-to-ten-lane roadway used to be the tailbone of the West Side Highway. At the moment, West Street is a car-choked, pothole-happy immensity, risky to cross on foot. As I waited for a clearing in traffic, a doorman warned me, "You gotta be careful, you get run over. You better run like hell!"

You can cross West Street by taking overhead pedestrian bridges, but this is an inconvenient hassle: raised walkways between buildings are unnatural for New Yorkers and break the pattern of pedestrian wandering. Getting across West Street might be worth the nuisance if you had an extensive neighborhood to explore; but Battery Park City is a thin finger of land, two or three blocks deep at most.

The strongest incentive for making that effort is to enjoy Battery Park City's extraordinary suite of waterfront parks and promenades, from the Beaux Arts order of the Esplanade, to the grand plaza of the World Financial Center, to the family-friendly Governor Nelson A. Rockefeller Park, with its children's playground and volleyball court, which curves behind Stuyvesant High School.* Starting at the southernmost end, next to the Battery, is the Robert F. Wagner Jr. Park, with its broad lawns. A rather stiff, monumental brick arch holds a café, restrooms, and a staircase that leads to a viewing platform that faces dramatically, across the bay, the Statue of Liberty. These Battery Park City parks frame, in as many different ways as possible, the Lady of the Harbor. The Robert F. Wagner Jr. Park also holds the Museum of Jewish Heritage and Living Memorial to the Holocaust, with its Mayan-pyramid-like stepped roof by Kevin Roche. (An outscaled new wing is presently under construction). I was initially dubious about the necessity for this Museum of Jewish Heritage,

---

*Though it is not part exactly a park, I would also like to mention the miraculously strange Irish Hunger Memorial: a replica of a bleak Hibernian hut and hill, perfect for seeing on a drizzly day, located in Battery Park City's Vesey Street and North End Avenue.

given that the city already has a Jewish Museum uptown; but I found the exhibits informative and moving. The large, bare, upper loft space with its myriad river-view windows is the place to be on a sunny day.

The next park moving north, South Cove, is to me the jewel of the complex. There is something mysterious and, above all, intimate about South Cove, with its haunting blue-glassed lanterns and wooden bridges that creak underfoot. Leaning over the wooden bridge, with waves slapping against the algae-covered pilings, you have the sense of being much closer to the water than at the nearby Esplanade. Alongside the bridge, the arrangement of rocks suggest a Japanese rock garden, while the wild rushes and other plantings present a rugged scene that might have been glimpsed by the first Dutch settlers. Incredibly, this serene retreat is but a half-mile from Wall Street, which can be glimpsed like a dream backdrop if you turn your head eastward.

All coves have something special about them: the world changes within their arms, becomes softer, more tidal. This insight seems to have guided the South Cove's designers: sculptor Mary Miss, landscape artist Susan Childs, and architect Eckstut. The result is a rare meeting of the natural and the constructed: curved metal bridges nicely complicate the choices for wandering, while a spiraling, tilted observation tower, whose oval top wittily quotes the Statue of Liberty's crown, offers a romantic outpost for lovers.

Just north of South Cove is the aforementioned Esplanade, a straight concourse edging the residential sector, and a perfect place to stroll, bicycle, jog, or meditate on the passage of the river. Tastefully done, its innovation, if you will, was to eschew novelty, and borrow a vocabulary of materials already familiar to New Yorkers from Central Park and Carl Schurz Park: the gray hexagonal flagstones, the curved iron railings, the comfortable benches that are replicas of those at the 1939 World's Fair, and the old-fashioned gaslight stanchions. Stan Eckstut, who designed the Esplanade, now says, "In hindsight, my biggest mistake was using those old-fashioned lampposts." He agrees with criticism that the Esplanade's New York's Greatest Hits design wasted an opportunity to evolve new prototypes for light stanchions and park furniture. But at the time, Battery Park City was an iffy proposition, and it was necessary to reassure investors with familiar visual touches. In any case, the Esplanade works beautifully as a public space. Let's leave it at that.

Farther north along the river's edge, you come into the spacious North Cove, with its marina and plaza, in front of the World Financial Center. The plaza is very large, and opens onto the river in a dramatic fashion that suggests, at sunset, the landing pier before Piazza San Marco in Venice. It could accommodate a huge crowd in a festival, and provide the sense of a ceremonial entrance to the city. Unfortunately, since it opened, the marina has essentially been a parking lot for luxury yachts going nowhere; post-9/11, the crossings of water taxis at least bring some maritime activity to the cove.

What makes the plaza itself special is the tremendously expansive openness of the vista. The multiple levels invite walking around. There is also a wonderful literary homage in the form of an iron fence: you walk along it reading, letter by letter, lines from Walt Whitman and Frank O'Hara. ". . . City of the sea! City of wharves and stores—city of tall façades of marble and iron! Proud and passionate city!" rhapsodizes Whitman. Frank O'Hara's wised-up voice tells us: "One need never leave the confines of New York to get all the greenery one wishes—I can't even enjoy a blade of grass unless I know there's a subway handy, or a radio store or some other sign that people do not totally regret life." As it happens, no subway comes into Battery Park City, and the shops of Radio Row were obliterated long ago by the World Trade Center. In fact, both quotes, meant to celebrate the ongoing spunk of New York, read like unconscious valedictions: in Whitman's case, for the bustling port whose demise led to this tame, provincial replacement, with its echoes of Baltimore Harbor; in O'Hara's, for the 1950s Manhattan street that generously threw up casual surprises—such as still exist across town, but nowhere near the suburban-mall premises of the adjacent World Financial Center.

Battery Park City's World Financial Center consists of four homogeneous jumbo towers, thirty-four to fifty stories high, comprising 8 million square feet of office, retail, and public space. The original guidelines by Alexander Cooper for this commercial office development had called for seven or eight buildings of a more slender, classically skyscraper form, all done by different architects. However, in 1979, Olympia and York, a Toronto-based realty firm (and at that time the largest developer in North America, before it came to grief in another new-town waterfront project,

London's Canary Wharf), pledged to build the entire World Financial Center. This major financial commitment, more than anything else, allowed Battery Park City to take off. The drawback was that it also consolidated too much land under one developer, who hired a single architect for the whole project. Cesar Pelli, an international star, had evolved from bolder projects in the 1970s, such as Los Angeles's blue-whale Pacific Design Center, to a suavely discreet, late-modernist style, the architectural equivalent of Giorgio Armani. The first financial giants who signed on to the World Financial Center—Merrill-Lynch, American Express, Dow Jones, Oppenheimer & Company—demanded huge, unbroken 40,000-square-foot floors; and Pelli obliged with a design that would accommodate these widebodies, at the same time trying to minimize the beefiness by a filmy curtain-wall skin with flat little windows and maroon or dark blue squares, which suggest a child's peel-off blocks. The resulting structures are like Macy's Thanksgiving Day Parade balloons, airless yet taking up considerable room—much chunkier than the old filigreed skyline of lower Manhattan.

As it is, the World Financial Center resembles nothing so much as an office park in Houston, like the Four-Clover Center, which Pelli also designed. It employs the same corporate campus vocabulary: a superblock; four "object" skyscrapers separated by uncomfortably large distances from each other and turning their backs to the street; a politely suburban grass slope; raised bridges between buildings to circumvent the weather; retail shops buried inside; and an overall visual monotony. Pelli has topped each of the towers with a different geometric configuration—mastaba, dome, pyramid, stepped pyramid—but essentially they are all the same building.

The interiors follow the same pattern of discreet corporate pomp: black columns, marble floors, rotunda lobbies that quickly dead-end. It's ironic that something grandiosely self-styled "the World Financial Center" should show so few public signs of the business activity ostensibly taking place within its walls. You come to a complex with such a name expecting to see, smell, or hear evidence of "filthy lucre" passing hands; and all you are given are boutiques, bookstores, temporary art exhibits, restaurants. At the very least, it would have been nice to have a public viewing gallery overlooking one of the trading floors, such as the New York Stock

Exchange offers. Compared with Wall Street, that narrow ghetto of passions, where the hoarse futures traders, elderly messengers, and young runners rub elbows, argue the headlines, and grab a quick hot dog before diving back into the fray, the World Financial Center has the abstract ambience of a new conference center. Some eerie social selection seems to have weeded out the colorful Wall Street characters, the old-timers, street vendors, shoeshine men, errand boys, loiterers, not to mention drifters or lowlifes, and left only men and women in dark suits and gray flannel decorously passing each other in cool, neutral hallways.

Many of the people who work in the World Financial Center are commuters from the tri-state area. What the center gives them is a work environment that quarantines them from the city: they can arrive on trains or commuter buses, take the elevator to their desks, do all errands within the connected buildings, and never have to interact with the ungainly streets of New York. The sadness of Battery Park City is that it may never feel part of the city; its smugness is that it may not want to be.

New Yorkers who work elsewhere have little reason to travel to the World Financial Center for shopping, since most of its retail outlets are branches of ubiquitous stores. There is, of course, the Winter Garden, the World Financial Center's dramatic indoor public space, with its sixteen palm trees and frequent free performances. At first I was swept away by the improbably giddy grandeur of the place: its ribbed, vaulted glass roof, its immense staircase ideal for royal balls. On subsequent visits I felt hemmed in by the retail outlets and food courts that made it seem less a true public space than a leftover from mall shopping. The celebrated palm trees, meant to suggest columns, are forbidding and severe, thanks to their spiky, plasticlike bark—not a tree you want to get close to. I would have preferred a real winter *garden*, lush, verdant and steamy.

The Winter Garden has recently been restored and reopened (it had to be closed, after taking a heavy blow from a pedestrian bridge shoved into its midsection on September 11, 2001). One feels guilty picking on Battery Park City after all it has gone through since September 11. Before that grim event, the complex was on a roll, full of new construction projects, its desirability as an address unquestioned. Then came the attack on the World Trade Center: residents living in nearby Battery Park City had to be evacuated; many could not return to their apartments for half a year or more; and once they were back, they were forced to deal with ashes, inoperative telephones, and damaged property, worry about toxic air, and bear witness to the solemn excavation at Ground Zero and the uncanny absence of the Twin Towers.

3

THE WORLD
TRADE CENTER

T HE WORLD TRADE CENTER HAD THIS FASCINATING
OPACITY: TWO STEEL-GRAY SLABS STOPPING THOUGHT.
THE MORE YOU LOOKED AT IT, THE LESS IT GAVE YOU
back. The Twin Towers came out of the minimalist aesthetic of late-1960s
Donald Judd sculptures: their only decorative adornments were those
elongated aluminum Y's, provoking you by their tight-lipped abstraction,
like the filigreed arches on the windows of mosques, or like a series of
whys. Were the towers clones derived from the DNA of some Platonic
ideal? Were they emblematic of containerization, which had destroyed the
Port of New York—the container being that standard, infinitely replicable
rectangle, everywhere the same height, length, and depth? Shining like
aluminum altars, 1,350 feet tall, the Twin Towers were our Stonehenge.
Their architect, Minoru Yamasaki, was asked why he made two of them,

side by side, instead of one gigantic structure, and he is said to have replied (the story may be apocryphal, but it's a good one anyhow) that double the height would have destroyed human scale.

I never found them offensive or overbearing, but neither did I love them; they didn't invite dislike, they were well-mannered, eight-hundred-pound gorillas in tuxes, having no need to beat their chests. (When they replaced the Empire State Building in the remake of *King Kong,* they offered the creature a too-smooth, unvaried façade to convey precarious mountain perching.) They were at once the most dominant and least assuming facet of the New York skyline: Don't mind me, they said.

It took seven years and a billion dollars to build them. Putting together the deal required immense muscle, supplied by David Rockefeller at the Chase Manhattan Bank, his brother Nelson, then governor of New York (who stocked one tower with state workers when the building failed to attract tenants), and the considerable resources of the Port Authority of New York and New Jersey. Austin Tobin, then head of the Port Authority, kept up the masquerade that the spanking new towers were somehow going to be given over to trade and port functions.

"How did the Port Authority—chartered to safeguard the economic health of New York's regional maritime commerce—become the agent, a half century later, of the port's displacement and decline? And what caused America's most venerable planning and development agency—once imbued with the high-minded public service doctrines of Woodrow Wilson—to transform itself into the world's biggest real estate speculator?" demanded Eric Darnton in his book about the World Trade Center, *Divided We Stand.* Though the agency probably could not have done much to keep the port in Manhattan, it does take gall to present to the public a real estate speculation as a consolidation of port services, at the very moment that these functions were being transferred to New Jersey. We were led to envision the twin towers as the vertical equivalent of all those shipping companies and countinghouses that once lined the docks, together with the shipbuilders, importers, commission merchants, marine insurance companies, brokers, and lawyers whose Whitehall Street offices had overlooked the harbor.

Still, you have to hand it to them: the World Trade Center went from being a white elephant, when it opened in 1972, to near-full occupancy of

10 million square feet of office space. Not only did it initiate the resurgence of Lower Manhattan; its dug-out foundation stones were reused as land-fill to make Battery Park City, the true center of that revival. By 2001 the World Trade Center was valued at $1.2 billion, and the Port Authority had managed to lease the buildings for ninety-nine years to a consortium led by Larry A. Silverstein for $3.2 billion. The city and the agency were lick-ing their chops, contemplating how they would spend the huge profits resulting from privatization. The electronics shopkeepers of Radio Row whose district had originally stood in the World Trade Center's path were long forgotten. But then, on September 11, 2001, the towers joined the palimpsest of multiple erasures, like a child's magic slate, which is New York.

Now that they are gone, their absence reasserts how much they cli-maxed the southern tip of Manhattan. Their silvered profiles shimmering against a blue sky, like matching cigarette cases, or at night, when they became moody and noir-ish, were poetic postcard effects achieved only at a distance; up close, they seemed blandly off-putting, and oppressive at street level, like most 65-mph architecture built in that era.

To the rest of the world—though, curiously, I would maintain, not to native New Yorkers like myself, who would always regard the twin towers as parvenus compared to the Empire State, Chrysler, and Woolworth Buildings—the World Trade Center symbolized the Big Apple and, beyond that, the might of America. Certainly the twins had the richest and most imaginative of meanings, a mystic temptation one can only spec-ulate on, to the Islamic terrorists who attacked them not once but twice. The first time, in 1993, despite the tragic loss of life and damage to the buildings, the towers remained standing, seemingly impregnable. The structural design had called for each tower's skin to be its main strength, through light glass-and-steel facing threaded by steel columns. These columns gave the buildings their stiffness, while a cluster of central columns and steel trusses helped hold up each concrete floor. "Redundancy" is what the engineers call that structural backup which ensures a building's resilience, even if damaged—a word that also fit the WTC aesthetically and, now, historically. The twin towers were very strong, nothing compromised in the way of construction, an engineering tour de force; but no building, as we discovered, is meant to take the brunt of a jetliner, gorged with jet fuel, shearing through its midsection. When they collapsed, they fell straight down, not forward. Like the good soldiers they were.

MY FIRST INKLING of an attack on the Twin Towers came from a FedEx man. He rang my doorbell around nine-fifteen, and when I started to sign for my package, he said, shaken, "Did you hear what happened? A plane crashed into the World Trade Center. You can see the black smoke from here." Indeed, looking down Sackett Street in Brooklyn toward the river on that infamously sunny day, I did see a plume of grayish black cloud at the end of my block. My first response was, So what? Planes do crash. As I went inside, the phone rang and it was my mother-in-law, telling me to turn on the television. My mother-in-law is something of a TV addict, especially if bad weather threatens; she'll keep the tube on just to track a storm. I had been looking forward to a day of writing, now that my daughter Lily was beginning second grade, and so I said rather testily that I couldn't turn on the television just now. But something urgent in her voice disturbed me, and so, against my usual practice, I did put on the TV in my office, and saw rebroadcast footage of a second plane crashing into the World Trade Center. Now I was gripped, shocked, queasy, as I realized something unprecedented was happening.

Still, I wandered over by habit to my desktop computer, and tried to punch in a few sentences. Maybe because I had been so fixated on this subject, I began to think the horrifying event was directly connected to the geography of the waterfront: Manhattan's slender, elongated shape, surrounded by rivers, made it easier for the hijacking pilots to hug the shore and spot the towers. My concentration, needless to say, was poor, but I resisted giving myself up entirely to this (so it yet seemed) public event. I am the kind of person who can write, and does, as a consoling escape from anxiety, in the midst of carpenters, street-riveters or other distractions. Around ten-thirty I was still writing with the television on, when my wife, Cheryl, called me from Lily's Montessori school and said she was sticking around, in case they decided to close and send the kids home. I replied— the resolve had suddenly formed in me and I needed to be out in the streets—that I was going for a walk by the Brooklyn waterfront, to see what I could. "Why don't you stop by the school afterward and look in on us?" she suggested. I said I doubted that I would, not adding that suddenly I felt a sharp urge to be alone.

The tragedy had registered on me exactly the same way as after my mother had died: a pain in the gut, the urge to walk and walk through the city, and a don't-touch-me reflex. I made my way down to Columbia Street, which feeds into the Brooklyn Promenade: the closer I got to the waterfront, the harder it was to breathe. The smoke was blowing directly across the East River into Brooklyn. There were not many people on Columbia Street, but most of those I passed had on surgical masks. I started choking without a mask. Cinders and poisonous-smelling smoke thickened the air, and ash fell like snowflakes on the parked cars and on one's clothing, constantly. It was what I had imagined war to be like.

This was two hours after the attack, and you could no longer make out the Manhattan skyline; all you could see was a billowing black cloud. Later my wife told me she had actually glimpsed the top of one of the Twin Towers in flames, and I envied her. I found myself envying everyone who had actually witnessed the buildings on fire or collapsing. Of course I had no one to blame but myself, having secreted myself indoors for the first few hours. I still can't imagine running *into* Manhattan to get a closer look, but I could have gone up to my roof. In the fury of the moment it hadn't occurred to me; probably because I was terrified, the spectating impulse had shut down. Now I saw thousands of people on foot crossing over the bridges into downtown Brooklyn.

When I reached Atlantic Avenue I turned east, away from the water, and began to encounter hordes of office workers, released early from their jobs. Not all of them seemed upset; there was a sort of holiday mood, in patches, brought on by unexpected free time. Two young men and a woman their age were even laughing as they recounted to each other the morning's events, how they had been stopped on their way out of the subway. The middle-aged and elderly, on the other hand, seemed profoundly disturbed, as if they had not expected anything so terrible as an attack on America to happen in the last quarter of their lives. Just as there is something unseemly when a young person dies, so the natural order of things seems wronged when the elderly, braced for their own diminishment, illness, and death, must absorb the bitter shock of how vulnerable and perishable their world is—the world they had counted on to outlast them. I myself felt, at fifty-seven, that the attack was a personal affront to the proper autobiographical arc, as though a melodramatic and unnecessarily complicated subplot had been introduced too late in the narrative.

All at once, I wanted to be with my family. My cocoa-colored shirt was flecked with white ash, like birdshit, when I turned in to my daughter's school. Parents crowded the lobby, many picking up their children to take them home. To my way of thinking, school seemed as safe a place for Lily as our house; I saw no reason to take her out prematurely. Cheryl was standing by the door of the multipurpose room, waiting for Lily's class to leave at the end of dance period. When she came out, Lily seemed happily surprised to see me, in midday; I hugged her. She trooped off to her next activity. Cheryl milled around with the other mothers and some of the fathers, who had returned from the financial district: they were all comparing personal accounts, and engaging in that compulsively repetitious dialogue by which an enormity is made real.

A few days later my wife reproached me for having shown up with ash-laden clothing, my shirttails left untucked. She said I could have frightened the children. I replied that I didn't think anyone had even noticed me. But, on some level, her reproach was justified: I was indulging the fantasy of being invisible, I was not being a team player. Some sort of communal bonding had started taking place, foreign to me, beautiful in many respects, scary in others. My wife and I both felt anguished that day and all week, but it was an anguish we could not share. The fault was mine: selfishly, I wanted to nurse my grief at what had been done to *my* city. I mistrusted any attempt to co-opt me into group-think, even conjugal-think.

That New York was the primary target I had no doubt. I felt so identified with my native city that it took a mental wrenching to understand all of America considered itself assaulted. I knew, of course, that the Pentagon had been hit and another plane had gone down in a Pennsylvania field, but I chose to see it as an attack on the values of urbanism, vertical density, secular humanism, skepticism, women's rights, and mass transit. The American flags that started appearing everywhere may have been fitting ways to honor the heroic local firemen and police who died in the line of duty, but the only banner I wanted to fly from my brownstone window was the orange, green, and white flag of New York City, with its clunky Dutchman and beaver.

People claim that the city will be changed forever by this attack. It is easy to say, less easy to understand exactly how. New York's history has not exactly been a stranger to tragedy. A few days after September 11, I did notice subway riders being unusually polite to each other, whether out of communal solidarity and respect for human life, or from wariness of the Other's potential rage, I cannot say. That nuance has faded. No New Yorker expected America's warm feelings toward the city to last very long; it was like getting licked by a large, forgetful St. Bernard dog. Meanwhile, the towers that anchored lower Manhattan are gone, *pfft*.

I ask myself how I have been changed personally. On the morning of September 12 I awoke and remembered immediately what had happened, like a murderer returning to the horror of his altered moral life. I sensed I would, perhaps, never be the same, though not necessarily better. I have never bought the idea that suffering ennobles people. Rather, I expect that this awful experience will add scar tissue to the other atrocities in life, like the death of one's parents, the illnesses of one's children, or the shame of one's nation (My Lai, for example), sorrows over which one has no control but that cause, for all that, the deepest regrets.

THE VOID LEFT in the heart of Lower Manhattan by the September 11 tragedy provoked considerable speculation about what should go there. Inevitably the discussion took on awkward tones from the start: the bad taste of dreaming design utopias or sending résumés around while bodies were still being excavated. Nevertheless, we all knew that after a suitable pause, with predictable wrangling between officials and developers, the area would have to get rebuilt. It was too important to lie fallow.

Much of the discussion seemed to me misdirected. How avant-garde the new buildings should be, what architectural brand should go on the site, mattered less to me than what sort of public environment ought to be created there. What would the streetlife be like? How would pedestrians, tourists, workers experience it on the ground? How could we most gracefully integrate the new complex into the surrounding area?

Lower Manhattan has a specific character. It is not Midtown, with its regular, flat-terrain blocks of high-rise density. It is the oldest part of New York, and the "grid" down there (if you can call it that) is more casually variable, the streets smaller and narrower, given to sudden surprises and winding perspectives. To the east are the canyons of Wall Street, a dramatic topography in itself, which it might be possible to prolong. Whatever gets built, there already seems a commendable push to extend the east-west streets river to river, as they originally ran, before the World Trade Center created an obstruction.

In many ways the World Trade Center marked a significant break with New York City's spatial form. Its superblock interrupted the circulation of pedestrians; its introverted, mall-life retail was hidden from the street; and it buried its transportation modes (the PATH and subway lines) deep within. It may have made an impressive contribution to the skyline, but it was not very effective at street level.

The design by Daniel Libeskind and Associates that was finally chosen to replace the World Trade Center, after a bitterly contested architectural competition, may or may not work better at street level, may or may not be severely compromised by the pressures of conflicting clients and a weak economy; it's too early to tell. Practically speaking, there is no reason why some of the 13 million square feet of offices destroyed in the attack shouldn't be replaced, though, partly because there is already a glut of office space downtown, I would prefer a more varied mix of office, residential, cultural (opera house or museum), retail, and transportation uses. Whatever gets built, there are better ways of doing it than towers set off in plazas.

Thousands of commuters will again pour into the area daily, as they have in the past. Some sort of terminal or overt transportation structure seems in order, to express with aplomb their entry to city's downtown area. Ideally, you could extend commuter rail from the Midtown terminals to the Lower Manhattan area, which would greatly enhance the attractiveness of the Financial District as a working environment.

A memorial must and will go up; the area is, after all, a massive gravesite. But I confess I am leery of the aesthetic range of contemporary monuments, pulled as they are between realist kitsch and tepidly tasteful abstraction, and I despair of any memorial doing justice to the victims and their families. As for the idea that a really spectacular memorial to

September 11 would rejuvenate Lower Manhattan's tourist business by itself, that seems to me craven if not delusional.

The greatest tribute we could pay those who gave their lives on this site would be to make it into a convivial, life-affirming, urbane place, which would most aptly express New York's street-smart character. (But all such rhetoric on the subject, however well intended, finally makes one gag.)

4

EXCURSUS

THE HARBOR AND
THE OLD PORT

And has it really faded from the port, the painful glamour? Has it really gone from them, the fiction that was always on the movements of the liners in and out the upper bay? Or has it merely retreated for a while behind the bluffs of the New Jersey shore, to return to us again to-morrow and draw the breast away once more into the distance beneath Staten Island hill?"
—PAUL ROSENFELD, *Port of New York*

FOR THE MAJORITY OF NEW YORKERS, EVEN NATIVE-BORN, THE HARBOR IS AN ABSTRACTION: ONE WOULD BE HARD PRESSED TO SAY WHAT EXACT TERRITORY OF LAND and water it encompassed. When the state agencies promoting tourism speak of a "Harbor Park" connecting the Battery, the Statue of Liberty, Ellis Island, Snug Harbor in Staten Island, and Empire-Fulton Ferry State Park in Brooklyn into one ferry-bound entity, they are essentially imposing a hopeful verbal scrim over what is to most people an empty stage. We know the harbor used to dominate the city's consciousness, but we don't feel it anymore. I am skeptical that tourists with limited time in New York—say, a week—would give a whole day to exploring this harbor concept, by taking ferries hither and yon to island monuments far removed from Broadway. But since there are many repeat tourists to New York, perhaps they might try it on a later visit; and happily so, less because of what they might find at the various stops than because there are few ways to experience New York as pleasurably as by looking at it from the water.

The recent proposal by the Metropolitan Waterfront Alliance for a harbor loop ferry system that would make up to fifteen stops in the Upper Bay, as an extension of the mass transit system, is exciting and sensible. Like a set of extra highways already in place, the waterways could cut down on travel time, expense, and pollution. But beyond whatever logistical, financial, and political problems may arise in instituting such a desirable plan, the harbor would have to be understood again by the public as more than an archaic abstraction—as something functionally real.*

I wonder what Ernest Poole would have made of such a turnabout. Poole, a journalist of the progressive camp, who wrote crusading pieces about the East Side slums, chose in his first novel, *The Harbor*, to portray the port of New York as the very symbol of reality. Poole used the terms *harbor* and *port* interchangeably, and when he wrote the novel, the Port of New York was the largest in the world, not only in the amount of commerce it handled, but also in the length of its available waterfront. In 1910 the U.S. Treasury Department, for purposes of customs law, established its

---

*The last writer to understand it that way was probably Alfred Kazin, who penned a 1986 essay called "The Harbor Is My New York." Can you imagine a young writer-about-town using that title today?

demarcations as "including all the territory lying within the corporate limits of the cities of Greater New York and Yonkers, N.Y., and of Jersey City,
N.J., and in addition thereto all the waters and shores of the Hudson River
and Kill von Kill in the State of New Jersey from a point opposite Fort
Washington to Bergen Point Light and all the waters and shores of
Newark Bay and the Hackensack River lying within Hudson County, N.J.,
from Bergen Point Light to the limits of Jersey City." This area had a
waterfront of 771 miles, of which 362 miles were developed with 852 piers.
Manhattan alone had a developed waterfront (measuring the area around
the piers) of about 76 miles.

The Harbor (1915) is a *Bildungsroman* about a young man, Billy, who
grows up above the Brooklyn waterfront, overlooking "a harbor that to me
was strange and terrible," with its "sweaty, hairy dockers and saloons." His
father owns a warehouse on the docks, and by Oedipal extension Billy
identifies everything that is patriarchal, brutal, and materialistic with the
harbor. "From that day the harbor became for me a big grim place to be
let alone—like my father. A place immeasurably stronger than I—like my
father—and like him harsh and indifferent." His ex-schoolteacher mother,
who "had come to hate the harbor," encourages Billy toward idealism and
the finer things in life. At the same time, he is drawn to the ragged waterfront kids, and mesmerized by the sight of "a big fat girl half dressed, giggling and queer, quite drunk" who seems to represent the life-force at its
greasiest and sexiest. Later, leaving no metaphor untried, Billy says, "I was
a toy piano. And the harbor was a giant who played on me till I rattled
inside."

Poole works the harbor symbolism so painstakingly that there is
scarcely room for the characters to come alive. Though the novel has its
moments, it's not a great book. I read it twice, wanting desperately to find
a lost masterpiece, so that I could rediscover and defend the neglected
Ernest Poole. As it happens, he writes with florid enthusiasm, like a poor
man's O. Henry or John Reed, in a boy-scoutish style (trying not to get
ahead of his character's naïveté) that has aged badly. Still, I find intriguing its one-track-mind fascination with the New York harbor as an
indomitable juggernaut that can never be stilled—especially since it *has*
been stilled.

. . .

IN 1915, THE SAME YEAR *The Harbor* appeared, the Russell Sage Foundation published Charles B. Barnes's *The Longshoremen,* probably the first in-depth study ever done of American dockworkers. The author's sympathy for the men he studied was apparent. Conveying with statistics and sober prose the dangerous, unremitting working conditions these men endured, Barnes reported that a longshoreman handled about three thousand pounds per hour, that the heavy lifting led frequently to hernias and muscular exhaustion, that the pressure to load or unload ships as rapidly as possible resulted in crews working thirty to forty hours straight, and that the ensuing fatigue increased the chances of accident.

Cargoes would swing through the air, barely missing men's heads, steel cables swayed precariously in the wind, a hundred competing noises distracted the focus, buckets of coal were dumped with a roar, releasing clouds of dust. At night the dangers increased, because of lowered visibility and the buildup of fatigue, and along with them came a curious indifference to personal safety, the men having successfully dodged so many close scrapes already. But however invulnerable a longshoreman might come to feel, virtually none were spared some incapacitating injury in the course of their careers. "One man who said he had never been hurt, was reminded by his daughter that his toe had been cut off while he was at work," wrote Barnes. And so on: these dockworkers seem to have been blessed with a mixture of stoicism and amnesia. Still, there was no way to put a good face on fatal accidents. Here, Barnes rose to grisly enumeration:

> The ways in which a man may meet death at longshore work are many and varied. . . . In four cases a heavy log or case rolled over and caught the men. Two men were overcome by the heat. Four were caught in the cog wheel of a winch or pulled around the drum end by the rope fall. Four were killed by the breaking of a boom or block. A sling thrown down the hatchway dragged two men from one of the decks to the lower hold. In two cases a draft on a lower deck became entangled, and as the power of the fall loosened it, it swung around in a circle and caught a man. While drafts were being dragged across one of the lower decks by the fall, they caught and crushed three men. Loads coming down with a rush, swung a little too far and struck four. In four cases a spiegel iron or other cargo fell from a tub

and killed the men. The insufficient foothold of ladders built too close to the bulkhead caused three men to fall. Where the vessel's rail was unshipped opposite the hatch, slight blows sent four men overboard. Two men were pulled off the deck by mooring ropes, or caught in a rope coil and dragged from the pier loft. The side door of the pier loft slipped and knocked two workers to the lower deck of the pier. In two cases a hand truck collided with a wagon and blows from the truck handles killed the men. Drums of chemicals exploded with dire result for two men. While a gangway man was leaning over the hatch coamings a box of tin slipped from a draft above and cut off his head.

Alongside the danger of accidents were more-subtle health risks attached to working on the waterfront: extremes of weather that would often lead to bronchitis, rheumatism, pneumonia, or heat prostration; the inhalation of harmful dust particles from, say, loading bulk grain, or dangerous fumes from sacks of potatoes, bone dust, rags, or sugar, strong enough to overcome the men. Barnes remarked as well on the toll taken by the irregularity of work on the piers,* which forced longshoremen into a debilitating pattern of idleness and drinking. Because there were so few dock structures in which the men could wait, and even fewer toilets, they had little choice but to hang out in saloons. Men were discouraged from straying to another pier to seek work, and each pier became a world unto itself, refusing to pool labor along the waterfront in the event of shortages. Imagine a situation in which one crew was forced to operate shorthanded, four men doing the job of five, increasing the chances of accident, while three blocks away a dozen men were sitting on their hands, desperate for work.

The workforce was changing ethnically, Barnes observed. Traditionally the waterfront had been an Irish preserve; blacks and Italians were initially introduced as scab labor, making them unpopular, but by 1915 the docks had settled into a cosmopolitan mix. Barnes described it thus: "Variety is as characteristic of the worker as it is of the cargoes he handles. Irishmen, Scandinavian, German, Italian, Polack, and Negro jostle one another on

---

*Longshore work tends toward the casual and irregular, dependent as it is on shipping schedules, the weather, seasonal variations in business, and global patterns of international politics and trade.

the piers of New York. And the impact is not physical alone. The clash of race, temperament, language, industrial and personal traditions, flare up in disagreements, more or less violent, or are smothered by the exigencies of the trade and overcome by time. Most often, good-natured indifference does duty for real toleration and the work proceeds." Lest we give Barnes more credit for lack of prejudice than he deserves, he added: "Always there is the shifting of races with the gradual increase of the less efficient types of worker; the substitution of the southern and southeastern European for the older, more easily assimilated Celt or Saxon." And he worried that this new breed was getting scrawnier: ". . . many are small and wiry, but . . . the eagerness of the Italians for work, their willingness to submit to deductions from their wages, leaving a neat little commission to be divided among foremen, saloon keepers, and native bosses—all these considerations insured the permanence of the Italian in longshore work."

Some of these European dockworkers brought with them a familiarity with radical politics, and at the very least a working-class solidarity, which made them ripe for unionization and willing to strike, if necessary. It was these same groups of politicized immigrants who helped get five Socialist Party candidates elected to the State Assembly from New York City. Indeed, in 1920, during the so-called "Red Scare," when the Lusk Legislative Committee investigated subversive activity throughout New York State, it went so far as to prepare an "Ethnic Map" of Manhattan, showing in which neighborhoods the non-Anglo-Saxon nationalities were concentrated, making an unapologetic equation between foreign birth and revolutionary activity.

Admittedly, the powers that be did have something to worry about. The era around the First World War saw the resurgence of a militant labor movement, culminating in a national wave of strikes during 1919. That year the federal government had decided to hold the line on wages, and shipping companies offered longshoremen only a five-cent increase on the regular sixty-five-cents-an-hour pay, and ten cents an hour on overtime. (This insulting five-and-ten offer was sardonically called the Woolworth Award.) When the longshoremen struck, in a wildcat action that paralyzed the port, tying up more than 600 vessels in the harbor, the head of the union, International Longshoremen's Association president T. V. O'Connor, who opposed the strike, said it was the work of "the Italian element, aided by German sympathizers." The press agreed that it was a "Bolshevik conspiracy," led by foreigners, chiefly Italians, men from "166 Sackett Street in Brooklyn." This address was the headquarters of the International Workers of the World—the "Wobblies," as they were called—above a fruit-and-vegetable stand. (By coincidence, I live on Sackett Street, in an old Italian neighborhood, and my heart raced when I saw that in print; but when I looked for number 166, I found the entire block had been torn down and replaced by the Brooklyn-Queens Expressway.) The truth was, the rank-and-file dockworkers had walked out in 1919 without either union or IWW leadership, and only afterwards appealed to the Wobblies for guidance.

"The strike ended in the first week of November," wrote labor historian Calvin Winslow. "It failed for many reasons: certainly the odds were overwhelming—the unwavering opposition of the union leadership, the shipping companies, and the federal government. Federal soldiers actually entered the Harbor in the second week of the strike, though their presence was mostly symbolic. They confined their activities to the army terminals and never directly confronted the strikers. The strikers themselves were undoubtedly exhausted by this conflict, as must have been their families, existing a month without wages or strike benefits."

There was not another major strike on the waterfront for twenty-six years, though working conditions for longshoremen remained as problematic as ever. Joseph Ryan, who ruled the International Longshoremen's Association throughout this period, getting himself elected the union's "president for life," saw to it that there would be no strikes, by promoting a system that kept the men weak and subservient. The cornerstone of this system was maintaining an oversupply of labor, which tended to depress wages and employ men on a casual basis, with no guarantees of an income from one day to the next. Long after most industries, even most other waterfronts, had gotten rid of the practice, the New York docks continued to be ruled by the infamous "shape-up," in which longshoremen would have to gather every eight hours outside the pier shed, usually in horseshoe configuration, and the pier foreman would select the workers lucky enough to form the crews that day. All troublemakers and organizers were excluded, thus limiting the possibility of reforming locals from within. Not only was the shape-up a demeaning way for men to seek work, but it gave hiring foremen the opportunity to profit by various extortions: kickbacks for jobs, bribes, payroll padding, loan-sharking (those wanting work had to agree to take out a loan), card games in which the longshoremen were expected to lose, and contributions extracted to phony charities.

Many of these hiring foremen were ex-convicts, who intimidated the men by threats as well as acts of violence, sufficient to ensure the "D&D" (deaf and dumb) response characteristic of longshoremen. Shipping companies condoned the use of thugs to run things because it kept the men in line. Ultimately this criminal element translated into racketeers taking over the union. Extensive pilferage of imported goods became routine, and the mob took a cut of everything that moved in and out of the port. Illegal immigrants who had jumped ship were given waterfront jobs immediately, so long as they bribed the foreman and bought a brass check. (A dockworker collected his pay by turning in a brass check or disc, but he could sell it to someone else before payday if he was hard up for cash.)

The International Longshoremen's Union both exploited immigrants and gave them a leg up. In this way the union was similar to the old, patronage-dispensing Democratic Party machine, Tammany Hall, which, on the one hand, was incorrigibly corrupt, and on the other, in its muzzy fashion, at least negotiated with the needs of newly arrived immigrants when the patrician Establishment could not be bothered. Joseph Ryan, the ILA president, was as much a creature of Tammany Hall as he was of the labor movement: a beefy ex-longshoreman with a sentimental streak he indulged in after-dinner speeches at testimonial banquets in his honor, his favor was sought by every important public official in the region, from Mayor Jimmy Walker to Governor Franklin Roosevelt. Ryan's indifferent stewardship of the longshoremen looks all the shabbier in contrast with his dynamic West Coast counterpart, Harry Bridges ("Red Harry"), who helped eradicate the shape-up by registering longshoremen and instituting a system of seniority and rotation in hiring, while fighting for better wages.

Though Ryan appeared in public as the union's leader, each New York pier was in fact a "pirate's nest," as one reporter called it, dominated by different "warlords." The Irish controlled the West Side's Chelsea piers, with the Bowers gang holding sway, and the Red Hook docks in Brooklyn were run by "Tough Tony" Anastasia, brother of Albert Anastasia, who was chief executioner for Murder Incorporated during the late 1930s.

One of the ironies of the Italian-American immigrant story is that Italian longshoremen were split into two factions, activist reformers and racketeering union officials, but popular culture remembers only the second branch. The most outspoken, courageous leader against the racketeering locals was a twenty-seven-year-old Italian-American named Peter Panto, who signed up more than a thousand supporters in 1939. Then he disappeared. According to the gangster Abe Reles, who offered to turn state's witness, Panto kept an appointment with some guys he didn't trust. He was taken to a shack on the waterfront where Albert Anastasia instructed Mindy Weiss to strangle him. His body was then dumped in a lime pit in New Jersey. Vito Marcantonio, the American Labor Party congressman, and author Richard Wright were enlisted to bring pressure for an investigation into Panto's demise. Reles "fell" to his own death from a hotel window while under police protection, and the case was dropped. The murder of Panto and the failure to prosecute his killers had a chilling effect for years on efforts to democratize the union.

In the postwar 1940s, the rank and file's appetite for struggle reawakened: the ILA's sweetheart contracts with shipping companies and the introduction of the sling load, a more onerous, injury-inflicting apparatus, had provoked the longshoremen's anger. There were wildcat strikes in 1945, 1948 (this one reluctantly backed by Joseph Ryan and the ILA), and 1951, with concessions won in the areas of increased hourly wage, overtime, guaranteed vacations, and the establishment of a welfare fund. Still, the union remained largely a tool of organized crime.

In Manhattan the loading racket had become the most lucrative scam of all. It operated this way: When goods were left on a pier-shed floor, truckers needed a helper or mechanical forklift to get the shipment onto the truck. Those who performed this task—the equivalent of public porters in a train station—came to control all movements on the pier. Lower Manhattan's narrow piers and antiquated cobbled streets near the waterfront exacerbated the congestion, as did the vast increase in trucking of freight. The greatest expense in shipping through New York became the waiting time for loading. Truckers in a hurry agreed to pay an extortionate fee to jump the line. In this way a group of middlemen ended up dominating the docks, with thugs and organized crime families fighting for the privilege. One especially brazen case occurred in 1947, when John "Cockeye" Dunn and Andrew "Squint" Sheridan, of the Bowers Gang, emptied a gun into John Hintz, the hiring boss of Pier 51, to gain control of that dock's public loading.

The loading racket, Daniel Bell notes in his book *The End of Ideology*, existed only in New York: "There has never been a loading racket in San Francisco, in New Orleans, in Baltimore or Philadelphia—the other major maritime ports in the U.S. . . . [T]he *spatial* arrangements of these other ports are such that loading never had a 'functional' significance. In all these ports, other than New York, there are direct railroad connections to the piers, so that the transfer of cargoes is easily and quickly accomplished; nor is there in these ports the congested and choking narrow-street patterns which in New York forced the trucks to wait, piled up 'time charges,' or made for off-pier loading."

All these arcane customs created an insular world in which the longshoremen, exploited by their overlords, nevertheless remained isolated from and suspicious of the surrounding community, unwilling to seek redress from it. Shape-ups continued to be a sham exercise, since the hiring foreman had a list in advance of favored names. Sometimes men who had placated the union officials would sport a toothpick in their hatbrims or behind their ears. That all this gangsterism should come down to a toothpick!

Many of these ingrown practices turn up in the film *On the Waterfront* (1954), some as central issues, others as researched, but throwaway, background details. For instance, in the shape-up scene, a dockworker is seen putting a toothpick behind his ear and instantly getting picked; the foreman subsequently throws on the ground some metal discs he calls "tabs," which are fought over by the remaining applicants, though what these actions mean could only be grasped by moviegoers already in the know. More familiar to 1950s audiences will have been the general problem of corrupt longshore unions, the code of silence, the fighting priests who crusaded against these practices, and the barrage of Crime Commission hearings investigating waterfront racketeering.

Since most people today know the New York working port only through this film, (which was actually shot in Hoboken, New Jersey, with the city's skyline tantalizingly backgrounded), it is worth reconsidering it. *On the Waterfront* is one of those film classics that, to me at least, don't hold up: shrill, rhetorical, its plot scheme of guilt and redemption rammed through to the percussive nudgings of an urban-jungle Leonard Bernstein score, its hysteria allows not a moment's relaxed cinematic breathing, save for one courtship scene on a park bench. Certainly Marlon Brando and Eva Marie Saint are still riveting—she translucent, powder-white, like a Kabuki lioness; he, the sensitive, inarticulate, darkly frowning star, on his way from Stanley Kowalski to Napoleon—yet at no moment can we accept her as a college girl from New Jersey taught by nuns, just as he, for all his charismatic charm, seems incredible as Terry Malone, the ex-boxer whose brains are partly scrambled, but whose pigeon-loving heart stays tenderly intact. The other acting is aggressively stylized: squashed-face secondaries recruited from the ring and the Actor's Studio, led by Lee J. Cobb in his snarling, Yiddish Theater Italian mobster mode; Rod Steiger's robotically mannered vocal hesitancies, meshing in the backseat with Brando's working-class lisp, all fun to watch, up to a point. But Karl Malden is unbearably hammy with his sermons, and the religious symbolism (Steiger dangling spread-armed from a hook, Brando browbloodied near the end, Malden yammering that every waterfront victim is a "crucifixion") seems maudlinly overdone. Schulberg and director Elia Kazan allowed themselves to interpret the waterfront zone as Calvary.

Harry Cohn, the head of the studio that produced *On the Waterfront*, had expected the picture to flop, partly because of its artiness, but the movie did well at the box office and even won several Academy Awards, including Best Picture. Only the unions were unhappy, protesting what they saw as an unfair emphasis on "labor crime."

THE WATERFRONT COMMISSION, established in the aftermath of the crime hearings, cleaned up the docks a good deal, especially seeing to it that ex-convicts were driven out of the locals. If anything, they became a little too puritanically strict in their rules against those with criminal records. Not that the New York waterfront lost all its ties with organized crime; but with the preponderance of shipping relocated, the problem became defused. The Port Authority simply moved the whole operation, lock, stock, and barrel, to container-port facilities in Elizabeth, New Jersey (whose marshland was a lot cheaper to acquire than Gotham real estate), and Port Newark, keeping only a few symbolic pieces of a container port in Red Hook, Brooklyn, and Howland Hook, Staten Island.

Could the city have done a better job of retaining its working port? Were the harbor commissioners asleep at the switch? Teddy Gleason, the head of the ILA, used to say, "You know what I see when I look down at Battery Park City? I see a container port that could have been." The union itself was partly responsible, having resisted containerization because it was not as labor-intensive as break-bulk cargo. Still, let's say that the harbor commissioners had overcome the union's hesitations, and built a containerized port where Battery Park City now stands. There would still be the lack of a rail hookup, insufficient backup space, and trucks stalled in cobbled streets in downtown Manhattan, probably leading to a new loading racket. Manhattan can never again have a working port. I reiterate this as an antidote to that aching nostalgia (my own included) for the old New York waterfront.

The New York waterfront treated its workforce as cruelly and crudely as any workplace can, while still making you wish it had continued to exist. In 1969 the same year that James Morris, soon to become Jan Morris, published a paean commissioned by the Port of New York Authority titled *The Great Port* (talk about your puff pieces)—the International Longshoremen's Union signed a contract to permit labor-saving mechanization and increased container shipping in exchange for a guaranteed annual income for its members, whether they worked or not. So the longshoremen finally lucked out with a golden parachute—or golden grappling hook—even if it meant trading their jobs in for retirement. The membership, 27,000 strong in 1969, has dwindled to a tenth of that: there are only 2,700 active longshoremen working in the regional port today. Many of them sit in isolation behind computers or in crane cabs, making sure that each container lands where it is supposed to, according to some prearranged master plan.

Sometimes I catch myself wondering—in that old-time liberal, prounion way one wonders—whether the unions were made the scapegoat for

the port's problems. It seems not entirely coincidental that the Port
Authority withdrew virtually all shipping from New York soon after the
well-publicized waterfront crime investigations, as if to say, It's the union's
fault we can't do business here. But one of the last of the shipping news
reporters, Bill White, set me straight: "The union was rotten. No doubt
about it."

White also wistfully told me that New York's working waterfront had
been one of the greatest spectacles in the world. With all that movement
and noise, and the smells of exotic spices, I don't doubt it: there is something intrinsically interesting about watching such work being performed,
as port-watchers in New Orleans or Barcelona can attest. How accessible
that spectacle ever was to the ordinary New Yorker, as opposed to a shipping news reporter, is a question. In Manhattan, certainly, there had long
been something of a fortresslike segregation between city and port:
"Rimmed off from the rest of the city by a steel-ribbed highway," Daniel
Bell wrote in 1962.

Even in 1915, before the highways were built, Poole described in *The
Harbor* "an unbroken wall of sheet iron and concrete" with "No Visitors
Allowed" signs and watchmen to exclude the public. Not that there weren't
good reasons: fear of theft, or safety and insurance concerns. In the end,
New York's working waterfront must have been a great urban spectacle, to
the extent one could glimpse it in passing, and a forbidden zone, parts of
which were as hidden from view as the Imperial Palace in Peking.

5
TRIBECA:
THE RIVER PROJECT

ACROSS FROM A JUMBO OFFICE BUILDING AND THE HIGHWAY SITS PIER 25, WITH ITS SCRAPPY CARNIVAL ASSORTMENT OF MINIATURE GOLF, BEACH VOLLEYBALL, kiddie rides, and soft ice cream. Next to that is Pier 26, on West Street and North Moore, just below Canal Street. Pier 26 is a wide concrete slab, looking out onto river-washed stubs of rotting timbers, which has been shared for the past decade by two exemplary nonprofit organizations, the River Project, which operates educational and exhibit programs related to river ecology, and the Downtown Boathouse, which runs kayaking and canoe programs.

The River Project, housed in a two-story wooden structure, with a trailer-office alongside, has been fondly described by John Waldman

(Heartbeats in the Muck) as "a resilient cross between a marine biology field station and a TriBeCa neighborhood clubhouse for the outdoor-minded." It gives off that odor of one-step-from-eviction squatter's idealism, klutzy if endearing voluntarism, and embattled overdrive which might be characterized as *essence de nonprofit.*

One Sunday in September I went over to the River Project to watch the scuba divers. On this brisk, windy day, an underwater trash-removal event had been scheduled to draw curious onlookers and raise consciousness about keeping the Hudson River clean. On a floating dock attached to the concrete slab, a young, rotund volunteer organizer in an orange life jacket was directing the flow of divers in the waters at his feet. "Who's going down next?" The eight divers, bobbing in the water like decapitated heads, looked uncertain, no one exactly rushing toward submersion. "Hold on to the dump-line," he said, "if you're going down. If you're not, clear the space for the others." The divers were all Hispanic inner-city youths in their teens, part of a group called the Kips Bay Girls and Boys Club (not from Kips Bay, of course, that would be too simple, but from the Bronx). One chubby girl, having completed her dive, half-flopped, half-climbed gracelessly onto the floating deck, saying "Help me!" The organizer did, reluctantly, then leaned over, asked a prettier girl in the water if she was okay, and she tapped her head, a signal that must have meant "everything's all right." Meanwhile, several people were videotaping the divers, part of that documentation process so dear to nonprofits. The organizer shooed one of the camera people off the deck because she lacked a lifejacket.

A young man, emerging from his dive, his mustache dripping river water, reported that he was unable to extricate any trash because he couldn't see a thing; the water was too murky. "Plus there's too many divers, you keep bumping into each other."

The adult leader of the Kips Bay Club surfaces a few moments later. Everyone calls him Michael. He is an articulate, gregarious African-American, shaved head, Fu Manchu mustache, handsome, body-builder type, with glittering eyes. Hanging on to the side of the dock, he answers admiring questions about his outfit: "It's a drysuit, Trilaminate, very comfortable. You can regulate the degree of warmth by the layers you wear underneath. See?" he says, peeling back the top to show his dark gray undershirt. "That's Polarfleece."

He explains that his group is part of the Boy Scouts: a "venture" club set up for thirteen-to-twenty-year-olds. He himself is over forty. It isn't clear to me whether he's paid to do this as a youth worker, or is a weekend volunteer. His rap is that the club is a good way to keep the kids off drugs. "When you've got activities, you don't do drugs, right? I take them lobstering and spearfishing out by Rockaway. There are three hundred wrecks underwater out there. You also come across chunks of the old FDR Drive, nasty concrete, iron poles that they sunk after the highway collapsed."

"So how was your dive?" a blond, slender, fit-looking woman in her forties, Danish or German, with sun-leathered skin, asks Michael flirtatiously.

"Terrible. Pitch-black. It's okay, I still had a good time."

"I think swimming, it's a better sport. Because diving you can't see anything."

"You don't go by visibility, you go by feel," says Michael. "It's like Braille. Anyway, this makes a good political statement."

"But there was no trash picked up," I object. "How is it political?"

Michael smiles, acknowledging the point. "It's more like, 'We dove the Hudson.'"

The earnest Hispanic teenager, who has been sitting on his haunches the whole time listening, pipes up, "Michael, can you help me improve my diving skills? I'm trying to go for underwater welder."

"That's cool."

Later, I wander around the various information tables. Some are distributing membership forms for diving clubs in the area. There is also a "Save the Rain Forest" group, with literature protesting the Department of Transportation's use of "wood logged from tropical rain forests for City construction projects." A gamelan group plays on the makeshift bandstand deck.

Inside the Estuarium, as the River Project's exhibit space is called, are research tanks with handwritten explanatory signs, showing the varieties of estuarial activity. In a tank housing oyster beds, fed by water drawn from the Hudson, a nerdy volunteer, rail-thin, is explaining to several younger girls: "Actually, see, the river is very clean, but there's muck at the bottom, and that's why when you stare down it looks as if it's dirty." This is a somewhat simplistic explanation of the Hudson's turbidity, but we'll let it stand.

I have set up an interview with Cathy Drew, director of the River Project. She is a middle-aged woman with straw-textured blond hair who walks with a cane, the residue of a serious case of the bends she got while diving. When I allude to that illness, she asks me suspiciously, "How much do you know about me?" I tell her I read about it in John Waldman's book, and she is mollified.

Asked about her background, she says she kicked around various careers, and then went to graduate school "later than most" and got a degree in marine biology. After her oceanographic accident, she was living in TriBeCa near Pier 26 and began to "do a few things there" around 1986, when it was still a parking garage with no electricity, run by the Department of Transportation. She asked the DOT if she could use one shed, then another. Nobody put up a fuss because the buildings were empty and standing idle.

Since then, the River Project has grown into an ambitious, well-used facility, overseeing scientific experiments about water quality, plant and fish life (so far, it has caught forty-six species) in the harbor, training interns to do research projects, conducting school tours of the Estuarium's exhibits, and acting as an advocacy group to improve the riparian environment.

At the core of Cathy's enthusiasm is the fact that New York Harbor is an estuary, where fresh water and ocean water commingle to bring about, in her words, "the highest diversity of plants, fish, and birds in a region which also happens to have the highest diversity of people." While she will speak mystically about "what it, Nature, wants to be," she also seems very much an urbanite. She relishes the irony that the harbor has been designated a "marine sanctuary," along with several other spots along the Hudson, and that the others are all pristine, though this place is "maximally stressed, the opposite of pure." Protecting and restoring the natural environment in this most populous, artificial, and stressed habitat appeals to her character as a New Yorker.

"There are three things you need for a healthy estuary," she tells me. "One, a mixture of two kinds of water; two, a wetland edge; three, a nutrient track. We no longer have a wetland edge. There used to be a wetland with rocky shoals, grass—all the right stuff for a spawning and feeding ground. Now you've got these competing uses: commerce, waste disposal,

transportation, recreation, and fishing. You can re-create freshwater wetlands easily—like ponds. They do it all the time. But trying to bring back
saltwater wetlands is very costly and usually doesn't take, in the long run.
Even when it starts to take, the other problem is that protecting the wetlands won't keep the developers from building right behind the wetlands,
so that when the water rises, the fish are driven back to the part that's built,
and they die in great numbers."

One of her trainees interrupts to ask her advice. Cathy Drew strikes me
as an inspired teacher rather than a polished administrator. Her approach
is casual, as in: Let's just do the experiment rather than wait for the fancy
equipment to come in. This trainee is trying to determine the movement
of fecal matter in the harbor between two piers, by tracking some oranges
as they bob around in the water. You can't get any more low-tech than that.
Another intern, a dark-skinned Pakistani girl about fifteen, has been doing
a feasibility study about establishing a beach somewhere below 14th Street,
on the Hudson. The girl is keeping track of water quality, by testing the
fecal matter to see on which days it would be safe to swim, and on which
not. The risks occur with rain, when excess runoff pours directly into the
river, bringing with it all the debris and excrement from the streets. For
days after a hard rain, the rivers around New York harbor are too polluted
to make swimming advisable; hence, locating a sandy beach on
Manhattan's shore remains a problematic, if alluring, idea.

"Aren't there devices for handling that runoff?" I ask Cathy.

"Yes. You can put filters in the rocks to capture some of it. You can put
filter drains in the streets. But the main way is to have holding tanks
inserted in the highways. When Route 9A [the replacement for the West
Side Highway] was first on the drawing board, there were provisions for
holding tanks, but they fell out of the plans somewhere, most likely for
budgetary reasons," she says. "You could *lobby* for holding tanks, I guess."
The old activist spirit surges back.

Cathy shows me an art piece, commissioned by the River Project, by
the sculptor George Trakas, which consists of two steel staircases leading
down from the pier to the water, with landing and seating areas. She wants
people to "get to the river," not to be afraid of it. Mix it up with the river:
a connection that's worked for her. She trusts it, why don't they? Originally
she wanted to have the staircases lead right down to the water, nothing

else, but the city regulatory agencies made her install two fences—
"two!"—as warnings that you were approaching the edge. "These people
don't travel outside of New York, they don't realize that in cities all over
the world you can get to the water. The Hudson River Park Trust put lots
of references to 'get-downs' in their literature, but then they didn't include
any in their final plans." So she made a get-down. And they made her put
up the fences.

For all the good stuff the River Project does, its continuing existence
on Pier 26 remains precarious. The Hudson River Park Trust, which has
jurisdiction over the property, would prefer to put some income-producing
facility on it: a slicker, theme-park-style estuarium, say, run by a university
or a prestige institution like the San Diego Aquarium, which would
become a magnet for tourist families, at eight dollars a head. The conflict
between the River Project's scruffy, improvisatory manner, all oaktag and
scotch tape, and the Hudson River Park Trust's corporate, buttoned-down
style, is alluded to, with barely concealed sarcasm, in a River Project leaflet:
"Now there is the opportunity to understand . . . them [the returning fish
populations] before the Park redevelopment eliminates these naturalizing
areas on rotting piers in favor of new pavements and managed landscapes."

It's the old story of the grassroots local organization that attaches itself
like a barnacle to neglected public land and performs a service no one else
will, only to be endangered when the whole area becomes desirable. For
the moment, the River Project and the Hudson River Park Trust are playing a cat-and-mouse game with each other, which could go on for years.

6

THE SOHO/GREENWICH VILLAGE CORRIDOR

And our landscape came to be as it is today:
Partially out of focus, some of it too near, the middle distance
A haven of serenity and unreachable. . . .
                                                —JOHN ASHBERY, *"A Wave"*

I AM WALKING ALONG THE NEW HUDSON RIVER PARK.
SOMEONE RUNS BY ME. I HAVE TO SAY THERE'S NOTHING
SO UNPLEASANT AS THAT SLIGHT BREEZE BEHIND YOUR EAR
of a biker or runner overtaking you: you have no warning, and then you
flinch, and feel like a fool for being so terrified. It's assumed, incorrectly,
that bikeway or running tracks are also congenial to walkers; in fact, we
are class enemies.

Hudson River Park has so far proven a godsend to bicyclists, joggers, and dog-trotters. It may not, I think, have the same appeal to recreational walkers like myself who, staring into the face of oncoming headlights, can never relax, never escape the sense of a jangling, if not scary, experience. Advancing in the face of oncoming traffic is never a pleasant experience, as it is hard to turn off your fear reflex. For the bicyclist, already vehicled, the car seems to be a friendly cousin, while for those morning runners high on pheromones, energy is eternal delight—they can match their speed with and even surpass the sluggish New York traffic; but for the walker, the sensation is something like the retreat from Dunkirk: trying to flee a battle while the enemy artillery keeps rolling in.

Hudson River Park, that outdoor temple of physical culture, has been designed as essentially a transit corridor; perhaps because the land available for a park is so thin, there was no other choice than a transit corridor. Watching the weekend joggers, rollerbladers and bicyclists exercising in the waterfront park around SoHo and Greenwich Village, however, I am increasingly bored and uneasy, until I realize why I am more drawn to the center of the island. It's that in the streets you see New Yorkers in their most purposeful, urgent aspect, their presentation of self is dramatic or at least emphatic, they are navigating from one compelling situation to another—between work, say, and going to the doctor or picking up the kids—and if their faces hold the burden of being overwhelmed with all they have to do in the next twenty-four hours, you also sense their pride, or at least workaday stoicism, which is the *genus loci* of this particular city. Whereas at leisure they could be anywhere—Spokane, North Carolina, Sydney. On a Sunday in the park, their placid, self-contented faces are emptied of content, save perhaps the strain of jogging one more half-mile, to burn off another centimeter of fat. And their costumes—shorts, T-shirts, sweatpants, sneakers—have no local or regional characteristics, they are the global uniforms of the body-snatched, those who have allowed their limbs to be turned over to machines for happiness. In contrast, compare the fashion-savvy suit or dress choices of office workers striding past Bryant Park at 9:00 A.M. on any given weekday: here you see something quintessentially New York. While everyone was worrying about the entry of the chain stores into Manhattan, fearing that the city would lose its local retail flavor to suburban shopping malls, the conformist forces of globalization sneaked in the back way through leisure. It is not consumerism per se that disturbs me—New York was always a mecca of shopping and fashion—but seeing the local populace come to rest and pirouette on skates in anonymous skivvies. At play, or at least this contemporary, puritanical cardiovascular exercise we call play, people look their most blandly bourgeois. Maybe it's just that I'm watching, for the most part, middle-class white people, the dominant demographic in Hudson River Park. Uptown, Hispanics and African-Americans capering on roller skates to a loud ghetto blaster in Central Park are much more entertaining. They know how to party in any public space, the point being to show off one's moves, not burn off one's calories.

Maybe Hudson River Park will be wonderful when it's finished. You can't tell yet. Still, it seems to me, as I'm walking along, that what should be on the waterfront is something fun, like—movie theaters. How great to be able to reach the river and see a large marquee featuring one, but at most three (okay, four) titles a day—anything more multiplex feels fragmented. I can imagine coming out of an Eric Rohmer film and wandering over by the water's edge, along the promenade, and smoking a cigarette (if only I smoked cigarettes), while I watch a lumbering tug, red-hulled with a striped stack. Or maybe all those cheap Times Square moviehouses that once showed kung fu, horror, or porn could be resurrected along the waterfront. What I miss is something outrageous that would honor the waterfront's raffish history: like a big Jones Beach–type amphitheater for *Song of Norway* revivals; or a pagoda-shaped gambling house festooned with neon, near Chinatown and Canal Street (first floor, mah jongg, second floor, cockfighting), or a floating casino supper club, run by Brooklyn gangsters, with reflections of little carmine lanterns bobbing in the water.

BY ALL RIGHTS, the waterfront should be the city's carnival release, the diastole to the workaholic's systole; but we've lost the habit, and now we're creakily, arthritically trying to regain it. That it *was* once a habit may be inferred from the opening pages of *Moby Dick:*

Circumambulate the city of a dreamy Sabbath afternoon. Go from Corlears Hook to Coenties Slip, and from thence, by Whitehall, northward. What do you see?—Posted like silent sentinels all around the town, stand thousands upon thousands of mortal men fixed in ocean reveries. Some leaning against the spiles; some seated upon the pier-heads; some looking over the bulwarks of ships from China; some high aloft in the rigging, as if striving to get a still better seaward peep. But these are all landsmen; of week days pent up in lath and plaster—tied to counters, nailed to benches, clinched to desks. . . . Strange! Nothing will content them but the extremest limit of the land; loitering under the shady lee of yonder warehouses will not suffice. No. They must get as nigh the water as they possibly can without falling in.

Melville's 1851 vision of a waterfront-besotted populace certainly jibes with Whitman's poems of the same decade; this must have been the very apex of the seaport's bursting youth. Yet, just a few years earlier, in 1843, the popular writer and editor Nathaniel Parker Willis—New York's first self-conscious *flâneur*—expressed a somewhat different view: "If quiet be the object, the nearer the water the less jostled the walk on Sunday. You would think, to cross the city anywhere from river to river, that there was a general hydrophobia—the entire population crowding to the high ridge of Broadway, and hardly a soul to be seen on either the East River or the Hudson."

So, which is correct? Melville's assertion that New Yorkers flock like lemmings to the river, or Willis's, that the crowds prefer the thick of Broadway, avoiding the waterfront like hydrophobic rats? Both, perhaps. I can only say that, walking the waterfront and finding myself often the sole human being on foot, I would not rule out the hydrophobic hypothesis as the deeper, more basic trait. In Manhattan you often forget you live on an island, much less one abutting a mighty ocean. You go about your business, deep in preoccupation. New York's granitic environment promotes living in your head, a cerebral, landlocked state just this side of paranoia, but perfect for an information capital.

It's not as though the New York waterfront ever was a place for ordinary citizens to walk much. Boys hung around it for fun and risk, jumping into the East River as their swimming hole, and those who made their living in the port felt comfortable at the river's edge. But except for the Battery, at the island's tip, there was very little opportunity along the water for strolling or recreation. It was not until the mid-1890s that a few downtown recreation piers and the first, rough version of Riverside Park were opened.

In the twentieth century the edges of Manhattan remained remote from the average New Yorker's everyday path, for the simple reason that the rapid transit system didn't extend that far. The main subway lines traversed the finger-shaped island in a north-south direction, rather than going east-west; also, the subways generally followed the densest residential or retail patterns, which left out the waterfront. Without a subway to take you to the far western or eastern edge, any riparian encounter would have to come after an excursion on foot, making it a more intentional, *marginal* experience. You might be a solitude-loving poet or an escaping thief or someone who lived nearby in one of the reconverted warehouses, but you could not be a member of a crowd, except in those rare, fiesta-like situations when the city embraced the river, usually for its unobstructed sightlines: Fourth of July fireworks, the Brooklyn Bridge or Statue of Liberty centenary. The very avidity with which millions of New Yorkers poured into the waterfront on those occasions suggested what an anomaly it was for them to be there, and only accentuated their usual indifference to the river's edge.

Now I pass by Pier 40, at West Houston Street. This enormous, fifteen-acre concrete bunker traversing three city blocks, probably the last substantial investment the Port Authority made on the island before it became crystal-clear that Manhattan's port was doomed, was built to handle cargo freight, and when it opened, in 1950, it was the largest precast structure in the world. A victim of bad timing, it sat redundant on the waterfront twenty years later. Thereafter it became a gargantuan parking lot—much-needed, by the way, in Lower Manhattan, especially for long-term commuters—that holds more than 2,000 cars and dozens of buses and trucks. It remains an immensely tantalizing site to planners, community activists, and utopian urban dreamers. The Van Alen Institute sponsored an architectural competition, which attracted 141 entries; the winning designs used all or parts of the existing structure, in some cases as a kind of picturesque scrim, leaving only the frame and opening the façade to the river breezes. For a while it was set to house a Home Depot super-store; now all the alternatives have been put on hold.

I brood about what might have been here, the proposal to build a new satellite Guggenheim art museum on Pier 40, designed by Frank Gehry. A tour-de-force, billowy wave of a building by the maestro of Bilbao at water's edge would have been magnificently dramatic, and where more suitably than at the cusp of two art-conscious neighborhoods, Greenwich Village and SoHo?* But it was shot down by the local community plan-ning board, which had long had its eye on the Pier 40 site for recreational uses (never mind that Hudson River Park and all of Battery Park City's recreation spaces were in the vicinity), and which did not appreciate the high-handed, empire-expansionist style of the Guggenheim's director, Thomas Krens, who had failed to consult the community before announc-ing the plan to the press. To me, the Gehry Museum proposal for Pier 40 was a casualty of a decentralized local planning process, by which what serves the city as a whole often takes a backseat to a community's parochial agenda.

I walk along the edge of Pier 40 next to the terminal building, where benches are set up and an old man is fishing. The sun flashing on the water, the sound of the slapping waves, idyllic: It does make a difference, getting a hundred feet out, away from the noise of the city. I try to think why I feel so comfortable on this pier, compared with some of the new sliver piers, which make me feel exposed and anxious. Of course! The side of the terminal building acts like a street-wall, giving the open space shape, structure, limit. All this emphasis on "open space" is not good for a native New Yorker like myself, who gets vague agoraphobia with no surround-ings to hem him in.

A Gehry-designed Guggenheim at Pier 40 would have set a good precedent for a highly visible public building on the waterfront. Unlike London, with its Houses of Parliament along the Thames, or Paris, where the Louvre's palaces front the Seine, New York's waterfront has a dearth of major public buildings. Its reason for being was commerce, not imper-ial display, so it turned the edges over strictly to port activities. "Virtually

---

*It was certainly a better site than the one chosen next, near the South Street Seaport, which would never have survived an environmental review process and which has since been jettisoned.

every foot of shoreline," wrote Kevin Bone in his superb book *The New York Waterfront*, "was occupied by some kind of maritime building: basins, docks, piers, wharves, and seawalls, as well as the headquarters of traders, haulers, shipbuilders, blacksmiths, rope makers, riggers, oyster merchants, brewers, carpenters, and all other conceivable maritime support trades. . . . [A] gateway village between the metropolis and the sea, for many, this tidewater frontier town was the only New York they knew. It had its own hotels, bars, and brothels, as well as at least one floating church."

One reason why exploring the waterfront is such a choppy, mystifying experience today is that you are walking over the bones of that commercial ghost town. There are still shards of it, in the form of the funkiest hotels and bars and (I assume) brothels you can imagine. Take the Liberty Inn Motel on Tenth Avenue and Fourteenth Street. I have always been fascinated by this modest, three-story, brick-faced, triangular structure, like a black-sheep offspring of the Flatiron Building: what is it doing out there, all by itself, near the water? It used to be known as a "hot sheet" hotel: a friend told me she would, in her youthful, promiscuous days, take her pickups from the clubs there. Today I force myself to go in and poke around, as a good reporter must. There is no lobby, just two chairs and a staircase leading up to the guest rooms; on one chair slumps an emaciated black woman, chin buried in chest, apparently nodding out; behind a Plexiglas divider an acne-faced Asian desk clerk eats a hero sandwich and chats on the phone. Misery. A set of rules posted beside the check-in desk states, "Guests must leave room together."

"What do you want?" asks the desk clerk behind the partition.

"I'd like to see a room. Some friends of mine are coming to town and I thought I might put them up here." The clerk looks me up and down: blue tweed jacket, white shirt, an obvious lie. She goes back to her friend on the phone. I wonder how far to push the masquerade. "I'll come back later," I say, leaving with relief. Surely the reader can imagine the kinds of rooms upstairs, without my having to inspect the decor.

Nor do I check out the remaining S&M/gay bars in the area, though I well remember how, at the height of the Stonewall era, this whole "west coast" of Greenwich Village was turned over nightly to men having sex in beef, poultry, and pork storage trucks, the irony of the term "meat-packing district" lost on no one. The writer Michael Lassell elegized that epoch in an essay for the anthology *New York Sex:* "Once upon a time the riverfront at the westernmost edge of Greenwich Village was a place for queer pioneers to lean between the uprights of the elevated highway, trolling for trade. . . . For decades, fearless, defiant men sucked dick and butt-fucked in the huge warehouses that loomed above the now-rotting planks that are off-limits big-time. . . . Nowadays the waterfront is 'Hudson River Park,' a hunk of to-be-developed green belt that is still a totally botched West Side Highway expansion. The once-dangerous turf has sprouted rules, regulations, and little green put-puts driven by dickless pissants in ugly uniforms."

ONE OF THE THINGS I LIKE about the waterfront is that it is ill-defined and still in transition. Maybe it's not such a bad idea for New York to hold on to incomplete zones that inspire dreams and anxieties. If you walk around Manhattan's waterfront today, you encounter a bewildering mix of edge-experiences that range from the blighted to the elegant, to the postmodernist pastiche, to the unfinished, to near wilderness. The sense you most often get is that everything the city doesn't want to deal with, everything "repressed," has been pushed to the water's edge. Salt mounds, auto salvage shops, beer-can recycling companies, defunct factories with smashed windows peeling in the sun, parking-violation tow pounds, huge parking lots for all the sanitation trucks on earth, S&M bars, public housing. Not for nothing do so many storage warehouses exist along the river, sheltering the old family dining sets, college books, and other obligations to the past that space-pinched New Yorkers think they need to hold on to, but are halfway to abandoning.

The repressed flourished best in the cracks of the decaying port, especially once it had begun to fall into ruin. The novelist Andrew Holleran once considered this phenomenon in an essay for *Christopher Street* magazine: "'Why do gays love ruins?' I said to my friends. . . . 'The Lower West Side, the docks. Why do we love slums so much?'

"'One can hardly suck cock on Madison Avenue, darling,' said the alumnus of the Mineshaft, curling his lip as we strolled down that very street. . . . 'When the shoreline is made pretty by city planners, and . . . the meatpacking district is given over entirely to boutiques and cardshops—

then we'll build an island in New York Harbor composed entirely of rotting piers, blocks of collapsed walls, and litter-strewn lots."

Today the meatpacking district is barely holding on, invaded as it is by boutiques and bistros. Meanwhile, the Greenwich Village waterfront is being transformed into a civic place, Hudson River Park. The Hudson River Park Trust is admirably, even radically, attempting to push forward a new public work along the water, from TriBeCa to 59th Street, a task every bit as difficult as building Central Park or Riverside Park—more so, actually, because it does not have landscape architects of genius like Olmsted and Vaux to oversee its design, or a powerful official like Robert Moses to cut through the red tape. It has only the conviction that New Yorkers want to get to the water, and that it is the city's manifest destiny to do so.

The former West Side Highway, now known as Route 9A, has been reconfigured as an "urban boulevard"—the model most often cited for it is Park Avenue—with traffic lights every three blocks and plantings in the middle. No longer a ten-lane, sixty-five miles-per-hour speedway, now it is to be a more "diminutive," eight-lane, optimally 25 mph glide. But it still looks and feels like a highway, not a boulevard. Nor does it resemble, in any way but the timing of its traffic lights, Park Avenue.

As I walk along the West Village section of the Hudson River Park, I find myself thinking: One of the best things you can do at the water's edge of a city is to make a street. Preferably a narrow street, providing only one car-lane apiece in each direction, so that it does not become another high-speed traffic corridor, but invites strolling, with fairly low-rise buildings that house shops on the ground floor, thereby bringing the vitality of the city to the edge. A promenade, be it in a beachside resort or a waterfront district, becomes energized when the walker can go from looking at the water to ducking into a shop or café on the street side (as in all those fatalistic French 1930s films, where Jean Gabin wanders down to the port to cast longing eyes at a ship leaving for foreign shores, then backs into a bar for a shot of *vin ordinaire*.) If you look at photographs of the Manhattan dockside in the early decades of the twentieth century, what you see—and it comes as a shock—is a real street, with automobiles parked two feet from the drink.

I suppose we must concede that West Street is technically a street, just not a very inviting, well-designed one. Certainly much of the success of the Hudson River Park, at least around SoHo and Greenwich Village, will hinge on what happens across the way, on the building side of West Street. At present it is a ragtag collection of holding-pattern uses: auto parts and garage repair shops, X-rated video stalls, printing firms on their way out, meatpacking plants in their twilight hour, next to boarded-up storefronts. The park will be served greatly if the street across from it becomes a lively area, with cafés and mixed uses and a steady stream of strollers. If it turns into nonstop luxury high-rises with private lobbies, as is already happening in parts of West Street, not so good.

7

EXCURSUS

OUTBOARD,
OR THE BATTLE
OF WESTWAY
AND ITS AFTERMATH

If a city has a memory, then the legacy of discarded infrastructural
works forms an important part of that memory.
—HAN MEYER, *City and Port*

NO UNBUILT PROJECT HAS HAD A GREATER IMPACT ON New York City's recent history than Westway, the plan to submerge the old six-lane highway under hundreds of acres of parkland and development along the West Side waterfront. The last three decades of the twentieth century were dominated by inflamed arguments for and against it, and, as a new century opens, the consequences of its defeat continue to shape all future development on the waterfront. Westway is the road not taken, and it haunts every choice made in its stead. Which is not to say that the man in the street even remembers it. The paradox of New York is that it is at once famously destructive and forgetful of its past, and forever walking in its oversized footprints. Those who wonder how a great city, capable of doing so much more along its riverfront, came to such an uninspiring compromise—a landscaped transit corridor that calls itself a park, a highway with a non-walkable divider that styles itself a boulevard—will do well to review the history of Westway, before it slides from our memory bank.

THE UNHAPPY CHOICE to ring the edge of Manhattan with highways, thereby cutting off the public from the water, is usually laid at the feet of Robert Moses, New York's all-powerful planning czar. Moses has become the hissed villain in the municipality's Passion Play, just as Frederic Law Olmsted, who, with his partner Calvert Vaux, gave the city its greatest treasures, Central Park and Prospect Park, is our hero. In fact, it was Olmsted who initially proposed a wide thoroughfare, or "park-way," along Manhattan's western edge, past his Riverside Park. Olmsted had a vision of adorning New York with a system of neighborhood parkways connecting up new parks, to serve the carriage trade (this was pre-automobile). As he and Vaux imagined it, the parkway was to be a pleasurably snaking, verdant route 260 feet wide, enough space to allow a wide path for vehicles down the middle, alternating rows of trees and walkways, then side-roads for vehicles to alight in front of buildings. They managed to build a few shining examples, such as Ocean Parkway and Eastern Parkway, which in turn inspired a nationwide parkway movement.

Olmsted's son, Frederic Law Olmsted Jr., also a prominent city planner, continued the work of his father in advocating a necklace of parkways around the perimeter of New York. But it was Julius Miller, as Manhattan borough president, who proposed the arterial roadway for the West Side in 1925 and oversaw the construction of its first section in 1930, and so it was Miller for whom the structure was named. (Few New Yorkers have ever called it the Miller Highway, taking almost immediately to the more impersonal nomenclature, the West Side Highway. A few years ago, ex-mayor Rudolph Giuliani, an unabashed Yankee fan, maybe forgetting that the road had already been named for an individual, chose to rename it the Joe DiMaggio Highway when the Yankee Clipper passed away, which designation New Yorkers have also largely ignored.)

Miller may have broken ground, but Robert Moses, expanding his domain from parks commissioner to highways and bridges, enthusiastically carried through perimeter-road construction around the whole island of Manhattan. If highways by the water's edge have proven to be a hideous idea, we must remember that many other cities in the United States and overseas were just as guilty of embracing that concept. It was in the air, not a demoniacal infliction by the Power Broker. Years later, in 1974, when perimeter highways were becoming openly reviled for robbing the public of waterfront access, a discarded Robert Moses wrote this defense, using passive tense and first person plural to suggest the more impersonal processes of collective reasoning:

"Not long after the turn of the century it became apparent that Manhattan's street system would not be able to cope with the inevitable growth of motor traffic. Congestion, particularly in the north-south avenues, was plain evidence of worse conditions yet to come. North-south arterials were needed, yet these could not be built in the interior of the borough. . . . The solution was obvious. Ring the borough with an arterial belt, remove the "Death Avenue" tracks* to a separate right of way, and along Riverside Park, cover them. Bring the park to the river's side, and create new waterfront parks and promenades in the process. Thus were the east side and west side improvements initiated." By these he means the

---

*"Death Avenue" referred to Twelfth Avenue and its freight railway spur, which took the lives of several citizens before being shut down.

East River (later renamed FDR) Drive, the Harlem River Drive, and the northern extension of Miller Highway above 72nd Street, all the way into the Bronx, where it connected with Westchester's parkway system.

"Such improvements were hailed as great achievements years ago. They rescued Manhattan from traffic strangulation that would have stunted the development of the business core. The Metropolitan region's worldwide eminence in commerce and industry is due in no small measure to them."

Here, Moses dodges the issue of why the roads had to be built in such a way as to leave a brutal gash in the urban fabric, and make it nearly impossible for people to get to the water by foot. He had shown, in his sensitive handling of Carl Schurz Park, the Brooklyn Esplanade, and parts of the Battery and Riverside Park, that he knew how to fold a highway underneath a public space quite beautifully, when he wanted to. But, aside from the greater initial costs entailed by covering perimeter highways, it was never a priority for Moses to make the waterside accessible to pedestrians, perhaps because he regarded himself as serving another constituency.

Moses shared with Olmsted a preference for personal transportation over mass transit. Though he has been portrayed since as Enemy of the People, it was probably more that he saw the middle class as Everyman (a common bourgeois misperception), and, since car ownership was the linchpin of American peacetime industry and the hallmark of citizenship and upward mobility, he regarded perimeter highways as a means of giving middle-class drivers and passengers alike something inspiring to look at as they tooled along.

In any event, the West Side Highway became a workhorse, the second-most-utilized road in the Greater New York area, next to the Long Island Expressway, and by the mid-1950s, a mere twenty-five years after construction, it was already dilapidated. Some traced the highway's crumbling condition to corrosive rock salt used during the big snow of 1947;[*] others, to pigeon excrement. "Nothing is to be gained," wrote Moses, taking the lofty perspective, "by carping criticism and second guessing as to why the highways were allowed to deteriorate to their present state." Suffice it to

---

[*] My first memory is of that 1947 snow, at four years old, when my mother tied my brother, sister, and me to a sled and pulled us down Havemeyer Street to do her marketing. What fun!

say there has always been more money in the city budget to build than to maintain infrastructure.

From 1956 on, plans were put forward to replace the West Side Highway, the most drastic being Moses' own egregious Lower Manhattan Expressway proposal, which would have barreled through parts of Greenwich Village and SoHo and shattered both communities. Jane Jacobs, whose paradigm-shifting 1961 book, *The Death and Life of Great American Cities*, awakened my generation to the value of multi-use neighborhoods and street life, and to the mistakes of urban planners seeking to impose excessive order, led the successful fight against this scheme. The Lower Manhattan Expressway proposal seemed the apotheosis of everything seigniorial and urbicidal in Moses' method of planning; and the relative ease with which it was defeated signaled that a new day of community activism had arrived.

John F. Kennedy was in the White House, and on the local level, the same fresh-start, glamorous spirit was exemplified by John V. Lindsay, the tall, handsome Lochinvar of a congressman from the Silk Stocking district. In 1965 Lindsay got himself elected mayor of New York on the Republican ticket (a rare event in a then-Democratic town), on a platform of giving neighborhoods more control over their destinies, through local city halls and community boards.

Lindsay brought in Edward Logue from Boston, where he had done great things as planning head. Logue, unafraid to wield power, was something of a dark hero to that new crowd of *urbanistas* who had sprung up in New York in the mid-sixties. Improbable as it sounds today, there was an almost rock-star excitement that surrounded city planning and urban improvement in that era. Under Lindsay's mayoralty, there started to be vest-pocket parks, traveling theater groups who performed in the barrios, free outdoor movies in summer, and all sorts of small-scale, contextual housing on the boards. Not much actually got built, but a perfume of limitless promise hovered in the air, the mystique of urban solutions drawing idealistic graduates from good universities, the progeny of Jane Jacobs and Paul Goodman. (I was one inch away at the time from becoming a city planner myself.)

Nelson Rockefeller, who served as governor of New York from 1958 through 1973, pried Ed Logue away from Lindsay (the two men hated each other; both liberal Republicans wanted to be president, with duplicate constituencies), and made him head of the newly formed Urban Development Corporation. At its outset, fully funded, the UDC had vast powers to construct housing, dormitories, hospitals, and schools across the state. Rockefeller had broken Moses' forty-year hold on the state, by accepting the Indispensable One's insincerely tendered resignation. Now Logue was given the authority, and he had more of a commitment to social justice and consultation with the community than Moses, his predecessor—which suited his new patron.

In spite of being born with the most silvered of silver spoons, Rockefeller, like all successful New York politicians, had the populist touch. "Hiya, fellow!" he would say, and wolf down pastrami at Katz's Delicatessen for the photographers. He wanted to be president, and got as far as vice-president, but was too liberal a Republican to make it all the way. The left could never say a good word about a Rockefeller, much less Nelson; but in retrospect he had a positive side, a passion for modern art and South America that helped establish the Museum of Modern Art and the United Nations headquarters; and he supported the UDC, which built a fair amount of decent mixed-income housing on Roosevelt Island and elsewhere. True, he made horrendous mistakes—the Albany Mall, the antidrug laws, his handling of the Attica prison riot—and that's what people tend to remember. In any case, he became one of the Westway proposal's earliest and most enthusiastic supporters.

THE WESTWAY PLAN was initially hatched around 1969–70, in the city's Housing and Development Administration (HDA), of all places. Sam Ratensky, a senior city planner at HDA, was, by all accounts, urbane and a mensch; he had apprenticed with Frank Lloyd Wright at Taliesen in his youth, and wanted to give a chance to young architects and planners bent on improving the city. He set up a shop of under-thirty aides, jauntily characterized by architectural critic Peter Blake as "Ratensky's Raiders," and they took on the problem of what to do with the West Side Highway. The team considered several options: restoring the elevated highway, building a new highway at street level, sinking a new highway along West Street with a deck over it, or the "outboard" solution—to build the highway in the river, alongside the waterfront—which was the one finally chosen.

Craig Whitaker, then twenty-nine, fresh from Yale architecture school and the Peace Corps, played a large part in developing the "outboard" plan, first called Wateredge. Originally the team had toyed with the idea of building a highway on pilings, but the federal highway officials had wanted it placed in a box, so they came up with the inspiration, as Whitaker likes to say, to "drop it in the drink."

Now a slight, professorial-looking man with thinning hair and pensive blue eyes, who teaches at NYU and wrote a book called *Architecture and the American Dream,* Whitaker seems a thoughtful survivor, less bitter than bemused. Westway is his Moby Dick, the whale that took thirteen years of his life. Having made more than 700 presentations to groups advocating the plan, and having spent years fighting to get it built, he is in no hurry to simplify the complexities of the battle story. He has devised a Westway slide show for his students, and his architectural office on lower Broadway contains what must be the world's largest archive of Westwayiana.

"Look, no sane person would have erected an at-grade or elevated highway again at the edge. The beauty of dropping it in the drink was that this way you got a broad new area, and people could walk to the water without being cut off from the highway. There was lots of parkland acreage. Landfill, yes. So what?" It would not eviscerate neighborhoods or cause massive relocation, nor would it tie up traffic for years with construction, since the downtown part of the old West Side Highway could continue to function at street level until Westway was opened. But, most important, it would bring people back to the Hudson, without having to cross a major highway.

As Whitaker tells it, Sam Ratensky got Ed Logue interested in the redesign. "Ratensky and Logue were rivals, but Sam was ill—dying of brain cancer—and about to retire. So Logue, who liked the outboard idea, hired Sam's whole crew, including me, into UDC, and Sam retired." The project now had a formidable protector in Logue.

"I was delegated to make the presentation to Governor Rockefeller. I was still pretty young, and no one knew me from Adam. But as soon as Rockefeller heard the word 'tunnel,' he went for it." Whitaker pauses in mid-thought, like a general recalling ancient errors of military strategy: "It was John Zuccotti [then Chairman of the City Planning Commission] who came up with the name 'Westway.' We should have just called it the Tunnel. People would have understood it better."*

It was not as if New Yorkers were unfamiliar with underwater tubes: they had lived for decades with the Holland and Hudson Tunnels, joining Manhattan with New Jersey, and the Brooklyn-Battery Tunnel, running under the East River between lower Manhattan and Brooklyn. The only difference was that this particular tunnel would hug the western shore of the island, rather than connecting two landmasses.

Certainly such a submerged tunnel, which would take an estimated ten years to construct, would not come cheap: the budget was projected for over a billion dollars, which would make it, foot for foot, the most expensive highway ever built. But the beauty part was that it would cost the city nothing. The Federal Highway Fund would pay for 90 percent, and the state would kick in the remaining 10 percent.

Westway was to run 4.2 miles from the Battery to 42nd Street, in the form of two tubes of three lanes each, plus a shoulder lane on each side. It would be considered part of the interstate highway system. If you wanted the Highway Trust Fund to fork over the money, you had to propose a high-speed interstate expressway. The irony is that the New York City Department of Transportation didn't particularly want a high-speed expressway. The transportation field's philosophy was shifting, from moving cars rapidly through and out of the city, to discouraging high-speed corridors in urban settings. As it was, the rush-hour speed on Westway was projected at only twenty miles per hour. But it still had to be presented as an "interstate highway" (largely a semantic issue) because that way the Feds would pick up 90 percent of the costs, whereas if it were for any other kind of road, federal funds would only pay 65 percent. Being a federal highway also meant that it would take trucks (a plus, removing trucks from the streets). But the very word *interstate* aroused the public's mistrust, understandably, as interstate highways had had a bad record nationwide of bulldozing through neighborhoods and increasing pollution. In fact, in

---

*What's in a name? The late Daniel Patrick Moynihan, New York's intellectual senator, who loved Westway to the end, said, "If only we had called it 'the Hudson Marshes.'"

1977 federal legislation was enacted to prevent interstates from passing through inner cities; however, Westway, being in a tunnel, would still qualify for federal highway monies.

One of the knocks on Westway was that it was put together to maximize drawing federal funds into the city. Merely because the money is available to us, argued critics, doesn't mean we have to take it, if the project is no good. We could "just say no." On the other hand, if one believed the project was worthy, why not take advantage of a federal cash stream? In a sense this was payback, since New York City had historically given much more in taxes to Washington than it had received back in services.

Part of what made the Westway plan so costly was that it offered far more than just a highway, encompassing a park and commercial and residential development as well. The project would have created 234 acres of new (via landfill) and reclaimed land, of which ninety-three acres were to be set aside for parks. Ada Louise Huxtable put the matter in perspective in her January 23, 1977, architecture column for the *New York Times:* "Westway is not just a billion-dollar road. It has never pretended to be only an answer to transportation needs. There are simpler answers, as opponents claim, but that misses the point. Westway possesses rare vision: it is large-scale, long-term land use planning for the city's future. It is a chance to reclaim the mutilated waterfront and West Side. It is an opportunity to do something extraordinarily constructive and creative—*provided that it is done well.*" For Huxtable, the challenge was to ensure that the design of the project met the very highest standards, and that real estate speculation in the areas adjoining the new parks was held in check by zoning restrictions with teeth.

The complexity that Huxtable saw as Westway's strength—that it was a comprehensive land-use plan, accomplishing several things at once—became one of its vulnerable points. Some critics would continue to insist that over a billion dollars was too high a price to pay for any road, ignoring the plan's other components, while others would portray Westway as dishonestly piggybacking a development scheme onto highway construction. Those who were for Westway asked why this merger of two aims, highway and community development, should necessarily be considered a boondoggle. In a society that was not afraid to plan for the future, it would only make sense to design the public areas—park and highway—and the private commercial and residential areas as one autonomous element, giving shape to the city.

THE PROPOSED WESTWAY was to run past several of the most contentious and politically active community boards in the city, Greenwich Village, TriBeCa, and Chelsea. Their support was essential for the project to go forward. As it happened, the NIMBY ("not in my backyard") factor played little part in the battle; the neighborhoods most affected were rather quiet during the Westway fight (perhaps preferring to have a highway submerged in landfill than run through their blocks). The main anti-Westway leaders, such as Marcy Benstock and Albert Butzel, lived farther uptown. The local community mistrust that did exist tended to center on the development issue.

So Mary Perot Nichols, in her *Village Voice* column dated November 19, 1970, alerted readers that the man just put in charge of waterfront planning, Samuel Ratensky, represented "a dead hand from the past. . . . Sources close to Ratensky claim he already has a plan, composed of highrise apartment buildings for the West Village. . . . Is Sam Ratensky going to give us a warmed over West Village Urban Renewal plan or has he turned over a new leaf? . . . Until we get these answers, maybe we should keep our paranoia alive but leashed."

The Greenwich Village community was mollified, to some extent, by the Westway team's agreement to limit the height of proposed new housing. In 1976 the selection of the innovative architectural firm Venturi, Scott Brown and Associates, to provide a design for the new park, won over much of the architectural set. The elegant, user-friendly plan they executed for the elongated Hudson River shoreline, much of which was to be created through landfill, redesigned the whole waterfront area as a public domain. An esplanade, running along the course of the shoreline, would be sunken in relation to the green park strip; there would be a bikeway and a promenade; and a wall would separate the park from the adjacent street, making for a much more enclosed, contemplative park experience, buffeted from the clamor of the metropolis, than the current Hudson River Park. But the park strip would be linked directly to the street network of the grid, and divided, in its entirety, into a series of smaller and larger parks, each of which would reflect the specific nature of the district bordering it. The Venturi, Scott Brown plan, improving on the best ideas of Olmsted and Moses, offered the chance for a great new piece of city-making to cap the end of the twentieth century.

A WATERFRONT PARK WAS ONE THING; but from whence came the landfill/development impetus? Nathan Silver, in his 1967 necropolis of a picture book, *Lost New York,* put the matter astutely:

> The New York Regional Plan of 1929–31, a proposal that was not timid about its new highway plans for Manhattan, nevertheless roundly disowned the West Side Highway. The planners found fault with it because its location cut people off from the Hudson River and made the development of new riverfront recreation facilities most difficult. The influence of the Regional Plan Association's comment was presumably modest, because the alignment of the new East River Drive soon repeated the mistake on the other side of the island. Since the penny-wise New York commissioners who laid out the 1811 grid of streets had reasoned that the City did not need many parks because of New York's healthful relationship with its river edges, one finds that official planning has, in its history, both turned people toward the water and then stopped them from getting there. This double bind may one day have to be resolved by means of expensive landfill and development.

Besides the statement's elegant terseness, what stands out today is that Silver, a champion of New York tradition and preservation, accepted without hesitation the solution of landfill. After all, Manhattan had grown physically, from the 1700s on, largely as a result of landfill: it had added Front, West, Water Streets, and more; it had connected the Battery and Castle Clinton, once surrounded by the water, to Downtown; it had filled in swamps and marshlands to support rail tracks and highways; it had rounded out shavings of land to the north; and, more recently, it had added nearly a hundred acres to make Battery Park City. In 1967 there was as yet no revulsion attached to the word. That taboo would come later, perhaps in the form of a delayed reaction.

The impetus for the inclusion of commercial and residential development in the plan had its own history; it grew out of Manhattan's anomalous possession of two competing business districts, Midtown and Downtown. Downtown was going through one of its periodic uneases: ever since the 1950s, the businessmen and realtors of Wall Street, headed by David Rockefeller, had been calling for some larger strategy to compete with Midtown, by making the financial district more attractive to new firms, meanwhile retaining the older ones. In 1958 the Downtown Lower Manhattan Association had outlined the area's problems, such as a lack of new building sites, gridlocked traffic, a monotonous single-use that made the area deserted after dark or on weekends, and a paucity of residential units and retail or cultural attractions to hold white-collar workers. The canyons of Wall Street being already crammed with skyscrapers, the obvious solution was to add onto Lower Manhattan, by building a whole new, day-night district on landfill—which is where the idea of Battery Park City came in. During the mid-1970s, with the city's economy approaching bankruptcy, and with Lower Manhattan neighborhoods' flattened growth seemingly in need of some economic boost, the billion dollars promised by Westway looked very tempting.

Here is how the anti-Westway attorney Michael Gerrard put it: "A remarkably successful effort to consolidate business and labor support for Westway ensued in 1975 and 1976, headed by the odd couple of David Rockefeller, chairman of the Chase Manhattan Bank, and Harry Van Arsdale, president of the Central Labor Council, AFL-CIO." Since New York City had just "brushed with bankruptcy" and "construction was in a terrible slump," Gerrard concluded: "The business community came to see Westway as a way to spur economic and real estate development; the construction unions saw Westway as a massive source of new jobs." To this picture of collusion among strange bedfellows, one might counter: How else could any massive public work, from Central Park to the water delivery system, have gotten built in New York without a broad alliance of business, labor, and government?

On December 15, 1973, the weight of a dump truck, hauling tar to fill the uncountable potholes on the West Side Highway, caused an elevated section of the roadway to collapse. The truck driver landed below, near West 12th Street, his vehicle upended like a turtle on its back, and eventually received $250,000 from the city as compensation for his injuries. The highway was then closed to traffic south of 46th Street, and that portion slated for demolition. In the interim, what followed was an urban idyll of sorts, in which bikers, strollers, and sunbathers liberated the deck for recreational uses. To the city government, the collapse of one highway section only increased the urgency to construct Westway or some other replacement road. But some citizens, especially those without cars, began to entertain the thought that maybe the metropolis could get along without new highways. A species of Luddite fantasy arose from deep within the bohemian subconscious of New Yorkers: a perpetual pedestrian be-in. The opposition to the Vietnam War had made any large government construction project suspect. Interstate highways seemed a domestic form of pacification, and cars were junior tanks, aggressive, lethal, spreading air pollution. Why should society's limited resources be squandered on that pampered convenience?

By 1974 the West Side Highway Project ('WSHP') had produced a final Westway design. Here was Whitaker's vision: start with the Downtown tunnel piece, from 59th Street to the Battery, and hook it up with the Brooklyn-Battery Tunnel at the bottom of Manhattan. Once that part had been built, and everyone saw how well it worked, with the barrier-highway removed and a generous-sized park giving the public easy access to the water, you could extend the submerged tube all the way north, to the George Washington Bridge, thereby freeing Riverside Park entirely of the highway that now mars some of its most beautiful waterside walking paths.

It was a clear, lucid vision, muddied at every turn by politics. The first occlusion involved a territorial squabble: the head of the Battery Park City Authority, a Governor Rockefeller appointee, was threatened by Ed Logue's infringing on his domain by proposing to run the tunnel underwater along Battery Park City's edge. (This was during the period when BPC still sat unbuilt, a tract of sand and mud.) He insisted that Westway connect *inland* and aboveground with a ten-lane Brooklyn-Battery Tunnel entrance, which meant it would need to surface somewhere south of Canal Street to gain enough altitude, and run at street level for the last mile or so. For whatever reason—cronyism, political blackmail—Rockefeller acceded to this stupid demand, which in effect doomed Battery Park City to isolation by a moatlike highway. This last section of construction, running as it would through Manhattan's streets, also greatly increased Westway's costs, absorbing almost 40 percent of the highway's proposed budget.

Meanwhile, the Upper West Side community was nervous about Westway, fearing it was a Trojan Horse that would gallop through Riverside Park. The district's state assemblyman, Albert Blumenthal, sponsored legislation that made it virtually impossible to disturb even a blade of grass in Riverside Park, for highway construction or any other purpose. The Westway team had no problem with that, since they had planned all along to build the northern extension of the highway underwater. Assemblyman Blumenthal, now reassured that Riverside Park was in no danger, became an enthusiastic supporter of Westway. However, the force of organized community suspicion, once unleashed, does not easily accede to fact. Whitaker recalls presenting to an Upper West Side community group the sketches showing how Westway would liberate Riverside Park of the present highway, and "dump it in the drink" alongside. At the meeting's end, an elderly woman approached him and said, "You seem like such a nice young man. Why would you want to destroy Riverside Park?" Years later, Whitaker, gray-haired, was still shaking his head at the memory.

One of the objections raised against Westway was that it would induce more traffic into the city. Roberta Brandes Gratz stated that position in her book *The Living City:* "[E]very new road in recent years has, by its very creation, stimulated new traffic. The reality of highway building is that highways encourage further automobile traffic." This notion, which started as a valuable corrective insight, has hardened into a mantra. Certainly, building new highways *may* generate more traffic, by enticing people to avail themselves of the new roads; but whether it actually will do so depends on duplication of routes and many other factors. As it turned out, Westway was not built, and traffic volume still increased in the 1990s along the old, patched-together West Side Highway. In the same years, subway ridership also increased, suggesting that the overall economic prosperity of the region during the 1990s led to more vehicles *and* more mass transit usage. In any case, the Westway plan called for the same number of lanes as the old West Side Highway, with no added capacity.

Again and again, it seems to me, the Westway team would answer some objection to the plan, only to discover their listeners had already made up their minds that these facts could not be trusted because they came from Satan. The irony of the Westway battle was that it pitted two groups of idealists against each other; but only one—the anti-Westway forces—was able to commandeer the rhetoric of virtue, perhaps because it was located outside the power structure. Ratensky's Raiders had started out with a pro-environmentalist perspective. Their willingness to compromise with opponents' objections stemmed partly from the fact that they were already sympathetic to the opposing point of view. "Everybody on that team hated highways," recalled Richard Kahan, Westway's counsel at the time, adding that these were not your typical gung-ho Department of Highways stalwarts, intent on moving traffic faster at all costs. If they had gotten involved with building a highway, it was because it seemed the only way to accomplish other purposes, such as waterfront access. But precisely because the Westway team thought of themselves as idealists and people of goodwill, they were never able to grasp the seriousness of the animus directed at them.

Community activists who had defeated the Lower Manhattan Expressway proposal rallied once more against this new highway proposal. The importance of the Lower Manhattan Expressway battle to the Westway saga is that anti-Westway activists could represent the proposal as the return of the old monster they had already slain. Never mind that Westway's design was an attempt to *avoid* the neighborhood-smashing of Robert Moses; the reform movement's collective memory requires the scenario that the same vampire arise anew in each succeeding generation.

So when Jane Jacobs, by now living in Toronto, was interviewed by *New York* magazine in 1978 about Westway, she attacked it not only on the basis that it was the second coming of the Lower Manhattan Expressway, but that it was the third coming of the New York Regional Plan Committee's 1929 report, with its proposed crosstown expressways traversing Manhattan. "Westway is only one small piece of a plan that would, piece by piece, Los Angeles-ize New York. It's an old plan that dates back to 1929." The advantage of a historical perspective is that an informed skeptic such as Jacobs can be appropriately on guard when newfangled ideas are proposed. The disadvantage is that one may be tempted to fight the old battles, ignoring important distinctions. "If Westway goes in, the Lower Manhattan Expressway will be revived," she told her interviewer confidently, though such an outcome, decimating Greenwich Village and Soho, would have been extremely unlikely.

Meanwhile, Robert Moses, the chief advocate of the Lower Manhattan Expressway, now in semi-retirement, issued a paper calling the Westway proposal a "fiasco," saying it would be too expensive, thereby incurring the resentment of Western and Southern congressmen, and that the better way was to repair the collapsed elevated roadway. "How much longer can such a shindig go on? Five years? Ten years? This is not orderly consideration. It is a mob dividing up stage money, an Anvil Chorus, a byword, a hissing and a yapping, a spectacle of bamboozlement. If this is the road to progress, I am the retired Gaekwar of Baroda," Moses concluded colorfully. For once, Jane Jacobs and Robert Moses were in agreement. Both hated Westway.

But look who was *for* Westway: three United States presidents (Gerald Ford, Jimmy Carter, Ronald Reagan) and every New York senator, governor, and mayor who served during its placement on the table (including such nationally recognized figures as Daniel Patrick Moynihan, Jacob Javits, Nelson Rockefeller, Hugh Carey, Mario Cuomo, John Lindsay, and Ed Koch), every construction and civil service union, the banks and business community, the three local daily newspapers, leading architectural critics (Ada Louise Huxtable, Paul Goldberger, Peter Blake), and various civic watchdog groups (Municipal Art Society, Citizens Housing and Planning Council)—all pressing to see this oddly visionary scheme become a reality. The Westway team was spearheaded by an undersecretary type with Washington influence (Lowell Bridwell), while able fixers like John Zuccotti, Abe Beame's deputy mayor, were working behind the scenes. It was easy for anti-Westway groups to put a single label on this broad spectrum of agreement: the Establishment. Formidable official pressure was being brought to bear to get this project built, making the end result doubly surprising.

ALBERT BUTZEL, the attorney who may have done more than anyone else to defeat Westway, acknowledges today that the project was designed in such a way as to avoid controversy. "Nobody had anything against Westway's being on landfill back then, it looked like a win-win solution. In fact, the genius of the Westway proposal was that it didn't tear down anyone's house. I even thought the tunnel was a pretty good idea," admitted Butzel. "It would bring people to the water. The fight back then was trading in highway funds for mass transit, shifting people back from cars to trains."

Westway became a litmus test for whether you were pro–mass transit or highways. Marci Benstock, another indefatigable leader of the anti-Westway forces, told the press that the driving force motivating her was her love of the subways. No one could argue that New York's subway system was rundown and in need of massive infusions of capital. For ridership to rebound, the fleet of trains needed to be replaced by newer models, and the shabby stations given facelifts. Through recent federal legislation, sponsored by New York congresswoman Bella Abzug, a mechanism existed for highway funds to be traded in for mass transit. It would never amount to a dollar-for-dollar exchange; at most, thirty or forty cents on the dollar. The federal government and Congress, having committed over a billion dollars for Westway, was not about to take kindly to New York City's saying, "On second thought, we don't really want that highway you thought so much of, can you give us a billion for our subways instead?"

The mass-transit-versus-highways choice was, from the start, a false one, since any balanced regional system needed both. As a *New York Times* editorial put it: "we deem false the assumption that Westway is an alternative to mass transit and that the two modes are irreconcilable. Westway forms a most significant part of a total transportation strategy. It will accommodate deliveries and services that never take the subway."

. . .

MUNICIPAL CONSTRUCTION PROJECTS that require a long while to win approval inevitably traverse several economic cycles, falling into and out of sync with the mood of the moment. So it was with Westway. Its redevelopment piece began as a way to boost a moribund area that needed development, then was transformed by a hot real estate market into something else. By the time the boom years of the 1980s had arrived, and there was a serious housing shortage, and co-ops in Greenwich Village, SoHo and TriBeCa were going for sky-high prices, and plans were afoot to throw up hideous high-rise apartment buildings at the end of every block that overlooked the Hudson River, the notion of the city government promoting upscale residential and commercial development—on landfill, no less—seemed obscene.

The educated public's visceral disgust with developers was in part a specific historical reaction against the transformation of Manhattan into an overbuilt vertical pincushion, and in part a revulsion against the spectacle of greed in the eighties, a postindustrial greed that thrived on fiscal manipulations. Just as there were sardonic jokes about lawyers in the eighties, there were developer jokes. In that climate of growing anti-development sentiment, much opposition to Westway came simply from the suspicion that the real estate lobby stood to make a lot of money from it. I felt that way myself at the time, and was in the anti-Westway camp, without giving it much thought, in lockstep with my peer group. Today I would characterize my changed position by saying that while I am not delighted at the possibility that a large public work may end up lining some pockets, I am unwilling to cease advocating civic amenities out of resentment that they will enrich others. Developers can be harsh, exploitative, damaging to community values and aesthetics, ruthless to the poor, all true; but they can also build great cities. What else is New York City but a huge real estate development?

THE COALITION OF GROUPS opposed to Westway included Marci Benstock's Clean Air Campaign, Action for Rational Transit (a

Manhattan citizen group that later evolved into the Straphangers), and the Sierra Club, all of which used the lawsuit as their principal weapon. Under the Clean Water Act and the Rivers and Harbors Appropriation Act, the New York State Department of Transportation was required to obtain a permit to place landfill in the Hudson River. The decision was left to the U.S. Army Corps of Engineers to decide whether to grant a landfill permit. The anti-Westway coalition argued against the project, on the grounds that it would promote air pollution and inefficient use of energy resources (highways instead of mass transit).

In 1977 the Environmental Protection Agency issued a report describing Westway as "environmentally unsatisfactory," and called for trading in the highway funds for mass transit. Years of lawsuits and delays followed; but the opponents of Westway were still never able to prove that the project would worsen air quality, at least to the satisfaction of the magistrate in charge, Judge Thomas P. Griesa of the U.S. District Court. In 1981 Judge Griesa dismissed all of the clean-air issues.

Albert Butzel remembers leaving the courtroom that day, thinking it was all over, they'd lost, Westway would get built. But a friendly soul asked him if he had seen the depositions by Michael Ludwig, a marine biologist with the National Marine Fisheries Service. Looking them over, Butzel noticed a passage about the landfill potentially interfering with the striped bass's favorite wintering site. Until that point, no one had taken the issue of marine habitat seriously, perhaps assuming that the harbor was too polluted to support much fish life. It so happened, however, that Butzel knew something about striped bass, because the fish had helped him and his law firm win a previous case that blocked Consolidated Edison's power plant at Storm King Mountain. If anti-Westway groups could prove that the tunnel might have a negative impact on striped bass migrating to the ocean, they were back in business.

TO GRASP THE STRIPED BASS'S SIGNIFICANCE to the lower Hudson requires some background about the abuse of the harbor. For a good part of New York's history, its harbor was used as a sewer and a dump. "[T]he rotting carcasses of horses and cattle were simply tossed into the rivers surrounding the city, where they remained for weeks, stinking and bloated, floating in and out with the tides," wrote Benjamin Miller in his informative book about New York's garbage, *Fat of the Land.* While the river disposal of dead animals was prohibited shortly after 1850, open-decked scows continued to dump garbage and mud into the harbor.

In that same period (1850–1890) there was increasing concern about the encroachment of docks into the Hudson and East Rivers, past the agreed-upon 400-foot limit. "Garbage, dredge spoil, sewer waste, ballast from ships, cinders and other materials coming either from city sewers or from docking ships quickly filled in the spaces between piers. What happened then was predictable," noted Marion J. Klawonn in *Cradle of the Corps.* "Dock owners simply extended their piers further out into the rivers in order to get into deeper water." Had the trend continued, Manhattan's Hudson River piers would have been, by 1900, within a quarter-mile of the New Jersey shore. But in 1855 the New York State legislature established a commission to survey and map the entire New York Harbor, in order to recommend definitive limits. The federal River and Harbor Act of 1888 established lines in harbors beyond which no building could take place without a permit and permission of the Army Corps of Engineers.

All these progressive pieces of legislation did not prevent unofficial dumping from continuing, as it was impossible for the overextended harbor police to patrol everywhere and enforce the laws. More important, the harbor was continuing "to receive staggering amounts of raw sewage—by 1910 six hundred million gallons a day of untreated waste was being discharged from New York City alone," according to John Waldman, in *Heartbeats in the Muck.* Seas of floating garbage and human fecal matter were washing back with the tides. Children who swam in the floating baths rimming New York were not protected from these incursions, and people caught typhoid fever from handling oysters, once a staple of the New York diet. Such were the good old days, before sewage treatment plants.

The harbor was polluted not merely by visible waste but, increasingly, by chemicals released by industry, such as dioxin, methane, and PCBs. No wonder many people had given up on New York's harbor, and assumed it to be biologically dead. But in 1972 (the same time the Westway proposal came into being), the Clean Water Act, one of the most radical pieces of legislature in our lifetime, was passed, and the Hudson River started to heal. In 1988 the U.S. Congress passed the Marine Protection Act, forbidding the ocean dumping of refuse.

Today New York Harbor is probably cleaner than at any time in the past hundred years,* and many fish species long absent have returned. But even before the effects of this cleansing could be felt, there was much more piscine activity in the lower Hudson than anyone except for a few hardy fishermen knew about. In 1969, naturalist Robert Boyle could write, in his study *The Hudson River* (which became a kind of holy text to the opponents of Westway): "As of now, the biological productivity of the lower Hudson is staggering. Fishes are there by the millions, with marine and freshwater species often side by side in the same patch of water. All told, the populations of fishes utilizing the lower Hudson for spawning, nursery, or feeding grounds comprise the greatest single wildlife resource in New York State. It is also the most neglected resource," he added.

The main reason for the fecundity of the lower Hudson, according to Boyle, is that it is an estuary, where ocean and freshwater merge. "Nothing ever really goes to waste in an estuary. . . . The rocking action of the tides keeps the lower Hudson stirred like a thick soup. . . . In essence, the Hudson estuary is a nutrient trap, a protein plant, a self-perpetuating fertilizer factory . . . a kind of Times Square" for fishes.

The Federal Highway Administration, in its 1977 report for the Environmental Impact Statement, described the Westway area as "biologically impoverished" and "almost devoid of macroorganism." The FHA and other pro-Westway agencies were obviously minimizing the loss of fish habitat so as to get on with the construction job at hand. To counter that stance, it was important for the anti-Westway coalition to demonstrate that the lower Hudson adjacent to Manhattan was still swarming with fish. But not just any fish: though plenty of winter flounder and tomcod could be found in New York Harbor, the case against Westway was built around the striped bass, because it was the premier recreational fish,

---

*Perhaps longer than that, but we have no way of knowing, because the city's water quality only started being monitored in 1909. The Department of Environmental Protection announced in 2001 that New York Harbor was cleaner than at any time since monitoring had begun, and that levels of fecal coliform bacteria, which come from human and animal waste, had dropped 98 percent since 1974.

the glamour fish of the East Coast. Its pursuit was big business; hundreds of charter boats and many coastal communities in the Chesapeake Bay, Connecticut, Long Island, and New Jersey catered to those who, as Boyle put it, "sacrifice their jobs, their marriage, and even their sacred honor to fish for stripers."

Curiously, very few sportsmen sought out stripers along the Hudson, in spite of the fact that, according to Boyle's 1969 estimate, the river held approximately 17 million striped bass, or 10 to 20 percent of the total run along the inshore Atlantic Coast. The reason given was that Hudson River striped bass are reputed to have an unpleasantly oily taste, thanks to the refineries in Bayonne. Hudson River striped bass are still officially frowned upon as eating fish, because they contain harmful concentrations of PCBs. But the economic potential for striper angling in the Hudson River remained high. In any event, it was easier to offer a case defending this well-loved fish than the tomcod or hogchoker. (As it happened, striped bass stocks in the mid-1970s were declining nationally, and federal legislation was passed to protect them, making for an even stronger case to protect them in New York.) So the opponents of Westway put aside their study of mass transit and went about learning the migrating patterns of the striped bass.

Hudson River striped bass spawn somewhere around Peekskill. A female striped bass produces more than a million eggs, which are fertilized by dozens of thrashing males; parental care is minimal, the eggs left to their own devices. At a few weeks old, the fish are silver in color; later they sport checkerboard sides; later still, they acquire the pretty horizontal stripes of the adult. Though a few swim north, they rarely get above Troy, because they are stopped by the system of canal locks; the vast majority head south, toward the Atlantic Ocean and New York City. Striped bass don't mind urban environments; they rather like cities. What they mostly like is structure, something to latch on to. While the smooth, straight-ruled bulkhead engirdling lower Manhattan would seem less latch-worthy than the original irregular coast, the downtown piers have come to offer a satisfying substitute.

The piers act like marshes, interrupting the flow of water and creating backwaters. For fish, the best parts of piers are the edges, which help bring about an "ecotone," an interface where habitat types can mix. The old finger docks of Manhattan were ideal for this purpose, because they were mostly all edge, and they did not have large platforms that would plunge the water underneath them in shadow. Fish tend to stay away from large pier structures: the darkness may scare them away, or else they prefer swimming in lighter waters where they can see their food and elude predators.

The so-called "interpier" area of the Hudson River, which the Westway landfill intended to occupy, was dotted with obsolete, deteriorating finger piers. The proposed Westway tunnel would be built out to the pier line, eliminating these piers. The first Westway survey ordered by the Department of Transportation found few fish in the harbor. But a second, taken during the winter months of 1979, determined that a diverse fish community did exist in the interpier area; that the striped bass present in that area were primarily in their first year (so-called "young-of-year") and second year of life ("yearlings"); and that a combination of adequate food and structural shelter seemed to have created a suitable winter habitat for these maturing, migrating stripers. A statistical spike in one area indicated that a population of striped bass was harbored in precisely the portion of the river slated for occupation by Westway.

From this point on, the hard science gets a little hazy. To begin with, patterns of fish movement and abundance are notoriously difficult to study. The fluctuations in population and distribution from season to season; the impact of weather—a mild winter versus a severe one, say—on the sample size; the techniques for collection, with the variants of depth distribution (bottom trawling as opposed to setting minnow traps, either one of which may privilege one species over another); the use of mathematical probabilities to determine best-case/worse-case scenarios, all may lead to very different results, and did, depending on who was doing the study.

With billions of dollars at stake, each side used the figures that best suited its argument. To the anti-Westway coalition, the discovery that young striped bass seemed to hang out at an interpier area in lower Manhattan indicated it was a crucial stopover, a "winter resort" in their migration to the ocean, allowing them to rest, conserve energy, and fatten up. To Craig Whitaker and other Westway proponents, the explanation was that striped bass liked garbage, and the only special lure of the inter-pier area was a sewage outflow that happened to be located there.*

Scientists on both sides recognized that the project-mandated experiments would have neither enough time nor funding to settle the point: a soupçon of science was being used to buttress a public policy decision. John Waldman, who was just starting out then as a young ichthyologist, recalls the Westway fish studies as both heroic and frustrating, because they were methodologically flawed. The U.S. Army Corps of Engineers kept maintaining that it had enough data, and issuing landfill permits, while the anti-Westway attorneys kept going back to court and obtaining delays, on the basis that not enough information had been collected. Two winters at minimum would be necessary for an adequate comparative study, at a direct cost of $9 million (and an additional $60 million for project delays). Above and beyond amassing sufficient data, it was in the interests of those opposed to Westway to stall. "The longer this thing is left out in the street," Ed Logue phrased it, "the more it's going to get kicked."

Delays had another negative effect on Westway, driving its projected budget up, as construction costs soared in the boom years of the eighties. Had the highway been built when it was first proposed, it would have cost slightly over a billion dollars. By 1984 the projected costs had risen to $2 billion, still able to be entirely funded by federal and state agencies. From this point on, however, the more construction costs rose, the greater the risk that the city would end up incurring some financial burden. As it was, the cost of the unbuilt Westway totaled over $200 million in planning, studies, lawsuits, and other fees, including an $80-million check that President Reagan released for New York State to buy the right-of-way from the city, which was never retrieved by the federal government, but which laid the groundwork for the Hudson River Park Trust.

The battle of Westway ended in the courtroom, as the same judge, Thomas Griesa, who had decided that the proposed highway did not present an additional air-pollution threat, ruled that it might endanger the

---

*"Silvery, sleek, and muscular, striped bass love to hunt by sewage outfalls, enjoy bumping and harassing commercial divers, and weigh anywhere from twenty to sixty pounds. . . ." (Anne Matthews, *Wild Nights*)

striped bass. Judge Griesa twice revoked the Army Corps of Engineers' landfill permits, in 1982 and 1985. And he did so, a reading of his brisk, scathing 1985 decision suggests, in part out of annoyance with the Corps's military-bureaucratic style, which he took to be evasive, bumbling, and dishonest.

Here we need to consider the internal culture of the Army Corps of Engineers. The Corps likes to build—it has an ethos sympathetic to large construction projects. Environmentalists had long felt that the Corps was reluctant to enforce antipollution statutes; its tendency was to stonewall the public and show obeisance to top industry officials. At times a cozy revolving-door employment policy existed between its officers and large contractors. In the matter of Westway, appearances were not helped when, in 1982, the Corps's district engineer, Colonel Walter Smith, after having decided that no new fish-sampling program in the Hudson would be necessary and that he was ready to grant a landfill permit, was discovered to have been seeking employment with the main engineering consultant for Westway.

Colonel F. H. Griffis was appointed to replace the retiring Colonel Smith as New York district engineer, and Griffis recommended a two-winter sampling study. But the Corps's problems with Judge Griesa did not end there. He found it in violation of the Clean Water Act because "the Corps simply ignored the views of sister agencies that were, by law, to be accorded great weight," acting instead "from an almost fixed predetermination to grant the Westway landfill permit." (The sister agencies he was referring to were the Environmental Protection Agency, the Fish and Wildlife Service and the National Marine Fisheries Service, all of whom had submitted objections to the landfill permit.) The judge criticized not only the Corps, but the Federal Highway Works Authority and the State Department of Transportation for their skimpy recordkeeping, and their inadequate public disclosure of materials detrimental to Westway.

Finally, Judge Griesa went tooth-and-nail after discrepancies between the Corps's preliminary environmental impact statement, which had found "significant" use by young striped bass of the interpier area, and the final environmental impact statement, which dismissed possible harmful effects of the project on the fish as "minor." Though the Corps's scientists tried to explain that they had been using the word "significant" only in the narrow sense of "statistically" significant, meaning it was "measurable" if minor, not in the broader, layman's sense, the judge remained unconvinced; he smelled a cover-up.

He was particularly incensed by the testimony of one government witness, William Dovel, who had developed the Corps's theory that the juvenile bass used the interpier area only briefly in the course of migrations out of and back into the river. Finding Dovel's wobbliness on the witness stand "bizarre," Griesa let him have it: "Dovel's testimony is a collection of assertions so irresponsible that it is shocking that the Government ever tendered him as a witness." Part of what made Dovel unreliable in the judge's eyes was that he seemed to have changed his mind regarding where the juvenile bass were overwintering, and acknowledged that his ideas were only "tentative hypotheses." But it did not help Dovel's credibility that he too had been caught in a conflict of interests: he had gone to Laurance Rockefeller's office, requesting funding for the preparation of a report on striped bass. "Dovel said that it could be most beneficial for Westway and that 'Westway could use it,'" Griesa summarized witheringly.

Against this background, Al Butzel, counsel for the Sierra Club, was able to raise a suspicion of self-interest and pro-development advocacy on the part of Westway's scientific hired consultants. In this David-versus-Goliath case, pitting feisty citizens' groups against state and corporate power, the anti-Westway witnesses were then seen as disinterested public servants. Judge Griesa had high praise for Frank DeLuise of the Fish and Wildlife Service and Michael Ludwig of the National Marine Fisheries Service: "There is no question about the honesty of these witnesses and the high degree of expertise they possess. Their knowledge of the relevant subject-matter is indeed profound."

The lawsuit has become the great equalizing tool for environmentalist causes. "Only in a courtroom," said Victor Yannacone, attorney for the Environmental Defense Fund, "can a scientist present his evidence, free from harassment by politicians. And only in a courtroom can bureaucratic hogwash be tested in the crucible of cross-examination." In this case, however, the courtroom process seems to have exaggerated the gap between the reliability of pro- and anti-Westway scientists. Shades of opinion, con-

tradition fueled by self-doubt, and principled uncertainty came out looking like "bureaucratic hogwash" and hypocrisy.

I spoke to Dennis Suszkowski, who had been a geologist at the Army
Corps of Engineers for thirteen years, and who helped prepare the Corps's
Westway case. Suszkowski is a thoughtful, undogmatic man who now
works for the Hudson River Foundation, an environmental group focusing on research. The picture he presents of the Corps is not nearly as
monolithic as Judge Griesa assumed. Suszkowski himself was against
Westway at the time, on the grounds that there were viable cheaper alternatives, and his then-boss, Colonel Griffis, also seemed opposed to the
project at first, before reversing himself and approving the landfill.
Suszkowski thought Judge Griesa had developed a bias against the project. Where Griesa saw possible collusion, Suszkowksi saw ineptness. Thus
the judge interpreted the difference between the language in the preliminary Environmental Impact Statement and the final EIS as suppression of
evidence, while Suszkowski thought it was simply that the preliminary
EIS had been poorly written, confusing, and never should have been
released. In the report's final draft, the language got sharpened and
improved, not censored.

In Suszkowksi's opinion, Westway was the last of the dinosaurs: it
emerged from the age of big projects and stepped into the regulatory age.
Its problem was not striped bass so much as bad timing.

Craig Whitaker winced when I told him that. "No, we weren't the *last*
of the dinosaurs, I like to think we were the first of the environmentally
conscious projects." Lost in the denouement, he felt, had been the state's
offer to invest as much as necessary to ease any impact Westway might
have on the striped bass, by driving piles, dredging shallow basins, and
sinking steel and concrete "fish houses," even making artificial habitats or
piers for the fish to congregate in, at a cost of over $52 million.

John Waldman acknowledged that he didn't think Westway would
have necessarily harmed the striped bass, but he still didn't want the landfill. Where a good fish habitat exists, why risk destroying it? Mike Ludwig
freely admitted to me that there were competent scientists on both sides.
"It was an honest difference of opinion—we're still friends. But my side
won and theirs lost."

Given the fact that Manhattan had so often resorted to landfill in the past, and the fish kept adapting to its shoreline's evolving profile, how can we know, I asked Ludwig, that the striped bass wouldn't have made an adjustment to Westway?

"We can't know," he said.

"Could they have adapted to the opposite shore?"

"That's what Ed Koch said," Ludwig laughed, and reminded me how the then-mayor of New York had remarked, in his inimitably truculent manner: "'Let 'em move to Joisey.'" Ludwig countered, "Look, you don't want to anthropomorphize these critters, they're pretty dumb. But they don't know New Jersey. The Hudson around lower Manhattan seems to have the proper mixture of saltwater and fresh water that they like."

The scientific debate may continue for years; the legal one is ended. I am struck that the fate of Westway was decided in court by some picayune inconsistencies of presentation and self-protective maneuvers typical of bureaucracy, some value judgments about what constitutes a significant adverse impact, which might have gone either way, and the judge's dislike of a witness.

THE BATTLE OF WESTWAY was a triumph of People Power over the Establishment. This time, however, the Establishment had the progressive vision and imagination, and the people, fearful and conservative, dug in their heels. Above and beyond the salutary effects on a community that had learned how to defeat the entrenched power structure, I am left with the sad reflection that New York City has entered its querulous middle age. It is ruled by a fractious civic culture, better suited to stop anything from getting built, than responding creatively and energetically to the need for fresh urban solutions.

"We have erected the art of paralysis," Louis Winnick, an urban analyst, reflected at the time on Westway's demise. "The city has lost its capacity to do monumental things." The political climate of New York is littered today with prospectuses for important public works that have either been shot down or hang on in a twilight of indefinite deferral: the Second Avenue subway, the 42nd Street trolley, Governors Island, Westway, the Brooklyn Navy Yard incinerators (or any sane way of dealing with our garbage, besides trucking it elsewhere). The metropolis that gave us the Croton Waterworks, Central Park, steam under the pavements, and the Brooklyn Bridge is afraid to undertake something new. The public is chary and tired. They have been burnt too often. There is a lack of conviction when it comes to generating new urban tissue, which is understandable, since nowadays the big projects always come out slightly bogus, pompous, denatured, and suburban. Who is to say that Westway would not have ended up looking like an urban waxworks, as have parts of Battery Park City? Still, I think it was a lost opportunity, the kind that only comes along once in a century.

As Edward Logue put it (and I think he was right): "Were Westway built, it would not have many enemies." The many enemies of an unbuilt Westway proliferated, however, in part because it remained an abstraction, a clumsy giant born of theory, unable to defend itself from charges of unreality.

THE DEFEAT OF WESTWAY brought many changes. Though the trade-off for mass transit came to only a few hundred million dollars, the infusion of capital did help the subway system improve: stations were redecorated, new trains and computerized monitoring equipment purchased. In the wake of Westway's defeat, communities across the country made out well in securing federal funds. The biggest recipient was Boston, whose sunken highway, the "Big Dig," inherited the billions of dollars that were there to be spent by the Highway Trust Fund, thanks to Tip O'Neill's authority in Congress. As a costly ("the most expensive highway in history") solution to heal the original rift and bring people to the waterfront, the Big Dig could be considered Son of Westway: it differed only in not building an outboard tunnel, but sinking the original perimeter highway in place and covering it over with a lid. There would be no disturbances of the aquatic environment; on the other hand, Boston traffic would be disrupted for over a decade.

As for landfill, it has become an utterly verboten, shudder-producing thought in New York City, at least for the next half-century,* which is

---

*It is still used widely elsewhere, even nearby in Newark, New Jersey, where the port is being significantly expanded to provide more backspace for containers.

probably to the good. Any large structures proposed for piers or platforms, such as a football stadium or a museum on the riverfront's edge, can anticipate years of obstructive litigation because of the shadows they would expect to cast on water routes frequented by fish.

The high-rise development close to the Hudson River that the West Villagers feared Westway would bring (and which, in fact, Westway might have controlled better, given its need to compromise) has occurred anyway, in the face of zoning and landmark restrictions. Some community planning boards approve larger buildings because of their star-architect cachet—*vide,* for instance, Richard Meier's vitrine-like twin towers, on West Street and Perry. For the most part, the West Village got a slew of view-blocking, high-rise apartment houses faced in hideously bland, chunky orange brick, with shower-sized balconies.

The old West Side Highway has remained in place, only now it is reconfigured as Route 9A, an "urban boulevard." Parts of this roadway are 140 feet wide, meaning you can't get across them in one light, short of breaking the hundred-yard-dash record, and it takes a minimum of two lights with a baby carriage.

WITH WESTWAY'S DEMISE, the old, decaying piers became the focus of plans to convert the waterfront to recreational use. Once thought nuisances and eyesores, these rotting structures were suddenly imbued with tremendous nostalgic value. In part it was the charm of ruins, and in part a more practical consideration: since no new structures could be built into the river, and since any replacement road for the West Side Highway would leave skimpy land at best for a waterside park, these piers represented significant splinters of potential public space. Whatever had once been a pier, however chewed-up by neglect or shipworms, could be "restored" (that is, reconstructed to its outermost original point and redecked) and turned into a place to stroll, bike, surfboard, or fish. Indeed, these piers were seen as offering New Yorkers a novel Sensurround experience of the river, by allowing them to leave the shore and go farther "into" the water for purposes of contemplation. "At the end of the day, Hudson River Park *is* the piers," I was told by Mike Ludwig, the marine biologist who had helped defeat Westway. Ludwig and Al Butzel were among the anti-Westway advocates who decided to salvage something positive from the campaign, and put their energies into building Hudson River Park. Marci Benstock, on the other hand, steadfastly opposed the new venture. Butzel and Benstock, former comrades-in-arms, fell out and became bitter enemies.

I spoke to both parties—separately, of course. Al Butzel was rangy and tall, wore blue jeans and a casual shirt, had glasses and a character-filled face, good-looking in a Sam Waterston way; eye contact very direct, with a slight smile playing around the lips, which marked his willingness to entertain opposing perspectives, though occasionally his intensity seemed to vibrate into a tremble. I feel an immediate rapport with him, as though he were a double of myself if I had gone into the law (as I had originally planned), or vice versa, if he had become a writer (as he has at times wanted to be).

He seemed smitten with the Hudson River, and eager to talk about it. "The Hudson is a great river. It's very unusual to have a great metropolitan area on a great river that connects the hinterland to the ocean. The Seine and the Thames are important because of the cities they flow through, but they're minor compared to the Hudson. It's a big river, bigger than most on the Eastern Seaboard. The ocean works a long way inland. It's an estuary, a fjord. It has great historical significance—it was thought to be the key to the American Revolutionary War, then there's West Point—and incredible commercial history, especially after the introduction of steamboats shifted the waterfront from the East River to the Hudson. And artistic significance: the Hudson River School of painters saw it as the image of God's America. Baedeker compared the Hudson to the Rhine and said it was finer, because the Rhine had been so industrialized, whereas much of the Hudson is still picturesque and pristine."

I switch the topic of conversation to his participation in the Hudson River Park, and the skepticism he picks up in my voice pains him somewhat.

"Sure, Hudson River Park is only a few acres, no one would mistake it for a large park space," he says. "But it's an experiment: the only park that has ever been built as a park space on piers. Very few cities are lucky enough to have so much public space along the waterfront. Cities like Boston or Baltimore have some nice open spaces, but they're dominated by commercial and residential use."

"And Hudson River Park will be dominated by Route 9A," I interject.

"I understand your objections, but the trees that the Department of Transportation put in along Route 9A will provide an overhang and give the park visual separation someday. It's like that famous photograph of ice skaters in Central Park and the Dakota Apartments in the background: today you wouldn't see the Dakota because the trees would be in the way. Okay, I'll admit that the Department of Transportation forgot to put in an irrigation system, so many of the trees they planted on 9A have already died. No one wants to take care of these trees, neither the DOT nor the Hudson River Park Trust. But they'll figure it out. And then you'll have a real, separate sanctuary. Look, this city is very intense. It needs places of retreat. I can imagine Socrates out on the piers with his students."

What about bringing some urban activity down to the water's edge?

"I'm not entirely opposed to commercial activity in the park, the way Marci Benstock is. I was for the proposal to keep three of the piers money-making, to help support the park. I would also hope that more maritime activities get associated with the piers. To be perfectly honest, clean air and clean water are not really the issues that drive me. But I feel deeply about wanting people to have the capacity in this city to connect with the world of water around them. To experience the river."

MARCI BENSTOCK has been characterized alternately as the heroine who slew Westway, an inspiration to environmental activists everywhere—and a paranoid zealot who does not know when to stop fighting. Marci, as everyone, friend or foe, calls her, is a youthful-looking, attractive woman in her early fifties, whose blackish shoulder-length hair is cut with trademark bangs cut straight across the forehead. The day we met, she wore a black sweater with a necklace of red and black carved stones, and a full, flaring houndstooth skirt.

I explained that I was not an investigative journalist, but thought her viewpoint was invaluable nonetheless in any discussion on Westway and the Hudson River Park.

She corrected me: "It's not a park. I call it the Hudson River Development Project. We're not just talking about what happens on the land. It's what happens under the surface of the water that matters for coastal systems. It's simple: you don't put structure in floodplains. The

Hudson River is the ocean estuary part of a floodplain. Why don't they place their development in underutilized or vacant parts of the city inland? It makes no sense. Besides, water has such destructive effect on a building's foundations; you have to keep repairing."

"So why do they want to do it?" I ask blandly, accepting for the moment her conspiratorial "they."

"It's an enormous boondoggle. Hudson River 'Park' and Route 9A are part of a long-range development scheme to turn the river into real estate. They'll do it by building out into the water, they don't care how—platforms, piers, floating platforms, landfill. The Army Corps of Engineers has already issued permits for major construction in the river as part of the Hudson River Park Trust and Route 9A."

"I was under the impression state legislation prohibits building in the Hudson."

"I've seen the permits! You have to know how to read them. I've had thirty years' experience and training. I have copies of them in my purse," she said, pointing to a rather large black handbag. As she did not offer to take them out, I did not ask to see them. Anyway, the moment was not right to interrupt her flow. "As further proof, the Army Corps has authorized the wholesale rebuilding of forty-odd piers with public funds. However nice an experience it may be to wander out into the water, you don't need more than five or six walking piers in Manhattan. Certainly not forty."

"I agree. So what do they want to put on these piers, in your view?"

"Housing, tall buildings, retail, other commercial use. The timetable for projects like these is very long. At first they say it's just to provide public access to the water. The excuse of having three piers that generate revenue for the park is just a crock. The amounts those three piers would generate is minuscule compared to the profits at stake. Views of the river are worth a lot in New York. A massive construction project like this will only become somewhat apparent by the end of five years, and only really apparent after ten."

As she sees it, construction firms, dredging and pile-driving companies, and construction unions form a powerful lobby "that make a living by turning water into land, give big political contributions, and the politicians pay them back by assigning them contracts on the waterfront, and setting up public authorities to funnel the pork. Private companies could conceivably put up the investment, but they prefer to use public funds. Money that flows through public authorities is notoriously hard to trace, and does not require as much accountability. The public authorities mutate and change initials, but they're still the same beasts. The same thing happens with stadium construction. Some private investors get burned, but a few at the top make out like bandits. That's how Roland Betts and Tom Bernstein, who now run the Chelsea Piers, made George W. Bush a millionaire down in Arlington, Texas. The reason the state is pushing to put stadiums on the water is that there's more pork when you are creating the site as well as building on it. Why are they scheduling all these marinas? Marinas have been going bankrupt in the other boroughs, but suddenly they have several planned for Manhattan. Because they want to choke up the habitat and turn it into real estate."

The longer she talks, the more mesmerized I become by her conviction. She is someone with a vision. However skewed or cynical, it all fits together. You might call it the "permanent government" thesis, that special interests have a stranglehold over the decisionmaking process of New York City.

"So why is there so much waterfront development internationally?" I ask, a touch faux-naïvely, but sure that she will have a ready answer.

"Because the water worldwide is free, like the air, so the politicians are taking it over to make a bundle for themselves and their friends. Also, the United States finished building the interstate highway system so they need to move onto the waterfronts, to generate more pork. All this talk about 'our crumbling infrastructure' is very cleverly used as a wedge to unleash more pork-barrel public funding."

"You don't believe our infrastructure is crumbling?" I ask. "What about the marine borers—the shipworms?"

"I have my doubts. That problem's overstated. The whole marine borer panic is being engineered to promote large-scale construction and restoration projects. It's all part of a massive public relations campaign to spread disinformation, and they are well funded," Marcy says with an emphatic look. "You don't believe me? Look at the way they've distorted my position in the media. I went from being portrayed as a saint to someone who's an—evil nut! I've no desire to see the edge returned to a 'pre-Colonial condition,' as they said about me in one newspaper article. In fact, I'm all for parks, I love parks! I just think it should be enough for people to be able to walk by or ride by and look out at that mighty river, and not build on it. The Hudson River is glorious and wonderful all by itself."

"You sound like Al Butzel."

"Al Butzel never really cared about the river," she says disdainfully.

THE NEXT DAY, sufficiently disturbed by her claims to want clarification, I drop in on Carter Craft at the Municipal Art Society. Carter, a pleasant, intelligent young man from the South, calm as a porpoise, with thick, dark-rimmed spectacles and dismayingly long sideburns, is also the most knowledgeable person I know about the waterfront. He heads an informational project within the venerable Municipal Art Society called the Metropolitan Waterfront Alliance. Carter is chomping down on a tuna sandwich in the conference room when he sees me, and he waves me inside. As usual, he takes an unruffled, objective tone after I repeat Marci Benstock's arguments: instead of scoffing at them, he tells me I should talk to So-and-So who assigns permits at the Army Corps of Engineers. In other words, check out the facts. If I were an investigative reporter, I would certainly do so. But I'm too lazy. I'm a belletrist, for God's sake! Finally I get him to fork over the information. According to the Hudson River Park legislation, there are only provisions for restoring sixteen piers, not forty, and of these, three will be habitat piers (that is, given over to wilderness growth, not people). He also says that legislation at present prevents construction in the water, though he understands Marci's fears, given the historical record, and he agrees with her that the state authorities are indeed largely unregulated: Battery Park City Authority was supposed to give back many millions of dollars for affordable housing years ago, and is still stalling. But he thinks the reconstructed piers are justifiable because 8 million people live in this city, these people could use more public space, and there can never be any extensive new public space created on the island of Manhattan itself.

. . .

IN THE AFTERMATH of the World Trade Center's destruction, many proposals were put forward to reknit the site to the surrounding urban fabric by placing a lid over the highwaylike West Street or otherwise submerging it. Though the tract being discussed was only the ten or so blocks adjoining Battery Park City and the old World Trade Center site, essentially what was being proposed was a Westway-type solution. The old bugbear even turned up by name in several articles. Ex-mayor Ed Koch was hauled in to reminisce: "Westway would have been wonderful." Jacob Weisberg, in a *New York Times Magazine* piece about how the city should rebuild after the World Trade Center attack, wrote: "High on many people's list of things that should have happened in those years [the 1980s and 1990s] but did not is Westway, the plan to submerge two miles of the West Side Highway and build a glorious downtown park and beach. After a fifteen-year struggle, environmentalists killed the plan in 1985, on the basis that the Army Corps of Engineers had not sufficiently proved the project harmless to striped bass—a far-from-endangered species that spawns in the Hudson." I was surprised and encouraged to see my private opinion corroborated in cold print, but dismayed to find it less excitingly heterodox than I had imagined. The pendulum was swinging back, apparently.

Taking the long-range perspective, in thirty or forty years the present highway along the West Side, Route 9A, will need to be done over, and at that time no one will have remembered Westway and it will be possible then to reintroduce the outboard solution. Taking a longer perspective still, global warming may raise the ocean levels and the shorelines may be flooded, in which case perimeter expressways will be passé, Canal Street will again be a canal, and Manhattan will have become as charmingly quaint as Venice, with the Woolworth Building its downtown campanile.

8

CHELSEA PIERS,
CHELSEA, AND
TROCCHI-LAND

CHELSEA PIERS IS A FASCINATING EXAMPLE OF WATER-
FRONT ADAPTIVE REUSE. OCCUPYING A THIRTY-ACRE
AREA BETWEEN 18TH AND 23RD STREETS, ON FOUR HIS-
toric but neglected piers (59, 60, 61, and 62) and the headhouse that connected them, it has been turned into an elaborate sports complex, with ice
skating, a golf driving range, roller rinks, gyms, a boxing ring, a volleyball
court, a batting cage, bowling alleys, an indoor track, a rock-climbing wall,
you name it. I know nine-year-old boys for whom Chelsea Piers is heaven
on earth; I also know urbanists who grit their teeth at the mere mention
of it.

I am in the ambivalent camp about Chelsea Piers, so much so that, were I to enumerate all my on-the-one-hand–on-the-other-hands, I would need as many hands as a Hindu goddess. As I've said, I have no purist objection to commercial development on the riverside; quite the contrary, it seems to me cities are inherent marketplaces, and commercial enterprises can help draw people to an underused waterfront. Chelsea Piers does attract considerable numbers (it is among New York's ten most frequently visited "destinations," according to one survey), and it fulfills a function as the largest sports complex in the metropolitan area. What pains me is that Chelsea Piers is so grudging, unneighborly, and suburban in its relation to the streetscape, thereby giving commercial development on the waterfront a bad name.

The term "suburban" as a derogatory shorthand in writing about cities can be overdone. However, when it comes to Chelsea Piers, I think it is apt. As if the chasm of Route 9A were not enough to distance the complex from its adjacent neighborhood, Chelsea, the center's signage and visual cues conspire to discourage pedestrians, while offering every incentive to motorists to drive in and park at the rather expensive lot. If you are walking along West Street (here its name becomes Twelfth Avenue), you see an elongated concrete bunker painted with aggressively ugly cartoons of sporting activities; there is no perceptible entrance door on the street itself, or any way of peering in at the activities. The leasing of some floor space for movie soundstages and fashion shoots may explain the lack of windows, but not the tacky façade presented to the public, which seems intentionally to mislead about the well-appointed facilities within.

Staring at this eyesore, you would be hard put to connect it with its original graceful façade, by Warren & Wetmore, the architects who built Grand Central Station and the New York Yacht Club. A photograph of the piers when they opened in 1910 shows a breathtaking repetition of arch-windowed doorways and pedimented roofs, fronting a West Street haunted by horse-drawn cabs. As the authors of *New York 1900*, Robert A. M. Stern, Gregory Gilmartin, and John Montague Massengale, describe it, "Warren & Wetmore invested the fashionable Modern French façades with a strikingly monumental grandeur and simplified but overscaled details. The river façades, which sheltered open observation platforms, were contrastingly festive transformations of the utilitarian steel piers which lay behind the street façades, and greeted the arriving passenger with a flutter of pennants and trophies."

In 1910, a day after the piers' official opening, *The New York Times* called them "the most remarkable urban design achievement of their day. . . . The Chelsea Piers replaced a hodgepodge of run-down waterfront structures with a magnificent row of grand buildings embellished with pink granite façades." The 800-foot-long finger piers were designed expressly for the new transatlantic luxury liners, such as the Cunard Line's *Mauretania* or the *Lusitania* (which departed from Chelsea Piers before being sunk by a German U-boat). Before it struck an iceberg, the *Titanic* had been scheduled to dock at Chelsea Piers. We tend to forget that many immigrants arrived first at Chelsea Piers, before being transferred by ferryboats to Ellis Island. The famous were frequently snapped waving from its gangplanks. In 1927 the *Ile de France* put in at its Pier 57, and introduced a new standard of ocean liner style. Chelsea Piers played an important role as a troop terminal in both world wars, but the Depression and jet travel cut into its luxury liner business, and container ships requiring larger berths spelled its doom. By the late 1960s Chelsea Piers' shipping days were over, and it became a municipal bus storage and a U.S. Customs impounding station. Decaying walls, shattered windows, and structural dilapidation led Mayor Lindsay's administration to employ the stopgap measure of enclosing it in a concrete casing, which gave it its present homely façade.

Thus the Chelsea Piers sports complex we see today cannot be accused of destroying an architectural landmark; if anything, it has preserved the bones of the original. It has also honored the site's maritime heritage with blown-up photographs and texts about the glorious history of the piers. Still, one wishes the owners would try to improve the façade, so that it at least begins to measure up architecturally to the distinction and quality of its predecessor.

There is also the question of striking a better balance between private and public space. In the past ten years we have embraced the profoundly desirable principle that the people of New York have the right of access to its waters, for their own enjoyment and spiritual nourishment. Chelsea Piers, born at about the same moment that the New York State legislature approved the Hudson River Park idea, raced to open its doors in late 1995, and seemed to operate on an older model of river access. I mean that the entrepreneurs operating Chelsea Piers did not make it easy for the walker interested in completing a circuit around Manhattan's shoreline. The so-called public space left at the water's edge by the sports complex is extremely stingy, and at the driving range it is almost nonexistent. The range's net, suspended from steel poles to keep golf balls from falling into the Hudson, terminates virtually at the river, inviting most walkers to leave the shore and cut through the enclosed parking lot and then through the complex itself. The central open courtyard at 23rd Street functions like a plaza in a shopping mall. On the one hand, Chelsea Piers generously offers free musical entertainment "to the community," or lets immunization vans park there; on the other hand, the signs that say WELCOME TO CHELSEA PIERS subtly tell you, if you are of a mind to wander by the river, that you are in a private enclave, with its own set of rules, regulations, and security guards.

Some of the prime river-view space has been taken up with two private catering halls, Pier 60 and the Lighthouse, rented out successfully for corporate meetings, weddings, "bar/bat mitzvahs and sweet-sixteen parties." Chelsea Piers also has several restaurants open to the public, suburban in décor and feel, but congenial for a drink with a friend in late-summer afternoons, on a deck overlooking the Hudson. The marina, another moneymaker, garages million-dollar yachts and an upscale version of the Circle Line, Bateaux New York, a sort of supper-club cruise that circumnavigates the island.

Chelsea Piers' profitable formula is based on a mixture of regular customers (annual club memberships, league play) and one-shot visitors (walk-ins and invitees to special events). On a tour of the complex, I was shown a beautiful, clean and airy, state-of-the-art gym, complete with its own sports medicine center, operated by New York–Presbyterian Hospital. While the interior spaces for children are knockabout-functional, all wrestling mats and primary colors, the adult facility's décor is an elegant white and maroon with sumptuous woods. The management of Chelsea Piers is thinking of franchising its concept, by setting up in cities around the world, particularly where there are large, architecturally intriguing, endangered structures on the waterfront.

The success of Chelsea Piers is especially remarkable when you consider how hard it is to get anything built on the New York waterfront, much less a 1.7-million-square-foot complex. Roland Betts, a financier of films, was originally interested in leasing just a small part of the vast, unused space of Chelsea Piers, to create an ice rink for his figure-skater daughter. Told that he would have to bid on the whole complex, Betts and his partner, Tom Bernstein, went ahead, using their own money, outlasting the bureaucratic endurance test of state, city, community, and environmental regulatory approval, securing a break on the rent and, eventually, a long-term lease that would allow for low-cost financing.

"There were two factors that contributed to the success of the Chelsea project: it was centered on recreation at a time when the Hudson was clean and its potential recreational benefits widely recognized; and, perhaps most important, all the interested parties genuinely wanted the project to succeed. In the end, sheer force of will, a readiness to be energized rather than discouraged by frustration, political savvy, and the ability to secure private financing finally broke down a portion of the walls that had closed off Manhattan's waterfront for so long," wrote Ann L. Buttenweiser enthusiastically in her useful book, *Manhattan Water-Bound.* Being more of a skeptic, I wonder if Chelsea Piers did not itself set up its own walls on the waterfront, even as it broke others down.

Sitting here at my desk and thinking about Chelsea Piers (I was only pretending to be walking around meditating), I am seized by diametrically opposed emotions: (1) a desire to run right down there and play, hit in the batting cages, try the bowling alley, the swimming pool, and make a day of it; (2) a nausea approaching disgust at the whole idea of this sports complex, springing not from any principled urbanist objections, but from my own estrangement from my body, and my fear and envy of people who celebrate life through their pores—I who live in my head, looking out at the world as if I were constantly reading a book, while my belly softens and my hair thins. When I was younger I did make more of an effort to live in my body, to *be* a body; to play tennis and have sex, both of which I still do, on occasion, but not as often as I would like. I see a tall woman jogging in the street, her breasts bobbing up and down in her sweatshirt, her pony tail orbiting with every cantered step, and am all too aware that she does not see me; she is concentrated, focused on the tightening sinews in her limbs, the pheromones spreading pleasure to her brain. Perhaps she is thinking of her lover, "I'll show *him!*" or "I'll show *her!*" or "I am making my figure as exquisitely proportioned as the Parthenon." Yes, I am glad she exists; glad that Chelsea Piers exists; but how can I not feel an outsider in this temple of the body, I whose only exercise is city walking, and that irregularly?

I AM COMING UP ON one of the structures I love most in New York, the Starrett-Lehigh Building, which fills an entire block, from West 26th Street to West 27th, between Eleventh and Twelfth Avenues. Its continuous, horizontal floors go on forever, the windows flush with the façade, a flapjack stack of fenestration separated by red-brick bands and a single brick column toward the center. If nothing else, it shows how graceful and grand a block-long building can be. I sometimes think that what's wrong with many of the city's new jumbo office towers, such as Battery Park City's World Financial Center, is that their bases are too broad—-they'd be prettier if they took up just half a block—but the Starrett-Lehigh (built in 1930–31) shows how you can ascend majestically on the widest possible foundation. Maybe the important distinction is not so much the size of the building's footprint as the materials used. Consider the solidity of Starrett-Lehigh's masonry versus the distressingly chunky airiness of the World Financial Center's curtain wall, what architectural critic Charles Jencks called "the difference between a brick and a balloon." Of course it's also true that the Starrett-Lehigh only goes up nineteen stories, making it stunningly horizontal: an impression enhanced by the brick-banded, blue-glazed spandrels that tear around the façade.

The interior was originally given over to lofts for factory or warehouse use. The floors were massive enough to allow for railroad cars to be brought into the ground level of the building. Train tracks ran from the pier at the end of West 26th Street right into the basement, where the railroad cars, brought from barges that had crossed the Hudson River, were unloaded. "They could also be carried into or taken out of the building through two immense elevators that open out onto loading docks at the center of nearly every floor," wrote a *New York Times* reporter. "But the building quickly became obsolete as other new architectural wonders, the Holland and Lincoln Tunnels and the George Washington Bridge, made the commercial shipping barges of the Hudson River give way to the trucks of the region's highways."

Perhaps the building stirs me because of my nostalgia for a time when New Yorkers still made things with their hands and New York was America's manufacturing capital—the blue-collar city of my father, a factory worker who would return from his ribbon-dyeing plant with the then-liberal *New York Post* carried lovingly like a Torah, and tell me not to cross picket lines. All I know is, I'm moved by the way the building towers over everything, yet seems largely invisible. Once acclaimed, now neglected, soldiering on in its functionality. A kind of background building, for all its bulk.

The background building is such an odd, poignant notion in itself. So much of this gridded city must inevitably turn into background music for the preoccupied stroller. Chicago has more four-star architectural masterpieces than New York, but New York is the greater built environment because it possesses a vaster, more continuous urban web, which is composed largely of background buildings, that is to say, barely noticeable, mediocre or simply average types holding up their end of the street-wall agreement. Background buildings are grunts enlisted in a great war against the horror of emptiness. The heyday of the background building was 1880–1950, when New York City's expansion required thousands and thousands of modest edifices that would do their part. Still, the question arises: is the designation "background building" a rationalization after the fact for failed ambition, or something intentional? When a background building was first thrown up, did its owners know it was only going to be . . . a background building? Certainly, if it was a brownstone or a six-story walk-up or a twelve-story apartment house or an ordinary speculative office building, they must have suspected they were not making architectural history. But they were content to do a little business, make a bit of money, using the stenciled formats that had proven successful. Occasionally, sure, they would sport a decorative touch that betrayed impatience with background status, a plinth or gargoyle or entablature of engraved stone; the persistence of vanity. The background building is like a good supporting actress, a

Thelma Ritter or Eve Arden, who is not above stealing a scene with a single line-reading of arch skepticism. The supporting actress knows she's a background character, but does the character she plays know it? A building may mutate from splendid provocation to background status to landmark in several generations. Such has been the fate of the Starrett-Lehigh, which, designed by Cory and Cory in 1930, was praised at its inception by Lewis Mumford in a *New Yorker* "Sky-Line" column ("Here a cantilevered front has been used, not as a cliché of modernism, but as a means of achieving a maximum amount of daylight and unbroken floor space for work requiring direct lighting. The aesthetic result is very happy indeed."), only to have its industrial-*moderne* charms fail to register on a new breed of glass wall/Mies-smitten modernists, then get rediscovered several decades later as a prototype of restrained elegance, "a landmark of modern architecture" (according to the *AIA Guide to New York City*).

Its forlorn beauty could not help but exert, in time, a hip appeal on the imaginations of design firms, shelter magazines, and dot-com entrepreneurs, and what is more apposite, it had huge floors of below-market raw space to offer, at a time when Manhattan commercial real estate prices were going through the roof. So tenants like Martha Stewart Living Omnimedia and fashion manufacturer Hugo Boss and SmartMoney.com moved in, at first drawn to the solitary charm of this industrial relic, then appalled by the pokey elevators, cockroaches, unreliable heat, and poor ventilation. Workers complained of the distance from the nearest subway, deli, drugstore, or diner. It has always been thus on the waterfront, especially when one tries to make it perform like a downtown office center.

One evening I attended the awards ceremony for the IFCCA (International Foundation for the Canadian Centre for Architecture) international design competition. The first site chosen for the triennial competition happened to be the western edge of Manhattan from 30th to 34th Streets, most notably the open railway cut and storage yards for New Jersey Transit and the Long Island Rail Road. In three years' time the architectural visionaries may be planning for Lagos or Singapore, but for the moment they were invited to bring their most untrammeled, cutting-edge imaginations to Old New York. The winner, Peter Eisenman, a respected ideologist for and practitioner of experimental architecture, had come up with a lofty scheme for a sports stadium over a platform extending into the Hudson River, which would certainly face decades of environmentalists' litigation if it ever threatened to approach reality. The ceremonies were held high up in the Starrett-Lehigh Building, the perfect setting for such a theoretical exercise, I found myself thinking, because it both overlooked the site under consideration and lived in a constant state of decaying futurist potential.

Part of what makes the Starrett-Lehigh Building so impressive today is that it sits in lonely eminence, the only large building for blocks around. It abuts the vast vacuity (for the moment) of the Penn train yards, rising above them like Gibraltar. In recent years there has been much talk of building a stadium, first for the New York Yankees, then for the football Jets, then for Olympics 2012 (should the city win its bid), and incorporating the facility as an extension of the Javits Convention Center. Meanwhile the land sits idle, a perfect foil to the Starrett-Lehigh's rugged, eminent sadness.

It has long been my conviction that New York is the saddest of cities, though I have no argument to support the feeling. All right, let me try. It has something to do with its precise age and built environment. Were it older, it would be a picturesque, Prague sort of museum city; younger, a Disneyesque novelty. But the dominant look of Manhattan (forgetting its few remnants from the eighteenth and early nineteenth centuries), is Industrial to Early Corporate, 1870s to 1950s, the cast-iron architecture of SoHo, the manufacturing and medical giants near the water, the background buildings, the somberly intelligent Garment Center towers on Seventh Avenue, the art deco setbacks along lower Park Avenue, everything so massive, gray, ineluctable. All of it perfectly, melancholically contextual—a way of being taken for granted. The Japanese believe that sadness comes from an awareness of the fragility of life at the same time one is captivated by its transient beauty. The cherry blossoms. But that is a very superficial understanding of sadness, may I say. True sadness arises when we realize that the world around us is imperishable, and rather ugly. Let me hasten to add that the ugliness of New York is instantly amenable to a mental flip-flop that converts it into beauty—but a *sad* beauty, such as the Starrett-Lehigh Building, since it cannot claim the beauty tiara on its own, unironically. The dated obduracy of the man-made is sadder than the radiant transience of nature, which explains why it gives you a more tragic feeling to look across the East River at the Bronx, Queens, Roosevelt Island's asylum in ruins, than across the noble Hudson at the Palisades forest with its scattering of condos. I don't mean to imply that New Jerseyans lack a tragic sense, only that the industrial vista across the East River is much more heartbreaking, and the proof is that Woody Allen would never have chosen a location on the Hudson River for his famous scene in *Manhattan* (looking out from Sutton Place at the 59th Street Bridge) to convey the tenuousness of love.

APPROACHING THE Jacob K. Javits Convention Center, which stretches from West 34th to West 39th Streets, I am struck by how little this bold lump of coal has been assimilated into Manhattan's bosom since it opened fifteen years ago. It was supposed to transform all the blocks around it, making Tenth and Eleventh Avenues bloom with hotels and shops; but of course the area has remained just as bleak and nondescript as ever. The only signs of new commercial enterprise serving the conventioneers are the silverfish dropped by hookers on the pavement.

I remember my excitement when the Convention Center was first under construction. I managed to sneak inside and clamber over sacks of dirt, and look up at that ebony glass roof, with its echoes of the Crystal Palace or some nineteenth-century Paris railroad station. Today I cast about for some explanation as to why this building, by the internationally renowned I. M. Pei, has had so little impact on New York's consciousness. The man who solved the Louvre's entrance problems with a pyramid must have thought to anchor the West Thirties with a stark, jagged rock. If only he hadn't compromised the shivery black glass with that superfluous off-white concrete bulwark on the river façade: was it meant to add a touch of monumental dignity, or protect the building's backside from out-of-control cars crashing into it from the adjoining highway? Pei may not be my favorite architect in any case, but I don't think that design flaws were the reason the Convention Center failed to click with the city around it. True, it was built for out-of-towners, hence never meant to be read as

"New York"; then, the moment it opened it was declared too small for some expositions; then it was bedeviled by corruption and kickback scandals. But the real problem, I think, was that it was too far west, inaccessible by subway, exiled to the lonely, geeky waterfront.

AT WEST 33RD STREET AND THE RIVER, we are in Trocchi territory.

In April 1956, Alexander Trocchi arrived in New York. The Scottish-born writer, already a very seasoned thirty-one, had come from Paris, where he had dazzled all with his literary promise and charisma (handsome and tall, he resembled Burt Lancaster, one friend wrote, though in the photographs I've seen, he looks more like early Jack Palance), had edited an avant-garde journal, *Merlin*, which showcased Beckett, Genet, and Ionesco before they were international names, had written several pornographic novels and one serious one *(Young Adam)* for Maurice Girodias's Olympia Press, and had gotten himself addicted to heroin. He moved to New York—why? he was never able to say, except that it seemed more downbeat than Paris, and he was on a downwardly mobile quest. After several months of mooching, Trocchi got hired as a scow captain with the New York Trap Rock Corporation. It was one of those jobs tailor-made for writers, like being a hotel night clerk or caretaker of an estate: no other gig, he said, paid so well for so little work. "And no supervision. That was important." All he had to do was catch the huge ropes, or hawsers, thrown by the tugs, and secure them to his post.

Operating a flat-bottomed scow or barge that possessed no locomotive power, but needed to be towed everywhere by a tugboat, must have seemed, to a junkie, the quintessence of apt passivity. The life of a junkie is austere to begin with, and his scow contained only its load of crushed stone (800 to 1,300 tons) and a small cabin—a wooden shack with a single bed, coal stove, cupboard, chair, and table, at which he could type or shoot up. In New York he spent much less time in literary circles than he had in Paris, but he wrote more seriously, producing his finest work. It was an ideal life for the solitary sort; the problem was that Trocchi could not bear to be alone much, he was feverishly social, a barroom entertainer, always looking to score drugs, and sometimes made anxious by the sight of Manhattan, with no way to get to it, stuck in "a low-slung coffin in the choppy grey water." One night he almost lost contact with the tugs and could have easily drifted out to the Atlantic, lost at sea.

Trocchi described the incident vividly in his autobiographical novel, *Cain's Book*, which came out in 1960. He also described picking up a Puerto Rican man and bringing him back to his barge to make love, and hitting on his scowman friend's wife, a beautiful one-legged woman ("she moved her stump between my thighs and pressed her belly close to me," wrote the ex-pornographer, though in a later conversation with Allen Ginsberg, Trocchi admitted that "I couldn't get a fucking hard-on! Now if I had got a hard-on that night, my whole life maybe would have been changed, and so would hers.") *Cain's Book* is a work of fragments, purporting to be a novel while taking the avant-garde, self-reflexive position that novels are an exhausted genre. Trocchi, given his fix-dominated, hand-to-mouth existence, could not have written it any other way than in fragments (his editor, Richard Seaver, got him to finish the book by doling out the advance thirty bucks a clip, the amount of a score, in exchange for some new pages), so he made necessity a virtue, building a kind of structure out of memory-pieces and short, tense scenes that had the veracity of diary entries. The best parts remain his descriptions of barge life and his memories of growing up in a boarding house in Glasgow, particularly the portrait of his father, a chronically unemployed Italian musician who seems to have "inspired" Trocchi's own congenital idleness.

Again and again, in *Cain's Book*, Trocchi returns to the monotonous, consoling daily routine on the New York waterfront, the slow-moving pace of scow-time, and the life of the "harbor gypsies," families or social sets who lived in instant villages of nine scows moored together. "Mine was the last scow and I sat aft at my open cabin door and watched the dark west waterfront of Manhattan slide away to the right. I thought of a night a long time ago when I had a girlfriend aboard for a short trip and how at the same kind of midnight we went naked over the end of a long tow, each in the hempen eye of a dockline, screaming sure and mad off Wall Street as the dark waves struck."

For every such exhilaration, there were four epiphanies of defeat. To work on a scow is to be a loser, Trocchi informs us; most scowmen are old, lazy, washed-up alcoholics, which is why tugboat captains despise them. By the mid-fifties the big cargo ships had already begun the move to New

Jersey, and scows like Trocchi's were left to haul sand and crushed stone, the detritus of a once-vast commerce. A few decades later the barges would become so much bigger that they could no longer be bunched together in floating communities; that whole way of life would be gone. If Ernest Poole celebrates the harbor at its zenith, Alexander Trocchi is the poet of the port in decline. The New York waterfront he describes would be an ideal location for a film noir:

"At 33rd Street is Pier 72. At the waterfront there are few buildings and they are low. The city is in the background. It has diners at its edge, boxcars abandoned and stored, rails amongst grass and gravel, vacant lots. The trucks of moving and storage companies are parked and shunted under the tunnels of an area of broad deserted shadows, useful for murder or rape. . . . After eight, when the diners close, the dockside streets are fairly deserted. In winter the lights under the elevated roadway shine as in a vast and dingy shed, dimly reflecting its own emptiness." Never does Trocchi make a historical observation about the comparative fortunes of the New York port: its "emptiness" is seen as a constant, a handy parable for his own exilic disquiet. Yet keeping a barge seems also to have liberated the otherwise self-absorbed Trocchi into a style of observant visual and aural notation, soaked in the attenuated present.

Perhaps heroin should also be given some credit for this perceptual patience. On the other hand, there is nothing more tedious than Trocchi's rants proselytizing for drugs, or his paranoid philosophizing about conformity. "While the mediaeval Church couldn't burn every heretic, it is just possible that the modern state can, even without recourse to the atomic bomb. . . ." If he seems to have had something of a persecution complex, reality sufficiently supported it: local narcs were on his case quickly, tailing and harassing him (mainly because he was pushing as well as using), and eventually he was caught selling drugs to a minor, and had to flee the country before sentence was passed, sticking his friend George Plimpton for the bail money while stealing two of Plimpton's suits.

Back in London, he registered as an addict, received his drugs from the state, and settled down to elder bohemian status, issuing Situationist manifestos such as "Invisible Insurrection of a Million Minds," which called for cultural revolt, sly subversion, and a life of play (he was very big on *Homo ludens*), helping to organize free universities with R. D. Laing, hanging out at the Edinburgh Poetry Festival with Ginsberg and Burroughs, signing and pocketing advances for sequels to *Cain's Book,* but never writing anything of significance again. Perhaps he'd already said what he had to.

I remember reading *Cain's Book* when it first came out, in 1960, and being drawn to its intimate, truth-telling narrative voice. Though it sputters in the last one-third, and doesn't quite add up to a satisfying whole, I'm amazed on rereading it how sharp and frank the best parts remain, what a fine writer he was in the traditional sense—strong sentences and vivid scene-making—but how irritating the bohemian rants have become. Trocchi's posturing about the hazards of drug addiction betrays more than a little grandiose self-pity, using the excuse of the Great Writer. You can agree that American antidrug laws are idiotic and still hold Trocchi responsible for the waste of his talent, not to mention the damage he brought to others (pimping his young wife, dealing to minors). He would have retorted that the others acted of their own free will.

Today, I put antennae out for the feel of Trocchi in his old waterfront hideout.

Here is the way he described it:

Pier 72 is the one immediately north of the new heliport which lies in the southern end of the basin formed by Piers 72 and 71. The remainder of the basin is used to moor the scows of a stone corporation with quarries at Haverstraw, Tomkin's Cove, and Clinton Point on the Hudson River. Piers 72 and 73 are close together. Nine scows at most are moored there. Looking in from the river you see the gabled ends of two large and dilapidated barns perched on foundations of stones and heavy beams, with a narrow walk around three sides of each. The gable-end of Pier 73 is a landmark from the river because it is painted with red, white, and blue stripes representing American Lines. At the end of Pier 72 there is a small landing stage-set with bollards and cleats of cast iron. A little wooden box painted green is nailed to the gable end of the shed. It houses lists from the dispatcher's office of the crushed stone corporation, lists which pertain to the movements of the scows.

From these lists Trocchi would learn whether he'd have to wait around on his barge all night to be towed somewhere, or was free to go into town and score, probably in the Village or Harlem.

Looking at the same tableau, there are no scows moored in the basin, and no gabled barns, dilapidated or otherwise. Pier 72 no longer exists; the stumps of a few timbers poke their heads up, suggesting the pilings' former outlines. That whole strip of waterfront is presently an orange ditch, while the Department of Transportation's tractors and earthmovers lay the groundwork for the Hudson River Park. The DOT's construction sheds, ocher and red, line the property. To its immediate south is the heliport Trocchi mentions, still in business, offering VIP helicopter tours: it consists of an asphalt landing strip and a rusty olive spud barge, where blue choppers take off and land, generating an astonishingly vehement noise.

The blocks facing the waterfront are taken up mostly by parking lots half-filled with storage trailers, FedEx delivery trucks, Greyhound buses. The train yards, now the repository of ailing or idled subway cars, await their apotheosis as a sports complex. Across the roadway from Pier 76 is the Javits Convention Center. Pier 76, still adorned with American Lines lettering, is now painted a faded battleship gray, and the several-blocks-long aluminum shed has been turned into a pound for cars towed for parking violations.

Two flags, as if contesting the tow pound's jurisdiction, fly from the roof: the Republic's stars-and-stripes and the city's tricolor. This *via dolorosa* for errant motorists, closed Sundays, is grimly surrounded by chain-link fence, with NYPD guards stationed at entry points to make sure any angry driver whose car was kidnapped by civil authorities will think twice about liberating it. Police department tow trucks, painted black-and-white, are parked in the front area. I feel certain Trocchi, with his borderline-paranoid fulminations about the coming police state, would have taken an I-told-you-so satisfaction at the American Lines' metamorphosis.

ENTER HERE TO REDEEM VEHICLES. You go up a ramp and into a hideous bullpen area, with puke-colored linoleum and too-low ceilings and cheap wooden wallboards: it is as though the humiliation of losing half a day and paying a steep fine to retrieve your car were not enough, the city wants you to feel like a criminal for parking in the wrong place. The seven clerical windows at the front (only three of which are manned at any one time) have an oddly whimsical touch: green and red "traffic lights" above each pane, which signal whether the civil servant is ready to receive you. There is a sign saying that if your car has been "booted" in the towing, you should proceed to the last window. The people in the bullpen awaiting their turn with the bureaucracy speak mostly Spanish to each other, and look philosophical regarding this latest sorrow. If you stay long enough, however, you will hear in English the various raps of people at the clerical windows trying to talk their way out of paying the fine, all quite unsuccessful.

9

EXCURSUS

SHIPWORMS

WITH THE CLEANUP OF THE RIVERS AROUND NEW YORK CITY, THANKS TO NEW SEWAGE TREATMENT PLANTS AND STRICTER ENFORCEMENTS AGAINST industrial dumping, and the waterfront's revival for recreational uses, the shipworm, which had been repressed by aquatic pollution, has returned to the harbor to chomp away at piers, causing major damage, and leading to an ugly outbreak of the word "ironic" in the media. New Yorkers, notoriously indifferent to the ecosystem's larger intricacies, can see no explanation for marine borer activity reaching its highest level in a century than that they are being made to suffer for their virtue, as in the cynical adage, "No good deed goes unpunished."

In 1995 the partial collapse of a pier platform underneath the FDR Drive, brought about by marine borer damage, required the temporary closure of that crucial artery. At the moment, one-half of Hudson River Park's $400-million budget is earmarked for repairing rotting piers and foundations. Battery Park City alone recently expended $90 million, using divers and advanced construction technology, to pour a 740-foot-long concrete wall under the water to reinforce a timber wall. Since waterfront work is the most costly type of construction, next to tunnels, it becomes clear why the final bill for repairing marine borer damage could approach a billion dollars, thereby devouring any future municipal surplus.

We must not take the shipworm's depredations personally. This "termite of the sea" or "ocean woodpecker," as it is sometimes called, has been around always. The oldest fossil shipworms are 60 million years old. Misnamed because of their resemblance to worms, they are actually a species of mollusk related to clams. There are other marine borers in the harbor, such as the gribble, a shrimplike crustacean that gnaws away at the surface of timbers, leaving them with an hourglass shape; but they are a less significant player at present than the shipworm, which burrows from within, making it difficult to assess until too late how much damage has been done. *Teredo navalis* (the pest's scientific name) attaches itself to any available wood, democratically reducing it, whatever its quality or density—soft pine, hard oak, mahogany, or scrap—in time to wet sawdust.

The first literary mention of the creature I have been able to find appears in a comedy by Aristophanes, *The Knights*, where the playwright imagines a dialogue between several ships, the eldest trireme saying that, rather than be sent on a dangerous expedition, she would prefer to remain at home, grow old, and be eaten by shipworms. Ovid, in a line almost too famous to quote, speaks of his heart constantly nibbled by sorrow, "gnawed as a ship is injured by the hidden borer" *(estur ut occulta vitiata teredine navis)*. Theophrastus describes the creature scrupulously, though Pliny mixes fact and fancy in his *Natural History,* mistakenly saying that "borerworms have a very large head in relation to their size," and confusing them with the grub of an insect. In the Middle Ages, the scholar-monk Yscolan wrote: "A full year I was placed / At Bangor, on the pole of a weir. / Consider thou my sufferings from sea-worms." Curiously, we find no mention of shipworms in Homer, Dante, Shakespeare, Rabelais, Goethe,

Pushkin, and other authors of universal genius. But it crops up frequently in accounts of the Age of Exploration, being blamed for the failure of Columbus's fourth voyage in 1502, when all his vessels had to be shelved because of problems with their bottoms. Sir Francis Drake's flagship was found riddled with shipworms when it returned from circumnavigating the globe. The "Zee-worm" devastated Holland in the 1730s. As Smollett reports, "the Dutch were greatly alarmed by an apprehension of being overwhelmed by an inundation occasioned by worms, which were said to have consumed the piles of timber work that supported their dykes. They prayed and fasted with uncommon zeal in terror of this calamity, which they did not know how to avert in any other manner. At length they were delivered from their fears by a hard frost, which effectually destroyed these dangerous animals."

Perhaps because Holland suffered so much shipworm damage, Dutch scientists led the way in investigating the malicious mollusk. Godfrey Sellius's 366-page Latin treatise, *Historia Naturalis Teredinis seu Xylophagi marini* (1733), is still regarded as a masterpiece of research. The British scientist J. B. Jeffreys observed about Sellius in his own nicely written *British Conchology* (1865): "The subject appears to have fascinated him, much in the same way as a capricious mistress does her lover, who now deprecates the cruelty of his fair tormentor, and then extols to the skies her beauty and gentleness. He calls the *Teredo* a wicked beast, the worst plague that angry Nature could inflict on man; but he defends it against the calumnies of certain anonymous writers who had preceded him, and he expresses in enthusiastic terms his admiration of its symmetry, economy, ingenuity, social harmony . . . and its wonderful perfection in every particular." Clearly the shipworm has the power to dazzle susceptible mentalities. Jeffreys himself fell under its spell, exclaiming, "I do not know any conchological study more interesting and important, and at the same time more difficult, than that of the *Teredo*.

Let us take a closer look at its anatomy. The clamlike creature has a bivalve shell that functions as a tool, the rough, ridged valve surfaces being used for boring and scraping. These ridges or "dentricles" are what Pliny mistook for teeth. It also has a muscular foot that permits crawling over surfaces and acts as a suction cup, holding the shell in place during burrowing. The creature's breathing siphons remain at the surface of the wood, taking in water and oxygen. Once attached to a piece of wood, the larva starts to turn into a proper shipworm—a metamorphosis, Jeffreys assures us, that is "not less wonderful than that which takes place in the frog, insect, or polyp." The adult form has a soft, almost gelatinous body and deposits a whitish, calcareous lining on its tunnel walls to protect its gentle flesh.

The shipworm requires three main conditions for life: proper temperature, salinity, and the presence of wood. A habitué of the sea, it does not fare well in freshwater lakes or inlets. It requires salinities ranging from normal sea water—averaging about 35 parts per thousand—to as low as 9 parts per thousand, according to Dr. Ruth Turner, the Harvard marine biologist who recently passed away at eighty-five, after devoting her life to studying the teredo. (Her obituary says she was affectionately called "Lady Wormwood," she scuba-dived until she was well into her seventies, and she never married, giving her heart, perhaps, to the shipworm.) Sellius, who experimented by thrusting shipworms into beer, rainwater, and milk, discovered, as one might predict, that they did not prosper. They dislike cold, breed in warm weather, and, when placed in a jar, invariably seek the sunny side. They also prefer shallow water, and are found most often around or slightly above the mud line. Though originally associated with one or another region, as a sort of local curse, they can be dispersed considerable distances by ocean currents, and may wash up anywhere on the globe, provided they have secured adequate ligneous transportation.

Their palates, well described by Sigerfoos (1908), are peculiar, tubelike structures that extrude siphons, which take in food and considerable amounts of water, which in turn help reduce the wood to a flocculent mass. These palates look like pieces of appendix, or asparagus stalks, or bent penises, hence the misnomer "worm." They soon outgrow the shell, which in any case is too frail to possess much protective function. If the shell is thin compared to that of other bivalves, it is perhaps because the shipworm finds all the protection it needs by lodging in a piece of wood. Once it has gained its hiding place, it escapes assault from other predators. Should another shipworm enter the abode, the first will make way. A single two-by-four may house three dozen teredos, recumbently sharing the space as in a crack den.

Sellius championed his creature's nondisputatious nature, Jeffreys tells us, arguing that the shipworm, while not of a sociable habit, "is actuated by a conscientious anxiety not to infringe on its neighbor. When a collision is imminent, it secretes a cup-shaped dome or plug in front, of a thinner texture than the rest of its sheath; and it shuts itself up. Sometimes it makes several of these outer walls, one after another. It then, being unable to eat its way through the wood and thus procure a supply of food, dies of starvation, preferring suicide to the alternative of invading and injuring its companions!" Sellius ascribed a fine sense of honor to his "hero," as he called the teredo. Whether the shipworm disdains to engage in territorial disputes out of chivalry or morose self-absorption remains an open question. That it is not always so pacific may be seen by the testimony of a later observer, Clapp (1951), who recorded the actions of one shipworm species, not sure whether he was witnessing fighting or copulation:

> This probing and tearing activity of the excurrent siphon is quite violent. The siphon arches and waves wildly in all directions with gyrations which might be likened to those of the trunk of a very active miniature elephant. . . . In spite of the struggles of the incurrent siphon, the excurrent siphon generally eventually succeeds in pushing the tip end for a considerable distance down the inside of the incurrent siphon and is able to maintain a firm attachment there. After a few seconds, active resistance by the incurrent siphon ceases, and the excurrent siphon may then remain in this position for several minutes. During this period, a minute amount of a somewhat transparent fluid may clearly be seen though the transparent walls of both siphons, being ejected spasmodically from the excurrent siphon into the incurrent siphon.

This sounds like sex to me. Unfortunately, we have no way of knowing if there was any sperm transfer, because Clapp did not collect the transparent fluid. Those who are interested in such matters may consult another paper, "Sexual rhythm in the pelecypod mollusk Teredo," by Wesley Roswell Coe.

As Sigerfoos first postulated, the shipworm's sexuality is protandrous, which means it is hermaphroditic, metamorphosing from a male to a female in the course of its development. In shipworms, the female is always more mature than the male. Propagation may occur in three ways: (1) both sperm and eggs are released into the water by the individual in vast numbers (100 million eggs in one spawning), and the pairings allowed to occur as they may; (2) the sperm may be extruded into the water and then stored in the gills of the individual, where fertilization subsequently takes place; or (3) an excurrent siphon of a male may eject semen directly into the incurrent siphon of a female, as vividly described by the eminent Clapp, above.

Within hours after the eggs are laid, the embryos become free-swimming. The larvae will navigate around, searching opportunistically for some minuscule opening in a piece of wood: "the hull of a vessel or boat, a harbour-pile, a shipping-stage, a floating tree or the roots of one growing on the banks of an estuarine river, a piece of bark timber, a fisherman's cork, a cocoa-nut, a bamboo rod, a walking-stick, a beacon or buoy, a mast, rudder, oar, plank, cask, hencoop, or other ligneous waif or stray of the ocean." (Jeffreys). The fry have a few hours, or at most a few days, in which to infiltrate their host medium. Once successfully inside, however, they can snuggle in and begin their burrow. Scraping diligently in a path that follows along the grain of the wood, they grow very rapidly, outstripping their shells and acquiring their look of waving asparagus. When they meet a knot in the grain, they often curve around it, though some will burrow straight through. They will literally eat themselves out of house and home. But a lucky shipworm, encountering sufficient food supply and no impediments, can grow indefinitely, attaining a size of two feet or more. Dr. Ruth Turner found one in the tropics that was three feet long, which borders on sea-monster dimensions.

Once a shipworm claims a home, it is stuck there for the rest of its life. Efforts to transplant healthy, intact specimens from one plank to another have all resulted in fatality. They are loyal to their habitat; give them that. You may think of the shipworm inching forward, carving its burrow like a crawling prisoner who digs an underground tunnel with a spoon; or a blind man tapping alone in the wooden dark.

The main diet of the shipworm appears to be plankton and other minute organisms. It remains unknown whether the shipworm actually eats the wood particles it shreds, or merely processes it into a pulpy substance. If the latter, you have to wonder why it expends so much energy on a task from which it does not specifically benefit. Eating wood is simply its mission, its fate, unquestioned, just as the scholar burrows through libraries, or the writer spends years piling up texts, secreting the unawaited vellum like a series of outer walls between the world and himself.

It would be a lovely revenge to eat "this villainous animal," as Massuet calls it, even introduce it as a delicacy at the Oyster Bar. Customers might be invited to select their own bunch at a wharf where shipworms are particularly plentiful and bring them to their favorite restaurant, for *Tournedos de teredo.* The celebrated Redi found it very eatable, excelling all shellfish with its exquisite flavor. But Jeffreys thought the smell of a fresh shipworm nauseating. In trying to assess what conceivable utility the shipworm might possess, he concluded dourly, "Perhaps it is one of the creatures made not so much for our use as for our punishment."

More recently, a chemist named Harold Griffin extracted a bacterium found in shipworms that can be used as a powerful stain remover for laundry detergents. Beyond that, shipworms perform a valuable if unsung service by reducing the amount of driftwood in the oceans. Wood being slow to deteriorate in salt water, shipworms help the process along, unclogging the waterways.

In the early 1970s, when the federal Clean Water Act of 1972 started the improvement of the coastal environments, New York's polluted waters were in fact choked with an excess of rotting wood. "As pier decks and pilings were worn or torn away from their structure, these boards, pilings, and pier components began to threaten the safety of boats navigating in the harbor. In 1974, the Army Corps of Engineers developed a program to cope with the monumental rot of the city's pier infrastructure, the New York Harbor Drift Removal Project," wrote Carter Craft, in his study *Piers as Public Infrastructure.* Meanwhile the shipworms, awaiting improvements in water quality, were getting ready to do their part. But they have overshot the mark, gnawing through sound and rotten wood without distinction. It has not helped matters that virtually all pier development in New York Harbor has been built on wood pilings.

One is tempted to say that maybe it would make more sense just to let the shipworms do their damnedest, and not even try to hold on to the piers. Millions of dollars would be saved. The problem with that strategy is that our current environmental laws will not permit any further incursions, be they landfill or construction, into the water, so that once a pier goes, it is lost forever, and with it the potential for being someday utilized as public space. Considering how narrow the Hudson River Park will be in certain stretches, hemmed in by the highway, the piers may afford the only opportunity to have a tranquil experience with the river, unimpeded by auto traffic.

So the shipworm must be stopped. Various coatings have been applied to wooden surfaces over the centuries to safeguard them against the marine borer, from tar to bacon and lime, but the most common wood treatments are creosote and CCA (a mixture of copper, chrome, and arsenate). Effective as creosote and CCA may be, it is now acknowledged that both treatments leach toxic chemicals into the water. Certain types of wood have proven more impervious to the shipworm because of their extreme density, such as rain-forest lumber, but these rare and difficult-to-replace timbers from the Amazon and Central American forests are increasingly placed off limits, as well they should be. You can wrap old wooden pilings in concrete or steel, as is increasingly done with pier reconstruction, though both materials encounter problems in aqueous environments: the former can be corroded by sulphate attack, the latter through oxidation. Stone, the best, most cost-effective material over time, has been neglected because it is the most initially expensive.

One promising new technology is to make new piers out of recycled plastics or composites (a composite is a plastic or other polymer combined with glass, carbon, or aramid fibers), which ought to be a much cheaper material than concrete and steel, as well as being more environmentally friendly. Most important, shipworms won't munch on plastic. Granted, plastics have a weaker load-bearing capacity than concrete or steel, necessitating closer-together pilings, and no one really knows how long they last underwater. But the time had come to test this intriguing solution. One such test occurred on the south side of Hunts Point, the Bronx: in the mid-1990s, the Tiffany Street Pier was constructed almost entirely of "plastic lumber," which came from millions of two-liter soda bottles. Less than a year after the recreational pier opened, to great fanfare, it was struck in a freak lightning storm and its deck incinerated. One might almost think the Almighty had intervened with lightning bolts to protect His lowliest creature, the shipworm, from extinction.

So shipworms and New Yorkers continue to coexist, uneasily. They have much in common: "Each lives alone in a crowd," Jeffreys says of the teredo, though he might be speaking equally of the Manhattanite; each is obsessed with finding a suitable pad or consoling cocoon; each adjusts readily to obstacles looming in its path, while remaining solitudinously, morosely driven; each has workaholic, if not bisexual, tendencies.

10

FROM 42ND STREET
TO RIVERSIDE SOUTH

BEYOND THE CONVENTION CENTER, ABOVE 42ND STREET
WALKING NORTH, IS THAT WHOLE BOLLIXED-UP TRAF-
FIC JAM OF AN AREA, THE AIRCRAFT CARRIER *INTREPID*
museum and the Passenger Terminal for ocean liners. The heyday of this
area was when all the Queens docked side by side—the *Queen Mary,* the
Queen Elizabeth, the *Normandie,* the *Ile de France*—and when Cole Porter
wrote, in "I Happen to Like New York," that he liked to "watch those liners booming in"; they came all that distance because they, too, "happen to
like New York." In those days, even Upper East Side snobs who said they
never went over to the West Side amended that with "except to go to the
French Line."

Now these piers seem drab and inhospitable. If there is any glamour
still attached to ocean liners, you would not be able to sense it from the

fortresslike vanilla concrete ramps designed for cars, not pedestrians. There are no sidewalks, period. I contemplate buying a ticket to the gunmetal gray *Intrepid,* but I've been on it, twice, and each time felt that the thrill of martial experience and historical sacrifice was eluding me. Instead, it seemed an ill-sorted collection of maritime junk. The glass box they've built in front to house a McDonald's doesn't help inspire feelings of nationalistic reverence. I may as well keep walking. It's supposed to be great walking along the waterfront, but around here I'm starting to feel lonely. Cut off. I'm not having a good time! I miss all the faces that would be rushing at me in the crowded streets. I'm starting to get that ominous sense of emptiness, the one that comes on me in other cities, where the dense urban web starts to thin out—like the warehouse district of Los Angeles, or the border between Houston's downtown and its ship channel—and suddenly there aren't enough buildings or color to support a walk for pleasure, and I'm thrown in on myself, that worm! that bluffer! that emotional disappointment to his friends and family, leaving them always feeling hungry, or judged. There'd better be something interesting looming up ahead, or I'll have to do a number on myself. That funny truck mounted on the roof of a one-story building, a species of folk art? No, nothing much there. The place where they make H&H bagels? So what? Hey, look at that weird sign on the World Yacht gate: DINNER AND BRUNCH CRUISES. Whoever heard of a *brunch* cruise?

The problem with writing a walk down is that the details are infinite, therefore not worth pursuing. As the poet Louise Gluck said: "We have made of the infinite a topic. But there isn't, it turns out, much to say about it."

At Pier 94, "The Unconvention Center," they are shooting an episode of *Law and Order.* Lots of actors dressed as cops stand about tensely. An empty canvas-back chair reads: Jerry Ohrbach. The star is nowhere in sight. I remember seeing him recently at a bistro in TriBeCa, looking frail, sitting with a young admirer. After contemplating his memory, I'm thrown back on myself: you fraud, you dope, you don't know anything.

Ah, but maybe it's not my fault, maybe it's because there really isn't a continuous path for walkers along the riverfront. The promise is in the air, but the reality is decades away. So I'm trying to make a coherent experience out of something that isn't one yet. All these pathetic little bike paths and dog runs that give out suddenly after three blocks. These makeshift "walkway" arrows that point you around a construction site, or the DANGER/PRIVATE PROPERTY/KEEP OUT signs. If you would walk the waterfront, you have to do it in the spirit of a trespasser: follow the legal pedestrian route until it becomes ambiguous, or the sidewalk disappears, and you find yourself in no-man's-land, dodging eye contact with the occasional workman who might shoo you away, or the derelict who might importune you for a handout—perfectly fine, under ordinary circumstances, but it bothers you now since you feel so illegitimate yourself. In any case, I tell myself, it's not my fault, I'm not a bad person, there are objective, tangible *reasons* for my malaise.

NOTHING MUCH TO SAY about this mostly forlorn stretch of waterfront along the West Fifties, until I come to West 59th Street, where a marine transfer station is being reestablished to ship the city's garbage someplace else. The transfer station is graced with a wacky Greek temple portal, designed by Richard Dattner, and neon-lit by artist Steven Antonakos, that tries a touch too hard to be playful, but at least it tries. Across the way is the stately old Consolidated Edison/IRT powerhouse, whose distinguished architectural pedigree (McKim, Mead and White) may protect it from demolition.

At West 59th Street and the Hudson River, you may also enter the new waterfront park, Riverside South. This piece of land, stretching from here to 72nd Street, was until fairly recently the West Side Rail Yards of the New York Central. Cornelius Vanderbilt, the "Commodore," had created that powerful railroad by merging several weaker lines in the nineteenth century. Not only did the New York Central offer passage north on both sides of the Hudson River, and westward following the Erie Canal route, it was the only railroad line actually to enter the island of Manhattan. The other lines, including New York Central's mighty competitor, the Pennsylvania Railroad, stopped short at the continental, New Jersey side of the Hudson River, and had to ferry passengers across, while loading freight onto barges pulled by tugboats.

It was New York Central's idea to split its Manhattan lines in two: one, the passenger line, would cross over eastward and terminate in midtown, at Grand Central Station; the other, devoted strictly to freight, would continue downtown along the West Side's perimeter, eventually concluding in St. John's Park Freight Terminal (which still exists), at Houston and Hudson Streets in Greenwich Village. In order to alert cars and pedestrians on Tenth Avenue of an approaching freight train, men on horseback would precede the train, galloping along the tracks.

One reason the practice was discontinued was that the trains occasionally struck an inattentive pedestrian or car driver, causing the route to be nicknamed "Death Avenue." The freight delivery system that replaced the open tracks was a viaduct built between the West 33rd Street train yards and St. John's Park Terminal, passing wondrously through and between buildings, known as the High Line. (There is now a worthwhile effort to preserve it from demolition and turn it into an elevated park.)

Even after the city ordered the removal of all railroad tracks at grade below 59th Street, the West Side Rail Yards continued in full operation. It was one of three major yards along the West Side, the other two being at West 33rd Street and West 130th Street (Manhattanville). The New York Central built all three between 1877 and 1882, shortly after it had erected its first version of Grand Central Station on 42nd Street. The West Side Rail Yards contained a roundhouse, a grain elevator, stockyards, sections to make up trains, an engine service terminal, and eight piers for barges and ships. The piers testified to the importance of the Rail Yards as a marine-rail transfer zone. Although the New York Central's monopoly of rail access into Manhattan at first gave it an enormous advantage in securing freight, the company found that rail freight was still costlier than barge (since water is cheaper to maintain than railroad track), and that its freight lines would also be difficult to expand in the routes available. Consequently, the New York Central began also employing a lighterage system between its Weehawken, New Jersey, terminal and the West Sixties rail yards.

"Lighterage" refers to the movement of freight within a harbor by barge. "Car floats" more specifically designate railroad cars loaded onto a barge. So prevalent became this means of freight transport that an estimated 3,000 to 5,000 railroad cars floated every day across New York harbor in the first half of the twentieth century. It is mind-boggling to think of all those flat-bottomed vessels piled high (one barge could hold eight or more carloads of freight), crossing very near each other on the crowded seas. In their heyday, the barges were almost as synonymous with New York's iconography as its skyscrapers.

The most complicated piece of equipment in the Rail Yards was probably the West 69th Street transfer bridge, built in 1911 and engineered to load 1,000 tons on a vessel in ten to fifteen minutes. A transfer bridge (sometimes called a "float bridge") was a technology perfected during the turn of the twentieth century; it could roll a railroad car from a train onto a barge, for transport across the river, without having to unload it. The hard part was that the car floats listed from one side to another when being loaded; the transfer bridge had to be designed to absorb these tortional motions and keep the cargo from falling in the river. The solution, invented by the engineer James B. French, was a "contained-apron" type (don't ask me to explain it). So successful was French's West 69th Street bridge that afterwards "all *new* suspended bridges built at the Port (twenty-one of them) were built to his design," concluded Thomas R. Flagg, the world's authority on New York harbor transfer bridges.

The West Side Rail Yards were located at the bottom of a sloping pit, separated from any residential neighborhood, which may be why they survived longer than similar waterfront facilities in Manhattan. The West Side Rail Yards were still on the scene when the New York Central merged with the Pennsylvania Railroad in 1968, and still on the scene when that amalgam went bankrupt two years later, in 1970, the casualty of public highways, air travel, and containerization. Pieces of the extinct Penn Central's routes were absorbed by Amtrak and local commuter systems; but the once-dominant water belt line, which had so capably moved freight on the backs of barges, had all but disappeared. As Carl Condit put it so well in his book *The Port of New York:* "One may plausibly debate the question whether the later city of vehicular bridges and tunnels and distant airports is an urbanistic and ecological improvement over the earlier city of railroads, lighters, carfloats, and ferries."

During the 1970s, when I lived on West 71st Street, I would frequently wander west a few blocks to where the street dead-ended in an overlook, and gaze down at the idled train yards. It gave me a mysterious feeling, looking north to the landscaped Riverside Park, which began at 72nd Street, and then south, a few hundred feet away, to this scruffy, sloping terrain and the unkempt, deserted tracks below. You knew even then, at the height of the city's fiscal crisis, that it couldn't remain that way much longer. Someone would begin to buy up the parcels and turn it into a huge, Upper West Side, Lincoln Center–oriented development. And that is precisely what Donald J. Trump did. This high-living real estate developer, whose fame rivaled that of rock stars, whose glowing good health, ego, money, and appetite for well-endowed blondes fed the tabloids' gossip pages, who wrote (or had ghost-written for him) best-sellers about how good it felt to have it all, to pull off successful deals and cut through the bureaucratic logjams of building anything in New York—this self-confident scalawag whose name was put forward at one time as a Republican candidate for president, and who represented, to a resentful faction of Democrats, Mammon himself, in 1983 purchased for $95 million, with the help of his mostly silent Chinese partners, these seventy-six acres of prime waterfront property, the then-largest undeveloped site left on Manhattan, on which he proposed to build the tallest tower on earth, 150 stories, plus the new NBC television studios, 7,600 units of housing, and a major shopping mall, all to be named—Trump City, or, on more-modest days, Television City.

But he had not fully reckoned with one of the orneriest, most combat-ready communities on earth, the Upper West Side, which expressed its legitimate unhappiness with the development's proposed density, with the thousands of air-polluting cars it would bring into the area, and with the additional stress it would place on the West 72nd Street subway station, already operating at or over capacity. An acrimonious stalemate and a blizzard of lawsuits followed, after which certain people of goodwill came forward and attempted to broker a deal. Among them was Richard Kahan, one of the most experienced and enlightened veterans of New York city planning. A small, soft-spoken, baldheaded man with a penchant for natty dark suits and a disarming smile, Kahan is not without ego himself, and had once started running for governor, before the reality of his utter lack of name-recognition or populist charisma sank in. But he understood government and real estate: he had been among the original Ratensky's Raiders (see the chapter on Westway); had helped push Battery Park City out of its sand trap as chairman of the Battery Park City Authority; had been instrumental in the rehabilitation of thousands of tenement units in the Bronx; and was now attempting to salvage the West Side Rail Yards debacle. The compromise he and other intermediaries worked out was that the developer (Trump) would scale back the project's density by more than half, would relinquish the world's tallest building and the world's largest television studio, would forget the shopping mall, and would settle for a dozen or so upscale residential towers, placed along a southern extension of Riverside Drive, to be called Riverside South, though later the name was changed to—Trump Place.

As Kahan recounted this episode to me, one of the novelties in the negotiating process was to have enlisted the watchdog civic groups, such as the Municipal Art Society, normally Trump's antagonist, to work with the developer on a satisfactory compromise. The collaboration might risk tarnishing the civic groups' reputations for integrity and autonomy, but the chance was worth taking, as Kahan saw it: not only would the project be scaled back considerably, and its buildings made to adhere to a sensitive urban design in the tradition of Central Park West, but the community would receive a splendid new public park, paid for and maintained entirely by Trump, and envisioned as a continuation of its distinguished neighbor to the north, Riverside Park.

The key to this amenity was moving the West Side Highway from its current elevated path and burying it under a deck, so that you could enter the park directly from Trump Place and walk down sloping banks to the river, without ever seeing an expressway. Kahan and several others went to Washington to lobby for this change, and the federal government agreed to pay for tearing down the highway and rerouting it underground. Everything looked wonderful, a great twenty-three-acre, car-less river-front park was within sight, when the project hit a roadblock: Assemblyman (later Congressman) Jerrold Nadler. This politician had a reputation as a fighting urban progressive, championing all manner of good things, such as burying the Gowanus Expressway in a tunnel, constructing a cross-harbor rail tunnel between Brooklyn and New Jersey, and returning freight trains to the region. One of the reasons he opposed burying the highway at that site, in fact, was that it would end the dream of resurrecting rail freight in the New York Central yards. (Not that such a possibility was even remotely in the offing.) The second reason, more personal, was that Jerry Nadler hated Donald Trump. If Trump was for it, he would have to be agin' it.

Nadler felt sure that Trump would never be able to rent his expensive apartments as long as a highway ran right outside their windows. Were the highway buried, it would profit Trump's sales efforts immensely; but if the elevated highway stayed in place, thought Nadler, Trump would get discouraged and give up the project. Kahan tried to convince Nadler that Trump was going ahead with construction, regardless of the highway's destiny; but Nadler was sure Trump would eventually cave in, and held to that conviction even after the first, the second, the third tower started to rise. . . . The shrewd developer, for his part, had guessed correctly that the New York real estate market was strong enough to attract plenty of buyers and renters to the new towers. Trump behaved with a surprising amount of restraint throughout this conflict, though he did rise to the bait once and call Nadler a fat slob, which was noted the next day in the tabloids. The rotund assemblyman took offense. This is how history in New York City is made. In the end, the West Side Highway stayed put, the park's potential was undermined, and the interests of the community were thwarted by their representative's spite. It was Westway all over again: the Federal government had expressed its willingness to pay for the removal of a highway along the waterfront, but the progressive reformers defeated the plan, because it would line the pockets of capitalists they detested.

What of Trump Place itself? You see it as you drive along the West Side Highway: looming, unavoidable, mediocre. Trump had enlisted Philip Johnson, largely because, to the developer, "Philip Johnson" had the most famous, resonant name of living architects, useful for marketing the apartment blocks. Of course, Philip Johnson is hardly the exciting architect he once was, but the marketing strategy worked. Then, too, the banal character of the towers done so far by Johnson and Costas Kondylis seems entirely in keeping with Trump's other buildings; he *likes* these suave, deluxe nullities, never exactly awful, but never enthralling: this restrained vulgarity is the Trump trademark.

The urban design guidelines, which sought to emulate the residential buildings of Central Park West, made for decent street layouts, while reducing the chance for more-original architecture. The *New York Times* architectural critic, Herbert Muschamp, who never tires of denouncing the sins of Contextualism, had these validly acerbic thoughts about the results: "Glass, in any case, is far more 'contextual' than masonry for waterfront locations: its reflective surface mirrors that of water; it yields a more radiant light. Context, moreover, is a matter of time as well of place. At Trump Place, ahistorical mutants masquerade as historical landmarks." In the end, the ensemble is no worse than the buildings just south of it—indeed, a fraction better. (The blocks behind Lincoln Center, going toward the river, are immensely dispiriting. Here the nightmare was enacted: mundane residential towers taking up whole blocks, without a speck of urbanism, no life at the sidewalk level, no invitation for nonresident pedestrians walking past, just privilege and dullness. I have been inside these apartment buildings: the construction is shoddy, the walls thin, niceties of detail nonexistent; you enter a barren box and are drawn immediately, and *only,* to the view.)

As for the resulting park, Riverside South, it is better than nothing. If you stand on the river's edge and look inland across the park, toward Trump Place, the elevated columns of the West Side Highway interrupt any bucolic sense you might have, chop up the space with industrial grime, and intrude their shadows over one whole stripe. You feel like Orpheus gazing through the mouth of hell toward a lost Eurydice. The one good thing about the highway being raised high at this stretch is that, if you turn your back to it, you can almost edit it out of your consciousness, or pretend the rushing sounds are surf—more so, anyway, than if the highway were barreling alongside you.

The park was designed by the dashing landscape architect Thomas Balsley, in an unobtrusive if underwhelming manner. Balsley's idea has been to move you from bulkhead to natural shoreline to pier to cove, and back to bulkhead. The old, disintegrating piers, victimized by fire and shipworms, are fun to look at. There is the "spaghetti carbonara" Pier D, a pile of blackened wire struck by lightning (or arson). There is the caved-in, sagging 64th Street Pier, looking like a rollercoaster that gravity has done a number on. Together they form a fascinating sequence, a narrative of decay and rot. I do not expect them to remain as they are for long, so appetizingly dysfunctional and dangerous to climb upon.

Balsley has designed the park's stellar new attraction, an 800-foot-long silver pier with scalloped edge. The pier's snaking profile suggests a natural shoreline. It zigzags like a lightning bolt that juts into the harbor. Sunday fishermen are out in good weather, angling for snapper or casting their crab traps into the brine; others sit on benches, taking in dramatic views. At walkway's end, you have the giddy sense of being on the water, yet remaining dry. To accommodate environmental agencies' concerns, the pier has been elevated several steps above its original height so that more sunlight can filter down to the fish.

Balsley's new pier sits next to the 1911 transfer bridge, which has been placed on the Historical Register, meaning that neither Trump nor anyone else is permitted to demolish it. In fact, he is responsible for *maintaining* it, and has already spent a quarter of a million dollars just to stabilize the structure. To restore it legitimately to its former glory, with all the bells and whistles appealing to railroad and waterfront buffs, would take an additional $3 million, but you would have a stunning monument to the city's industrial history.

Another plan being bruited about is to turn the West 69th Street float bridge into a landing for small, high-speed ferries. Though some critics of the plan wonder how passengers would connect with further transportation, once they deboarded (imagine having to walk up through the park two blocks to hail a taxi!), it would be grand to see the transfer bridge given a new lease on life.

THIS TRANSFER BRIDGE WAS, incidentally, the abode of one J.R., a homeless man who squatted there in the early 1990s. In a photograph from that period, taken by Margaret Morton, it was emblazoned in graffiti with the name "Tooney." Those hardy enough to ascend the gantry to the cabin aloft were met with a hand-lettered sign that read: STAY THE FUCK OUT OF MY HOUSE!!!!! (Morton has done two remarkable books, *Fragile Dwelling* and *The Tunnel,* which document with words and pictures the individual men and women who give a human face to that abstraction "the homeless.") J.R., an ex-convict and onetime bounty hunter, was forced to move out of his transfer bridge outpost by the bitter winter of January 1994, into one of twenty-seven concrete vaults under some West Side Rail Yard tracks. (These particular tracks had originally been built for milk trains, which delivered much of the city's milk, cream, condensed milk, and pot cheese between the hours of 11:30 P.M. and 3:30 A.M.). Each concrete vault was eventually occupied by a homeless person or couple, some of whom went to great lengths to personalize and decorate them.

When it took over the New York Central Rail Yards, Trump's development corporation wasted no time seeing to it that the homeless people nesting there were removed. Without warning, bulldozers crushed the makeshift homes and filled the cubicles with dirt and debris taken from the Trump Place excavation project. Earlier, fifty or so homeless people living in the tunnel to the north, which ran almost the entire length of Riverside Park, from West 72nd Street to 123rd Street, were also evicted.* In the late 1980s and early 1990s, a population of homeless had stumbled upon the underground crypt and found it to their liking. But the Trump construction staff did not want vagrants around its staging area, and put pressure on Amtrak officials to have them removed, along with the Rail Yard squatters. Margaret Morton wrote: "When city police razed the Rail Yard encampment on February 26, 1997, they demolished the last shantytown in Manhattan. Since then, the numbers of homeless poor have not diminished, but they have become less visible. Fearful of police, the dispossessed journey the streets alone, urban nomads forever on the move: riding subways throughout the night; sleeping on dark, silent streets; hiding in the shadows of construction sites; tucking themselves into decaying structure along the waterfront; disappearing before dawn."

THE WATERFRONT IS A NATURAL REFUGE for the homeless. It is out of the way, less policed, and those who wish to "sleep rough" without being hassled eventually make their way to the city's edges. As the New York Coalition for the Homeless director, Mary Brosnahan Sullivan, told me, "They've already marginalized themselves internally, so why not geographically? They seek out the waterfront because they want to be left alone."

---

*Technically, the Riverside Park structure should be called an "overbuild" rather than a tunnel, because it was erected on top of preexisting tracks, rather than dug in the ground: Robert Moses had it constructed as a sensible way of keeping trains away from park-goers, and protecting the air from the train's befouling coal emissions.

The first homeless population on New York's waterfront to receive attention were vagrant children: the so-called "dock rats," who lived in and around the wharves along the East River. There were estimated to be at least 15,000 unreclaimed children roaming the streets of New York in the late nineteenth century. They lived by their wits, often pilfering from ships' cargoes. "Anywhere along the docks are facilities for petty thieving, and, guard as the policemen may, the swarms of small street rovers can circumvent them. A load of wood left on the dock diminishes under his very eyes. The sticks are passed from one to another, the child nearest the pile being busy apparently in playing marbles. If any move of suspicion is made toward them, they are off like a swarm of cockroaches, and with about as much sense of responsibility," wrote Mrs. Helen Campbell in the 1893 guidebook *Darkness and Daylight; or, Lights and Shadows of New York Life.* Another dodge was for the dock rat "to dive under a wharf and fasten one end of a wire rope to one of the rafters. Then he'd sneak along on board a lead-loaded schooner and fasten the end he'd carried with him to whatever came handy." He would drop the pilfered object—maybe a metal bar or a ship's chronometer—with the weighted rope attached to it into the water, and fish it out at his convenience. Fences and junk shops along the waterfront were only too happy to purchase the stolen goods.

These child waterfront thieves became a favorite journalistic subject throughout the nineteenth century, along with their nemesis, the harbor police. An unsigned article in *Harper's Magazine,* October 1872, reported:

The thoroughly untamed and wild-animal character of the "dock rats" is frequently evinced by a singular tendency which they exhibit for making themselves dens or nests of their own under the very piers themselves, and amidst the stench of the oozing tides and sewerage. Here they will patch together odds and ends of plank and driftwood, and even set up some sort of contrivance for warmth and cookery, if they can so arrange that the fumes of their coke and charcoal shall not too speedily betray them. Their nests are great places for the reception of plunder when the junk-shops are too closely watched, and every few weeks the harbor police make thorough searches for them, boating and wading, to the great detriment of tempers and uniforms, and at the cost of severe fatigue and personal disgust.

Children's aid societies were formed to set up lodging-houses and provide support for these unsupervised waifs, but there were too many to be accommodated. Others did not want to be; they preferred the lawless freedom of the docks. "Whence this army of homeless children? is a question often asked," Jacob Riis posited in his 1890 crusading classic, *How the Other Half Lives*. "The answer is supplied by the procession of mothers that go out and in at Police Headquarters the year round, inquiring for missing boys, often not until they have been gone for weeks and months, and then sometimes rather as a matter of decent form than from any real interest in the lad's fate. The stereotyped promise of the clerks who fail to find his name on the books among the arrests, that 'he will come back when he gets hungry,' does not always come true. More likely he went away because he was hungry."

The West Side waterfront has long had a history of adult homelessness, dating at least from the 1850s, when the railroad first entered there and found squatters occupying the mud flats along the Hudson River. In the Panic of 1893, brought on when the Philadelphia & Reading Railroad declared bankruptcy, a serious economic depression ensued that closed the Gilded Age and threw many Americans out of work for nearly a decade. Meanwhile, an estimated 60,000 men rode the rails, looking for work. "By the early 1900s both the homeless community and the railroad had expanded: a tarpaper shantytown with 125 occupants lined the four tracks of the New York Central and Hudson River Railroad where it stretched six miles along an area known as Riverside Park," wrote Margaret Morton. Hoovervilles were a common sight along the West Side Rail Yards and Riverside Park during the Great Depression. In the 1980s and 1990s, a squeeze on affordable housing, combined with a loss of manufacturing and entry-level jobs, again saw the homeless take up positions along these rocks, coves, and underpasses.

The picture that emerges from Margaret Morton's interviews with the waterfront homeless is of a proud, resourceful, self-reliant group, almost all of whom disdain street begging or the social welfare system, preferring instead to scrounge for food from supermarkets, schools, and other institutions that throw out their day's extras, and to support themselves by collecting cans for deposits, washing cars, helping supers with recycling piles, or holding down odd jobs off the books. They pick up discarded furnishings that might improve their makeshift quarters, and hook up wiring to the lampposts for TVs and record players. They use the playground restrooms and hydrants for water. Contrary to the caricature of laziness, they tend to be active all day and much of the night, as a necessary condition for survival. Most have had awful experiences with homeless shelters, and prefer the outdoors or the tunnel system, partly because shelters are dangerous, violent, unhealthy (fear of tuberculosis is not unfounded), and restrictive regarding freedom of property and choosing one's company.

The tendency to demonize the homeless as shiftless or crazy can inspire an equally dubious countertendency to sentimentalize them as heroic, salt-of-the-earth rebels or philosophical *clochards*. The reality would seem to be somewhere in between: perhaps a third suffer from mental illness, a third more from alcoholism and substance abuse. There are indeed normal, sober homeless people who are simply down on their luck, but forced to adapt to economic hard times by living on the street; others become homeless after an injury has temporarily cost them their livelihood; still others have had their immigration papers stolen (or, illegal in the first place, make up this story of stolen papers); some have been traumatized by the death of a child, divorce, or combat stress.

The paradox is that the homeless are labeled as pathologically "disaffiliated" from society, but when they try to form a society of their own, they are dispersed; they are characterized as "rootless," yet when they embrace domestic values by building fragile dwellings, their chambers are bulldozed. Recently, starting under ex-mayor Giuliani's reign, they have been forced into the much more dangerous, asocial, nomadic situation of sleeping alone, and then having to take up their cardboard boxes or blankets each morning and move elsewhere. If they gather in groups of three or more, some offended citizen is apt to call the "quality of life" hotline, and the police are sent to break it up.

Often, in walking the waterfront, I have seen traces of homeless encampments, or come upon a group around a fire burning in a barrel. During the warm-weather months, the population turns younger; there are "summer punks" who sleep in the parks. On the waterfront, the homeless bunk down under a bridge or inside the anchorage, beneath a highway ramp, along the seawall, in riverside parks, around abandoned piers and railroad transfer gantries, and tucked into weedy brownfields.

11

RIVERSIDE PARK
AND MANHATTANVILLE

Riverside Park has long been the jewel in the waterfront crown, the best recreational facility on the edge of Manhattan Island. Central Park is for the world, the tourists, the outer boroughs; Riverside Park is a neighborhood amenity, not a guidebook "destination." It is the garden reserve for Faubourg Upper West Side, and as such enjoys a cozy mirror-relationship with its comfortably well-off, Parisian-style residential surroundings.

One block east of the park runs West End Avenue, a respectable quarter of stout apartment buildings that epitomizes the virtues of the middle class. The appreciation that Christopher Morley, learned scribbler and belletrist, wrote of the street in 1932, still holds true today: "West End Avenue is incomparably the most agreeable and convenient of large residential streets, second only to Riverside Drive. . . . When it goes residential at 70th Street, [it] does so in solid fashion, without freak or fantasy. For thirty-five blocks it has probably the most uniform skyline of any avenue in New York. It indulges little in terraces or penthouses; just even bulks of masonry. What other street can show me a run of thirty-five blocks without a shop-window?"

Those who own co-ops in the spacious, prewar apartment buildings on West End Avenue or Riverside Drive, and are lucky enough to have a view of the park and the river as well, will tell you they could not live anywhere else in New York City, they *need* the park for their sanity. And you register the note of bourgeois complacency and feel a bit put off by it, if you are an outsider, when you walk the park itself. It is heaven; but is it *your* heaven?

Once or twice it was, in fact, my heaven, though I used it roughly and unconsciously, too young to appreciate urban sublimity. When I went to Columbia as an undergraduate, my head full of dark paradoxes, I would sometimes buy a meatball hero and take it to the park and chew it on a bench overlooking the river, or stride through the brown leaves in autumn. Years after that, in my bachelor phase, I would bring dates to the 79th Street marina in summer, with the fireflies twinkling around us. While none of these cycles *took,* and I had never fully bonded with Riverside Park, in the way of those who had made the commitment to live in one of those big, oppressively nice, prewar apartments and work and die in the park's vicinity, still I came to feel an ongoing private connection to the place.

In 1873 THE CITY COMMISSIONED Frederick Law Olmsted, the chief designer of Central Park, to build a park on a narrow strip of shoreline alongside the already-functioning Hudson River Railroad. Olmsted made use of the steep bluffs and rocky outcroppings left by prehistoric glaciers to create a rustic hillside landscape, through which passed one of his patented parkways. Neglected, its features effaced, by the 1920s Riverside Park had become "a wasteland," wrote Robert Caro in *The Power Broker:* "the 'park' was nothing but a vast low-lying mass of dirt and mud. Running through its length was the four-track bed of the New York Central, which lay in a right-of-way that had been turned over to the railroad by the city half a century before. Unpainted, rusting, jagged wire fences along the tracks barred the city from the waterfront; in the whole six miles, there were exactly three bridges on which the tracks could be crossed, and they led only to private boating clubs." In one of his greatest, most populist acts, Parks Commissioner Robert Moses seized the opportunity, during the construction of the West Side Highway and the Henry Hudson Parkway in the 1930s, to double the park's size and improve, if considerably tame, its design: the railroad tracks were covered over, granite walls and concrete paths were introduced, ballfields, a playground, and tennis courts added, and a complex, three-level traffic circle, jet fountain, and grand staircase were put in at West 79th Street, overlooking the 79th Street Boat Basin.

With its allées and terraces, woods, marina, and open, sloping lawns, Riverside Park is a neighborhood treasure that continues to be used, casually and effectively, by a variety of different groups at different times of day. (I am talking here of the southern end of Riverside Park, which begins at West 72nd Street and ends at 125th Street; the lesser-known upper end, which picks up at 135th Street and continues all the way up north to 152nd Street, serving poorer neighborhoods, is more ragtag, starved for landscaping services and left in disrepair.)

Today I walk down to the water at West 72nd Street, skirting a homeless man with matted hair who sits up on the grass next to his shopping cart, looking dazed. At the river's edge, a film crew is taking a lunch break, munching sandwiches on the benches. As usual, whenever I stumble on a film being shot, nothing is happening, and I am too impatient to wait for the action to start.

I pass a Hispanic fisherman in green jogging outfit, around forty-five, thin mustache, lowering a rod into the water. "Any luck?" is on the tip of my tongue, but I don't say it, fearing to sound boorish. *Any luck?* I repeat to myself. What a glorious day! At the marina, three mothers are showing their preschoolers some ducks in the water. They're laughing among themselves, with that solidarity of moms looking after kids. Suddenly I feel bereft. I want to tell them I also have a small child. I start thinking about Lily, and the waterfront recedes.

There's a jogging woman running up the curved, sweeping fieldstone staircase, holding on to the reins of two dogs, not one, while pushing a baby stroller. She's determined to get her exercise. She looks like a woman named Sarah I know, which puts me in mind of Sara Teasdale, who haunts the park. Sara Teasdale wrote an Edwardian make-out poem, in 1915, called "Summer Night, Riverside." It begins:

In the wild soft summer darkness
How many and many a night we two together
Sat in the park and watched the Hudson
Wearing her lights like golden spangles
Glinting on black satin.
The rail along the curving pathway
Was low in a happy place to let us cross,
And down the hill a tree that dripped with bloom
Sheltered us,
While your kisses and the flowers,
Falling, falling,
Tangled my hair.

The frail white stars moved slowly over the sky.

And so on. Teasdale no longer enjoys much critical cachet, but I am a sucker for her romantic-poetess style, all that sorrow and astronomy, curiously localized to New York settings. She lived around Riverside Park for years, unhappily if sedately married, before moving down to Greenwich Village, to be more "with it," and eventually, realizing she had fallen permanently out of fashion (which had shifted to literary experimentation), to kill herself, taking pills in a rented Village flat.

Riverside Park has the effect of slowing down the senses and making you more conscious of the seasons. I also associate Riverside Park with Paul Goodman, the novelist/social critic/lay psychoanalyst/poet/planner, etc., who played guru to several of my Columbia classmates during the early sixties, both because of his youth-flattering book, *Growing Up Absurd,* and his Socratic charisma. My classmate Richard Tristman (now dead, alas) spoke excitedly to me on a Riverside Park bench about Goodman's all-purpose brilliance, and dangled the possibility that he might someday take me around to the great man's apartment, which was nearby. It seemed improbable, like meeting Goethe, and in fact it never happened. Goodman, à propos, wrote that loveliest of Upper West Side waterfront poems, "The Lordly Hudson," which goes:

"Driver, what stream is it?" I asked, well knowing
it was our lordly Hudson hardly flowing,
"It is our lordly Hudson hardly flowing,"
he said, "under the green-grown cliffs."

Be still, heart! No one needs your passionate
Suffrage to select this glory,
this is our lordly Hudson hardly flowing
under the green-grown cliffs.

"Driver! Has this a peer in Europe or the East?"
"No no!" he said. Home! Home!
be quiet, heart! this is our lordly Hudson
and has no peer in Europe or the East,

this is our lordly Hudson hardly flowing
under the green-grown cliffs
and has no peer in Europe or the East.
Be quiet, heart! home! Home!

Communitas, the wise, sane little primer on city planning that Paul Goodman wrote with his architect-brother, Percival, in 1960, is skeptical about many neatnik, utopian schemes for separating activities into zones, insisting instead that "urban beauty is a beauty of walking" and holding up for emulation the European piazza: "Squares are not avenues of motor or pedestrian traffic, but are places where people remain. Place of work and home are close at hand, but in the city square is what is still more interesting—the other people." Nobly put. Still, so attached were the brothers Goodman to Manhattan's rivers that they had published a rather mad vision, anti-mixed-use, in *The New Republic* fifteen years earlier, and retrieved it as an appendix to *Communitas.*

"A Master Plan for New York" proposed that business and industry be concentrated into a continuous axis running up the central spine of Manhattan (even though this would mean filling in Central Park!), that the through avenues on either side of this axis should be removed and the land developed as park/residential neighborhoods, right down to the rivers, with the shores turned over to beaches for swimming, boating, and promenades. Arguing that there had always been something wrong about Manhattan's turning inward, instead of being encouraged "to open out toward the water," they justified the conversion of the greater part of the island's twenty-nine-mile shoreline to sport and residence, by "recognizing that the riverfront in Manhattan proper has diminished in commercial importance and may now be put to another use." I find it astonishing that these words were written in 1944; evidently some observers, even before the advent of containerization, had already intuited the Port of New York's decline, though it was still playing such a crucial role throughout World War II.

As for their proposal that New York's most beloved creation, Central Park, be totaled, the Goodmans blithely stated, "We should not for a moment venture to destroy this wonderful strategem of the central parks, were it not the case that more and more the river parks have proved their value. . . ." Their love of Riverside Park inspired them to extend the model and turn New York upside-down. Of course much of what they proposed would have been folly, but it provided a template for the many schemes since then, some quite recent, designed to turn the shoreline of Manhattan into a playland of recreation and residence.

As soon as you get above the 79th Street marina you start becoming conscious of the undulating shoreline, which is one of the central beauties of the water's-edge experience. (In retrospect, you register it as an experience that had been denied you farther south, in Downtown and Midtown Manhattan's straight-ruled bulkhead edge.)

Today I am met in the park and shown around by an old friend in publishing, Ann, who overcame cancer a few years back—partly, she is convinced, by learning to cut back on stress and to be more peaceful inside herself. "I would come down to Riverside Park every day and do my cancer-cell meditations while watching the sunset." To hear Ann talk,

Riverside Park saved her life. Her relationship with it has deepened since she acquired a dog, a little gray poodle named Augie. "The city changes when you have a dog," said Ann. How? I (skeptic and cat owner) asked. "It becomes friendlier, for one thing," she answered. Now when she takes Augie on his morning and afternoon walks, she has all sorts of instantaneous engagements with other dog owners, which help construe the park as a community. Some dog owners can be a pain, of course, but when she wants to break away she just blames it on Augie.

Her daily walks with Augie all tend to amble *through* the park's sloping woods and fields, which the dog prefers, though sometimes she takes the route along the water. Today, just to humor me, she accompanies me up the newly installed Cherry Walk. This paved path from about 105th to 125th Streets, painted with a middle stripe to separate walkers from joggers or bicyclists traveling in different directions, hugs the rocky shore. One of the few places along the island's edge you can get down to the water, formerly it was a weedy, flotsam-strewn area, with crushed milk cartons, cellophane wrappers, bottles, newspapers, discarded underwear from derelicts' encampments; but now it is—designed, the precise shades of gray road surface and lime-green stripe obviously much pondered over, and chosen for their tasteful restraint. It looks clean and intended to be walked, no longer an accidental residue of nature. By the waterside is a meadow with dandelions and London plane trees, boulders and riprap; Cherry Walk somehow gives better definition to this wild scrap of Hudson River School vista.

Ann leads me through the Bird Sanctuary (which I never thought in my college was anything more than scruffy woods), and we end up in the 105th Street Dog Run. The coy sign outside it reads DOG RUN 105/CURSUS CANIS CV, to let us know we are near Columbia and Morningside Heights, the Acropolis of America. Ann tells me that in the morning there's a little cart with tea and coffee outside the dog run. At noon, the hired dog-walkers bring in fifteen dogs on leashes, and the locals stay away. The enclosed area is certainly pleasant-looking and well kept; the graveled ground, the wrought-iron fences, all bespeak an attention to aesthetic detail one rarely sees in dog runs. I am willing to go on record and say it is the nicest dog run in the city. (What do *I* know?) There is a small, enclosed run for Pekineses or puppies, so they won't be threatened by the rowdier, bigger dogs. A man says to his Airedale, quite as if he were at a children's playground, "Come, sweetie. Let's go, Daddy's cold."

I LEAVE ANN AND GO ON ALONE. There's handsome, gray Riverside Church in the distance, commanding the skyline for miles around like an ecclesiastical office tower. How Lewis Mumford hated what he regarded as its "fake Gothic," stained-glass eclecticism when it first opened in 1930, calling it one of America's "dead colossi." Now no one would think to see it as a betrayal of modernism. If a building stays in one place long enough, all its retrograde sins are forgiven, or better yet, forgotten.

The other major landmark adjacent to Riverside Park is Grant's Tomb, located at West 122nd Street and Riverside Drive. Talk about your dead colossi! This monument was once the destination spot for tourists and locals. Now it is mostly frequented by schoolkids, who listen tactfully to the National Park Service Ranger's rap, before going outside to play kick-ball on the wide plaza fronting the monument. What to make of the struc-ture itself, that granite neoclassical wedding cake, with Doric columns and a raised rotunda? Once it symbolized respect and dignity; now, it's, well, a mausoleum. (It was in fact partly copied from the original mausoleum, Mausoleus's tomb at Halicarnassus, as well as Napoleon's tomb in the Invalides). Inside, it's pleasantly cool, and severe and empty enough to impress, with "a scale that seems pitilessly Poe-like in its grandeur," noted the poet David Shapiro. Beneath the dome are two polished black sar-cophagi side by side, wherein repose the remains of General Ulysses Simpson Grant and his wife, Julia. (The old joke went: Who is buried in Grant's tomb?—No one, his body is in a raised sarcophagus. Har! Har!)

Placards inform us that the fund-raising campaign for the monument, organized by Richard T. Greener, the first black graduate of Harvard, attracted ninety thousand donors. On its opening day, April 27, 1897 (declared a full holiday by the State of New York), enormous crowds of a million-plus filled the streets! President McKinley officiated from the grandstand. Grant's Tomb remained near the top of America's most pop-ular monuments until the end of World War I, by which time most Civil War veterans and their families had died out. During my lifetime, it lay graffiti-marred for years, before it was lovingly restored, under the care of the National Parks Service.

What does it say about us as a people that a monument that once drew respectful millions now barely registers on the public's consciousness? Is it that Americans are amnesiac, or that our taste in monumental architecture has improved? Grant's reputation did go through a slide during the first half of the twentieth century, when he was seen as an alcoholic and an inept administrator; but now that a revisionist movement among historians would rank him higher as a general, chief executive, and memoirist, does that mean his tomb will receive more visitors? Unlikely. Perhaps it is not our taste in monuments so much as our notions about vistas and the sublime that have dramatically changed. A century ago, visitors, still under the influence of the Hudson River School of Painting, wanted to look down on the city and the river from a detached height. The skyscraper negated the power of the landscaped overlook, by making it possible to glimpse the city from on high while still in the middle of it.

Finally, Grant's Tomb is "merely" a tomb, with no slide show, no video presentation, no educational outreach program, no temporary exhibits of Civil War gold. Outside the monument is a set of benches, mosaic-tiled and cheerful in a child-friendly, Miró-derivative manner, installed around the monument, to the chagrin of the Grant family. Their faux-naïve sweetness clashes with the chill neoclassicism of the tomb.

AT 125TH STREET, Riverside Park terminates in a parking area whose grubbiness tells you immediately that you are leaving the realm of the privileged and designed, and entering the fringes of Harlem. There begins Manhattanville. To fathom this mysterious neighborhood to the north of Columbia and Riverside Park, I needed a guide; someone suggested I contact Eric Washington, the unofficial historian of Manhattanville. He agreed to meet me at 125th Street and Broadway, where the grandiose arch of the elevated train confronts the Golden Arches of Big Mac.

Eric turns out to be a gentle, cultivated black man of medium height, who makes his living as a freelance writer. After having been asked to prepare the landmark designation for St. Mary's Church, he became more and more interested in Manhattanville's history, collecting old postcards and prints of the area (many appeared in his book *Manhattanville: Old Heart of West Harlem*), and now conducts walking tours of the neighborhood. Though he speaks knowledgeably about architecture and urbanism, he has no formal training in these areas, and describes himself modestly as a "neighborhood buff." Where would local history be without such buffs?

For purposes of definition, he tells me, Manhattanville is the valley that extends north from 125th to 135th Street, and east from the Hudson River to St. Nicholas Avenue. But in its heyday, its name could refer to places below 125th Street (Morningside Heights as an entity did not yet exist) and north of 135th Street.

In 1609, Henry Hudson anchored the *Half Moon* near the inlet of future Manhattanville, and was met by four canoes of natives. A crew member, Robert Jouet, recorded in his journal that "we suffered none of them to come into our ship; they brought very great store of very good oysters aboard, which we bought for trifles."

In September 1776, the area figured prominently in the Battle of Harlem Heights. George Washington, headquartered slightly north in the Roger Morris house (later the Stephen Jumel Mansion), was debating whether to quit New York. In view of the vastly superior numbers of British troops that General Howe seemed about to land there, and the Continental Army's inexperience, evacuation of the city was inevitable, but after the ignominious defeat on Long Island, Washington hoped to fight a campaign in Manhattan that would at least help season his raw troops. On the first day of skirmishes, in which the Continentals panicked and ran, "Washington promptly came down with two New England brigades to give them mettle and, galloping on his charger to the scene, endeavored to rally the men before they completely dispersed. In a moment of rage, he dashed his hat onto the ground and exclaimed, 'Are these the men with whom I am to defend America!'" wrote Benson Bobrick in his history of the American Revolution, *Angel in the Whirlwind*. Somehow the New York garrison managed to escape up the island's west side. The next day, Washington planned to use the strategic advantage of the steep bluffs at Harlem Heights to stave off the British, and surround them in the low valley of Manhattanville, which was then called the Hollow Way.

As Bruce Bliven tells it in his vivid account, *Battle for Manhattan:* "The

General [Washington] did not mean to risk an engagement with the full British force, whatever it was, nor to try to drive the British back toward their camp. But he thought he might be able to lure Leslie's confident light infantrymen a little further north, down from the high ground at Claremont into the Hollow Way, and then cut them off by sending a strong detachment around to the west, up the rocky Morningside Heights bluff, to the rear. Two separate, coordinated actions would be required: a feint in front of Claremont as if the Americans meant to rush up the hill, which would draw some of the British down into the valley, and simultaneously a stealthy encircling march around the left by a force which would be masked from the British by the terrain and the trees. It was among the most elementary of tactical schemes. On the other hand, it was more, in terms of control and synchronized action, than the Americans had yet pulled off."

As it happened, it was bungled by a premature order to fire, ruining the surprise, and two American commanders, Knowlton and Leitch, were mortally wounded in the process. But the Continental troops recouped and, by the end of the day, had the British in retreat. Though the Battle of Harlem Heights proved inconsequential in terms of territory held, it was immensely important for lifting the troops' morale: it gave the Americans "the pleasure of seeing the backs of British uniforms," and the knowledge that they could prevail against this enemy, if they were but stalwart enough.

After independence, the Hollow Way became incorporated as Manhattanville. A notice in the 1806 *Spectator* advertised that "Manhattan Ville is now forming in the Ninth Ward of this city, on the Bloomingdale road, in front of Haerlem Cove.... The corporation have opened a road, or avenue ... from the North [Hudson] to the East-river.... The proprietors of the soil are now laying out the streets, which are to be wide and open, to the Hudson river, where vessels of 300 tons may lie in safety." Manhattanville became a populous village, one of two uptown, the other one being Harlem. A settlement of Quakers lived there. Bloomingdale Road, a meandering thoroughfare that would later become upper Broadway, wandered through it.

The Shiefellens, a wealthy family who had an estate slightly north, in Hamilton Heights, donated the land for Manhattanville's St. Mary's

Church, which was attended by Alexander Hamilton's widow. (Hamilton himself did not have much time to enjoy the Grange before his fatal duel with Aaron Burr.)* St. Mary's is an Episcopal church, and was the first in the city to offer free pews. Eric has brought me there, knowing I will find it interesting. The rectory, wood-slatted, painted yellow and white, dates from 1851. The present St. Mary's Church, dating from 1900, was designed by Carrère & Hastings (famous for the great Fifth Avenue branch of the New York Public Library) and T. E. Blake, and is one of the prettiest churches in New York. Its scale manages just the right balance between awe-inspiring and intimate. Its ribbed roof and stained glass put one in mind of a country church.

The nineteenth-century village that was Manhattanville had a pigment factory, D. F. Tiemann's Dye Works, a worsted mill, and piers for port and ferry functions. The Tiemann family was important in local and downtown civic affairs; one of them even unseated Fernando Wood as mayor, briefly. From the start, Eric tells me, a third of the population was black, either free laborers or slaves. Manhattanville was eventually home to Germans, Irish, and Jews, and a smattering of other ethnic groups. The area remained fairly rural until the subway was built. There were big dairies near the water, including the white terra-cotta building on 125th Street, built in 1906, that once housed Sheffield Farms and now is a Columbia University chemical engineering laboratory. Meatpacking plants, slaughterhouses, and coal storage firms also sprang up near the water, and the railroads that ran through Riverside Park serviced those businesses.

When the newly elected President Lincoln was traveling on his way to New York and Washington, his train stopped at the Manhattanville depot and he greeted the (mostly silent) citizens. After his assassination, his funeral train again stopped at Manhattanville, the first station north of midtown New York, en route to Albany.

Manhattanville being a valley (and one of the few places in Manhattan

---

*To show what a small world upper Manhattan was then, Burr married the former wife of Stephen Jumel, Elizabeth, to whom Jumel had already gifted the Morris mansion which had served as George Washington's headquarters! She was apparently a stunning beauty, an adventuress and an ex-prostitute, who went on to divorce Burr and die the richest woman in America.

where topography still matters), it became necessary to construct two extraordinary structures traversing the dip, both running parallel to each other in a north-south direction, that have come to dominate the neighborhood and provide much of its iconographic identity: the elevated section of the IRT subway lines, and the Riverside Drive viaduct. Both have an Erector Set monumentality, and create eerie, suggestive spaces underneath, which are frequently photographed or used as exotic locations for movies. Both were originally designed for travelers to look out at the city and river below—the Riverside Drive viaduct even had wooden slats to peep through, and elegant viewing balconies, though these have been largely blocked off or filled in, perhaps to evade the cost of maintaining them.

The Riverside Drive viaduct opened in 1901 and was written up in *Scientific American* as a feat of engineering. Some aesthetes criticized its engineer, F. Stewart Williamson, for using steel pillars instead of a more dignified material, like marble or granite (he defended himself by explaining that stone would have required much fatter bases, which would have cut into the adjoining property lines.) Today these viaducts have the chic of industrial architecture in its unselfconscious engineering glory. Eric sees them as part of America's love affair with Paris: the lampposts suggest to him those along the Seine, while the visual corridor leading south to Grant's Tomb is reminiscent of the Alexander III Bridge approaching the Invalides.

These viaducts cry out to be more celebrated than they are, with seasonal fiestas in the streets underneath, illuminated by special night lighting. Now the undersides mostly serve as parking lots for schoolbuses. Underneath the Riverside Drive viaduct, at 125th Street and 12th Avenue, you can still see the last vestiges of a trolley turnaround: some tracks and a manhole that reads Third Avenue Company. It was this same Third Avenue Company whom Elizabeth Jennings, an early-day Rosa Parks, successfully sued for putting her off a trolley downtown because she was black.

In the distance, looking east toward 131st Street, may be glimpsed the top of the handsome, castellated Studebaker Building, once part of an uptown Automobile Showroom Row, now occupied by Mme. Alexander's Doll Factory, the largest employer in Harlem, making collectible handcrafted dolls. The Warren Nash Building, across the street, is rumored to have been part of the Manhattan Project that led to the A-bomb.

The area is surrounded by educational institutions, which, Eric feels, could do more for Manhattanville. There is of course Columbia (never forget that the university bought the Bloomingdale Insane Asylum to reestablish its campus uptown). Manhattan College started here; it has since located to Riverdale, but its buildings and grounds are incorporated into the southern campus of nearby City College. Teachers College was directly responsible for the public housing in the area, having conducted a house-to-house survey in the 1940s, which ascertained that the Manhattanville tenements were unsanitary and unhealthy. Robert Moses went on to raze them and build the General Grant Houses, Manhattanville Houses, and Morningside Gardens, each for a different economic group.

I am drawn to a Hopperesque row of low-lying brick and carved sandstone buildings just east of "Marginal Street" and the river, which continue to house remnants of the once-booming meatpacking, slaughterhouse, and fish-packaging industries of Manhattanville; you can tell from the powerful smell as you pass them on a hot summer day, wow. They have mostly been acquired by Fairway Supermarket, which runs a phenomenally successful gourmet produce business in the area, catering to Westchester or New Jersey customers who stop off at the Manhattanville waterfront and stock up on endives and Brie and smoked salmon, then drive away. Fairway grows under the viaduct like a giant toadstool, and has a constant need for storage and parking space (it has already usurped waterfront right-of-way for parking); and these ramshackle meatpacking blocks stand a good chance of being knocked down for parking lots. A shame, because they give such a clear idea of the historical streetscape that once prevailed here. Eric hopes the little meatpacking buildings remain, but he's afraid of making too big a deal about preserving them, because that might invite an "accidental" fire or other preemptive strike, before they can receive landmark protection.

Servicing the meat and fish packers is the West Market Diner, with its Budweiser sign and stainless-steel façade: it used to be a train car, or two dining cars stuck together. Inside, you find the classic greasy-spoon decor, stainless steel and Formica and black ridged signs with white letters announcing the bill of fare. The place has been in business at least since the 1940s. The owner is a retirement-age Greek who started working here in 1963, having just come to this country. When I ask him his name, he turns me aside playfully with "Call me Bill," in a thick Greek accent. "What do you want to know? Ask me anything."

"Has it changed a lot?" I ask.

"It used to be like Times Square around here." There our conversation ends. I can't be bothered to question him further about the past while decoding his accent, so I finish my grilled cheese and my Pepsi in silence. Besides, what is there to ask? He washed up on our American shores thirty-eight years ago, and this is as far as he got. Joseph Mitchell would have squeezed at least twenty pages' worth out of him.

We leave the diner and wander down again to the river's edge, from 125th Street to 132nd Street, where Henry Hudson put down anchor, and where the New Jersey ferries landed,* and where the dye works and dairies loaded their goods. It seems to offer an incredible missed opportunity for a lively public space on the porch step of Harlem. Not that no one's thought of it: the community board has long dreamed elaborate plans, focusing attention on this site. The Cotton Club, a white stucco structure looking very L.A., with neon lettering (it has more in common with Coppola's 1970 cinematic fantasy, *The Cotton Club*, than with the original Harlem nightspot of that name), accumulates dust at the base of 125th Street. It was

---

*To learn more about this service, which started in 1866, one must consult the research of two ferry buffs, Raymond J. Baxter and Arthur G. Adams, in their ragingly learned *Railroad Ferries of the Hudson* (Fordham University Press, 1999): "In modern times, the principal line to upper Manhattan was the Edgewater ferry to 125th Street, sometimes known as the Public Service Ferry. This line was started in 1894. In 1900, it was acquired by the then newly organized New Jersey & Hudson River Railway & Ferry Co., which operated an extensive network of electric railways in New Jersey. The line had good connections with the Broadway IRT subway near its Manhattan terminal. Also, Day Line and Night Line steamers stopped at an immediately adjacent pier, and the Iron Steamboat Co. had a pier at 129th Street and operated service downbay and to Coney Island until 1932, making this a popular excursion route. There was also a crosstown trolley car on 125th Street, connecting with the New York Central and New Haven Railroad Stations.

"In 1911, the ferry and electric railways were taken over by the Public Service Railways, a division of Public Service Electric & Gas Company, which also operated a ferry line from Bayonne, New Jersey, to Staten Island. In 1938, the last trolley rolled out of Edgewater Terminal, over the switchback route up the cliffs, and Public Service put on buses in substitution. Public Service soon lost interest in the ferry and began running most of its buses directly across the George Washington Bridge, or through the Lincoln and Holland tunnels, to Manhattan."

supposed to spark a whole club scene, an entertainment-district revival of Manhattanville. Now it's mainly used for group celebrations, such as Sunday after-church get-togethers. No headliners perform there.

"A lot of what would help revitalize the area is the awareness that it *is* an area," says Eric. In the 1920s, the vesting of Central Harlem with glamour and panache led to the eclipse of Manhattanville as a separate entity. In effect, Manhattanville became absorbed in the public's mind into Harlem. And so it remains.

12

SEWAGE TREATMENT PLANT AND SALSA PARTY

THE RIVERBANK STATE PARK SITS ON A 28.5-ACRE SITE ON TOP OF THE NORTH RIVER SEWAGE TREATMENT PLANT. IT RUNS BETWEEN WEST 137TH AND WEST 145TH Streets, high above Riverside Park, and is a glorious contribution to New York's public space, one of the very best amenities added to the city in a long time. Drivers heading north along the West Side Highway (as I persist in calling it) have no idea what a splendid recreational complex they are missing, because their angle of vision is too low to see it as they ride by. But those who take the trouble to enter the park by foot, from one of the staircases on the northern end of Manhattanville or from the pedestrian bridges that cross over the highway from Harlem, will discover an entrancing collection of ballfields, tracks, an indoor swimming pool, a covered ice-skating/rollerblade rink, an athletics building for basketball, volleyball, and gymnastics, a multipurpose cultural center, a restaurant, an amphitheater, even a carousel, all clearly and intelligently distributed.

On weekends, in anything approaching good weather, kids swarm the park to use the athletic facilities; arts-and-crafts tables are set out for small children; couples stroll the grounds or occupy benches by the esplanade overlooking the Hudson River. Operated by the state, not the city, the park has more money to spend on upkeep and staff, and looks tidy and well maintained. The buildings and pavilions, with their bold red and green accents, tan bricks, and cool fiberglass pyramid roofs, have a light, friendly, beachhouse look, perking up the open spaces of the playing fields without in any way dominating them. Richard Dattner & Partners designed Riverbank State Park in a manner characteristic of the firm's work: warm, unimposing, vaguely tropical. Dattner was the fourth architect hired on to the job, and he saw it through a tempestuous fifteen-year process (1978–93) of planning and construction.

That controversy came about because New York's city and state governments, concluding that they needed to do something to clean up the harbor's polluted waterways, decided to site a sewage treatment plant in West Harlem, after several other Manhattan communities had successfully resisted it. The Harlem community was understandably up in arms against what seemed a blatant instance of environmental injustice; already taxed with more than its share of noxious bus depots and waste-transfer stations, and suffering some of the highest asthma rates in the country, it looked askance at the threat of more harmful chemicals released into the air. The state offered a compromise, or rather a consolation prize: to build a spacious park on the roof of the pollution treatment plant. At first community leaders fought the offer, thinking that if they could stop the park they could stop the sewage treatment plant. When residents realized it was too late to derail the plant, they became resigned to accepting both—though they were prodded again to outrage once it opened. Especially in its first years, there was this stench; but the state sank millions of dollars into solving the problem, and now it seems to have gone away, though some say there are still offensive odors. (I have never smelled anything untoward in my visits, but then my perennially sinusitic nostrils are not the sharpest). No concentrations of harmful chemicals have been found in the air nearby. On balance, the North River Sewage Treatment Plant has done so much good for the city's aquatic environment that it would be hard to second-guess its existence. And the neighborhood now loves the park, which draws close to 4 million visitors a year, thanks in part to Richard Dattner's tactful yet jaunty design.

Dattner is committed to what he calls "civil architecture": public design that will have a "civilizing force" on communal behavior. His childhood refugee background, fleeing Nazi-occupied Poland with his parents in 1940, and bouncing around from Italy to Cuba to the United States, influenced his determination to produce welcoming, ordered, cosmopolitan public urban spaces responsive to the communities in which they are sited. Certainly no other architect has worked so often at, or in close proximity to, the New York waterfront in our era. Dattner's projects near the Manhattan waterfront, besides Riverbank State Park, include the award-winning public school, P.S. 234, on Chambers Street and Greenwich Avenue, near Battery Park City; the Asphalt Green AquaCenter, beside the FDR Drive in the East Nineties; the Marine Transfer Station on West 59th Street; Columbia University's football stadium in Inwood; the Children's Services Center, at First Avenue near 29th Street; and the Con Edison Service Building, a curved curtain wall of green glass at East 16th Street and the FDR Drive. He has also designed a number of treatment plants along the Brooklyn and Queens waterfronts.

Though he has worked for corporate clients outside New York, he is essentially a local architect who specializes in municipal projects, understands the city's maddeningly fractured community politics, feels comfortable with its layered, multicultural viewpoint (he speaks Spanish fluently), and has the patience to withstand its tormentingly slow public review process. "Any architect willing to endure the often brutal process of working for a government agency deserves a Purple Heart," the *Times*'s critic Herbert Muschamp has written. "An architect like Richard Dattner, who has been through the process repeatedly and nonetheless sustained a level of quality as high as that shown by his designs for Riverbank State Park, sewage treatment plans and public school buildings, should be given a ticker tape parade up Broadway."

Notwithstanding this accolade, Dattner has received little recognition from the architectural press, given how successfully he has molded parts of New York's public environment. He is not a superstar architect who gets written about constantly; his style is pleasing and charming, but he does not do "signature" buildings (and the client be damned). Rather, he adjusts pragmatically to each site's specific rules and budget restrictions. Certain stylistic motifs run through his work—an uncluttered clarity, with colored panels, curved canopies, and patterned brick bands by way of ornament— but the pizzazz is discreetly and tastefully meted out. In truth, while I really admire his work, I have to admit he is a not a master. Nothing he does bowls you over; but it is *so* superlatively adequate and user-friendly that it makes you wonder why there is not more of an enthusiasm for the quintessentially gifted minor architect, as there is for the minor writer or minor independent filmmaker.

Dattner's office is on West 57th Street, down the block from Carnegie Hall, in an elegant, Gilded Age, bay-windowed building with double windows for artists' studios, which was once home to the likes of William Dean Howells and Childe Hassam. On first meeting him, one is struck by his gentle, non-hornblowing manner, rare among architects, who tend to be even more egomaniacal than writers. A lean, good-looking man in his mid-sixties with a shock of white hair, a prominent beaked nose, and a warm, skeptical smile, who speaks with the slightest trace of a European accent, he seems, like his buildings, modest, friendly, approachable, cultivated. He wears glasses on a chain, which, when he puts them on, give him a nannyish look. After a while you realize that he is not without satiric judgments or competitive ego. He might wish he was more celebrated for what he does best; but if it is not to be, so okay, he will continue executing commissions, assisted by his partners and a staff of forty.

Asked whether he works differently near the waterfront than inland, he says that each time he has faced different challenges. In addition to the community's dubiousness about Riverbank State Park, he needed to build very lightly, to "put the architecture on a diet," as he says, because of the limited load-bearing capacity of the plant's roof. So he came up with "a quasi-Japanese look, the light panels functioning like shoji screens." The platform was also six hundred feet out from the mainland; it was like being on the deck of an aircraft carrier,* which created its own set of aesthetic problems.

With Asphalt Green, at East 91st Street and the FDR Drive, the challenge was to create a building that had sufficient presence to be seen from across the river, while still deferring to the older icon next to it, the Asphalt Plant (a 1940s loop of exposed concrete over a parabolic, arched steel frame that has become a kind of beloved found object to design modernists). Dattner had to wedge a community athletic facility next to it, and this structure had to house a large pool on a fairly small site. The resulting Aquacenter is a sensuous building, with a wavy façade of alternating tan brick and green windows that recalls swimming in ocean waves; it looks smashing, especially lit up at night.

With P.S. 234, he wanted to convey the point that the water's edge used to be at Greenwich Street, before landfill extended the island. So he put in a form at the corner of the schoolyard that is both lighthouse and bell tower. Each day a different schoolchild rings the bell. The artist Donna Dennis's fence, with its lighters and tugboats, makes manifest the site's maritime history, and her porcelain medallions evoke the old Washington Market that used to be there.

How do you get a successful social mix, I ask, at a place like Riverbank or Asphalt Green, so that these public spaces are not seen as just for one class or ethnic group? He replies, "You try to nurture as many activities as you can: basketball for the Dominican teenagers, swimming classes for the old Jewish ladies, and so on. And you provide enough security so that it

---

*The North River Sewage Treatment Plant marked the last time that a major structure could be built above on the water on piles, without assessing its impact as a sort of landfill. Because the plant was under development in the late 1960s, it was not subject to the environmental laws passed in the 1970s which prevented waterfront construction from impacting negatively on marine habitat (i.e., the controversy regarding shadows cast on striped bass, which undermined Westway). It seems ironic that such an environmentally positive project as the Sewage Treatment Plant should have been the last to cause a shrinkage of striped bass habitat; but in retrospect it was a logical tradeoff.

feels safe." Still, he worries that the Internet and cell phones will further erode the civility of public space. People are losing their sense of place-ness, he feels, and as they become attached to these virtual spaces they will pass through the real ones without taking notice. (Although in the main an optimist, he does have this high-minded, cultured-European, grouchy side.)

Dattner and his wife live in Washington Heights, on Cabrini Boulevard, where they enjoy great views of the Hudson, he says. "I live on the river and always will. On summer nights my wife and I go up on the roof and watch the sunsets. Fabulous."

His preoccupation with the Manhattan waterfront goes back a long way. In 1967 he headed up a team of seventy architects that came up with a Hudson River plan. He wonders whether there is still a copy of it some-where. "I've always been fascinated with the conjunction of buildings, river, and park. I like folding buildings into a park." Now he has returned to the West Side waterfront, having been given the commission to design a segment of the Hudson River Park, from 26th Street to 59th Street. Dattner's first design proposal for his section of the park called for steps leading down to the water, such as exist in Paris; it was rejected on the grounds that seals might waddle up the steps and be fed the wrong kind of food! He shrugs; he is used to compromise. He invites me to attend an upcoming public meeting of the local West Side Community Planning Board, which will be discussing his latest Hudson River Park design.

At the last moment, I decide to go. It is midsummer, still broiling in the early evening. As usual, the community planning board meets in a hos-pital conference room, which they can use for free. (It does give these meetings a clinical, medicinal air.) Before the meeting even starts, I hear the insiders at the back of the room plotting their strategies and attacks. "How can you put a little hill on that pier? It will cut off sightlines to the water." "You bring that up. I'll bring up the point about the highway ramp—."

The meeting starts at six-thirty, and Dattner makes a low-key presen-tation. The moment he has ended, audience members line up at the micro-phone and begin zestfully nitpicking it apart. One half of me is thinking, *What a display of democracy in action! It's wonderful how involved and how committed these neighborhood people are to improving the design of their sur-*

roundings. The other half thinks, *A bunch of petty wannabe architects—why don't they get a life?* I'm wondering how a nice fellow like Dattner can take this public abuse year after year; he must have a masochistic side. To my surprise, he walks out of the meeting after an hour, leaving his associate to field the audience's gripes. Either he's less patient and open than I'd thought, or he had a prior dinner engagement. Maybe he just wanted to take in one last summer sunset with his wife, from their roof in Washington Heights.

ON MOST HOT WEEKEND NIGHTS during the summer, and even into the fall, there is a section of Riverside Park that gets turned into a giant salsa party. I've passed it by automobile many times, intrigued by that blur of carnival clangor along the Hudson River, wondering what it would feel like to stand in the middle of it. One August night I plucked up my courage enough to try.

You take the Number 1 train to 145th Street and Broadway, head in the direction of the water, and follow the pedestrian bridge over the West Side Highway into Riverbank State Park. If you pause on that overpass, looking down, you'll see giddy convoys hurtling into or out of the city. I happened to arrive around 7:30 P.M., when a clouded-over, indigo sky was smeared with a pink arc over New Jersey, and the nearby George Washington Bridge was already styling a dowager choker of lights. Riverbank Park beckoned, but this time I was determined to get to the salsa party below. I could hear the invitation of blaring trumpets, and see the cars parked thickly below highway girders, and the revelers milling around.

A long, twisting metal staircase extends from Riverbank Park's upper platform to the ground below; and because this part of the Riverside Park is cut off by highway, it is the only practical way you can get to the water by foot. In daytime, when the park below is usually deserted, I don't mind admitting I feel a bit nervous going down that staircase alone. But tonight families wander up and down, and the scene is completely benign. At the bottom, a man and two boys wait patiently with bikes for an elevator to take them up; I do not stay long enough to find out if the elevator is out of service or arrives eventually.

On the lawn near the base of the stairs, there's a dark-skinned Latino father pitching to his preteen daughter, in a family baseball game of three against three, and cheering her as she smacks one and rounds the bases, her long braid flapping, as if she were Sammy Sosa. Close by, a fenced-in playground holds kids racing around playing tag, letting off steam. Some teenage boys kick a soccer ball. Some lucky families have commandeered benches and are setting out mountains of food and coolers. What strikes me immediately is that, although it's nightfall, this Latin American community has no compunction about bringing little kids to the park at this hour, letting the bigger ones run free around the swings and slides, while dandling the infants up and down to the salsa rhythm. Because it is a genuine community, children and grandparents belong to the bacchanal. On the one hand, it's a family outing, a chance to picnic, play catch, loll about on a Sunday night, before the soul-sapping work week begins. On the one hand, it's a massive, sexually heated *paseo* for people to scrutinize, flirt, dance, pick each other up.

I am headed down a footpath of trees toward the booming sound, the center of life. To my left is the river, and I wonder what its presence means to those gathered here. Is this the re-creation of waterside picnics in Santo Domingo or smaller villages? Or is it only the large public space that matters, the park itself, and the river but an incidental throw-in of mise-en-scène? Some teenage girls sit by the rocks, talking quietly. A motorboat approaches. For the most part, however, people stand with their backs to the river, seemingly ignoring it. No doubt they've subliminally registered its presence, and are glad it's there, but they're not "communing" with the river god. They're here for the salsa party, that huge roofless nightclub under the stars.

And now I've come to the magical center: I enter it through a modest break between cars and grass. What it is, this magnetically pulsing zone, is essentially a parking lot. In addition to the cars parked everywhere, a stream of vehicles waits to filter in from the north, while a small group of early leavetakers tries to edge its way out. Along the rim of this parking lot, portable stoves and food tables have been stationed to cook and vend roast chicken, pigs' feet, *ropa vieja,* empanadas, potatoes, cabbage, pork chops, salted cod, rice and beans, and just about everything greasy or fattening that sends "crave" signals to the brain. The overall, enticing smell of fried onions holds within its envelope many individual, piquant aromas. The servers stack the paper plates high with helpings; it's assumed you will want a taste of everything. People eat standing up, or crammed behind steering wheels. Appetite, not comfort, calls the shots.

NO ALCOHOLIC BEVERAGES PERMITTED IN THIS AREA, a sign by the staircase had warned. Too bad, I'd thought, it must be hard to strike a down-home party spirit without liquor. Not to worry; as soon as you enter the zone you see vans with cases of beer stacked inside, adding an outlaw quality to the festivities. I look around quickly, wondering, where are the cops? In the distance is the familiar NYPD blue and white car, and thereafter, all through the night, I notice patrol pairs on foot, and police cars cruising around. But the sense you get is that they're being tactful, nonintrusive—more there to keep the peace, should a fight break out, than to enforce the liquor laws.

I can't get over the paradox that a makeshift parking lot—especially if you find parking lots as ugly as I do—should have the power to attract and hold these many enchanted people. But as I begin to make my way around the rectangle, I realize that it's not just a parking lot, it's also become a *plaza mayor*, in the classical Latin American sense, a square around which the communal energies gather, and from any point of which you can watch the townspeople's comings and goings. The Upper Manhattan Hispanic community has taken this flat, nondescript area of Riverside Park, originally intended for pastoral retreat, which happens to be near the exit ramp of the West Side Highway, and "liberated" it, with their genius for city-making, bringing the congested vitality of the street to the Olmstedian woods.

Second, it's not the physical surroundings that matter here, but the aural surround. Every thirty feet a different salsa tune is blaring; yet the effect is not cacophonous, but rather like variant melodic streams all feeding the same sonic lake. Maybe because so many salsa tunes have that same steady mambo rhythm, neither slow ballad nor up-tempo but ongoing, insistent, hip-grinding, they mesh. What had sounded from a distance like a single powerful sound system is revealed close up to be decentralized: some cars sport ghetto blasters, some have raised hoods filled with speaker drums—the entire vehicle turned into an amplifier, only secondarily a means of transport.

I watched a very handsome young couple doing a merengue, with that insinuating, gliding mastery of good Latin dancers everywhere. At first they seemed as close as you could get to having sex in public, so synchronized were their pelvic movements. But at one point the man tried to brush his hand against the woman's breasts, and was reproached with a prim smile, establishing the boundaries of affectionate display. They were in their own world, focused intently, as though under a pink, spotlighted cone of glamour, rather than in a shabby parking lot. Were they passionately in love, I wondered, or would-be ballroom dancers competing for an imaginary gold medal?

Around the zone, stout, middle-aged couples danced, enjoying themselves, relaxed, with less at stake. What caught my eye again and again, however, were the *princesas* in their pride of beauty, slender yet full-figured, with long black hair, who moved confidently though the salsa party with a young woman's pleasure in her supreme moment of arrival. You had to respect the self-assurance of the mating spectacle, each gender carrying out its role to the fullest.

Making my way out of the parking zone, toward the river, I passed two Hispanic men who looked like graduate students, engrossed in learned conversation, and again it was borne in on me that this was a community event, not just something for the sexy and beautiful who provoked my envious fantasies.

The 151st Street handball courts acted as a sort of northern barrier to the salsa party, somewhat as Richard Serra's *Tilted Arc* had functioned puritanically downtown. I wanted to make my way out of the park, without having to backtrack to the Riverbank Park staircase. But it wasn't easy to find an exit from Riverside Park across the highway. I realized one of the reasons that cars play such a dominant part in the salsa party is the lack of pedestrian access to this part of the park. Which came first, limited pedestrian access or working-class Latino car culture?

At 155th Street, I locate a pedestrian overpass. You still have to cross two highway lanes to get to it, but that only requires patience, not foolhardy courage. I walk up the stairs and find myself in a creepy tunnel, dark, deserted, filling me with trepidation at this late hour. Fortunately, no one with evil intent lurks in the shadows: beyond the tunnel, just ahead, are a few teenage couples making out in the cool night air. To my left looms the stately, white-columned American Academy of Arts and Sciences, whose annual function I once or twice attended, and the Museum of Hispanic Culture, with its distinguished names carved into the pediment, next to which is Boricua College. Strange to come upon this sober campus of cultural institutions after a night of populist carousal! I am on Broadway again, and wave to an oncoming taxi to take me home.

IF YOU WERE TO STAY in the park and keep walking northward, through a dirt path surrounded by high weeds, you would come to one of the loveliest, most harmonious, and yet least-known spots on the Manhattan waterfront. I am speaking of the river's edge along Fort Washington Park. The Hudson River looks magnificent here. There is a particular, covelike indentation in the Hudson, with an oak tree in the foreground, the sun beating off the water, and the proud Little Red Lighthouse in the distance, dwarfed by the George Washington Bridge, which is one of the most stirring sights I know. Here the natural undulations of the shoreline swell and curve with great beauty; a green meadow slants down to algaed rocks, which invite you to clamber and bend down to touch the water; there are occasional picnic benches, tennis courts, a paved gravel road. In recent years this riverside stretch of Fort Washington Park has received pampering attention. To the east, on the other side of the train tracks and highway, the slopes of Fort Washington Park remain debris-laden and badly tended, as are most of the parks beside poor, minority neighborhoods; but this particular spot leads a charmed life.

One of the reasons it remains so secret is that it is not easy to get to. Descending from the streets above, a city-within-a-city of pain and its therapeutic remedies, where Columbia-Presbyterian Hospital holds sway, I tried my usual bullheaded method of proceeding down the vine-scrabbled hill until the Henry Hudson Highway cut me off, then made a mad dash for it. Actually, the highway bifurcates within the park, so that you have to risk your life twice to get to the water's edge. I got halfway across the first highway when a police car screeched beside me and a highway patrolman with the sternest expression said to me, Did I know I had just broken a law? I was aghast with astonishment; Claude Rains in *Casablanca* could not have been more "shocked." He let me off, after telling me about the legal way to get across: a pedestrian bridge somewhere above and to the left. There are, in fact, two—and only two—footbridges that cross the highways and bring you down to the riverside, between all of Fort Washington Park and Fort Tryon Park, the equivalent of fifty city blocks (two or three miles): one, near the mouth of 168th Street and Riverside Drive, difficult to find amid the entangled highway ramps, and the other, a few blocks north of the George Washington Bridge, around 182nd Street and Riverside Drive. My own preference is to take the stairs at the northern end of the waste treatment plant down to the park, and hew to the shoreline.

In any case, if you are lucky or persistent enough to find yourself on that enchanted stretch of riverfront park, walking north, you will come to the Little Red Lighthouse, which dates from 1880. In their 1942 children's classic, *The Little Red Lighthouse and the Great Gray Bridge*, Hidegarde H. Swift and Lynd Ward told us: "Once upon a time a little lighthouse was built on a sharp point of the shore by the Hudson River. It was round and fat and red. It was fat and red and jolly. And it was VERY, VERY PROUD." With its beacon of light and, on foggy nights, its bell, it warned the boats on the river against crashing into the shore, until the strange new bridge was built, which "made the little red lighthouse feel **very very small**." Eventually they sort it out, each has its role to play, the giant and the midget. In truth, once the George Washington Bridge was opened in 1932, the Coast Guard closed the lighthouse. It was put up for auction, but schoolchildren wrote letters of protest, and it was turned over to the Parks Department. Thenceforth it fell on hard times, its concrete base cracked, its doors welded shut, until finally it was restored. Today it wears a gleaming coat of red, and its interior (re-equipped with a genuine Fresnel lens, operating on a timer) has been made available for school field trips.

The bridge itself dominates not only the lighthouse but the whole northern Upper West Side of Manhattan. It was built by the great engineer O. H. Ammann with the assistance of architect Cass Gilbert, and has an austere profile—nothing fussy about it. Le Corbusier himself was moved to write, after he visited these shores, in *When the Cathedrals Were White* (1947):

The George Washington Bridge over the Hudson is the most beautiful bridge in the world. Made of cables and steel beams, it gleams in the sky like a reversed arch. It is blessed. It is the only seat of grace in this disordered city. It is painted an aluminum color and, between water and sky, you see nothing but the bent cord supported by two steel towers. When your car moves up the ramp the two towers rise so high that it brings you happiness; their structure is so pure, so resolute, so regular that here, finally, steel architecture seems to laugh. The car reaches an unexpectedly wide apron; the second tower is very far away; innumerable vertical cables, gleaming against the sky, are suspended from the magisterial curve which swings down and then up. The rose-colored towers of New York appear, a vision whose harshness is mitigated by distance.

Magnificent as this appreciation sounds, it is the enthusiasm of a traveler, and a doctrinaire one at that. I can't imagine locals on either end of the span, in Fort Lee, New Jersey, or Washington Heights, Manhattan, gushing this way, nor have I ever sensed its steel architecture laugh. Not even a giggle. A lower traffic level was added in 1962, which mars the perfect simplicity of the child's sailboat design; I always try to edit it out visually to imagine the shivery purity that so captivated Le Corbusier.

A year after *When the Cathedrals Were White* was published, a very different sort of tribute to Ammann's span appeared. It was right here, near the base of the George Washington Bridge and the Little Red Lighthouse, that John Garfield found Thomas Gomez's gang-murdered body, tossed on the rocks, at the end of Abraham Polonsky's 1948 noir masterpiece, *Force of Evil.* This film, after claustrophobically shuttling between bookie joints and nightclubs, "opens up," as they say, catches a gulp of air in the larger, more unimpeded vistas of urban riverside, as Garfield's character, holding the corpse of his older brother in the gray dawn, vows to give up his dirty, corrupted life.

If you wish to proceed north past the George Washington Bridge, you can take a path that leads you steeply uphill and away from the water, until it joins with the Cloisters at the summit-top of Fort Tryon Park. Should you want to cleave to the water, however, you will have to scramble along some tide-wetted, pointed rocks for about a mile. I did this one time, edging past two officers of the law placed there after 9/11 to guard the bridge against sabotage, who were sleeping in their car (one of the less heralded uses of the waterfront is that is supplies a hideout for napping policemen), and ventured forth along the rocky coast—the only natural stretch left on Manhattan's shoreline, by the way, being neither riprap nor bulkhead—all the way to the Dyckman Street marina in Inwood. It was arduous going, as I progressed boulder by boulder, partly upright, partly on my hands and knees and ass; but it had become a point of pride to travel as far as possible alongside the river.

Whenever I chanced to look up, pausing from the decision as to where I could least perilously place my next shoe, I saw an inspiring, postcard view of the Hudson, with the sun blinking its flanks. I could have been on some rocky coast of Nova Scotia, for all its remoteness to human life; and yet this was still Manhattan! The only sign of civilization I came across was a homeless person's shack wedged into the rock face, tarpapered and trimly square; the occupant was absent and, peering inside, I saw a sleeping pallet below a picture of Jesus. Otherwise this stretch of rocky shore must be the least-trafficked segment in the New York parks system. For more habitable sights, it is advisable to take the hilly path at the base of the bridge, leave the park entirely, and venture into the neighborhood on the cliffs above, Washington Heights.

13

WASHINGTON HEIGHTS AND INWOOD

W ASHINGTON HEIGHTS IS ONE OF THE MOST DRA-
MATICALLY HILLY SECTIONS OF MANHATTAN. HERE,
FOR ONCE, THE GRID HAS BEEN OBLIGED TO adjust to
topography. There are steep stairs linking one street to another, as in
European cities; and the catacomblike subway stations with cavernous,
arched ceilings and elaborate tilework are built into the rock face at such
a depth as to require elevators. Certain east-west thoroughfares, such as
West 181st Street, accommodate the land by gently curving to their termi-
nation at the peak of the cliffs. West 181st Street, once the heart of a Jewish
neighborhood, retains a few kosher food stores and restaurants; and the
street still acts as an unofficial barrier, dividing the southern end of
Washington Heights, which is largely hospitals and Hispanic tenements,

from the more Irish and Jewish northern end, with its middle-class coop-
erative enclaves and nursing homes.

If you walk downhill toward the Hudson River on West 181st Street,
you come to Cabrini Boulevard (formerly Northern Avenue), one of New
York's tucked-away treasures. Here are some remarkable apartment house
enclaves, built during the 1920s and 1930s, when city developers still
thought it economically viable to erect castles for the middle class. On the
eastern side of the street is the older Hudson View Gardens, a Tudor
extravaganza in brown brick, with simulated half-timbering of dark brown
wooden diagonals crisscrossing the façade. The apartment houses were
built by George F. Pelham in 1924–25, and stand at attention along the
street wall, correctly if somewhat stodgily, like a regiment of Tudor cot-
tages on growth hormones. Across the way from them, on the western side
of Cabrini Boulevard, is Castle Village, built by Pelham's son, George F.
Pelham II, in 1938–39. This is a more frankly up-to-date and, to my mind,
fascinating high-rise apartment complex, stretching all the way from West
181st to West 186th Street. It has been maintained in tiptop shape: the
white window frames all look newly painted, the apple-red brick façades
spanking clean. The "architecture" of Castle Village, if one can call it that,
attempts nothing ambitious; it is meant to convey cozy comfort, familiarity. The one original touch is that all five buildings are in the shape of a
cross, which maximizes river views (eight out of nine apartments get them
on each floor).

It was this X shape that caught the eye of Lewis Mumford, and
prompted him to write a "Sky Line" column about Castle Village in *The
New Yorker*. Mumford, to his credit, was not merely focused on cutting-
edge architecture but was curious about the actual built environment going
up around him. After praising the complex's attention to "Light, air, space,
gardens—the substance and ornament of all good architecture," and the
"simple vernacular of our period: wide, steel casement windows; a plain,
unadorned façade," Mumford nitpicked the brick's color, the "barricade"-
like repetition of the five identical buildings and the X plan's space-
wastage compared to "a zigzag or sawtooth layout." He concluded evenly:
"The builder of Castle Village is to be congratulated for going as far as he
has gone, but he is to be reproached for not going further, since he had
perhaps the finest site remaining in New York for residential purposes."

It remains a fine site, with the cruciform buildings set discreetly back from the generous grounds. What captivates me most about Castle Village is the broad lawn sweeping down to the ledge that overlooks Fort Washington Park, the George Washington Bridge, and the Hudson River. In the late afternoon, this secluded garden is a pleasance out of an Italian countryside, with quaint stone fence, benches, sitting nooks, and magnificent trees, which give form and shade to the whole. Whether the public has the right to enjoy this view—a sign on the lawn says FOR RES-IDENTS ONLY I always partake, and no one ever stops me. The former, Gothicized estate of Dr. Charles Paterno that once rested on the site may be gone, but you can still imagine, from the grounds' placement and from one remaining fragment, a pergola on the northern end of the garden, its picturesque configuration atop this hill overlooking the Palisades of New Jersey.

If you continue north along Cabrini Boulevard, past Mother Cabrini High School and Cabrini Chapel, the buildings suddenly cease along the western side of the street and give way to a mysterious wooden rail-ing, which overlooks a steeply treacherous, pathless, and largely impass-able forest on the border between Fort Washington Park and Fort Tryon Park. When I lived in Inwood, in the mid-1960s, I used to be fascinated by this stretch of rural wildness. With no trouble at all, merely editing out distant traffic noise, I could imagine it the setting for some feral hermit's existence. At twenty, prematurely embarked on my first mar-riage, I was soothed by the wilderness glimpsed from Cabrini Terrace, so at odds did it seem with the surrounding *gemütlich* apartment build-ings and bungalows of Washington Heights and Inwood, where elderly German Jews lived out their span and doctors' families occupied the spacious ground floor. These amiably middle-class homes soothed me as well, but in a different way: we were lucky to have found refuge among them. Upper Manhattan, though thoroughly respectable, wasn't fashionable enough to be pricy; and financially needy newlyweds such as we were could still find decent apartments at bargain rents. I remem-ber living there with Carol during my last year at college, 1964, and sev-eral years after, and that feeling of still technically being on Manhattan, but far removed from the careerist energy and pulse and glamour, "the rat race," as we enviously called it; how East Village poet-friends had to be coaxed to visit us, and took several books with them on the subway uptown, as if for a three days' journey; how I'd show them around, proud of the area's obscurity, its backwater charm: those private bungalows on Payson Avenue, with bricks the color of dried blood and casement windows with black hinges overlooking hilly Inwood Park, which Carol and I, mocking their propriety, would nonetheless fantasize retiring to in old age.

The dream of that first marriage was to bypass youth and ascend straight to a responsibly shared life in double work-harness. The goal seemed reasonable at the time, since we got along so companionably, but it proved impossible because we were far too young and exaggerated our maturity—a fact that only surfaced when life began to test us.

I was twenty-two when the screws tightened. I mention my age partly to exonerate myself in advance for bad behavior. It was not that I behaved so despicably, which could at least allow me the retrospective allure of villainy, as that I was so passive and overwhelmed and inadequate to the challenge. My wife was also young at the time, but she behaved with far more womanly self-respect; age is not the whole story. Nevertheless, we were babies: two baby literati, presuming ourselves writers with no assurance from the world that we ought to have. For the moment, we supported ourselves by freelance editing, tape transcribing, ghostwriting—"taking in wash," we called it. We barely survived, using nearby Columbia-Presbyterian Hospital's emergency room as our family physician; and when starvation threatened, Carol went out and got a full-time job. I'm especially embarrassed to recall that part—but there seemed to be an implicit understanding between us, typical of the period, that I was the literary genius of the house and needed to hone my writing, whereas she could develop hers any old time.

One day Carol came home and told me she was pregnant. We had been wondering what had happened to her period, but I took the firm position that there was no point in worrying about what might not be the case. Now it was the case. What to do? We began by taking long walks, up and down the hills of Manhattan's northern tip, analyzing the pros and cons. I cannot think of those discussions without associating them with the terrain, the Cloisters and Fort Tryon Park where we picnicked if the weather was good, the frozen-in-time residential sections of Inwood, and our feverish agonizing, dropping our voices in the presence of passersby when our vocabulary became too explicit ("curettage," "trimester"). One night on Broadway, near the Dyckman House, we were stopped in our tracks by a couple clouting each other outside an Irish saloon, and we were unsure how to take this: as a recommendation to start a family or not, since everything that crossed our path seemed an omen.

The most painful part of these increasingly nippy walks (it was autumn, edging over into winter) was that neither one of us seemed able to express a strong opinion about what he or she wanted. We had that young lovers' symbiotic habit of sympathizing with the other's viewpoint; and, like detectives hired to shadow one another, we watched carefully for signs of deep, unequivocal feeling, the better to support it. Not sure what my true feelings were, I told myself: If Carol really wants this baby, I will back her up, we'll somehow make ends meet. I had always imagined having children someday. The fact that the opportunity had come sooner rather than later—well, I could adjust to the challenge of fatherhood, I guessed. I had a great desire to be an adult. I also wanted to act nobly in a crisis, to shoulder my end of responsibility, or at least to appear in public to do so. Why should Carol have to make a sacrifice and give up a baby she wanted? If, however, she feels not yet emotionally ready for a baby, or thinks it will get in the way of her career, I'll support her decision to end the pregnancy. So far, she said she wasn't sure she *did* want it. But perhaps she was only saying that because she was uncertain whether she could depend on me, my being such an egotist. If I were to start saying I was *sure* I wanted this baby—which felt in any case like the mature, adult thing to say—she would undoubtedly—or most probably—come around to a certainty of wanting it. My pretend-decisiveness would conquer her hesitation, and once the baby was born, she would, I felt confident, become a wonderfully devoted mother, and this devotion would in the end dissolve what remained of my own ambivalence. In fact, she might never even notice my ambivalence if I played the pro-baby role with enough conviction.

But of course, nothing goes unnoticed in marriage. And the fact that it was thought of as a role, not intrinsic to my character, meant that it could be superseded by another role ("If you really want this abortion, I will support you all the way"), which is indeed what happened, until the two roles began alternating in such quick succession, as we went over and over the same ground, that in the end, understandably, she stopped listening to me. She turned inward. I began to sense a quiet will gathering inside her and hunkering down; we were no longer belaboring the topic as much. In truth, I began to miss that operatic agonizing; a part of me could have gone on and on with it. At about that time, my wife began seeing a woman psychotherapist, and I suspected that they were working it out between themselves. Whether or not this suspicion was correct, the day came when Carol calmly informed me that she had made up her mind to have an abortion. It was fixed, final, no more discussion.

As abortions in 1966 were illegal, we would have to become outlaws. We asked around, and heard about a saintly woman physician whom I'll call Dr. Elizabeth, in Philadelphia. Carol made an appointment to see her, and we took the train to Philadelphia. At first it seemed like a tourist adventure: we talked about seeing the Philadelphia Museum, and exploring a city neither of us knew. On the day in question we were too nervous to look at paintings, but we killed an hour or two walking around the historic district, admiring the old iron lampposts and cobblestone streets and Federal-style rowhouses in which ordinary people still lived; and, with that hunger for normal life which must have sprung from the desperate little act we were contemplating, I predicted aloud that we would someday come to live here, in one of these same charming historic townhouses, as a reward for our current hardships.

The doctor's waiting room was crowded. We sat there patiently, and finally it was Carol's turn. I glimpsed Dr. Elizabeth for a few seconds, beckoning my wife inside; she was an elegantly poised brunette in a navy blue angora sweater, nicely put together (I placed her in my harem of erotic fantasies instantly, jerk that I am). Thirty minutes later Carol reemerged, looking thoughtful and sad. For some reason I can no longer remember, Dr. Elizabeth had refused to perform the abortion. Perhaps she felt the police were watching her too closely, or she had decided to perform abortions only for in-state women, or else truly indigent cases. Whatever her reasons, they could not have been mercenary, because afterwards we did not think critically of her, only of ourselves: you would think we had failed a stiff entrance exam. We had a hollow feeling, as though our insides were already scraped out, while we waited at Union Station to catch the return train. Someone at the food counter had on a soul station, Diana Ross singing "My World Is Empty Without You, Babe," and this, too, seemed an omen.

Back in New York, Carol found another abortionist, on the Lower East Side, and went alone to the appointment. The first curettage did not take; she was obliged to return to the same bungler (we could not afford two fees) and have it done all over again. I shudder to think how close we came to tragedy. No, I don't want to think about it. Half a lifetime later, she's alive, I'm alive. Both married to different people.

I cannot say that the abortion alone inflicted a mortal blow to our marriage (there would be others), but it did uncover veins of mutual mistrust we had not known existed. It left me feeling ashamed of myself, aware of my untrustworthiness and eager to cover it up better next time. And I think it left Carol not only wounded and weary, but resentful—either because I'd been unable to protect her from the sorrow she had gone through, more or less alone, or because my failure to lobby harder for baby and family had alerted her to a secret (even secret to myself at the time) inconstancy on my part toward the marriage, a footloose streak that would one day lead me to go off and fulfill some bachelor destiny.

"Destiny" is what you know about your life in hindsight. Or maybe it's the stubbornness that takes over once your character, colliding with the world's barriers, has coalesced into a set of rigidities. "There is a point beyond which there is no going back. That is the point that we must reach," said Kierkegaard. He was speaking of faith, but I would apply the same idea to love, monogamy, or the decision to have a child. Precisely what I was missing as a young man—now I have it almost too much—was a conviction of limits and the irrevocable: many paths seemed equally provisional, equally capricious (like the choice of trails from the Cloisters down to the street below), and so I felt a fraud asserting any one in particular.

AT FORT TRYON PARK, which can be entered around 190th Street, I pass the familiar herbal garden and the medieval tower of the Cloisters, all the generous bequest of the Rockefeller family to the city of New York. Not only did the Rockefeller family bequeath the land and the buildings, they bought up the Palisades across the Hudson, on the New Jersey side, so that visitors to the Cloisters would have a wooded vista to contemplate, protected from future development. Say what you may about the Rockefellers' cupidity, none of today's billionaires would even think to give this or any other city so magnificent an enhancement.

Descending from the Cloisters, I see Inwood stretched out below. Its comfortably lower-middle-class mix of three-story retail along Dyckman Street and Broadway, and six-story walkup apartment houses along the cross-avenues, has not changed much since the sixties, at least from this angle; its chic-resistant personality rejects gentrification.

I remember how Carol and I used to walk down to the river along Dyckman Street, at dusk on a summer's night, past a carpet-cleaning factory, and how scandalously intimate with the Hudson we were able to get, close enough to trail our hands in the swift-moving water. Yes, this is where we always entered, through the fence at the edge of Inwood Park, right next to the marina (which has undergone improvements since I lived here). You can walk along a narrow dirt path above the black rocks leading to the water—or over the rocks themselves—but I prefer the path. To the west is the river, broad and consolatory, and the Palisades cliffs, fortunately untouched, or just barely, by condo construction at this northern point, so that it must be almost the same vista the Lenapes and Wiechquaesgecks saw. To the east, as you walk along the dirt path, are the fenced-in ballfields of Inwood Park. I am walking along at five o'clock, the setting winter sun licking the trees golden, and I am absolutely elated. Why so happy, I begin to wonder, when I have been walking along the waterfront all day? Is it that this stretch feels particularly wild, as though I were actually in the country (leaving aside the ballfields)? Is it the magical hour of day? I am the only walker here, which frightens and exhilarates me a bit, though just as I think that thought, a jogger whizzes by me, an elderly, bespectacled man with stringy calves. He is older than I by a decade, and yet in better shape. Well, never mind; walking is good exercise, too. I am happy, happy, happy. Farther downtown, so many obstructions, fences, and roads kept me from the river. Only here, on the northern tip of the island, with highways nowhere in sight, do I feel in direct contact with the river, I smell it, I lustily breathe it in.

After walking about two miles along the Inwood Park shoreline in this contented state, ahead of me I suddenly see a fence blocking my way. The dirt path is drawing to an end. I call out to the elderly jogger, who is circling back in my direction, "How do you get out of here?" He yells back, "You don't!" then, looking annoyed that he will have to break stride and play Good Samaritan, comes to a halt. "You either have to go all the way back to Dyckman Street, or halfway back to that footbridge"—he points to a green structure with steep stairs—" or I guess you could try squeezing under the fence and proceeding that way." I am for going forward, no turning back! All day I have been moving north, north, north, and am not going to be deterred at this point from savoring the uppermost curve of the island.

I thank him and approach the chain-link fence, which is twisted out of shape in one corner of the base, suggesting others have ducked under here before. I crawl on all fours through the tangled vines, then stand up, banging my head against the fencepost. Just then a train hurtles by, so close as to give me a fright. Ohmigod, I must be on the Metro North train tracks. Posted signs say, PRIVATE PROPERTY AMTRAK KEEP OUT! Gladly would I, but I am trapped in a cage: beyond the tracks stands a chain-link fence too high to scale.

I have no choice but to follow the tracks. I walk along the gravel by their side, reasoning that another train will not be coming anytime soon. I now start crossing a narrow rail-bridge over a body of water—the Spuyten Duyvil, I believe. In other words, I am leaving Manhattan! I have left Manhattan Island, I will never caress the giant's rounded shoulder. It is getting darker, and also colder. I need to put my gloves on, but the wind is so vigorous that I'm afraid if I let go of the railing even for a second I will fall into the river. I look down below, past the meshed metal path I am standing on (is it even designed for walking?), to see if I am getting dizzy. Just keep moving forward.

Finally I make it to the end of the bridge; I am at the edge of the Bronx, which used to be part of Manhattan before the dynamiting of Hellgate channeled the Harlem River through. Just beyond is Riverdale. Some beat-up train tracks lie ahead, not a human being in sight. I feel like a hobo, walking the tracks. If I keep veering east, I will get to those apartment buildings looming up ahead. The underbrush is too thick; I can't find a path along this abandoned, funky set of train tracks. I'll have to walk right down the middle of them! They're probably no longer in operation. Sure enough, they dribble off into the grass. I push through dense shrubbery and find myself looking up at substantial apartment houses in the distance. The problem is that I am separated from them by a new set of train tracks, and these are much more serious-looking.

As I get closer to the outside track, I read with alarm: 1700 VOLTS, DANGEROUS, DO NOT TOUCH EVER, or words to that effect. I wonder what 1,700 volts would do to me. Across the tracks, waiting for me, is a glass-enclosed train station: SPUYTEN DUYVIL, says the station sign. Now I have to calm myself and mentally picture stepping casually yet carefully over the third rail, under no circumstances tripping or grabbing the rail for support. The fact that I am notoriously clumsy enters into the imaging process. Well, I may be clumsy in general, but I will not be clumsy this time. No: I will step with a high arc over the rail, going nowhere near it, as soon as I feel calm enough. And so I do. Then I step high over the second and the first rails, not taking any chances touching them, although they are not marked with warnings. Looking up, I notice an old woman in a babushka who has been watching me all this while, behind the Plexiglas, with a scared expression. Is she frightened of me, or for me? Do I remind her of the Creature from the Black Lagoon, or some crazy mugger who lives beside the tracks and is going to attack her? At the moment I'm no menace to anyone but myself: not sure how to pull myself up onto the platform, it is too high to belly-flop onto, but I'd better do it before the train comes. Luckily, I find a metal ladder at the end of the platform, I climb it and ascend the steps of the station and cross over, past Babushka Lady, into civilization.

I scramble up and then down Marble Hill, legs now shaking with exhaustion, and find myself on Broadway, by the elevated Number 2 line. A Manhattan-bound bus happens to be standing there, with a sign that promises 168 STREET. I board it, and look around in the pitch-black Bronx night at dingy stores with neon lights lining the street. As we are crossing the bridge into Manhattan, the tiny Filipino nurse sitting next to me says, "Mister—Jesus loves you. Mister—the Lord Jesus Christ loves you."

"Okay. I get the picture."

. . .

DETERMINED TO GO BACK and explore the rounded shoulder of upper Manhattan, I return eight months later, this time accompanied by a labor historian I know, Steve Fraser, who lives in an apartment with spectacular views overlooking Inwood Park. We enter the park at Isham Place near 211th Street. A broad, open green slopes gently down to the water. The prettiest part of Manhattan, it seems at that moment. A large pond is awash with ducks on a warm June day. At the artificial lake's edge sits a white art-deco-style park building, now used as an Urban Ecology Center. Steve tells me that after World War II there were plans to redirect the Harlem River into the park and establish a public marina there, but the city ran out of funds, or rethought the scheme, so now you have just a little canal filtering water into a pond. At one of the pond's indentations, the city is trying to establish a little beach, the beginnings of a wetland mitigation project. So far, all you can see over in that corner are some rocks, dirt piles, and shade trees: it gives a scruffier sort of edge than elsewhere on the geometrically engirdled pond.

Across the river, on the Bronx side, is a cliff with a giant *C* on it, my alma mater's imperial mark, which both embarrasses and pleases me, the sky-blue edged in white repainted each year by fraternity boys suspended on ropes, to signify Columbia's territorial claims in the area, through its operation of team athletic facilities: Bakers Field football stadium, a tennis club, and a rowing boathouse. Steve, seeing me stare at the orgulous *C*, shrugs, as if to say, "What are you gonna do?" He is more interested in the Inwood Little League field, founded in 1950, in which his son hit several home runs, and which he assures me has "perfect" ballpark dimensions for that playing level.

Steve is justly proud of Inwood Park, which he says is very safe, especially in summer, when there are always plenty of residents from the community using it. In September, Native American tribes gather in the park for an annual shad festival, either bringing the fish in to cook or catching them at the shore. Here, too, a plaque informs us, is where the settlers supposedly bought Manhattan from the Indians. That it was an important site for local tribes is well established: archaeologists have found middens, mounds of shellfish shells, left by Native Americans in Inwood Park, and these historical sites are now protected, more or less, from souvenir hunters by chain-link fences.

We start ascending into the woods. Inwood Park is much wilder than, say, Fort Tryon Park, it has no Cloisters or rose gardens. It has, in fact, the only native forest left in the city. There are still great tulip trees and oaks, Manhattan's oldest and largest wild trees, mixed in with bitternut hickory, flowering dogwood, and black cherry. The hilly, wooded terrain is much like you might encounter in the country, which makes this landscape a complete anomaly for Manhattan. Perhaps less has been made of it than seems proper because it so serenely resembles a familiar landscape—elsewhere.

"Instant air conditioning," says Steve, beaming, "even in summer during heat waves, it's cool here." He points out the caves where homeless people used to live during the Great Depression, and perhaps more recently. The park was also a big hangout for teenage drugs and drinking in the 1970s, according to the poet Jim Carroll's *Basketball Diaries.* Irish teenagers especially would hang out in the woods and play basketball in the courts by the water: they looked strong and athletic till their mid-twenties, after which their bodies would sag, deteriorating from booze.

"I used to bring my dog, Baron, over here for hours each day," says Steve. "That dog would get into fights with squirrels, raccoons, even rats—he was a real hunting dog. When he died, my wife said, 'That's it, now no more dogs in the house!'"

Still ascending, we pass a shed for tollbooths over the Henry Hudson Bridge. Swerving back into the forest, we could swear we were on a country road. The farther away you get from the highway and the river, the quieter it becomes. Steve starts looking for the ruins of the School and Home for Wayward Girls. It used to exist high up in Inwood Park, sometime in the late nineteenth century. Finally we happen upon it: a stone wall, waist-high, and various granite foundation blocks. Steve is excitedly telling me the background of the institution, who is thought to have started it, what the philanthropic ideology at the time was, when I notice, atop one of the low stone walls, an unpleasant surprise: the word KIKE has been formed out of twigs. I feel suddenly unwanted in this Eden. And I feel sorry for Steve, also Jewish, whose pride in his neighborhood park has been deflated. We say something banal about how deep and enduring anti-Semitism remains as a world force, but it also strikes us as just bloody strange that such an archaic derogatory locution would crop up today.* In Philippe Soupault's *Last Nights of Paris,* the narrator says that he walks all night through the city in hopes of encountering a corpse. I walk and walk, it seems at that moment, in order to encounter a sign that will tell me to get lost.

---

*On the other hand, I later learned that "Kike" is sometimes used by Dominicans (who also proliferate in the Inwood area) as a nickname for "Enrique," in which case it would be perfectly innocent. We will never know.

PART TWO

THE EAST SIDE

A tugboat, wheezing wreaths of steam,
Lunged past, with one galvanic blare stove up the River.
I counted the echoes assembling, one after another,
Searching, thumbing the midnight on the piers.
Lights, coasting, left the oily tympanum of waters;
The blackness somewhere gouged glass on a sky.
And this thy harbor, O my City, I have driven under,
Tossed from the coil of ticking towers. . . . Tomorrow,
And to be. . . . Here, by the River that is East—

—HART CRANE, *The Bridge*

14

INTRODUCTION: ON THE AESTHETICS OF URBAN WALKING AND WRITING

F OR ALL BUT THE DISABLED, WALKING IS A BASIC HUMAN ACTIVITY, RANKING JUST BELOW EATING AND SLEEPING. CONSEQUENTLY, PERIPATETIC LITERATURE IS VAST: rarely does a novel or poetry volume lack some walk. But it's a strange sub-genre: a writer can't help wondering how to put a leash on the infinite. How do you begin to impose a structure on what could easily degenerate into shapeless listing? How do you distribute your attention between nature, passersby, architecture, social issues? What needs does the literary walk fulfill for the writer?

Most written-down walks are undertaken alone. The walk becomes a technique to deal with, act out, dramatize, defend, or deplore one's solitude. With solitude, of course, comes a danger: self-preoccupation. The literary walk inscribes the struggle between self-absorption and self-forgetting, between the poison of ego-brooding and the healing parade of sensory stimuli. One of the classic preoccupations of peripatetic literature is how a mood changes in the process of traversing a city on foot. In the meantime, perception is sharpened, by charting the precise movement between interior monologue ("the daily fodder of my mind" is how Rousseau put it in *The Reveries of the Solitary Walker*) and outward attentiveness, like the rack-focus in movies that pulls first the foreground, then the background into clarity.

Walking also offers the chance to sample other class realities: sipping the life above one's station as well as below it. This peripatetic "slumming" (a combination of envy and disdain, voyeurism and sympathy, held in temporary abeyance) yields, at its worst, a numbed indifference to social inequities, by reducing them to spectacle, or by inspiring the fantasy that one knows how the other half lives; at its best, however, it can open one's eyes to the realities of destitution, which beats a refusal to look at all.

The urban walk-poem or story is a species of travel literature—one in which, without going anywhere, you often adopt a stance of unfamiliarity in your own town. In New York, precisely because it is so polyglot and international, the walker-writer can turn a corner and imagine being in Prague, say, or Montevideo. Some walks follow habitual routes, and are intended to reassure; others are undertaken to disorient oneself in a strange neighborhood—to court, as in childhood, the sensation of being lost and afraid, albeit in safe, small doses.

Such walking requires leisure. Idlers and literary bohemians, looking down on nine-to-five "wage slaves," try to swallow their guilt toward the worker and promote walking into a sacred vocation, much like the nineteenth-century *flâneurs* who strolled around Paris, and whom Walter Benjamin called "connoisseurs of the sidewalk." A wine connoisseur appreciates the best and often the most expensive vintages; but the connoisseur of streets, while charmed by the leafy quiet and exclusive shops in a wealthy area, is more likely to grow enthusiastic over a section a bit more ragged. Street connoisseurs are often drawn to borders between neighborhoods, which inherit the different, high-low, *joli-laid* personalities of both. It's this sort of cognitive dissonance that the urban connoisseur takes pride in recognizing and then resolving aesthetically.

The urban connoisseur is also an amateur archaeologist of the recently vanished past. Not surprisingly, an elegiac tone creeps into this genre, as personal memories intersect with what had formerly existed on a particular spot. The walker-writer cannot help seeing, superimposed over the present edifice, its former incarnation, and he/she sings the necropolis, the litany of all those torn-down Pennsylvania Stations and Les Halles marketplaces that goes: Lost New York, Lost Boston, Lost Tokyo, Lost Paris.

IN EXPLORING THE MANHATTAN WATERFRONT, I've felt myself returning to an old habit, rambling around New York. I used to have a passion for walking; now it's something I recognize I can do naturally, like falling back on an old coping strategy.

I first began coming to Manhattan on foot, from Brooklyn. My family would walk across the Williamsburg Bridge at sundown on a Saturday night, like many of our neighbors, to mark the Sabbath's end with a meal at a Manhattan dairy restaurant, usually Ratner's or Rappaport's. Not that my parents were particularly observant Jews, but living in an Orthodox/Hasidic area, they adapted to the local custom. Later, as a teenager, I took to walking across the bridge myself, a poeticizing adolescent mesmerized by motes in air. These spots, which I told myself *only I could see, thanks to my sensitivity,* floating before the housing projects that already walled off the Lower East Side's edge from the river, represented the possibility of a transcendent escape from the ghetto where I felt imprisoned. Not motes but money, I came to see later, was the ticket out.

"Before him, then," wrote James Baldwin in *Go Tell It on the Mountain,* "the slope stretched upward, and above it the brilliant sky, and beyond it, cloudy and far away, he saw the skyline of New York. He did not know why, but there arose in him an exultation and a sense of power, and he ran up the hill like an engine, or a madman, willing to throw himself headlong into the city that glowed before him."

This passage epitomizes a literature about sensitive provincials from the Midwest, the outer boroughs, or Harlem, approaching the city with a lump in their throats. I do not propose to add my lump. Rather, let me fast-forward through adolescence, college, a first marriage at twenty, conjugal cocooning in Washington Heights, divorce at twenty-five, a California-runaway period; skip ahead to my late twenties, when I returned to live in New York, this time on the Upper East Side, and to search out the city, as an avid bachelor this time.

I walked. How I walked! In Midtown Manhattan you walk as though on a conveyor belt, the grid pulling you along. It is not a restful sensation, true: there are none of those piazzas, like in Rome, where you can cool your feet in a sidewalk caffe and stare across at a fountain. You keep moving, you feel purposeful, wary, pointed, athletic. You can gauge your progress to an appointment by the rule of thumb that a block takes roughly a minute on foot, and, given the vagaries of traffic and subway delays, walking is often the most reliable transport option, as well as the most economical. Meanwhile, the grid acts as a reassuring compass, always ready to orient you. It pulls your eye straight up the avenue, to those long, unimpeded vistas; looking left or right, if you are anywhere near the waterfront, you can catch a peripheral glimpse of river, or a sunset made lovelier by the city's atmospheric pollutants; and so your gaze keeps adjusting astigmatically between long distance and middle range, and all the while there is so much coming at you that you have to attend to the immediate surround, dodging bodies and seizing openings. You take in the street by layers: this guy with the hat stepping too close to your shoulder; the storefront signs and window displays prompting impulse purchases; the stone-cut ornaments just above your head (cornices, cherubs, lions), and sometimes a whole second-story tier of retail or an upstairs restaurant; the wall posters on construction sites selling movies, politicians, rock stars; and, finally, the tops of buildings, for which the best touches are often saved: Babylonian roof gardens, green copper domes, medieval castle turrets, Mayan setbacks, Greek temples, and all manner of pointy needles symbolizing the heavenward aspirations of commerce.

I also loved the ability of Manhattan's streets to absorb without fuss the most varied mix of people. Rich or poor, white or black, gay or straight, for the moment, at least, everyone in the pedestrian swirl is assigned the same human value: you are either in my way or not.

Around this time I began to appreciate the performance art of pedestrianism. Each New Yorker can seem like a minor character who has honed his or her persona into a sharp, three-second cameo. You have only an instant to catch the passerby's unique gesture or telltale accessory: a cough, hair primping, insouciant drawing on a cigarette, nubby red scarf, words muttered under the breath, eyebrow squinched in doubt. Diane Arbus used to say that in that split-second of passing someone, she looked for the *flaw*. I would say I look for the self-dramatizing element. How often you see perfectly sane people walking along grimacing to themselves, giggling, or wincing at some memory. Once I passed a man in a three-piece suit who let out a sigh as intimate as if he had been sitting on the toilet. The expression worn on the street is perhaps more unconscious, therefore truer, than at work or at love. The crowded streets bring out, on the one hand, a pure self-absorption unembarrassed by witnesses, and on the other hand a secret conviction that one is being watched by Higher Powers, the anxious eyes of pedestrians all seeming to ask: Oh Lord, why hast Thou forsaken me?

WITH WALT WHITMAN, I encountered an even more omnivorous appetite than mine for walking in crowds. Whitman celebrated Manhattan at a time when it was elbowing aside Boston and Philadelphia as the most populous American metropolis. His positive love of crowds was unusual for the nineteenth century, when many American intellectuals were expressing a fastidious scorn for the "mob." Whitman's fellow New Yorker, Edgar Allan Poe, who said that "democracy is a very admirable form of government—for dogs," wrote a short story, "A Man of the Crowd," in which he equated the boulevard walker with an automaton who "refuses to be alone." Whitman saw no contradiction between joining a crowd and being alone. His solitary, essential self was not threatened by the masses; rather, he took energy and comfort from their surrounding bodies. William James said admiringly of Whitman: "He felt the human crowd as rapturously as Wordsworth felt the mountains. . . ." It's certainly true that Whitman substituted the crowd for nature as a fit poetic subject, and made it a metaphor for American democracy, but the crowd fulfilled another function for him: it turned him on. His gaze peeled beneath the city's houses to the ghosts of remembered or fantasized erotic encounters. The crowd was for him a continually tantalizing, pullulating field of sexual potential: attraction, arousal, frustration, resignation, sometimes even fulfillment, a point he made clear in "City of Orgies":

> . . . as I pass O Manhattan, your frequent and swift flash of eyes offering me
> love,
> Offering response to my own—these repay me,
> Lovers, continual lovers, only repay me.

Whitman's impact on walking-round literature was vast, partly because his all-embracing, synthesizing persona helped organize the streets' random stimuli: what we now call the problem of "sensory overload." Specifically, Whitman perfected the list-poem or inventory. It was a megalomaniac solution, perhaps, with the "I" becoming a vacuum cleaner that sweeps up everything in its path and warms it with the empathic suction-blast of self. This gargantuan process of assimilation, engorging the world by looking at and naming it, was fueled by the desire to make it with everything in the cosmos. "I Am He That Aches With Love," he writes. In the process, Whitman ennobles the walk: his long verse lines are streets we're asked to saunter along.

Many writers since have linked the physiology of walking and writing. The mind relaxes through the calming, repeated movement of a stroll, while the legs' cadences trigger the rhythms of poetry.

Another solution for organizing peripatetic experience on the page was to shave the walk down to an anecdote. The master of this approach was Charles Reznikoff, the Objectivist poet who died in 1976. Reznikoff was a great walker, putting in twenty miles a day, usually starting from his home on the Upper West Side of Manhattan. He walked, as much as anything, to get material. But he felt no responsibility to give a full report of the walk; on returning home, he would focus on only that image or situation that had moved him. Many of his poems are miniature narratives, told in spare, plain language.

Reznikoff was particularly interested in how different ethnic groups—Italians, Jews, Southern blacks, Puerto Ricans, Poles—adjusted to New York. He sympathized with the poor, suffering, resilient city folk he met on his walks, and his poems conveyed the impression that accidental encounters with strangers or gregarious shopkeepers could be among the most nourishing experiences of city life. It was the unexpected rapport that touched him. Walking was both a way for the poet to be alone and—controlledly, indirectly—with others, knowing the spark of intimacy would last only a short while and incur no further obligations.

I knew Reznikoff slightly, and used to come across him in the Éclair, an old-fashioned German pastry café on West 72nd Street. Baldheaded, with glasses, dipping his nose in his coffee like a bird's beak, he wore a somewhat resigned, defeated air, which made me associate him with the Depression years. Knowing he had received less recognition as a poet than he deserved (at times even publishing his own books), I thought I saw traces of bitterness and disappointment in him, fiercely suppressed behind a set of gentle shrugs. Alongside the manifest tenderness in his work, there was a preoccupation with cruelty, though the cruelty was often directed at himself—as in this walking poem, where his stale solitude is not mitigated by any invigorating encounter:

> I am alone—
> and glad to be alone;
> I do not like people who walk about
> so late; who walk slowly after midnight
> through the leaves fallen on sidewalks.
> I do not like
> my own face
> in the little mirrors of the slot-machines
> before the crowded stores.

Self-dislike is the doppelgänger dogging the walker, who must evade it all costs by immersion in the present. We know that feeling of suddenly catching a reflection of ourselves in a car-mirror and not liking what we see.

AFTER I RETURNED TO NEW YORK and resumed my habitual walking, it so happened I fell under the tutelage of a Jungian shrink who encouraged me to attend to the present moment—a hopeless proposition, in the long run; but for a while I schooled myself in concrete detail (the opposite of motes), in the street's one-thing-after-anotherness. No thera-pist alone could have gotten me to live in the present, but this was also a general recipe among poets I admired, such as Reznikoff, Frank O'Hara, and Edwin Denby, and I wanted at the time to be a poet, like them, of proudly urban verse. In the meantime I kept diaries, telling myself: You need not seek, the streets will deliver all in due time.

In front of Carnegie Hall near the Russian Tea Room, there was a crazy man screaming his lungs out, something about "Man is an animal!"—in any case, not very interesting from the viewpoint of language or ideas. People were swerving away from him, but he was tyrannizing the whole street with his insane yelling. Finally I had had enough: I said, "Oh, shut up!" Straightaway he got a happy gleam in his eye. I made a beeline for the coffee shop across the street and sat down at a table, but he came in right after me, and in front of the cash register man and a dozen customers on stools, he began poking his finger at me. I realized now that he was much taller than I had thought. I started making the motion with my hand of patting the waves, the now-wait-a-minute-buddy-calm-down gesture.

"You want me on your back?" he yelled with satisfaction. "Huh? You want ME ON YOUR BACK, mister?!" I had to admit he had a point.

The truncated anecdote: so often this was what I brought home from my walks and tried to work up into something literary. I was squeezing the sidewalks for free entertainment. Often enough, they obliged. Urbanists are fond of comparing the streets of a metropolis to a theatrical set—a tricky metaphor and, by now, a tiresome one. The American theater being what it is today, the streets are probably a more reliable source of diver-sion. But what they give you, for the most part, are curtain-raisers.

I WALKED, I WALKED. In cold weather I appreciated the chestnut sell-ers, the Christmas tree in Rockefeller Center, the chalky elephant-gray lighting of Radio City and the RCA Building, and the way various tow-ers around midtown were suddenly competing to illuminate their crowns. In hot weather I became a connoisseur of halter tops and sidewalk book vendors.

After years of this peripatetic lyricism, the effect began to wear off. Alone, I'd walk the avenues annoyed, too indrawn to appreciate detail. At times the city bored me with its density, its celebrated this-that-and-the-other. But then, whenever it suited me, I'd fall into my walker-in-the-city act. With Kay, for instance, a woman who dated me, off and on, for years, obligingly playing my femme fatale: when she and I went for a walk, and she began dissecting her depressions, sometimes, to change the subject, I'd show off my famous affection for the streets, pointing out brickwork, mansards, gargoyles, quoins, lampposts attracting snow, cute dogs with curly tails, the asphalt rainbows after a summer storm. She'd say "It's only when I'm seeing you that New York has that shimmer of enchantment. Because you love it so."

There is about this walking (usually in the case of men, though not exclusively) an imperialistic vanity, as though you could possess a city by marking it with your shoe leather, side-by-side with a conviction of incurable solitude, that stems from early feelings of powerlessness: mind-locked, onanistic, boastful, defensive, and melancholy (as all flirtations with the infinite must be). Perhaps, like Whitman, I also walked looking for erotic adventure, and, though I never actually picked up anyone on these peregrinations, they were all undertaken under the sign of Venus. I was not looking to find romance itself, so much as to be invaded by sharp glimpses of heart-stopping beauty, to take back with me and muse over in my rooms. It seemed to me that with so many of the women I passed, I could achieve happiness. While my actual bachelor experiences ought to have chastened this naïveté, I never succeeded in rooting out the utopian dream of finding my soulmate, or at least her fleeting paradigm, in the street.

Then I fell in love in my late forties, and remarried. At first I wondered, since the aesthetic response to beauty never dies, if the streets might pose a continuous challenge to my fidelity, mentally if not physically. Of course I still look at pretty women, sometimes longingly, but one main result of marriage has been that I find myself walking less. Manhattan, that mecca for singles, has become less purposefully fascinating, now that the hunt is over. Besides, I am expected at home.

These days, when I walk around Manhattan, often I don't really see the city: that is, I see it in a blur, taking in only what I need to navigate its streets. At times I'll even perversely read a book as I walk, espying only as much of the streetscape as peripheral vision around the volume's borders will allow. I resent the pressure (which I've put on myself—nobody asked me to!) to find grace in the old lobbies and water towers, or piquancy in the physiognomies of my fellow citizens. Yes, New York is amazing, but must I always pay it homage? As a native son, don't I have the right to take it for granted? How often have I conned myself into being astonished by the Flatiron Building, making believe I was a tourist seeing it for the first time! No more. If New York is going to astonish me, it had better do so without my lifting a finger.

It still does, even if the astonishment is milder. In late May, I love to walk around Greenwich Village in the afternoon and see the three-o'clock sun on the façades of red-bricked, Federal-style townhouses. I think there's some mystery to the light at this time of year, but then I realize it's only that the trees are coming into bloom, and I'm seeing the light filtered through and softened by erose leaves, which cast delicate shadows against the building walls. Also, there's a perfect correspondence in scale: one tree, one townhouse. An equivalence, a relationship. By July, you are so used to the fullness of the trees that you don't notice the light anymore—you notice the heat. And of course in winter the sun is dimmer and the trees are bare. But there really is something miraculous about the sun-licked façades at that time of year. And your energy is higher, because it's fun to walk around in spring with a nip still in the air.

ONE WOULD LIKE TO THINK that fine-grained descriptions at street level, such as can only be provided by a walker's unhurried perspective, will be with us always. Still, I wonder if future writers will continue to walk around the city for the same inspiration. Such Whitmanesque Adamic naming seems passé—worn out partly by the very success of earlier peripatetic writers, who may have exhausted temporarily the impulse to catalog the street's biota.

"We are bored in the city, there is no longer any Temple of the Sun. . . . We are bored in the city, we really have to strain still to discover the mysteries on the sidewalk billboards. . . ." So wrote nineteen-year-old Ivan Chtcheglov in 1953, in a Situationist manifesto titled *Formulary for a New*

Urbanism. Between 1953, when Chtcheglov wrote his beautiful whine, and today, the mood has changed: we are no longer bored in cities, because we can no longer take them for granted; we are afraid for them. Svetlana Boym put the matter succinctly in her book, *The Future of Nostalgia:* "In the nineteenth century the nostalgic was an urban dweller who dreamed of escape from the city into the unspoiled landscape. At the end of the twentieth century the urban dweller feels that the city itself is an endangered landscape."

The destructive impact of cars on the urban fabric has made pedestrianism almost counterintuitive. Today's *flâneurs* are mere shadows of their former selves. Today the very notion of a "walking city" begins to sound precious, or curated, like the specially set-aside pedestrian zones in Italian cities that bring people, mainly tourists, together in a fragile mausoleum of an old historical center (called "Downtown" in America) to practice the ancient ritual of walking. What if walking ceased to be a form of entertainment, and became a cultural duty, something "good for you"? Will all future literary meditations take place from behind the wheel? Or is there, as I still believe, an intrinsic, powerfully organic connection between walking and writing, pen and foot, that will survive all future suburbanization of city life?

I don't know: me, I continue to walk around, torn by the conflicting evidence, and writing down my confusions—which are perhaps more a perplexity about my place in the changing urban environment than about the city itself. We now understand, I would hope, that New York City is too big and complex to die; despite apocalyptic predictions in recent decades that New York was doomed, all that happened was that one of its earlier narratives wore out. For now, New York City is between mythologies. There are moments when it pierces you with its dramatic presence; then it fades, gives off an intermittent signal. Nowhere is the idea of New York more variable or inconsistent than on its waterfront, where the void left by the departure of industrial and maritime uses still awaits imaginative replenishment.

15

CAPTAIN KIDD
AND PEARL STREET

I AM WANDERING AROUND THE BASE OF MANHATTAN ISLAND,
TRYING TO FIND 119–21 PEARL STREET, WHERE THE PIRATE
WILLIAM KIDD LIVED WITH HIS WIFE AND DAUGHTER IN A
house built by the previous owner, a Dutch New Yorker named
Loockermans. This was desirable waterfront property at the time, as Pearl
Street then lay at the foot of the East River, before landfill had extended
the island. Loockermans had come over to New Netherlands as a cook's
mate, and then gone into the trading business, from which he prospered,
being a tight man with a guilder. He also married a widow who owned
some property on Pearl Street, and acquired several more houses, including the one he died in, 119–21 Pearl, which was subsequently bought by the
not-yet-infamous Captain Kidd.

In *The Iconography of Manhattan Island*, that remarkable, obsessive, labyrinthine work by Isaac N. Phelps Stokes, a six-volume compendium of maps, prints, and known and obscure facts that took twelve years to compile, between 1913 and 1925, we read:

> Valentine's statement in *Man. Com. Coun.* (1858), 515, that Capt. Kidd owned a lot, and built a house upon it, in Liberty St. (see Vol. IV, p. 392), is an error. It probably arose from the fact that there is a record of his buying a lot in Tienhoven St., and that this name, according to Post (*Old Streets*, 46) was indiscriminately used for both the present Liberty and Pine Sts. According to the records of the Title Guarantee and Trust Co., Kidd bought land in Tienhoven (Pine) St., at the present Nos. 25, 27 and 29; but so far as known, he did not improve it. His home was undoubtedly on Pearl St., where he lived with his wife in the house built by Loockermans.—See Vol. II, p. 329, and L.M.R.K., III: 950.
>
> It is interesting to note that Robt. W. Chambers, the novelist, who made thorough researches regarding the life of Capt. Kidd in New York before writing his recent historical novel, "The Man They Hanged," says in answer to inquiry: "This legend of Kidd's house on Liberty St. crops up every few years. I am convinced that it has no foundation, and that the land in question was on the present Pine St. I know of no evidence to show that he built there."

So get it out of your head that Captain Kidd lived on Liberty. The man lived on Pearl Street, nowhere else.

But where on Pearl? In our day, the street commences across from Battery Park and State Street; I enter it there, conscientiously, determined to explore every inch and grasp its innate piratical soul. Around me is a phalanx of glass towers, with none of the step-backed grace or marbled dignity of the old skyscrapers that formerly constituted your exhilarating, first-glimpse-from-the-ferry skyline of Manhattan. The Broad Financial Center, built in 1986 by Fox & Fowle, is a sort of in-your-face-but-don't-look-at-me black hole stopping thought: curtain wall, indeed. At street level are a few franchise amenities, Starbuck's Coffee, Au Bon Pain, Health and Racquet Club, which could be anywhere, like downtown Minneapolis.

Before embarking on this quest to find the site of Captain Kidd's old house, I had asked the librarian in the Maps Division of the New York Public Library, who knows his stuff, how I could be sure the present property designated 119–21 Pearl Street bore any relation to the seventeenth-century address, and if not, how I could find out exactly where the 1695 property was presently located, and he told me, "Trust your instincts," which was tantamount to getting rid of me. He did show me a few maps from 1695 and a staff member's handwritten research notes on the changing designations and demarcations of the old streets; from these sources I gleaned that the Pearl Street of Kidd's time had extended from Broadway to Broad Street, after which it changed its name and became Dock Street, then, a bit farther north, altered its name again to Queen Street. In 1725, all three appellations were consolidated into the one, Pearl Street, which currently extends all the way into Chinatown, culminating in the courthouses of Centre Street.

Back to William Kidd. His trade was that of sea captain and, only secondarily, pirate. Besides, in those days, many ships crossed the thin line between commercial, exploratory, and privateering activities. Sir Francis Drake, knighted in his day by Queen Elizabeth, had been a pirate as well as a navigator. There was such a thing as "officially sanctioned piracy," in which private merchants and governments subsidized buccaneering ventures, splitting the booty with their captains. Kidd had been a sometime pirate in the West Indies, though not quite industrious enough for his cutthroat crew, who ran away with his ship. Giving chase, he tracked them to New York, then a haven for pirates.

Piracy, as Robert C. Ritchie notes in his interesting book, *Captain Kidd and the War Against the Pirates,* was a growth area for the New York economy. Pirates could come to New York "to refit and reprovision their ships." The local New York merchants also got involved in a clever entrepreneurial triangle trade with Madagascar: the Indian Ocean buccaneers could be outfitted and their booty exchanged for luxury goods, which, at enormous markups, could then be transferred to ships headed to Europe, thereby escaping the scrutiny of customs agents. All highly illegal, but New York merchants were shy neither about employing pirates nor about bribing the British colony's governor to look the other way.

"Encouraged by such lack of oversight," writes Ritchie, "New York became notorious as a pirate haven and center for supplying the Indian Ocean pirates. Its streets and alehouses were filled with buccaneers, and its citizens were kept awake by their lewd activities with prostitutes. 'Turkey' and 'Araby' gold and strange coins of all kinds added to the city's diverse currency. In a depressed economy this influx was highly welcome, and while New York was not quite as outrageous as Port Royale in its heyday, it enjoyed a similar reputation. It resembled any of the out-of-the-way places on the periphery of imperial control that enjoyed a living from sea robbery."

This was the New York that now drew in Kidd. His ex-confederates had already left, but he found an interesting political situation. The town was split between the proponents of Jacob Leisler, a staunch Dutch New York Protestant who had led an insurrection against the British patricians and Papists, and the anti-Leislerians, who were the Establishment. Kidd threw his support (and cannons) behind the anti-Leislerians, which proved the winning faction. He was rewarded £150 for his services. He also now had powerful New York friends who helped set him up in business. Looking about, he took a bride in 1692, the wealthy widow Sarah Bradley Cox Oort. Soon after, they were ensconced in 119–21 Pearl Street.

There seems to have been much marrying of widows. It was, among other things, one of the easiest ways to secure local properties. But one mustn't cast mercenary aspersions on Kidd's conjugal motives; perhaps this was a love-match. As one who married a widow myself, let me say that those who bring consolation to widows, a second chance at love, deserve a special place in heaven. How often we must win back the recidivist hearts of our mates, who keep being drawn to the shades of their first husbands, finding them that much more perfect and empathetic, in retrospect, than ourselves.

So I sympathize with Kidd. He seemed to have every intention of settling down as a respectable burgher; he and his wife had a daughter, and purchased a pew in Trinity Church. In fact, he provided the block and tackle for hoisting the stones of the newly constructed church. "After a few more years," the authors of *Gotham* (Edwin G. Burrows and Mike Wallace) cheerfully tell us, "Kidd had acquired fine silverware, a large plot of land north of Wall Street, and an excellent wine cellar; his wife was the proud owner of the first 'Turkey worked' carpet seen in New York."

After such splendor, he plateaued. Kidd saw his old compatriots, the pirates, spending their gold coins freely in the streets, having a good time, reeling with grog, while he, nose to the grindstone, slaved away for more Turkish carpets. It made him itchy. Had to. But he was not ready just yet to throw off the legitimate life. So, with two of his patrons, wealthy merchant Robert Livingston (Scottish-born, like Kidd himself) and the powerful Earl of Bellomont, he cooked up a scheme to extract a royal commission from the King of England to—*capture* pirates, in exchange for part of their spoils. It seems that piracy was undergoing a moral transition in people's minds, from a socially sanctioned activity to a deeply disapproved-of one: the age of scampish maritime risk was nearing an end; British merchants now wanted the seas made more orderly, to extend their trade in a safe, regulated manner. Kidd knew the hangouts and habits of privateers, he knew the players; what better use of his background skills could be made than to convert him into a sort of bounty hunter?

The King agreed. So Kidd was given a ship, the *Adventure Galley* (wonderful name), in 1696 for the purpose of catching pirates, and also to seize any French merchant ships he chanced upon, England and France being then at war. Having selected from the docks of New York a large crew of 155 rough-and-tumble sailors prepared for fights at sea and lured by a promise of shares, forthwith he set sail for Madagascar. Of course it would be Madagascar, because that was where the pirates hung out those days, in between runs—Madagascar and the Malabar coast; and the third place, we know now, was New York. Why he should not have stayed home and trapped pirates from his snuggery in Pearl Street, I am not entirely sure. At any event, such was his poor luck that when he got to Madagascar, it happened that all the pirate ships had already left that place in search of prey. He sailed on to the coast of Malabar, but here too he was unsuccessful. "His provisions were every day wasting, and his ship began to want repair," reported Captain Charles Johnson in his book *Lives of the Most Notorious Pirates*. Most contemporary scholars now suspect Captain Johnson was none other than Daniel Defoe: *Lives of the Most Notorious Pirates* has the founder of the English novel's documentary flair, his wryness, his quick adoption of a persona; and, as we all know, Defoe loved pirate stories. To quote further from that charming account:

It does not appear all this while that he had the least design of turning Pirate, for near Mohill and Johanna both, he met with several Indian ships richly laden, to which he did not offer the least violence, though he was strong enough to have done what he pleased with them; and the first outrage or depredation I find he committed upon mankind, was after repairing his ship and leaving Johanna, when he touched at a place called Mabbee upon the Red Sea, where he took some Guinea corn from the natives, by force.

After this he sailed to Bab's Key, a place upon a little island at the entrance to the Red Sea. Here it was that he first began to open himself to his ship's company and let them understand that he intended to change his measures; for happening to talk of the Mocha Fleet which was to sail that way he said, *we have been unsuccessful hitherto, but courage, boys, we'll make our fortunes out of this fleet.* And finding that none of them appeared averse to it, he ordered a boat out, well manned, to go upon the coast to make discoveries, commanding them to take a prisoner and bring to him, or get intelligence any way they could. The boat returned in a few days, bringing him word that they saw fourteen or fifteen ships ready to sail, some with English, some with Dutch and some with Moorish colours.

We cannot account for this sudden change in his conduct, otherwise than by supposing that he first meant well, while he had hopes of making his fortune by taking of Pirates; but now, weary of ill-success and fearing lest his owners, out of humour at their great expenses, should dismiss him and he should want employment and be marked out for an unlucky man; rather, I say, than run the risk of poverty, he resolved to do his business one way, since he could not do it another.

The rest of the story is an illustration of the adage that one might as well be hanged for a wolf as a sheep. Kidd plunders and seizes ships, robs the Indians, and even kills one of his crew, the gunner Moore, in a fit of rage by striking him over the head with a bucket, after Moore had railed at the captain for ruining them all. Yet what surprises us in the contemporary accounts is how cautiously Kidd acted, for the most part, even when his crew threatened to mutiny because he was being insufficiently piratical. Kidd was by no means the most ruthless pirate; but he became the most notorious, the subject of ballads and speeches in Parliament, largely because of bad timing. His protector, the Earl of Bellomont, being a Whig, the Tories seized on this connection to bring about a change in government; so Kidd became the fall guy, the symbol of all who flew the Jolly Roger. Bellomont put as much distance as possible between himself and his former protégé. When Kidd sailed back to New York, in fact, he walked into a trap set by Bellomont, and was quickly arrested and sent to Boston, before being shipped to London for trial. Captain Kidd spent several years in the hideous Newgate Prison while awaiting trial (there were actually four trials of Kidd and his confederates). Later, Bellomont's damage control included a curious pamphlet issued in 1701, "A Full Account of the Actions of the Late Famous Pyrate, Capt. Kidd, with the Proceedings against Him, and a Vindication of the Right Honourable Richard Earl of Bellomont, Lord Coloony, Late Governor of New England, and other Honourable Persons, from the Unjust Reflections cast upon them, By a Person of Quality." This whitewash of Bellomont shifts the blame to Kidd and Livingston. Kidd, for his part, insisted in court that his men had forced him into piracy, threatening to kill him if he did not do so, and that the case against him was based on perjured testimony. Defoe summarizes: "But the evidence being full and particular against him, he was found Guilty. . . . Wherefore about a week later, Capt. Kid, Nicholas Churchill, James How, Gabriel Loff, Hugh Parrot, Abel Owens and Darby Mullins, were executed at Execution Dock, and afterwards hung up in chains at some distance from each other, down the river, where their bodies hung exposed for many years."

No question, Kidd engaged in piracy, though the moral meaning of that fact had shifted in his lifetime. Ritchie argues that ultimately he was "crushed by the forces of bureaucracy and the modern world." Even his old haunt pulled away from the practice. "In New York the loss to pirates . . . of three of the four ships that went to Madagascar in 1698 dimmed the ardor of the New York merchant community."

As I wander down Pearl Street, I already know it is unlikely I'll find a shred of Captain Kidd's residence here, amid these glass towers. In 1695 New York, 119–21 Pearl might theoretically have fallen somewhere between Broadway and Broad Street; but in today's New York, that stretch covers a mere two blocks, and the buildings are so large that, by Broad Street, we have only arrived at number 32. Nevertheless, I am unwilling to surrender, determined to find 119–21 Pearl Street and commune with *it,* because, even if it turns out to be located ten blocks away from the original site of Kidd's residence, it may still have some numerical, cabalistic significance.

How can this bland passageway with so little character be Pearl Street? Do streets have immortal souls? Will they speak to us still of what they have seen, even when they have been completely made over, inch by inch?

Pearl Street has gone through so much. The Dutch named it "da Paerle Straet," from the mounds of oyster shells left behind by the Lenape Indians. When fewer than a hundred structures existed on the island, strings of houses already clustered on Pearl, as well as the first church built in Manhattan ("Edwardus Bogardus, Dominie, 1633," the plaque informs us), along the East River shore. In typical Dutch fashion, they put in a Strand, a row of tall houses with stepped gables along the water. The city's first mercantile exchange was located on Pearl Street, and the Dutch West India Company erected a large warehouse there. When the English took over the colony, Pearl remained a thriving business street, with auction houses, retail shops, and wholesalers, who stacked their goods on the sidewalks, forcing pedestrians "to jump over boxes, or squeeze yourself, as best you can, between bales of merchandize," wrote a contemporary witness. African slaves were traded in Pearl Street's countinghouses. Fraunces' Tavern, on the corner of Pearl and Broad streets, was *the* fashionable watering-hole. Herman Melville was born on Pearl Street, the logical place for his successful merchant-father, Allan, to locate, before he overextended himself and went bankrupt. Georgian mansions gave way to Greek Revival style in the late 1820s; the Pearl Street House, a fine hotel for the business class, opened its doors. After the great fire of 1835, which burned down much of the district, the dry-goods and hardware establishments relocated uptown, which left Pearl more purely a financial center, honeycombed with bankers, brokers, and accounting and law firms. Orators railed against the sins of Wall Street and Pearl Street in one breath.

The blocks parallel and to the east of Pearl Street, which were added by landfill—Water Street, Front Street, and South Street (begun in 1798)—absorbed the brunt of waterfront vice—the taverns, brothels, and crooked boardinghouses that shanghaied sailors—insulating Pearl, for the most part, from those depredations. Still, by the mid-nineteenth century, women had taken to sitting on the decaying stoops of Pearl Street's tenements and brownstones, accosting men from the financial and waterfront districts. Then Chinese and Jewish residents started moving in, spilling over from their ghettos in Chinatown and the Lower East Side. Pearl Street was losing its identity as a premier thoroughfare, on the way to becoming an afterthought in the consciousness of New York.

I pass by some Georgian and Federal style houses, including Fraunces' Tavern, reconstructed from scratch in 1907 in a hopeful manner. I like the way Ada Louise Huxtable calls it, in her *Classic New York,* "a fine, educated guess" and "a scholarly fake." (New York schoolchildren, myself included, were brought here on field trips and told without qualification that here George Washington made his farewell address to the troops.) I pass by Coenties Slip, once an inlet of the East River, and then on to Hanover Square, where other vestiges of old New York, such as the brownstone-façaded India House (first a brokerage house, then the Cotton Exchange, next a consulate, now a club) and Delmonico's Restaurant, continue to share the limelight with postmodernist behemoths. Hanover Square, formed by winding streets all debouching into it, and enclosed like a stage set, has a certain spatial resemblance to an Italian pizza, quite unusual for New York. From the second half of the eighteenth century to the early nineteenth, this square was the city's business center. You can still see elegant basement restaurants—like the oyster cellars of old, where New Yorkers once guzzled oysters as their birthright—now catering to a dignified, gray-suited, broker clientele.

All the buildings on this continuation of Pearl Street sport Hanover Square addresses. Farther north, their lobbies and numbers are located on the side streets, such as Pine or Liberty—a sure sign that Pearl Street has become a less-than-prestigious address. Slowly it dawns on me that there is not going to be a 199 Pearl Street. I am well into the 200s before I come upon the next Pearl Street address. How can I lay the ghost of Captain Kidd to rest, in the middle of dour Wall Street? Oh, William, you would still find New York a land of hazardous fortune, where it helps to have friends in high places, but their loyalty cannot always be trusted. (Consider the fates of Ivan Boesky and Michael Milken, pirates of the modern school). At the foot of Centre Street I double back and sniff around like an alley cat for oyster shells and the bones of pirates and widows.

POSTSCRIPT: I now have it on good authority, the historian Edwin G. Burrows (coauthor of *Gotham*), that William Kidd's home faced Hanover Square on Pearl Street. Burrows also writes that the city's privateering phase lasted longer than I thought: "In fact, more privateers would operate out of New York during the eighteenth century than out of any other Atlantic port, and they returned home with prizes worth something like two million pounds sterling—an immense accession of wealth and the basis of more than one family fortune."

16

EXCURSUS

SAILORS AND MERCHANT SEAMEN IN NEW YORK

Arm in arm they careened up Pearl Street under the drenching rain. Bars yawned bright to them at the corners of rainseething streets. . . . Laplander Matty stood with his arms round two girls' necks, yanked his shirt open to show a naked man and a naked woman tattooed in red and green on his chest, hugging, stiffly coiled in a seaserpent. . . .

—JOHN DOS PASSOS, *Manhattan Transfer*

THE SAILOR IS A LIMINAL FIGURE. HE PASSES BETWEEN SEA AND LAND WITHOUT EVER FULLY COMMITTING TO EITHER. WHEN IN PORT, HE OFTEN REQUIRES ANOTHER liquid (alcohol) to console him for the loss of his mother element. A risk to others, he is even more a danger to himself; and those who do not fear his approach—tavernkeepers, streetwalkers, shipping agents—systematically take advantage of him.

The working waterfront is at once a site of cleansing and defilement. In most religions, water purifies, renews, and washes away sins. (Followers of Shinto, Yoruba-influenced Baptists, Zoroastrians, Hindus, Christians, Jews, Muslims, and Native Americans all perform rites today around New York City's rivers.) On the other hand, only the truly amphibious may pass without harm from one medium to the other. "Danger lies in transitional states, simply because transition is neither one state nor the next, it is undefinable," writes the anthropologist Mary Douglas. Waterfront districts have been traditionally associated with sin and peril. A port, no less an authority on the transgressive than Michel Foucault informs us, in *Discipline and Punish*, "is—with its circulation of goods, men signed up willingly or by force, sailors embarking and disembarking, diseases and epidemics—a place of desertion, smuggling, contagion: it is a crossroads for dangerous mixtures, a meeting place for forbidden circulations."

The experience of sailors and seamen in New York harbor is an essential part of the waterfront's history. Though the terms "sailor" and "seamen" often get used interchangeably, and mariners have frequently exchanged one role for the other, we might say for purposes of definition that the merchant seaman signs on with a commercial enterprise, while the naval sailor enlists in a military organization.

Of course, sailors did not always enlist. When New York was still a colony, the British navy would send armed press-gangs to enter houses and taverns and seize local men, whether they had seafaring experience or not, to fill its manpower needs—a practice known as impressment. The British navy had been losing recruits steadily to privateering, a more lucrative affair, especially during the French and Indian War. But impressment was so hated that those targeted for it would often run for their lives, or put up a struggle, and little boys would bombard the press-gangs with stones. Historian Jesse Lemisch has argued that these violations of sailors' civil liberties, and the sometimes violent resistance they provoked, laid the groundwork for the American Revolution. In his book *Jack Tar vs. John Bull: The Role of New York's Seamen in Precipitating the Revolution,* Lemisch demonstrates that during the Stamp Act riots, the mobs in New York were led by seamen discontented with lack of employment and the British government's high-handed practices. Admitting that the colonial American sailor (personified as "Jack Tar") often brawled, shed blood, and committed petty thefts, Lemisch nevertheless construes him as a member of a revolutionary proletarian vanguard:

> The picture of Jack Tar which emerges from a close consideration is complex and at least double-faceted. On the one hand he is simply the American at sea. He is young and optimistic, and rightfully optimistic, for his prospects are good. . . . But the other Jack Tar is quite different. His temper is Ishmael's. He is a dissenter from the American mood. His goals differ from his fellows' ashore; he is the non-conformist, the rebel, the extreme individualist, the man without family ties. He has no steady employment but rather a series of separate jobs. When he is ashore he is unemployed; released from the discipline of shipboard life he is apt to be explosive and irresponsible rather than cautious and sober. . . . He is, except for his personal possessions, propertyless, his income is unstable, and he does not build up any significant savings: he is a sea-going proletarian.

Even after the Revolution, the sailor could expect long hours of constant labor in stormy seas, and unremitting busywork in calm weather. His diet consisted of salt meat, biscuit, an occasional mess of hot "scouse" (pounded biscuit, chopped salt beef, and a few potatoes, peppered and boiled together), and rations of grog. Ships on the high seas were autocracies—only pirate crews operated with a smidgen of democracy—and the captain's word was unchallengeable and reinforced by floggings. A memorable scene in Richard Henry Dana Jr.'s classic 1840 personal account, *Two Years Before the Mast,* captures the cruelty of the system:

> "Can't a man ask a question without being flogged?"
>
> "No," shouted the captain; "nobody shall open his mouth aboard this vessel, but myself"; and began laying the blows upon his back, swinging

half round between each blow, to give it full effect. As he went on, his passion increased, and he danced about the deck, calling out as he swung the rope—"If you want to know what I flog you for, I'll tell you. It's because I like to do it!—because I like to do it!—It suits me! That's what I do it for!"

It was certainly a harsh, dangerous life—sailors had the highest mortality rate of any occupation in nineteenth-century America—and there were only a few weeks' port leave to rest up during the year. Land was not such a safe place, either. No sooner had a mariner docked in New York than he risked being set upon by a team operating in concert: "touters," who hung around the docks and steered sailors to certain boardinghouses; "crimps," who worked as agents for shipping companies and saw to it that a full crew signed on, even if it meant drugging a sailor with spiked liquor and shanghaiing him; prostitutes, who sometimes robbed their clients; and innkeepers and boardinghouse proprietors, who found ways to fleece the seaman of his wages by padding the bill or charging extortionate interest rates. In the late 1860s, investigators reported that 15,000 sailors were robbed annually of over $2 million.

Jesse Lemisch tries to put a sympathetic, pro-labor spin on the tie between sailor and tavernkeeper: "For the seaman in New York the only welfare agency which really functioned was the 'public house'—the bar. In these houses the seaman was free of the authoritarian atmosphere of the ship and the alien ways of the landman. Here, among his fellows, the unemployed or unpaid seaman could drink his frustrations away, sure that his credit was good. Here were women, cards, and dice. Here too was information about jobs, and advice on such technical problems as making out a will. Between proprietor and seaman there was sometimes enmity but always mutual need. . . ." Still, the system worked to impoverish the seamen, who had to fork over his first month's pay to the crimps as an employment fee, and who were overcharged for purchases such as clothing and tobacco from the ship's store, generally operated by the captain.

The Christian evangelical movement became interested in the New York seaman's plight and established floating churches, in and around the waterfront taverns and brothels, and in competition with them, as it were. Some of these waterfront preachers were so popular with genteel New York that the floating chapels had to set aside a block of seats for the mariners they were originally intended to serve. However, when it became clear to the religious societies that the vast majority of sailors remained lukewarm about their souls' salvation, they shifted the focus of these operations to minister to the men's social welfare, for which there was never a shortage of need.

Herman Melville's lively autobiographical novel, *Redburn,* which offers an incomparable account of life in the nineteenth-century merchant service, comments on these efforts "of ameliorating the condition of sailors." Redburn lists ironically the remedies employed so far, such as distributing "clever religious tracts in the nautical dialect," or providing "evangelical boarding-houses," or "the really sincere and pious efforts of Temperance Societies, to take away from seamen their old rations of grog while at sea:— notwithstanding all these things, and many more, the relative condition of the great bulk of sailors to the rest of mankind, seems to remain pretty much where it was, a century ago." He concludes that the only way to improve the sailors' lot is "by ameliorating the moral organization of all civilization."

Melville was being unduly pessimistic: the conditions for seamen, at sea and ashore, did improve, thanks in part to technological advances in shipbuilding, which made vessels safer and crewmen's quarters less cramped, and in part to the ongoing pressure of reformers and the creation of seamen's unions. In 1850 flogging was outlawed; and in succeeding decades legislation was passed to regulate the hiring and paying of seamen, to set standards for licensing steamboat engineers and pilots, to eliminate imprisonment for desertion and all corporal punishment, and to establish maximum hours of work and minimum requirements for living spaces on board.

Meanwhile, New York philanthropists and charitable institutions endeavored to improve the seamen's life in port. Robert Randall, who had inherited a fortune from his father's privateering operations, left his entire estate for the establishment of what became Sailors Snug Harbor, in Staten Island, "for the purpose of maintaining and supporting aged, decrepit and worn-out sailors." In 1900 it housed almost 1,000 retired seamen. A hospital known as the Seamen's Retreat opened on thirty-five acres of Clifton, in Staten Island. The Seamen's Exchange opened its building on Water Street, with a savings bank, reading room, clothing and outfitting store, bowling alley, lecture and meeting hall, and shipping offices with listings of ships in need of crews. Waterfront boardinghouses began to be licensed and inspected. In truth, seamen had always enjoyed more-sober options in New York than the lurid "sun-and-shadow" guidebooks of the nineteenth century would have had us believe. While the waterfront certainly had its share of vice dens, many sailors found decent boardinghouses in other parts of town, or boarded with their parents, or stayed with other sailors' families, or started families of their own.

Still, the Port of New York's reputation for debauching seamen lingered, as something perhaps too colorful to relinquish. The legend was given delicious representation in Josef von Sternberg's 1929 *The Docks of New York*. This masterpiece of the silent cinema begins with documentary-like shots of the East River and the Brooklyn Bridge from a passing ship, the only footage actually shot on location in New York. Von Sternberg always preferred to re-create his stylized worlds on a studio set, where the lighting on faces and fishnets could be better controlled. The New York docks were given a soupy, fluid, moody atmosphere, along the lines of the title: "Night and fog met the stokers coming ashore." A big galoot of a stoker, Bill Roberts (played by George Bancroft), with only one night ashore, and looking for fun, sees a woman throw herself in the river. He takes another drag on his cigarette—the matter-of-fact pause is priceless—and tosses the butt, then dives in to rescue her. She, a chippy named Sadie (played by the touching Betty Compson), is alternately grateful and annoyed at her rescue. Faced with her despairing insistence that he should have let her die, he tells her to lighten up: "You left all that slush in the river, baby. All you need is a good time." Her sage reply is, "I've had too many good times." They repair to the waterfront saloon downstairs, the Sandbar, where seamen are fighting, getting tossed by bouncers, or dancing with prostitutes, while a player piano performs by itself, as mechanical as the pleasures available to the stuporous clientele. Bill impulsively decides to "marry" Sadie on the spot, sans license, and a mock ceremony occurs before the leering, cheering patrons. He assures the parson he'll take care of the license in the morning, though he has no intention of doing so. The next morning he leaves for his ship, or, as the film says, "gives her the air." Sternberg's sympathies surround these fallen angels without moralistic judgment: they've been through it and they know the score. In the end, the reluctant gallant, Bill, has his moment of redemption, jumping overboard and swimming back to her. The film ends in night court, a fitting venue for any mariner passing through the treacherous New York port.

NOT ALL THE ACTION near the docks was heterosexual. Hart Crane described, in his allusive manner, in the "Cutty Sark" section of *The Bridge*, picking up a tall sailor with a "shark tooth" on a chain, and a host of confused sea yarns. The Ohio-born Crane, who became a habitué of the New York waterfront, portrayed the city's edge in this poem as a site of amorous opportunity, quenched torches, and inevitable separation:

> Outside a wharf truck nearly ran him down
> —he lunged up Bowery way while the dawn
> was putting the Statue of Liberty out—that
> torch of hers you know—
>
> I started walking home across the Bridge. . . .

Michael Berube, in his book about homosexuals in the military, *Coming Out Under Fire*, wrote that a different "sexual folklore" about each branch of the service existed among gay civilians during World War II. "Generally they believed sailors to be the most available and marines the least. Sailors acquired this reputation because they were out at sea without women for long stretches of time, they were younger than men in the other branches and their tight uniforms looked boyish, revealing, and sexy . . ."

Those tight white uniforms were featured prominently in the postwar 1949 movie *On the Town*. But the New York awaiting the sailors in port for the day was a Technicolor-benign, tourist place—a far cry from von Sternberg's sinful docks. The MGM musical begins at 5:57 A.M. on the Brooklyn docks, with a romantic view of the New York skyline in the background. The pier, a white battleship moored next to it, is nearly empty, except for a yawning watchman making his early-morning rounds. Three minutes later, at 6 A.M., a whistle blows, and hundreds of sailors pour out of the ship as if shot from a cannon, ready to make the most of their shore leave in the big city. Our heroes, Gene Kelly, Jules Munshin, and Frank Sinatra, leap about as they sing the wonders of New York, and, in the montage that follows, seem almost jeté-borne, careening from the Brooklyn Bridge to Wall Street, Chinatown, the Statue of Liberty, Washington Square, Grant's Tomb, Central Park, Rockefeller Center, on to Times Square. (This opening ten-minute "New York, New York" number was in fact the only part of the film shot on location; the rest was filmed on the Metro lot in Hollywood.)

Let us leave the U.S. enlisted sailor here, in this afterimage of frolicsome tourist enthusiasm and good fortune. With the closing of naval bases in the metropolitan region, the cute white uniforms of our sailors were seen less on the streets of New York, except for the annual Fleet Week or an occasional celebratory parade of ships.

But what about his brother, the merchant seaman? How is he faring these days? To get an idea, I went down to the Seamen's Church Institute on Water Street in the South Street Seaport. It is the oldest institution of its kind, having continuously served merchant seamen in New York from the mid-nineteenth century. Affiliated from the start with the Episcopal Church, the Seamen's Church Institute (SCI) helps seamen regardless of religion or nationality. For fifty-odd years, from 1913 on, it operated a seamen's residence and meeting-place out of a large Dutch Colonial building on 25 South Street, nicknamed "the Doghouse," which became something of a landmark. With most of the shipping transferred to New Jersey, and with the newer ships spending less time in port, the institute realized it had less of a hotel function to perform. To stay close to its served population, it opened a large clubhouse, the Institutional Seafarers' Center, in Port Newark, New Jersey (the gender-neutral term "seafarers" has become preferable to "seamen," more accurately reflecting the increasing presence of women employees—some 20 percent of the cruise-ship labor force, for instance). The SCI also had a new headquarters built for itself in Lower Manhattan. This shiny red building is discreetly contextual, designed by James Stewart Polshek and Partners to fit in with the older, Federal era, red-brick structures on Water Street, its tower alluding to a lighthouse and its roof to the deck of an ocean liner.

The new building has a chapel, a gallery exhibiting some of the institute's extensive collections, and a recreational wing; when I visited, I saw a half-dozen elderly seamen hanging out in a café, silently watching or pretending to watch television. But the bulk of the building is taken up with administrative offices, devoted to SCI's educational programs in computer navigational skills, its training program for clergy to become port chaplains, and its Center for Seafarers' Rights, which protects mariners who encounter legal or labor problems, while lobbying for their improved well-being.

In his 1992 book, *Trouble on Board: The Plight of International Seafarers*, Paul K. Chapman, a former SCI chaplain, analyzed some of the shipping industry's labor abuses. To keep wages depressed, it has increasingly employed a maritime workforce from the Third World, which is over-whelmingly Asian (the Philippines and China being the main suppliers), along with a growing number of seamen from Eastern Europe (the Ukraine, Russia, and Turkey). The workers, often coming from economi-cally depressed areas, are reluctant to make complaints for fear of being blacklisted in the future. Very few Americans work on foreign-owned vessels today, because the pay scale is too low and because they are considered too demanding and are therefore passed over for employment. They *are* desirable as officers; even so, there is a worldwide shortage of trained mar-itime officers, now approaching crisis proportions.

Of the two kinds of vessels, cargo and cruise ships, the worst labor abuses have occurred in bulk cargo ships that fly under "flags of conve-nience"—that is, the owner of the ship may be of one nationality, but chooses to register the vessel with an obliging country such as Panama or Liberia, thereby enabling the owner to skip paying certain taxes and to dis-pense with certain inspections. As ships have become so labor-intensive and expensive (it costs at least $100 million to build a cargo ship, and more for a cruise liner), it is hard for any individual to own one, so that often the "owner" turns out to be a syndicate or corporation, dispersed over several nationalities; and when trouble occurs on board, it becomes exceedingly difficult to track down the owners, much less get them to take responsibil-ity. The sorts of troubles Chapman encountered (the port chaplain not only ministers to seafarers' spiritual needs, but visits every ship in port, to ascer-tain if conditions on board are amiss) include officers beating mariners bloody; owners defrauding mariners of some or all of their wages; vessels being maintained so poorly that they keep breaking down and become unsafe; and crews being compelled to inhabit filthy, cramped quarters with stopped-up toilets, or to eat miserable slop, or to sleep on floors without bedding. Women employees often complain of sexual harassment.

Maritime unions, which might otherwise come to the workers' rescue, tend to be weak, especially in Third World countries; and united union action is hard to organize, when so many members are scattered over the seven seas. As for getting the nation under which the flag is registered to administer justice, that objective seems close to impossible. Chapman concludes: "There are no enforceable international standards of operation for the internal affairs of the ship. International practice does not impose any particular responsibility on the ship's flag state. . . . In effect, the internal management of the ship is no longer controlled by a sovereign state but a sovereign shipowner." In this laissez-faire maritime climate, is it any wonder that piracy is making a comeback?

Beyond flagrant rights violations, seafarers routinely suffer the more-subtle stresses of boredom, physical constriction, lack of recreation (on cruise ships they are forbidden to mingle with the passengers, or to be seen in many areas of the ship), and long separation from their families. Even the luxury cruise, an expanding and highly profitable part of the shipping industry, often provides stingy living quarters and substandard fare for the crew. Finally, contemporary ships are more automated, employ smaller crews, and, time being money, stay for only the shortest periods in port. Hence the whole waterfront-district culture, with its boardinghouses, saloons, exotic pet shops, and opportunities for sin and redemption, has become a thing of the past. While this may not seem like much of a loss so some, it means the modern seafarer is basically trapped on board year-round, with scant opportunity for any release, carnivalesque or chaste.

You begin to wonder whether conditions have actually improved for the seafarer over the past 150 years, since Melville's first voyage, or whether these improvements are now in danger of getting rolled back. The good work of the Seamen's Church Institute continues, defending seafarers, for instance, against recent attempts by the industry to cut back traditional provisions for medical care. With ship tonnage worldwide predicted to double or treble, the quiet struggle of a seagoing, low-income workforce to maintain itself in the face of increasing technical skills requirements and cost-cutting managerial measures can only become more visible in the years to come. New York may once again have to take notice of the concerns of these peripatetic laborers who touch, however fleetingly, on its shores. In the larger scheme of things, they are not going away.

17

THE SOUTH STREET SEAPORT AND THE FULTON FISH MARKET

W HENEVER I WALK AROUND THE SOUTH STREET SEAPORT, IT BOTH DEPRESSES AND BAFFLES ME. IN THIS DISPIRITING MALL (THE HISTORIC DISTRICT was "saved" by extracting every last ounce of its vitality, then injecting it with the formaldehyde of Ann Taylor, the Gap, and the other national franchise stores), the only authentic remnant of the old area is Carmine's, a decently garlicky Italian restaurant that you can still smell a block away. I go in and order a plate of spaghetti with garlic and oil and a Bass Ale. Fortified, I am ready to explore the new Seaport. I enter a stationer's, which is self-consciously done up like an old printer's shop, with antique presses in back, ready for demonstrations, à la Colonial Williamsburg. The people behind the counter are so friendly, and business so slow, that I end up buying a scratchpad I don't need for three dollars, with a drawing of a galleon on the upper left-hand corner. Everything has nautical imagery: the note cards, stationery, pen sets. What a life, I think, to be stuck in such a contrived spot day after day; and yet the owner looks contented enough.

Outside, there are signs for the South Street Seaport Museum, and I do find a storefront gallery with an exhibit about steamship travel, but aside from that, the museum is one of those fata morganas of the waterfront. "We are a museum without walls," Peter Neill, the museum's president, explains. I suppose its main collection consists of historic ships located on the nearby piers: the four-masted *Peking*, built in 1911; the *Wavertree*, a three-masted square-rigger from 1885; the steel-hulled *Ambrose Lightship*, built in 1908; and three working vessels—the schooners *Pioneer* and *Lettie G. Howard*, and the tugboat *W.O. Decker*. Still, when they say "museum" I keep expecting to find a regular edifice with serious, room-after-room exhibits. How old-fashioned of me.*

As for the surroundings themselves, I am grateful that they did not tear down these Federal-style buildings when so little is left of the texture of old, early-nineteenth-century New York, and to have them as a connected ensemble is even more worth cherishing. And yet they seem mummified, so sandblasted and repointed and sign-cutesified are they. Is it a neighborhood? A theme park? An architectural cemetery? Part of the confusion comes from the lack of demarcation between the museum and the retail components. It is as though the museum were three-fourths gift shop. The dispersed, uncentered nature of the South Street Seaport Museum is disturbing: we are asked to see the old ships in the harbor, and the façades of the buildings, and the prints or photographs in the gallery, as all part of the "collection." It won't do, unless we are to edit out the brew-and-burger joints, the Banana Republic boutiques, as also part of the collection. Yet the Seaport Museum continues to put out materials suggesting it is doing exactly what its mission meant it to do, making me feel that I am not get-

---

*To be fair, the South Street Seaport Museum says it is getting ready to open a much larger indoor installation of exhibits, any day—or year—now, which may considerably improve its curatorial profile.

ting some secret Masonic-type connection that is being confidently asserted. Perhaps the reason may be that the museum is run by seafaring buffs, for whom the sheer display of scrimshaw and schooners within sight of water is enough to arouse in their minds the synthesizing romance of the Old Port. Whether they have communicated to the lay public their arcane passion is questionable, but perhaps it is because we are unsure what standard we are asked to bring to this "museum." Surely not aesthetics, as we might at an art museum: the scrimshaw displayed is not the best example of any folk artist, nor it is asserted to be. Historical resonance? But how can we grasp the history of a place so full of animated, jumbled sensation as the old working port, in an atmosphere so stripped of any pulse? How can New York, having strangled to death its port (whatever the valid reasons for doing so), turn around and ask us to celebrate that once-mighty engine of commerce, in the most sterile and manicured of surroundings, frequented mostly by tourists.

Well, what's wrong with having an area just for tourists? you might ask.

The problem is that tourists travel long distances to observe daily life in a foreign setting, and then they are lured to a "festival marketplace" where all they see is T-shirt and taffy merchandising, of a sort the locals won't go near.

Were there an outdoor market with stalls, we could at least pretend that we were experiencing the same hurly-burly. But the Seaport Museum's founders were, from the start, less than happy with the Fulton Fish Market; they wanted its smelly, strenuous trade out of their midst, and will shortly be getting their wish. The Federal-style buildings that presently house the fish stalls will probably be redeveloped as expensive housing units, with a retail mix of Seaport Museum expansions and gentrified shops.

Perhaps the whole nature of honoring history through preservation and similar embalming devices should be reexamined. Isn't the true way of honoring the life of a historic district to make something happen in it that recaptures that vitality? For instance, in the South Street Seaport, instead of kicking out the Fulton Fish Market, they should be expanding it into a day-and-night affair, an open-air food market with covered stalls, such as the Markt in Vienna. What cities can't seem to do any more is create true bazaars that mix recreation and work, attracting all classes of strollers.

Those with disposable income will come to a street fair or flea market if there is sufficient density of urban spectacle, even if only to slum. This casual kasbah feeling used to be the genius of cities, something in their blood, but now it is almost impossible to design; and when shopping centers do go up in the heart of the city, they tend to be filled immediately with big-box stores, the easiest (because national chains will sign long leases) if dullest way to rent the space. By contrast, in Istanbul's covered bazaar, each shop was meant to support just one owner and his apprentice; merchants were not allowed to expand businesses into the next space: a radical idea, impractical in our society, but it makes for a lively parade of stalls.

Historically, public marketplaces were extraordinarily important to the New York waterfront, along both shores. Around 1650, on "market-day," the city's inhabitants would wait on the strand at the East River shore to buy fish or animal skins from Indians in canoes, and produce from the Brooklyn and Long Island farmers. Later a succession of more-permanent structures—Broadway Shambles, Custom-House Bridge Market, Old Slip Market, Coenties Slip Market, Fly Market, the Exchange Market, Peck Slip Market, Catharine Market, Greenwich Market, and Washington Market—were built on or near the waterfront in Lower Manhattan, usually close to the ferries. For instance, the Old Slip Market developed because there were several large shady trees on the shore, near the end of Hanover Square and Old Slip, where country people coming from the Brooklyn ferry would stop and rest. The slaughterhouse butchers also prospered on the edge, though there were efforts to dislodge them, both because their activities were considered noxious and because they were in the habit of keeping bulldogs, who helped corral the cattle but also ran loose in the city, biting the local citizens. Thomas DeVoe, himself a butcher and an amateur historian who collected all the information he could about New York public markets into a fascinating, curious tome called *The Market Book* (1862), defended the early slaughterhouses: "They were public institutions—built and conducted for more than a century and a half by some of the first men of that day, several of whom have given their names to certain public streets, as Cortlandt, Beekman, Bayard, &c.; and withal, they are noted or marked down on many of the early maps of the City in the most prominent form; and if they are an eye-sore or an evil, they are a necessary one, where people will be carnivorous."

Some of these waterfront markets had quite a healthy run, and became favorite subjects for guidebook writers. The talented reporter George G. Foster described in *New York by Gas-Light* (1850) the tumult of the West Side's Washington Market, which began in 1812 and grew into the country's largest food market:

> But we are here at Washington Market. What a squeeze—what a crowd! It is not here mere elbows and knees, and brawny chests and broad stout backs that you are to encounter. Now you stumble against a firkin, and now are overset by a bag. And there is a woman who has somehow—it is impossible to tell how—squeezed through between you and your next neighbor: but her basket, to which she clings with death-like tenacity, appears to be made of less elastic material than herself. It has assumed the position of a balloon, and forms a target for a score of noses pushed on from the rear. There is no chance of its coming through, that is certain; and the woman will *not* let go of it—that seems equally clear. There is nothing, therefore, for you to do but to crawl under it. As you are in the act of performing this difficult and delicate passage, a couple of salt mackerel, at the bottom of the basket, as if in sympathy for your sufferings, bedew your Leary with their briny tears, while a piece of corned-beef, with a large slice of the fat, lovingly reposes on your coat-collar. You at length regain your feet and ascertain that you have been kneeling in a basket of stale eggs, to the imminent ruin of your new black pants. The Irish huckster-woman who owns them, seeing this wholesale destruction of her brood of incipient chickens, pours out a volley of abuse upon your devoted dead, and loudly demands full compensation for her irreparable loss. You gladly pay whatever she requires; and by dint of pulling and squeezing, and being pulled and squeezed, we at length make our way through the lower walk, past the butter and cheese stands, and stalls for carcasses of dead hogs and sheep, now ankle-deep in mud, and so on to the fish-market.

At the end of the Civil War a separate wholesale section of the Washington Market was built a dozen blocks north of Vesey Street, on North Moore Street. In 1927 it was still going strong, when the English travel writer Stephen Graham described "the great market" in his book,

New York Nights: "It was two o'clock [A.M.], and New York here was very much alive. There were horse wagons and motor wagons, cases and baskets of vegetables and fruits, and porters innumerable hurrying hither and thither with gleaming white-wood boxes on their shoulders. . . . There were crates of greens stacked higher than men. There were cabinets of blackberries and raspberries. The nose whispered to the heart 'Raspberries, raspberries' as it tasted the air."

The retail portion of the Washington Market was closed by the city in 1956, and the wholesale component lasted until 1967, when it was relocated (to Hunt's Point Market in the Bronx) to make way for Battery Park City. Today the only remnant of Manhattan's proud waterfront-market tradition is the Fulton Fish Market. A boisterous open market at the river's edge, such as some present-day stroller might just happen upon, would have to overcome the problem of the waterfront's isolation and remoteness. Most successful open markets in Europe and Asia are centrally located—they let you out at important, busy streets with public transportation on either end—whereas the Fulton Fish Market (in keeping with the evolution of the city's waterfront from beehive to isolated strip) is uninvitingly tucked under the highway, and deserted and boarded up in the daytime. Nevertheless, in full nighttime swing it remains as fascinating and as compelling as its companion, the South Street Seaport, is not.

AT FOUR IN THE MORNING, the Fulton Fish Market is lit up like a stadium night game. The lights, mounted high on lampposts and rooftops, render "day for night," as they say on movie sets. The wholesale firms have unloaded and set out their wares in the post-midnight hours, and now the customers (mostly restaurants and retail fish stores) start arriving. For the next few hours it's like a performance piece, an elaborate opera about fish love. Approaching from the north end, through an ample parking lot that lies under the viaduct supporting the FDR Drive, you'd better look lively, because panel trucks, forklifts, and hand trucks bear down from all directions. Here, pedestrians don't have right of way; if you're just there to gape, you'll be dissonantly conspicuous in this symphony of purpose. Loaders, journeymen, salesmen, wholesalers, watchmen, inspectors, bosses, filleters, everyone's got a function: the overall impression is that of old-fashioned, proletarian sweat, such as one had almost given up seeing on the streets of postmodernist New York.

A fish market has stood on this same site, between East River Piers 17 and 18, since 1834. It began as part of a larger, all-purpose market, open day and night, that sold everything from petticoats to books to hardware—to fish (its oysters enjoyed a worldwide reputation); but the market butchers pushed the fish stalls to a separate site across the way, claiming that its smells and wetness were a nuisance. The present Fulton Market spreads onto both sides of South Street: the smaller, more-modest fish-sellers operate in cavelike stalls carved out of the ground floors of Federal-style brick buildings, while, across the street, on the river side, two tin-roofed sheds that constitute the Market Building house the larger wholesale firms. The 1930s art-deco-lettered Fulton Fish Market was built in the La Guardia era, and the Little Flower dedicated the building. The much older Tin Building, which dates from 1907, was burned down by a fire in 1996 (some say it was set vengefully by mobsters during the period of their extirpation), and replaced—despite strong misgivings the Giuliani admin- istration had about the Fulton Fish Market—mainly because you couldn't leave a charred wreck facing the South Street Seaport, it was too unsightly and dangerous. It has been restored to a frontless, functional, breathtak- ingly unadorned state.

I meet up with Dave Pasternak, chef and co-owner of one of the city's best fish restaurants, Esca. I am not sure I would have had the nerve to explore the market in the wee hours without a guide. Dave, an athletic- looking man with a crewcut, is twitchy from lack of sleep and foodie inten- sity.

"When do you sleep?" I ask him.

"Never. Sunday. Though this Sunday I'm supposed to go tuna fishing on Long Island." Pasternak loves to fish. His fantasy is retiring from the restaurant business to indulge his hobby full-time.

Pasternak usually starts his rounds at David Samuels's Blue Ribbon Fish Company, one of the more established, respected firms, begun in 1931 by Samuels's grandfather. Traditionally the fish market has been the province of Italians and Jews, though in recent years Koreans have entered in numbers. Very few blacks find it a comfortable place to work.

"What do you got that's *stylish?*" Pasternak asks Samuels.

"We got some pretty good monkfish." Samuels shows them to his customer. "I'll take a box," says Pasternak, who starts to launch into a fishing story.

Samuels interrupts with an aside: "I have no idea what he's talking about. I never caught a fish in my life." A nice moment: retailer detaching himself from the obsessions of his customers. Samuels, in his soiled white apron and jeans, looks a bit like Walter Matthau, and has some of that actor's rumpled world-weariness and humor. A third-generation fishmonger (though that term, with its "cockles and mussels" wheelbarrow associations, hardly seems applicable to a successful businessman who lives in Greenwich, Connecticut), he began working summers at the market on his sixteenth birthday. He says he was so innocent he didn't even curse. A dead body turned up that first day, and he thought, "Oh boy, this is going to be an experience." No dead bodies have turned up since.

"Got any red snapper?" asks Pasternak.

"Come on, I'll show you. This is a ten. This is as good as it gets," Samuels says, but with a trace of self-mockery. The two men seem to enjoy each other. Regular customers are crucial to the Fulton Fish Market, and it is equally important for buyers to establish close ties with wholesalers, because here everything is based on trust. "If he gives me bad fish," Dave explains later, "he'd be hearing from me next day, so what's the point? He always tells me the truth." Conversely, if a customer stiffed a wholesaler, he would never be sold to again. It's a closed world, a club, like the New York Stock Exchange, where one's word of honor means something. They even have a uniform: the men here are all dressed in knockabout *zhlub* (I'd been warned to do the same, and when I got home, I found fish scales stuck to my sleeve). Footwear consists of boots and old shoes, because the floor is one big puddle.

Watch your back, watch your back. It's impossible to stand idly in one place for very long. "Excuse me!" a journeyman says, aggrieved, pushing a hand truck, coming through no matter what.

Without my having noticed, Samuels has faded from Pasternak's side. There's a protocol to this dealing: the facts of inventory emerge little by little. A circling, with very little eye contact; the pressure to buy is minimized that way, conversations break off easily, the customer wanders over to another aisle, comparison-shopping, then back to the first. If anything, it seems a seller's market: the buyer has to keep pressing to get straight answers from stall operators. The old Italians who like to gab with each other are in no hurry to push their goods, as though sure the lot will be taken off their hands before daybreak. Maybe their customers have already put in phone orders. On the other hand, one hears a good deal of grousing about slow business. The prospect of both local teams, the Yankees and Mets, getting into the playoffs is aired pessimistically from a Fulton Fish Market perspective. "Restaurants'll be dead. Everybody'll be staying home, or in bars eating burgers and chicken wings."

Dave is now over at the northern shed, where an Italian-American named Gino is holding forth. A man in his sixties, grizzled three-day growth, teeth missing, easily roused to volatility, which no one takes that seriously, Gino is offering slices of raw octopus to sample. I munch on one. It's good. I have the sense that I'm being watched, my manly mettle evaluated.

"Bet you never ate octopus at four in the morning," he says to me.

"You're right about that."

Dave needs sea urchins, and he's trying to coax Gino. For a good customer, there is often "something in back" when the supply seems exhausted in front.

"Come on, give me half a box."

"I can't, I promised it to the other guy."

"So tell him half for me, half for him."

No dice. This time Gino really has no more sea urchins, in back or front. Also, there's very little shellfish tonight: "The truck broke down in Long Island." I get a vision of an eighteen-wheeler pulling off the Sunset Highway, grounded till morning.

It's a male environment, with the exception of several middle-aged Asian women buyers. Samuels's handsome cousin struts around with a halibut held priapically at his fly. "Hey, don't hurt anybody with that thing," a co-worker yells. Pasternak turns to me and explains, "All these guys are related." Fathers pass the job down to sons, with very little mobility from one generation to the next; workers stay workers, and bosses, bosses. Nicknames abound, there's an atmosphere of camaraderie, based partly, I would imagine, on the sharing of tough working conditions: night hours, outside in all weathers, doused by fish water, dodging seagull droppings, digging one's hands into ice. Those who work in the fish market are prone to rheumatism, arthritis, heart trouble, cancer, and a shorter lifespan. These are men for whom family comes first, but their crew is like a second family. When the Organized Crime Control Bureau investigated the fish market for shylocking, extortion, income tax evasion, and "tapping" (the practice of swiping a few fish out of the box), they were frustrated by a wall of silence. Though the mob seems mostly cleaned out, or submerged, there are still knots of men standing around affecting a wiseguy swagger. "If he owes you money, go and get it," one says to the other, with an ominous wink. "Go and *get* it."

I am introduced to an affable, beefy Italian guy with an enormous chest and spindly legs. "This guy used to be an enforcer."

"Get outta here," the man says modestly.

"He used to collect checks."

"If I can't get a Czech, I'll take a Polack."

A coffee wagon in the middle of the shed dispenses caffeine and crullers. I notice a little recreational area along the river's edge, Peck Slip, where a few workmen are taking a cigarette-and-coffee break. This sliver of park has benches and informational plaques that say ships used to tie up here, and warehouses received their goods. All that are left of those days are some souvenir iron bollards waiting for mooring ropes that will never come again.

Pasternak points out a young, athletic-looking Korean stall-owner, who is climbing over his stock, looking for the moment more eager to unpack crates than to sell, moving emptied boxes out of the way with a grappling hook. "See that guy? He's big. He's the one who first brought in white salmon." Nowadays there are many more imports; fish is flown in from all over the world—yellowfin tuna and mahi-mahi from Fiji and Hawaii, halibut from the West Coast, exotic species from the Caribbean—thanks in part to Styrofoam, inexpensive, lightweight insulation that has made air freight more attractive. Fifty years ago, New Yorkers used to eat little more than flounder, codfish, and shrimp, but their tastes have grown more adventurous and cosmopolitan, keeping in step with the city's changing demographics. Philippine, Thai, Korean, West Indian, Dominican, Haitian, and Indian cuisines have all widened the New York fish-eater's palate, just as Japanese sushi taught people to appreciate the once-disdained tuna. Fish also has to be much fresher now, as the nouvelle-cuisine methods of preparing it have edged toward medium-rare, and the clientele has grown more demanding.

I am following Pasternak, trying to ascertain his principles of choice. He sniffs a bluefish here, pokes a mackerel there. "What are you looking for?" I ask.

"If it's stiff," he says, as if the answer were self-evident. Clear eyes and blood-red sacs are also signs of freshness. "With tuna, it's all in the color or the fat."

He bumps into an old buddy, a Montauk fisherman, and they exchange info. On the one hand, the buyers and sellers live for fish. They're like enthusiasts at a comic book convention: they'll talk about different species by the hour, how to catch this, how to prepare that. ("Whiting is great for frying up. A little tartar sauce on the side—mhm!") On the other hand, there's a nonchalance bordering on disrespect. Filleters, master craftsmen in their art, who carve with precision up to twenty-five hundred pounds of fish in a night, dribble cigarette ash with one hand, slicing and boning with the other. One guy drags a decapitated swordfish along the ground, not even bothering to lift it. Why should I? he seems to be saying. Dead is dead.

It's a little different, I think, at a fish market where they still bring the product in by boat. One of the greatest urban spectacles a city can offer is a really jumping fish market: I saw one such example in Pusan, South Korea, with the fishing boats moored just outside the stalls, and their wooden crates stacked onto the pier, wriggling with live critters, and the dockside restaurants where you point to your dinner, still swimming in the tanks. Fulton Fish Market used to be thick with sailing vessels: twenty or thirty smacks, sloops, and schooners discharging their cargoes at once, and live fish stored in the East River in slatted boxes that floated behind the building. But fish stopped arriving by water in the early 1970s, partly because New York Harbor was too polluted to supply a local catch (or store it in the river, once caught), partly because it was less labor-intensive to load the fish onto refrigerated trucks in New Bedford, Baltimore, Canada, and Florida.

Thursday morning is the busiest selling day at Fulton Market, because the restaurants stock up in advance for the weekends. A buyer for the Grand Central Station Oyster Bar—round cheeks, professorial glasses, spotless white apron—chats with Pasternak at the Blue Ribbon stalls, talking about fish prices and one of their competitors, who can afford to spend outrageous amounts for the most exotic types. Pasternak says gloomily, "People don't understand that quality fish costs *us*, too."

Pasternak does a quick tour around the stalls on the east side of the street. (Here the firms tend to be smaller, and the fish cheaper and more commonplace). Everything he has bought so far gets shipped to one stall and taken away from there in a truck. I'm still dodging crowds, wherever I look there seems to be activity, but my guide apologizes: "Tonight the market's slow. The weather was lousy earlier in the week, and the boats didn't go out, so there's less product than usual."

I have been told by old-timers that there used to be a lot more fish, quantitatively speaking, in the market. The number of firms has shrunk from 187 a few decades ago to 50 today. I ask David Samuels if he thinks fish markets themselves are an endangered species.

"Fresh fish is something that has to be purchased by eye," Samuels answers. "There'll always be a need for a wholesale fish market." And the Fulton Fish Market remains one of the largest wholesale fish markets in the world.

That doesn't mean it will always be in Lower Manhattan. Somehow the fact that the fish gets motored in makes the present Fulton Fish Market seem vaguely arbitrary; I mean if it's just a truck depot, it doesn't have to be on the water anymore. It could be anywhere, even Hunt's Point on the Bronx waterfront, where a produce and meat market already exist, and where a string of mayors since the 1970s have been pushing to relocate the reluctant fishmongers to a bigger, "state of the art" fish market. During his mayoral administration, Rudolph Giuliani was especially adamant about moving the market to the Bronx, perhaps because he had made his earlier reputation as a prosecutor by promising to rid the Fulton Fish Market of organized crime, and retained his distaste for the milieu. City officials justify the move by saying that federal health regulations prohibit selling fish outdoors and require that it be refrigerated at the point of sale. The fishmongers who want to stay in the Fulton Market insist that they can get around that problem.

Those, like myself, who love the old market where it is, say it's about preserving a piece of living history, and keeping it in an accessible part of the city (close to Chinatown as well), so that even civilians can drop in and buy a dozen fish for a party, while veterans can continue doing business where they and their families have for generations. With all the forced, artificial connections that are being foisted on the New York waterfront in its twenty-first-century transformation, a fish market on the river's edge continues to feel like the most appropriate of functions.

I used to come down to the market in my early twenties, mostly to eat at a great fish restaurant named Sweets, on the corner of South Street and Fulton. It was upstairs on the second floor, and had sawdust on the planks, and the slanted look of a ship galley out of Melville's time, and it wasn't even pricey but quite reasonable, and you could get a piece of fish grilled to your liking with a minimum of fuss or sauce, and the old black waiter didn't treat me like an impostor, though I felt like one, an aspiring writer pretending to be as worldly as the bankers in gray flannel suits at the next table. Most of the legendary eateries—Sloppy Louie's, Dirty Ernie's, Sweets, the Paris Bar—are gone (the Paris Café presently on South Street is a parvenu establishment that appropriated the name); and the suburban-type restaurants of South Street Seaport have little connection with the market adjoining it. For the moment, the Seaport and the Fulton Fish Market coexist pragmatically if uneasily; the refrigerated trucks are gone and the streets washed down if not cleaned by 10:00 A.M. in time for the parking lot to be filled by the Seaport's tourist and white-collar clientele.

At six-thirty in the morning, when the market is starting to wind down, I go around the corner to the Market Grill on 40 Peck Slip, which is open all night, and serves omelets with fried potatoes and other breakfast staples. Fish does not seem particularly featured on the menu, though that may come as a relief to the market workers who frequent it. The TV is on to CNN, the waitress is talking sports with one of her regulars, and a group of Koreans hang around the back tables, laughing.

As I leave, I pause to take in a last whiff of the fish market. Joseph Mitchell, tireless habitué of these streets and stalls, once tried to pin down that "heady, blood-quickening, sensual smell." He found it to be a mixture of the harbor, the oyster houses, tar, smoke from the fish-curing lofts, wet boat nets, the coffee-roasting plants on Front Street, a spice mill, and the tannery district to the north. Gone are the coffee-roasting plants and the tannery district and the spice mill, and the boats themselves; but you can still be brought up short by the ripe pungency of the Fulton Fish Market and the brackish East River, now augmented by the burnt-rubber tire smell of the FDR Drive, and the starched odor of fax paper and modems from nearby brokerage houses.

Fish are the most transitory of human delights, next to cherry blossoms. If a week-old newspaper's prose is said to be good for nothing but wrapping fish, the week-old haddock claims not even that utility. As the commodity is perishable, so is the venue. The Fulton Market, the last fish market of a city in the Western world that is still on its original site, hangs on, vibrant, raunchy, but under siege. My prediction is that in a year or two it will be gone. So maybe you had better get over there some 4:00 A.M. and see it and smell it for yourself, before it turns into another page of *Lost New York.*

18

EXCURSUS:
THE ELUSIVE
JOSEPH MITCHELL

No one wrote more passionately or intimately or well about the New York waterfront than Joseph Mitchell. When I first began telling people I was working on a book on the same subject, many would get misty-eyed and ask me if I had read *The Bottom of the Harbor* (which of course I had), with the clear implication that he'd already done the job. Joseph Mitchell became a tiger in my path, the patriarch I would first have to slay. Some part of me began to dislike Joseph Mitchell. Well, "dislike" is too strong a word; I itched to disparage him, the only problem being that he was such a good writer. I adored a number of his essays, such as

"Up in the Old Hotel," "Mr. Hunter's Grave," "The Cave Dwellers," "The Rats on the Waterfront," and "Joe Gould's Secret." Still, I'd never been a total Mitchell fan; the long technical passages about catching and cooking fish bored me, I could not sign on to the romance of the saloon, and the quaint old geezers sitting around the fish market gabbing in the "Old Mr. Flood" stories did not do it for me.

Perhaps what put me off Mitchell most was that he exemplified a certain objective-sounding, reticent ideal of nonfiction prose that many educated people respect the most, but that seemed the opposite of the kind I practiced, the personal essay, which dramatically foregrounds the contradictions of a subjective outlook. Mitchell was a first-rate reporter, and he would go forth and hang out and bring back an impeccably researched study of some unsung character or way of life, written in that unobtrusive, fact-filled, clarity-and-precision style advocated by Strunk and White, and filtered through the narrative voice of a non-egotistical first-person singular. Oh, occasionally Mitchell would permit glimpses of himself to peep through his profiles, but they conveyed mostly a generalized-observer sensibility, rather than the particulars of one man's experiences and struggles with his self. Even as I was entertained and moved by his pieces, I felt frustrated by the hide-and-seek, watery aspect of Mitchell's persona.

This aqueous quality is not surprising when you consider that, after a certain point, the man wrote mostly about fish and alcohol. To list the topics he shied away from—power, sex, money, youth, glamour, class, politics—is one way of getting at his world-view's stubborn boundaries.

Every now and then, seeking to rid my mind of thoughts of death and doom, I get up early and go down to the Fulton Fish Market. I usually arrive around five-thirty, and take a walk through the two huge, open-fronted market sheds, the Old Market and the New Market, whose fronts rest on South Street and whose backs rest on pilings in the East River. At that time, a little while before the trading begins, the stands in the sheds are heaped high and spilling over with forty to sixty kinds of finfish and shellfish from the East Coast, the West Coast, the Gulf Coast, and half a dozen foreign countries. The smoky riverbank dawn, the racket the fishmongers make, the seaweedy smell, and the sight of this plentifulness always give me a feeling of well-being, and sometimes they elate me. I wander among the stands for an hour or so. Then I go into a cheerful restaurant named Sloppy Louie's and eat a big, inexpensive, invigorating breakfast—a kippered herring and scrambled eggs, or a shad-roe omelet, or split sea scallops and bacon, or some other breakfast specialty of the place.

So begins Mitchell's great essay "Up in the Old Hotel." Typically, he alludes to his morbid cast of mind, but with such glancing swiftness as to invite the reader to take it ironically, then goes on to list the physical details of a grubby place he loves, where he finds anew the consoling, simple pleasures. Impossible to write better prose. You read a paragraph like that and think, "Why do I even bother?" But then, I tell myself, Joseph Mitchell spoke for those who know the names of things, every fish in the ocean and nautical rope; I'm going to speak for those who are ignorant, like me. He wrote unfailingly well; I'll write badly, or at least unevenly. There's room for both of us on the bookshelf.

It was a good try, but not enough to clean up my Joseph Mitchell problem. I still wanted to grapple with his achievement and ease out from under his shadow. So I sat down and reread his oeuvre, which, this time around, I liked much better, overall, albeit retaining some of my earlier reservations. I also came to the conclusion that I knew the man; this time he hadn't kept quite as hidden as I once thought. Whether or not I can convey this intuitive flash of knowledge on the page remains to be seen.

IN 1929, Joseph Mitchell arrived in New York City from North Carolina. He was twenty-one and determined to find a job on a newspaper, just as the Great Depression was dawning. For the next eight years he worked at the *World*, the *Herald Tribune*, and the *World-Telegram*, where he honed his skills as a crime reporter, celebrity interviewer, and feature writer. This newspaper work formed the basis for his first collection, *My Ears Are Bent* (1938), all of which he omitted from the big selected-prose volume that appeared shortly before his death, *Up in the Old Hotel*, explaining merely that "It was a different kind of writing." So were several very weak short stories he chose to include in his selected prose, which suggests he would rather be known as a failed fiction writer than as a professional newspaperman. In any case, the superb, energetic *My Ears Are Bent*, recently reissued by Pantheon Books, makes for delicious reading, especially in light of the author's later avoidance of the sensationalistic and racy. In these pieces on electrocuted murderers, strippers, anarchists, dope fiends, voodoo doctors, pickpockets, movie stars, and other journalistic staples of the day, Mitchell is more unbuttoned and forthcoming as a narrator, his comic impulse bobbing closer to the surface. (For instance, in his piece on voodoo, he cavalierly dismisses the ingredient known as "goofer-dust" as, "after all, only earth stolen from the fresh grave of an infant sometime around midnight.")

Just as striking, and different from the later Mitchell mode, were his street scenes, composed of overheard conversations or notations of almost nothing, tenderly and artfully strung together:

"In summer the East Side lives in the street. The young mothers are in love with the sun, but the old ones sit in the shade. The babies doze in their carriages and whimper and play with their toes. The old mothers mutter unceasingly, but the young ones sit in the sun in clean print dresses and read confession magazines."

Such a verbal snapshot by a young, belletristic reporter high on lyrical urban detail is the literary equivalent of photographs by Walker Evans, Rudy Burckhardt, and Berenice Abbott. The thirties gave us an aesthetic of the Common Man. Suddenly it was enough just to catch the way ordinary people passed the time.

Every so often *The New Yorker* would pluck some street-smart, salty newspaperman from the city's dailies and put him on staff. They did it with A. J. Liebling and John McNulty and Joseph Mitchell. McNulty was a hard-drinking, economical writer who wrote funny, poignant vignettes about barflies, taxi drivers, ambulance drivers, and nuns, capturing the common parlance of New Yorkers with a disjunctive, native surrealism that partly came out of the bottle. McNulty did not change his terse style much in transit from the New York *Daily News* to *The New Yorker,* but Mitchell took the opportunity to remake his subject matter and fine-tune his prose.

Over the years, Mitchell distanced himself from what he had called the "melodrama of the metropolis" and its cast of freaks (Olga the Bearded Lady would be his last such profile), shifting interest from the lurid to the stoical, from flamboyant extroverts to unsung artisans who did the world's work, or retirees who viewed the passing scene *hors de combat*. Typically, he described these later subjects as "companionable but reserved," "self-sufficient," "sad-eyed," lacking "an itch for money," and rheumatically past caring about sex. His pieces, which grew longer and more complexly structured, thanks to *The New Yorker's* encouragement of serious investigation, tended to circle around knowledgeable professionals (a restaurant owner, a dragger captain, an exterminator, a detective) or tribes (Gypsies, Mohawks working in construction) or milieus (McSorley's saloon, the harbor). If something spontaneous had gotten lost in the transition from newspaperman to *New Yorker* regular—if his scrupulously fact-checked prose, with its careful descriptions of work processes, felt dry at times, like the soundtrack of an industrial documentary—it was also true that his writing on the whole had deepened, becoming fuller, wiser, and more reflective.

And Mitchell settled into his fundamental subject: inertia. In a world changing too fast, he sought out those who were through evolving, content to guard their posts (a harbor boat watching for poachers, a ticket-seller's cage) or reminisce about the old days. Ever the polite Southern son, he sat next to old codgers and drew out their expertise. The transcribed monologue became a perfect form for this purpose, emphasizing as it did patterns of repetition and monomania; many of his subjects seem gripped by an idée fixe. "I have been tortured by some of the fanciest ear-benders in the world," he wrote in the preface to *My Ears Are Bent*, "and I have long since lost the ability to detect insanity." Re-creating, wherever possible, the static atmosphere of a sleepy Southern square in the modern metropolis, he wheeled out his "opinionated and idiosyncratic" old men and women.

Mitchell's eccentrics have been compared—validly, it seems to me—with Charles Dickens characters: they have that Victorian consistency and one-sided frontality which fits E. M. Forster's famous definition of "flat characters" in *Aspects of the Novel*. A humorous writer, Mitchell practices what might be called the comedy of decrepitude, part of which is shown by a descent into rambling speech. ("Tonsils, adenoids, appendix, gall bladder, prostate," enumerates Joe in "The Rivermen." ". . . I've got varicose veins from walking around on wet cement floors in Fulton Market all those years, and I have to wear elastic stockings that are hell to get on and hell to get off and don't do a damned bit of good, and I've got fallen arches and I have to wear some kind of patented arch supports that always make me feel as if I'm about to jump, and I've never known the time I didn't have corns—corns and bunions and calluses.") Mitchell once listed his favorite authors as Twain (his favorite book was the peerless *Life on the Mississippi*), Dostoevsky, and Joyce; the first two delight in ranting monologues, the third in stream of consciousness.

Clearly the monologue is also a quick, practical way of establishing the character and biography of a profiled subject. But it had to be the monologue of someone who was going nowhere. Mitchell had little regard for tycoons or men of action. He listed, in *My Ears Are Bent,* his least favorite interview subjects as "industrial leaders, automobile manufacturers, Wall Street financiers, oil and steel czars, people like that. . . . After painfully interviewing one of those gentlemen you go down in the elevator and walk into the street and see the pretty girls, the pretty working girls, with their jolly breasts bouncing under their dresses and you are relieved; you feel as if you had escaped a tomb in which the worms were just beginning their work; you feel it would be better to cheat, lie, steal, stick up drugstores or stretch out dead drunk in the gutter than to end up like one of those industrial leaders with a face that looks like a bowl of cold oatmeal." This is partly the young Mitchell talking, full of Great Depression populism, bohemian reverse-snobbism, and newspaperman swagger. Later, when he moved to *The New Yorker,* he would restrain his rhetorical dislike for high society. Still, toward those who had no interest in getting and spending, Mitchell continued to extend a courteous, warm interest bordering on sentimentality. These urban peasants had achieved the simple pleasures, paradise on earth. Their advanced age may have also indicated, for this death-haunted author, always fleeing "a tomb in which the worms were just beginning their work," that only by hunkering down and staying clear of ambition could you cheat the Grim Reaper, who would not think to look for you in such backwaters.

As the monologues became more and more freighted with background exposition and procedural information, they lost some of the quality of individual speech. ("As a rule, people that drown in the harbor in winter stay down until spring. When the water begins to get warm, gas forms in them and that makes them buoyant and they rise to the surface," explains a Mr. Poole, helpfully if less than colloquially.) At a certain point, Mitchell's goal of capturing character through the way a person talks came into collision with his desire to document physical processes. The speakers all began to sound the same, sanded down to a personality-less smoothness, or, rather, taking on what had become the classic Joseph Mitchell informant personality: patient, thorough, slightly ironic, and emotionally reserved.

What was often missing in these profiles—intentionally, even perversely so—was a sense of drama (for if everyone has settled into his or her rut, and no one is trying to achieve any new ambitions, even romantic ones, we are left with a fairly undynamic model of human behavior); what was being asserted in its place was a depressive's pastorale. It was as though Mitchell were trying to see how far you could go as a writer in sustaining interest without resort to conflict. The burden was shifted to small comic effects, the textured pleasures of syntax and vocabulary, a boundless curiosity about how things worked, and a serene melancholy.

The denizens in one of Mitchell's most celebrated essays, "McSorley's Wonderful Saloon" (1940), are described as "insulated with ale against the dreadful loneliness of the old. 'God be wit' yez,' Kelly says as they go out the door." Compare the kindly regard the author bestows on these rummies with another work from the same era, Eugene O'Neill's play *The Iceman Cometh* (1946), also set in a Bowery bar, but much harsher and less forgiving of the alcoholic's rationalizations. It was Mitchell's chivalric way to take people at their word—not to trip them up. Sometimes, as in his magnificent profile "Mr. Hunter's Grave" (1956), the interviewed subject, given enough rope and the force of his own honesty, leads the reader to a full comprehension of his tragically riven nature. But if the subjects themselves remained unaware of their contradictions, he was not going to be the one to force the issue. Nor did he interrogate in print his own role as regards slumming or exploiting his subjects. The result was a somewhat public, decorous presentation of human character, which barely acknowledged how divided, mendacious, or self-destructive people could be—it was almost pre-psychological in its refusal to recognize unconscious motives. In piece after piece, Mitchell gave the impression of guarding his subject's secrets.

With one exception, and that is his masterpiece, "Joe Gould's Secret." Here, for the first time, he was forced to admit that someone had been lying to him. In an earlier piece, "Professor Sea Gull," Mitchell had fondly portrayed a derelict bohemian named Joe Gould, who cadged handouts in Greenwich Village by reciting scurrilous poems and imitating sea gulls. "Although Gould strives to give the impression that he is a philosophical loafer, he has done an immense amount of work during his career as a bohemian. Every day, even when he has a bad hangover or even when he is weak and listless from hunger, he spends a couple of hours working on a formless, rather mysterious book that he calls 'An Oral History of Our Time.' He began this book twenty-six years ago, and it is nowhere near finished. . . . He estimates that the manuscript contains 9,000,000 words, all in longhand." The problem was that it wasn't true. After the profile appeared, Mitchell finally realized that Gould had conned him and that the entire "Oral History" was a bluff. Why a man as worldly and intelligent as Mitchell, who knew the conditions under which serious writing generally occurs, should have taken so long to figure out that the manuscript didn't exist is the real mystery; but some of the reasons may lie in Mitchell's own fascination with oral history, and his ambitions along that line, which allowed him to imagine Gould as a sort of non-co-opted alter ego.

In any case, in "Joe Gould's Secret," published in 1964, after Gould's death, Mitchell does something he never did before: he lays bare his own thought processes, reactions, and ambivalence. And he becomes a character himself in the process. In his other profiles, Mitchell would sometimes refer to the subject as "my friend," but then quote the person at length with journalistic impersonality, not allowing the give-and-take of a genuine friendship to appear on the page. This time we see Mitchell's relationship to the profiled subject vividly: the "I" character, Joe Mitchell, perennially oscillating between generosity and self-protective indifference, charmed gullibility and disenchantment. In this, the longest piece he ever wrote, he charts the course by which Professor Seagull became an albatross around his neck.

I find especially intriguing his revisiting the first set of meetings with Gould, the very material he had shaped in "Professor Sea Gull," this time admitting to his uneasiness, boredom, and revulsion at the time, which led him on occasion to put off the importuning wraith. Even after Mitchell's

narrator has divined Gould's secret, he can still not entirely shake this dop-
peländer—or his lingering feelings of responsibility for him. In the end,
Mitchell's narrator comes to discover that Gould has been merely rewrit-
ing (without improvement, necessarily) the same two essays over and over,
his entire life: one about the death of his father, one about tomatoes. The
pathetic stack of manuscripts left posthumously, all with the same two
titles, induces textual vertigo, like something out of Borges. When he concluded, however, with "'God pity him,' I said, 'and pity us all,'" I bet
Mitchell was thinking not of Borges but of Melville's "Ah, Bartleby! Ah,
humanity!"

The psychological depth and rounded characterizations achieved in
"Joe Gould's Secret" can be read backwards as a self-critique of the earlier
profiles. Of course, by calling "Joe Gould's Secret" Mitchell's masterpiece,
I am in part expressing my own literary preferences, because here is a true
personal essay, and a double portrait, with a fully developed, shaded narrative persona—the kind of thing I like best.

THE ACHIEVEMENT OF *The Bottom of the Harbor*, which is Mitchell's
strongest essay collection overall, was based less on individual portraiture
than on his success in rendering a complex environment. Combining the
perspectives of marine biologist, geologist, urbanist, anthropologist, and historian, he succeeded in unraveling the interdependent strands of past and
present, nature and humanity, predators and prey, economics and culture, all
in the most elegantly accessible prose. His vision of the harbor had a startling ecological prescience: in the 1951 title essay, he was writing about water
pollution, landfill, garbage disposal, dredging, and all the interrelationships
between creature and environment that were being altered by modernity.

"The bulk of the water in New York Harbor is oily, dirty, and germy.
Men on the mud suckers, the big harbor dredges, like to say that you could
bottle it and sell it for poison. The bottom of the harbor is dirtier than the
water. In most places, it is covered with a blanket of sludge that is composed of silt, sewage, industrial wastes, and clotted oil. . . . Nevertheless,
there is considerable marine life in the harbor water and on the harbor bottom. Under the paths of liners and tankers and ferries and tugs, fish school
and oysters spawn and lobsters nest."

Mitchell's uncanny ability to envision the world undersea is reminiscent of the dragger captain he profiles, Ellery, who "thinks like a flounder," or Roy, who has "got the bottom of the harbor on the brain," or the old rivermen who "fish around in their memories." Mitchell's imagining of the ocean floor has an allegorical dimension: the harbor is the inside of his skull.

The essays hint at other allegorical meanings, some topographically derived ("Up in the Old Hotel," "The Bottom of the Harbor"), some expressing a whimsically Gothic inclination. When Louis, the owner of Sloppy Louie's, finally makes his way into the boarded-up floors above his restaurant, the decor of decay he finds has echoes of Poe and Hawthorne. There is a Gothic sensibility working as well in the claustrophobic, obsessive accumulation of detail—or the rats that leap out of drawers, "snarling." Mitchell confesses a persistent Southern taste for cemeteries, hell-and-brimfire preachers, and "people with phobias, especially people who predict the end of the world." Foreshadowings of apocalypse keep wandering into these harbor essays: "The Last Judgment is on the way, or the Second Coming, or the end of the world," says a boatman looking at the New York skyline; others warn that the world is going to hell in a handbasket; even the equable black deacon, Mr. Hunter, broods, "It'll all end in a mess one of these days," and worries about "the prophecies in the Bible," when "the dead are raised." The occult and the esoteric are never far removed: they are to be found in biblical visions, in the secrets of old men and women, and in Joe Gould's "underground masterpiece," hidden somewhere. It is as if Mitchell were always hoping to decode signs of eternity in the prosaic world around him. Few writers possess a sense of the daily and the apocalyptic in such close proximity.

In "Joe Gould's Secret," Mitchell confessed that as a young man he had planned to write a novel about a reporter, coming to New York, who "often sees the city as a kind of Hell, a Gehenna." While he never wrote that overly symbolic novel, neither did he ever give up entirely his Revelations-inflected reading of the modern city. There is a dark, morbidly transcendental undercoating to his otherwise sunny pieces, at once powerful and frustrating, as in any private allegory whose meanings can only be partly surmised.

. . .

JOSEPH MITCHELL published nothing else after "Joe Gould's Secret." For the last thirty years of his life, he continued to report to work. Sitting in that office year after year, not writing (though his typewriter could sometimes be heard: then let us say, not writing anything he deemed of sufficient worth to let into print), he became, in a sense, Joe Gould, a malingerer bluffing a great manuscript that no one would ever see. He was allowed to retain his *New Yorker* office for decades after he stopped publishing, becoming the sentimental mascot of the magazine, even more principled for keeping his silence, or for refusing to relax his high standards by venturing again into vulgar print. He was the dotty but lovable uncle in *You Can't Take It With You,* who would emerge from his room from time to time and be given a choice seat at the banquet.

Many have speculated on his writing block. Could be he'd said all he had to say. Could be that the implications and vistas opened to him by "Joe Gould's Secret," of planting himself in the narrative, frightened him. Moreover, it wasn't only Mitchell who stopped writing profiles of the common man. As the city's demographics altered, it seemed more awkward for white journalists to cast the newer, darker-skinned faces in the role of New York's Everyman. All those amusing sketches of curbstone characters, such as A. J. Liebling's cigar store owners and tummlers, came to a halt, as white journalists hesitated to portray minority entrepreneurs or street-corner society in droll, local-color profiles, and minority journalists were in no mood to patronize their own. Perhaps, too, regardless of ethnicity, the new reporters with their journalism-school degrees felt farther away from the man in the street than their school-of-hard-knocks predecessors had.

Russell Baker, in an appreciation of Mitchell for *The New York Review of Books,* asserts that the author stopped writing because the city had grown too harsh and uncivilized: "But the New York emerging in the 1960s was not a city that lent itself to his particular 'cast of mind.' It needed writers who had grown up hearing the roar of the bullhorn, not the voice of Aunt Annie talking about the people down below." Also, Baker says, the age had grown too narcissistic for Mitchell: "He was trained in the hard discipline of an old-fashioned journalism whose code demanded self-effacement of the writer. A reporter's effusions about his own inner turmoil were taboo." Myself, I don't see the point of invoking Joseph Mitchell as the last decent man whose writing block chastises the rest of us for our vulgarity and egotism. There was plenty of unsettling loud noise in New York during Mitchell's prolific periods, and there were plenty of star journalists who put themselves in the story. No, I rather think his silence had more to do with aging. It is hard for an elderly man to keep seeking out those still more ancient, and he refused, reasonably enough, to learn from youth.

In the interim, a cult had grown around him. His out-of-print books, which he refused to allow reprinted (in the same way that he refused to be anthologized), were collected and hoarded by bibliophiles, especially those with an interest in urban sketches, old New York, or the golden age of *The New Yorker*. I remember once visiting some journalists in Hoboken, who had made a sort of shrine to Mitchell in their bookshelves. Eventually he accepted an offer from Pantheon Books to reissue a large, handsome edition of his work, in 1992: *Up in the Old Hotel*, for which he received the Brendan Gill Award, given to the year's greatest contribution to New York culture. Sitting at the awards luncheon among his admirers, he seemed a courtly, birdlike presence, enjoying his meal and rising to accept the compliments of strangers (including myself).

A few years later, in 1996, he passed away. And now he is both one of the gods of American nonfiction, and largely forgotten and unread—a combination not entirely paradoxical if you consider the low esteem in which belletristic, nonfiction prose is held in our culture.

When I walk the waterfront, sometimes feeling a courtly apparition at my elbow, I am tempted to call out, "Joe, is that you? What do you make of what they're doing to your harbor?" He found *his* waterfront real. That was the whole thing in a nutshell. It seems a dubious, wishful idea: that reality only adheres to the poor, the derelict, the grimy, the wet; that the powerful are abstract and unreal. Still, we've all had that feeling at times.

19

THE SOUTH STREET SEAPORT (CONTINUED)

I WAS WANDERING AROUND THE SOUTH STREET SEAPORT AREA WITH BARBARA MENSCH, A PHOTOGRAPHER WHO HAS LIVED IN THAT NEIGHBORHOOD FOR DECADES AND HAS SEEN all its changes. Barbara did a great series of photographs on the Fulton Fish Market, which became a book. She remembers when Peck Slip was a very important part of the fish market: on winter nights all the oil cans were lit with fires, the fish were laid out, and the hand wagons rumbled over the cobblestones. At 40 Peck Slip, she says, there used to be something called the Club on the second floor (above the present Market Bar), where numbers, loansharking, and other recreational activities of an illegal nature went on. Crime, says Barbara, was an accepted part of the fish market scene. Security guards who had just gotten out of the can themselves for theft would be hired by the stall owners. The market, she says, was not about fish so much as it was about survival, trying to keep afloat a way of life ("call it *goombah* or white ethnic working class or street smarts"); it was living by your wits with improvised cons at the border of legality. In the end, that way of life could not survive here: it fell to the corporations and realtors who call the tune in this city, and who practiced a smoother type of dishonesty, breaking their promises to the fish-dealers.

Barbara spoke warmly about that period in her life when she was gradually accepted by these rough, sentimental men, enough to let themselves be photographed and interviewed, and to let her hang around all night watching the market operate at full blast. The only other women who were down there were prostitutes, she said.

Barbara is slender, small, and intense; everything she brings into a conversation she cares so deeply about that, finally, neither of you knows how to get her back to a calmer, more mundane place, except by interrupting her brusquely and changing the subject, which tactic she seems not to mind at all. A single mother, she exemplifies a certain type of scarred, courageous New York City woman; then she'll lighten up, especially looking at the city she loves, and start to laugh.

She remembers when an icehouse stood on the old dock where Pier 17 is now, and the fish were sorted there, fresh off the boats. She remembers going to community meetings and trying with others to talk the Rouse Corporation into saving more of the fish market and the surrounding atmosphere. But New York was undergoing severe financial difficulties at the time, and the Rouse Corporation, which had made such a success of Boston's Faneuil Hall (and was about to do Baltimore Harbor), held the upper hand in negotiations with the city, and demanded several concessions that would make it more like a shopping mall: some old buildings at Peck Slip were torn down, the sidewalks were widened, and a large, signature "festival marketplace" pavilion was built out on a pier. Pier 17, this big, red, barnlike structure with its chain boutiques and overpriced, vista-offering restaurants, which I hated when it first appeared (what do red barns have to do with the waterfront?), now seems to me tolerable, harmless, almost benign. Its best feature is a bleacher view of the harbor—one of the most dramatic places from which to watch what is left of the East River boat traffic; and, if not the "instant urban landmark" of "vernacular waterfront architecture" the *AIA Guide* proclaimed it to be, in any event it is not what is essentially wrong with the South Street Seaport. For that, you have to cross the street to the inland side.

There you find the 1883 Fulton Market Building, where all manner of goods that came in off the boat or from the neighboring district (fruits, vegetables, meats, rags, paper) were once sold at indoor stalls. There the Rouse Corporation "preserved" the structure's exterior while dividing up the honeycomb-stalled interior into a few large retail boxes. The first stores leased were more local and oriented toward the maritime trades, based on the model of Mystic Seaport, Connecticut. But as these folded, they were replaced by national chains. In fact, nothing seems to succeed here for long. Currently the Gap shares the building with Bridgewater, a private club. Shades of Chelsea Piers, where once-active public spaces overlooking the waterfront have given way to private catering halls. A shame; if only they had tried harder to retain the crowded market-stall atmosphere, they could have created a genuine magnet.

But when you look west up Fulton Street just beyond the restored Seaport, to the gigantic steel-and-glass financial-service skyscrapers rimming it, you realize that it barely matters whether the stores placed in the Fulton Market made it or not; their true importance was in providing a quaint, sanitized backdrop for the new towers.

Barbara remembers when the river-end of Fulton Street, which is cobblestoned, had an ordinary asphalt surface; the workmen had to dig up the asphalt and lay down fresh cobblestones to get the proper Ye Olde Seaport effect, and when they ran out of cobblestones, they stole some from the adjoining streets. The irony is that many of the streets surrounding the Seaport Museum are truly, convincingly old; along narrow, cobbled alleys, grimy brick walkups with Dutch gables and boarded-up windows are still allowed to present a tenement face to the world. She shows me a part she especially likes, on Front Street, where the jerry-built, pitch-patched backs of the fish market buildings look irresistibly picturesque; probably they were once sailors' boardinghouses. After the Fulton Fish Market is relocated to the Bronx, Barbara thinks, these ancient abandoned wrecks that have seen more than their share of crime and murder will be renovated and sold as townhouses for over a million apiece. "It'll be like Georgetown," she says.

A community of serious artists once lived in the Seaport neighborhood: Agnes Martin, Mark di Suvero, Clyfford Still and Ellsworth Kelly, Red Grooms and Christo all occupied semi-illegal lofts in these abandoned warehouses. The fish market also drew a plethora of drifters ("smokeys," they were called) and alley cats, says Barbara. She points to a parking lot in front of the Fulton Market Building and says that it used to be a dry dock for boat repairs. Another parking lot on Peck Slip once contained some fine old buildings, but they burned in a fire. All empty spaces previously filled by market functions or habitations are now, automatically, it would seem, given over to parking. In addition, much of the area underneath the highway viaduct, just south of the Seaport, is turned over to tourist buses, whose engines are kept running in idle most of the time.

On a winter day in March, temperature in the low thirties, we have an adventure. Barbara has told me about some fascinating rooms *inside* the Brooklyn Bridge, which she was permitted to photograph during a recent period of maintenance work, when a supporting beam needed replacement. I've long known about the vaults on the Brooklyn anchorage side, and even attended gallery exhibits there, but these interior spaces on the Manhattan anchorage side are news to me. I insist on her showing me them. As we approach the chain-link fence that cordons off the bridge from the street, she notices that a metal door in the bridge's stone façade is off its hinges, a good sign; it means that, theoretically at least, we can get inside the bridge if we can manage to scale the fence.

After some discussion about who is going to lead the way, and much looking nervously about, she climbs over first, tearing her jacket in the process. I start to hoist myself up, though I am having second thoughts about this, worried about tearing my own jacket, when some beat-up guy with front teeth missing, who has been watching us and smiling at our efforts, says, "There's an easier way. Just go down to the end, the second fence gate, you can pull it apart easy and slip in." I climb down and make my way to the gate he has described, Barbara meanwhile crossing the lot from her end to meet me. Sure enough, it's simple to wedge my body inside there.

The concrete lot between the fence and the bridge is home to mounds of abandoned tires, black garbage bags, and smelly debris. The chain-link fence has RESERVED SPACE signs hanging on it, left over from a period when the lot was leased for parking. It's amazing that such a trashed-out area should adjoin one of our most beloved national monuments. I mean, can you imagine such a dumping ground allowed to fester near the Eiffel Tower or Mount Fuji? That's New York for you. We pass a black homeless man warming himself by a wastebasket with a fire lit at the bottom. By looking away, he gives us to understand that he is not a threat.

Barbara moves the metal door aside, reassuring me that it will be all right, and slides in on her back, through a hole about three feet by three feet. Somehow I too manage to squeeze in on my back, and find myself in a pitch-black chamber. "Give yourself a minute or two for your eyes to adjust to the dark," she says. "Usually I take a flashlight with me, but I didn't know we'd be doing this today." She grabs my hand and leads the way, cautioning me to move slowly. The floor feels like a combination of wood and earth. I am beginning to make out dim shapes, pieces of discarded wrought iron on the floor, and, up ahead, a staircase. "This used to be a factory," she says. We inch toward the staircase, which has an elegant iron bannister, very old, rusty and dirty. I notice a lightbulb dangling from the ceiling and wonder if the power is still connected. Maybe the city is still paying the electric bill from its last maintenance job. The bannister has a gap of about a foot somewhere up ahead. Barbara tells me to shift my weight to the other side when we reach that hiatus. One of the steps is very tippy, but I feel reasonably secure, moving slowly, testing every footfall. We reach the second floor, which seems much more like a factory studio. Little half-moons, holes in the brick façade, give us all the daylight we need. I see a toilet bowl ripped out and on its side. The ceiling has a series of arches in it. A small shaft of light triangulates a corner of a wall, revealing a verdigris pattern of decay. The walls are brick—I am tempted to say "exposed brick," as if this were a decor decision, though the only decorative principle operating here is total abandonment. It is fantastically beautiful—a combination of the architecture's original nobility and the serendipitous outcropping effects achieved by ruins—and sad. To think of the derelict state this national treasure has been allowed to fall into! I had always thought the Brooklyn Bridge was well maintained.

On the third floor there is much more light, because on either end of the floor an entire arched window has been punched out, and nothing but sky left in its place. I walk over and look down at the cars struggling up the ramp onto the Brooklyn-bound side, a road I have taken hundreds of times myself. Now I am above them, looking down at them/me. Still farther above me, on the structure's roof, hundreds of cars pass unseen. From inside the Bridge I can hear little, it's fairly quiet. What's most amazing on this third floor is the vaulted wooden ceiling, which looks like the keel of a canoe. Barbara tells me that different materials were used on each side: brick and wood in the Manhattan anchorage, and stone on the Brooklyn end. Incongruously, a basketball hoop sits atop a wooden pole in the middle of the room.

It seems, according to Barbara's research, that John Roebling, the first designer of the Brooklyn Bridge, had planned the largest vaulted spaces as a market hall, which, in his words, would "sooner or later supersede the old Fulton Market." He had also envisioned some of the fortress-thick tunnels and vaults being used to store bonds or currency—exploiting the bridge's proximity to Wall Street. But when the banks showed no interest, the lofts were adopted for light industry and warehousing. A Department of Bridges report, 1898, lists a rent roll of twenty-eight tenants for these spaces, with purposes such as cold storage, machinery, radiators, leather, printing, wine, lamps, stables, grocers' supplies, filtering, iron, junk, cooperage, and ship chandlery. The last business to be listed, the Hide and Skin Trucking Corporation, moved out of the anchorage by the beginning of the 1970s. If these rooms were ever cleaned up, they would make idyllic artists' lofts. Barbara says she would love to have a studio here, as would every Downtown artist she knows. I am thinking they would also make wonderful screening rooms. With a mixture of regret and relief, we crawl back out into the early evening.

YOU GET AN INKLING of life alongside the Brooklyn Bridge when it was first built from this passage in *Darkness and Daylight* (1893) by Mrs. Helen Campbell, one of those sun-and-shadow guidebooks that revealed the secret squalors of New York: "Under the great Bridge stands a tenement house so shadowed by the vast structure that, save at midday, natural light barely penetrates it. . . . The women who cannot afford the gas or oil that must burn if they work in the daytime sleep while day lasts; and when night comes, and the searching rays of the electric light penetrates every corner of their shadowy rooms, turn to the toil by which their bread is won. Heavy-eyed women toil at the washboard or run the sewing-machine, and when sunrise has come and the East River and the beautiful harbor are aflame with color, the light for these buildings is extinguished. . . ."

My late friend Rudy Burckhardt, the Swiss-born photographer and experimental filmmaker, made a twenty-minute film, *Under the Brooklyn Bridge* (1947), a city symphony that captures indelibly, as in a time capsule, what the industrial area around the bridge looked like immediately after the Second World War. I have watched it dozens of times and still ache to possess its elusive beauty by heart. In the first scene, the ornamental details of an already-hoary warehouse-and-factory architecture—the massive arches, the stone-carved heads, the beam-anchoring stars implanted in brick façades—are placed against the larger, fabulous, gossamer-granite, spectral structure of the bridge itself. The second scene shows the demolition of a substantial building facing the bridge: workmen hammer at the stone, tie rope to both ends of a wall and pull it apart, cart bricks away in wheelbarrows, dump debris down a chute into a waiting truck, drive tractors through rubble mounds, while a supervisor stands by, chewing gum. Time-lapse photography shows the sturdy warehouse coming down floor after floor, like a chocolate layer cake consumed by tiers. In scene three, the men are on their lunch break, eating packed sandwiches on a building deck or crowding into a workers' café. Their faces are suspicious, appetite-driven, sharing a craggy obduracy with the materials they demolish. A lifetime of physical labor has left them hardened but calm. The waiters and countermen who serve them look equally battered. In the distance, through the window glass, looms the Brooklyn Bridge, a favorite Burckhardt touch. Episode four is an urban arcadia of a half-dozen boys swimming in the East River. These neighborhood kids look Italian or Puerto Rican: they make their way past grass, weeds, and rotting pilings, improvise a plank as a diving board, and leap in, some buck naked, their penises wagging like bell clappers, others in underpants; one crossing himself before the dive, another sunning on a rock afterwards. Theirs is a private boy's world of audacity and laughter, before the public's awareness of

PCBs. The East River was polluted back then, but evidently not enough to stop the young and intrepid. In the next scene, women workers, white and black, leave their factories and head for the subway. Together they walk with an unhurried ceremoniousness tinged with bone-fatigue under monumental, arched vaults and past empty lots. Some have on half-moon forties hats; all wear either blouses and skirts or dresses, and look pin-neat at the end of the workday. Burckhardt ends his film with a few long shots of the area, deserted now, to the haunted piano score of Robert Fitzdale and Arthur Gold, and one last glimpse of a tugboat cutting under the mighty span at night.

20

THE BROOKLYN BRIDGE

ONFRONTING THE WORLD'S MOST RECOGNIZABLE, REPRODUCED MONUMENTS ̄THE EIFFEL TOWER, THE PYRAMIDS, THE ACROPOLIS, THE COLOSSEUM, THE Brooklyn Bridge—the mind tends to go numb. So much devotion has been lavished on these by-now primal shapes, they seem hard-wired into our imaginations, iconically omnipresent and therefore refractory to awe. Still, we long to feel the same shiver our ancestors did; and sometimes we have what approximates a religious experience in their proximity, either because of or despite the programming we've received. The rest of the time we must scrape away apathy and make a conscious effort to rekindle our wonderment, by exploring the historical ground against which they first stood out as miraculous.

Of all the world's grand monuments, the oddest, I would think, is the Brooklyn Bridge, because it is so purely functional. This paradox was articulated by America's first important architectural critic, Montgomery Schuyler, when he wrote in 1883, the year it opened: "It so happens that the work which is likely to be our most durable monument, and to convey some knowledge of us to the most remote posterity, is a work of bare utility; not a shrine, not a fortress, not a palace, but a bridge."

The Brooklyn Bridge has remained celebrated and cherished, long after its technological achievements have been superseded. It was not the first successful suspension bridge in America; it is no longer the longest in the country, or even necessarily the most beautiful in New York; some, like Le Corbusier, would argue for the George Washington Bridge. Yet it is hard to imagine the GW Bridge receiving the lavish national attention on its hundredth birthday that the Brooklyn Bridge generated on its 1983 centenary. Why has the Brooklyn span remained so alive in the popular culture?

Because it has had the capacity to make itself lovable. Beautiful it may also be, but "lovable" is a different quality; it suggests the knack of inspiring tenderness. If the Brooklyn Bridge began as a magisterial, solitary alpine range connecting the two great cities of Manhattan and Brooklyn, it soon enough had company across the East River: the Williamsburg Bridge opened in 1903, the Manhattan Bridge in 1905. These siblings forever gamboling at their elder brother's side, elbowing their raw profiles into view, meant that the Brooklyn Bridge had to be revered for something other than its riparian-spanning properties. Aesthetics and tradition both came to the rescue.

First, aesthetics: the Brooklyn Bridge is, without a doubt, soaringly, stubbornly handsome. There is the elegance of the catenary curve (the natural form taken by any rope or cable suspended from two points) as it swoops down to the center, and then scallops upward toward the towers; the visual cross-thatching of vertical cables and diagonal stays, yielding an effect that has been compared to a harp, a spider's web, angels' wings; the unearthly collision of materials: the airy steel wire of the cables and stays—it was the first bridge to rely solely on steel for such purposes—against the staunch granite towers. Its towers seemed at the time the one opportunity to make a consciously monumental statement. In an architecturally eclectic period, faced with the option of borrowing from any historical style (neoclassical, Gothic, French Renaissance), its makers chose Gothic for the gateways to the two cities. It was this very dissonance of sleek steel and old-fashioned granite that annoyed Montgomery Schuyler in his early, proto-modernist assessment, "The Brooklyn Bridge as Monument." After acknowledging that the bridge was perhaps the finest, most enduring structure of the day, Schuyler took issue with the anachronistic heaviness of the Gothic stylings, wishing instead that the towers could have better "revealed" structurally the cables they contained within. It was as though he had in mind a pure steel structure like the George Washington Bridge, which is indeed more harmonious, from a modernist aesthetic viewpoint. But the Brooklyn Bridge is more endearing, more—lovable, precisely because it exemplifies that tension, held in stately balance, between old and new, handmade and industrial, granite and gossamer.

Adding to its endearing qualities are the heroic legends about its four-teen-year construction, which still cling to its girders. That Iliadic tale of the struggle to build the Brooklyn Bridge has been told many times, most definitively in David McCullough's fine book *The Great Bridge:* how the stern, brilliant German immigrant engineer John Augustus Roebling, ex-student of Hegel, having successfully solved the riddle of making suspension bridges safe (maximum stiffness), was offered the assignment to span the East River; how he became its first victim, his toes crushed in a pier accident, leading to tetanus and death; how his son, Washington Roebling, he of calm integrity and superhuman persistence, took over the task, assembled a loyal projects team, mostly fellow alumni from Rensselaer Polytechnic Institute, and set about resourcefully meeting each of the challenges with technological inventions; how they battled the elements and turbulent tides and geological surprises of the East River; how they built two enormous compressed-air foundations, or caissons, each weighing 6 million pounds, and sank them underwater to dredge and anchor the towers; how the laborers, working eight-hour shifts with primitive equipment (no power tools!) in these ill-lit, poorly ventilated, sweltering underwater conditions for two dollars a day, began to suffer from caisson sickness, or "the bends," which crippled them; how their boss, Washington Roebling, investigating a fire in the caisson, himself contracted the illness and became an invalid for life, forced to attend the bridge's construction from his window with a spyglass; how he developed, along with the physical disease, a nervous disorder—a neurotically unsociable manner close to misanthropy; how his devoted wife, Emily, played the "bridge" with his associates and employers, smoothing over public demands for her husband's resignation as chief engineer; how gluttonous William Macy Tweed, ruler of Tammany Hall, saw this massive public work as a splendid opportunity for graft and almost took it, but the Tweed Ring was exposed and busted in the nick of time; how a corrupt supplier of steel wire, a bigamist mountebank who gained the contract through political kickbacks, managed to smuggle in substandard materials, despite Roebling's orders that every yard of wire be personally inspected; how it didn't matter, finally, because Roebling had already factored in that the bridge be built to six times its necessary strength; how it mattered only symbolically, in that there would always be invisible weaknesses woven into the bridge's near-perfection, just as blood was admixed into its joints and bolts from the deaths of more than twenty workmen.

As Alan Trachtenberg has pointed out in his excellent study, *Brooklyn Bridge:* "For many Americans in 1883, Brooklyn Bridge proved the nation to be healed of its wounds of civil war and again on its true course: the peaceful mastery of nature." It was the age of engineer-heroes (de Lesseps, Roebling) and engineering feats, and nothing stirred the public's romantic sentiment more than bridges. "Babylon had her hanging garden, Egypt her pyramid, Athens her Acropolis, Rome her Atheneum; so Brooklyn has her Bridge," boasted a shopkeeper sign on the holiday of its opening. The bridge had been strung with lightbulbs, making it the first electrified span over water. But such innovations, again, are easily forgotten: what kept the Brooklyn Bridge alive in the minds of people was its significance in the mythos and daily life of New York City. The bridge unified two great cities as physically as a rope tied around their waists: it had been purposely designed in such a way as to connect New York's City Hall with the City Hall of Brooklyn; to extend, as it were, Broadway to Fulton Street. The success of the bridge preempted charter revision: it made the amalgamation of the five boroughs a few years later, in 1898, into one super-metropolis, a kind of inevitability, an afterthought.

"I hereby prophecy that in 1900 A.D. Brooklyn will be the city and New York will be the suburb," wrote George Templeton Strong in his diary in 1865. "It is inevitable if both go on growing as they have grown for the last forty years. Brooklyn has room to spread and New York has not." Brooklyn was the coming place; no one anticipated Manhattan would grow vertically. It was Brooklyn, then the fifth-largest city in the nation, that had agitated most for the bridge, thinking correctly that it would drive up the value of its Heights real estate and attract middle-class businessmen, by making their commute easier than the unreliable, icebound ferries. It was Brooklyn that had supplied the vast majority of planning and political energies for the building of the bridge, and paid the lion's share of its construction costs. So it was only fair that what had been originally called "the East River Bridge" would undergo a name change to honor its sponsoring agent. The irony is that the bridge both put Brooklyn on the map and diminished it forever, by undermining its urban independence. However much the residents of Kings County might cling to their faith that Brooklyn was still the emerging urban hub, its destiny was to be a provincial, if eccentric, bedroom borough to Manhattan.

For Manhattanites, the bridge became, as David McCullough put it, "a highway into the open air." One of Roebling's great design decisions had been to been to build an elevated promenade, which would arch ever so slightly, so as to bow *above* the traffic. The walker would have the freedom of the city: to look down at vehicles crossing the bridge (first horse-carriages and elevated trains; later cars), or else to ignore them and gaze uninterruptedly in every direction, at the water, the boats (innumerable, during the East River's heyday as a port), the skyline, and the sky itself.

From where else can one see the whole city today? From skyscraper observatories, certainly, such as the Empire State Building, but one has to pay a fee, and then, once aloft, the pacing possibilities have distinct limits; whereas the Brooklyn Bridge promenade is an extension of the street system, a great free thoroughfare.

Governor Al Smith, in his autobiography, *Up to Now,* recalled: "In those early days the bridge served as more than a utility for transportation between the two cities. It soon became a place of recreation and of pleasure. So much so that it was referred to in songs and popularized on the variety stage. I can still sing 'Danny by my side.'

The Brooklyn Bridge on Sunday is known as lover's lane,
I stroll there with my sweetheart, oh, time and time again;
Oh, how I love to ramble, oh, yes, it is my pride,
Dressed in my best, each day of rest, with Danny by my side."

The lordly position of the pedestrian on the promenade must have suited Washington Roebling, who refused to enter a motorcar in his lifetime (he died in 1920). On the other hand, there is irony in the fact that this superb public space was built by a man who, after his bout with caisson sickness, hated to be in crowds, and found it a torment to socialize with anyone but his wife for more than a few minutes.

The bridge was also inspiration to poets and loners. Lewis Mumford, in his autobiography, *Sketches From Life,* told how the Brooklyn Bridge figured in a key experience of his dawning manhood. On a March day, the then-youthful Mumford was walking into Manhattan at twilight, and "as I reached the middle of the Brooklyn Bridge, the sunlight spread across the sky, forming a halo around the jagged mountain of skyscrapers, with the darkened loft buildings and warehouses huddling below in the foreground. The towers, topped by the golden pinnacles of the new Woolworth Building, still caught the light even as it began to ebb away. Three-quarters of the way across the bridge I saw the skyscrapers in the deepening darkness become slowly honeycombed with lights until, before I reached the Manhattan end, these buildings piled up in a dazzling mass against the indigo sky.

"Here was my city, immense, overpowering, flooded with energy and light. . . . And there was I, breasting the March wind, drinking in the city and the sky, both vast, yet contained in me, transmitting through me the great mysterious will that made them and the promise of the new day that was still to come." Mumford, looking backward half a century, remembers being filled with an exaltation he compares to "the wonder of an orgasm in the body of one's beloved." He says: "In that sudden revelation of power and beauty all the confusions of adolescence dropped from me, and I trod the narrow, resilient boards of the footway with a new confidence that came, not from my isolated self alone but from the collective energies I had confronted and risen to."

Here the Brooklyn Bridge is a cradle for self-creation. Like Rastignac in Balzac's *Père Goriot*, waving his fist at Paris below and swearing he will conquer it someday, Mumford vows to extract the fullest from his talents, and to affect the city stretched tantalizingly around him. The bridge's elevated, 360-degree vantage point inspired feelings of wholeness bordering on omnipotence.

The Russian poet Vladimir Mayakovsky, in his poem "Brooklyn Bridge," compared the structure to a dinosaur, one of those "huge giant lizards" from which future geologists could re-create our world, and whose bones alone would survive the apocalyptic twentieth century. Henry James, returning to his native city after years abroad, recorded with something like horror, in his travel book *The American Scene*, his reaction to the span as an enormous steam engine and power loom, as well as a sort of Frankenstein monster: "One has the sense that the monster grows and grows, flinging abroad its loose limbs even as some unmannered young giant at his 'larks,' and that the binding stitches must forever fly further and faster and draw harder; the future complexity of the web, all under sky and above the sea, becoming thus that of some colossal set of clockworks, some steel-souled machine-room of brandished arms and hammering fists and opening and closing jaws."

For James, writing in 1907, the Brooklyn Bridge was still too new—too suggestive of the ominous threat of industrialized conformity—to be cherished as a work of local genius. But Hart Crane saw and understood the lonely grandeur and achievement of the bridge from a more sympathetic, historically removed perspective. He had researched the Roeblings with an eye toward writing their biography. To inhabit their inner world, he rented the same apartment on Hicks Street, in Brooklyn Heights, from which Washington Roebling had overseen the bridge's construction. "Brooklyn Bridge," wrote Crane to his family, is "the most superb piece of construction in the modern world, I'm sure, with strings of lights crossing it like glowing worms as the Ls and surface cars pass each other coming and going." He chose it as his symbol of American affirmation in *The Bridge* (1927–30), his response to Eliot's *The Waste Land.* Among its many gorgeous, exhilarating lines are these in the prologue, addressed directly "To Brooklyn Bridge":

O harp and altar, of the fury fused,
(How could mere toil align thy choiring strings!)

Crane encircles the bridge with spiritual connotations: a "curveship," like an alien spaceship dropped down from the galaxies, it redeems the prophet's pledges, sets up heavenly choirs, lifts night in its arms, condenses eternity, and, to top it all, lends its own myth to a God who seems in need of one, in our secular age.

It is interesting that so many of the most memorable paeans to the Brooklyn Bridge, in poetry (Crane, Mayakovsky, García Lorca), prose (John Dos Passos, Thomas Wolfe, Henry Miller), and paint (Joseph Stella, John Marin, Albert Gleizes, Marsden Hartley,) were fashioned just after the First World War through the twenties and thirties, when the structure had already been standing for a number of decades. It no longer was a technological novelty, but its glamour had, if anything, skyrocketed. Why this should be may have as much to do with the development of modernism—and American modernism in particular—as with any singularities of the Brooklyn Bridge.

In his 1924 *Port of New York,* Paul Rosenfeld gathered a collection of his essays on fourteen American moderns, who included Arthur Dove, John Marin, William Carlos Williams, Alfred Stieglitz, Georgia O'Keeffe, and Marsden Hartley. He analyzed what he called "the drama of cultural awakening" in America of the 1920s, using the Port of New York as a central organizing image. No longer was it necessary for bohemians and artists to go abroad, Rosenfeld argued. "For what we once could feel only by quitting New York—the fundamental oneness we have with the place and the people in it—that is sensible to us today in the very jostling, abstracted streets of the city. We know it here, our relationship with this place in which we live. The buildings cannot deprive us of it. For they and we have suddenly commenced growing together." If the buildings were entwining roots into the artists' souls, how much more so their beloved Bridge, the mother of local modernism, which spanned this self-same, essential Port of New York?

SUCH FERVENT, MYTHIFYING WORSHIP could not continue at the same heat. It was too much to put on any bridge, even the most awesomely endearing. The literary tributes fell away, though Roebling's wonder continued to be the most photographed bridge in the world.

Crossing it today, you are made aware of the tense play of light and shadow in the Brooklyn Bridge's form: the granite arches that loom like minarets beckoning the traveler to prayer; the haunting shadow of the bridge on water; the serpentine plunge of the span's railing, like a roller-coaster descending into the high-rise city. Then there is the relationship between the bridge and the metropolis: on one side, flamboyant, vertical Manhattan; on the other, a more horizontal, spread-out Brooklyn.

I remember admiring the terrifying acrobatic cool of ironworkers, these sky-walkers who function, as the saying goes, without a net, when they repaired the bridge some years back. (The nets that were strung up, incidentally, were installed to protect the vehicles and pedestrians, not the repair workers.) How calm they looked in their hardhats as they perched over the river, one misstep away from catastrophe, drinking their coffee through ski masks necessitated by the bitter cold.

"When the perfected East River bridge shall permanently and uninterruptedly connect the two cities," predicted a reporter for the *Brooklyn Eagle*, Thomas Kinsella, with some regret, "the daily thousands who cross it will consider it a sort of natural and inevitable phenomenon, such as the rising and setting of the sun, and they will unconsciously overlook the preliminary difficulties surmounted before the structure spanned the stream, and will perhaps undervalue the indomitable courage, the absolute faith, the consummate genius which assured the engineer's triumph." Seeing those ironworkers restoring the bridge returned me to the original romance of its making. "How could mere toil align thy choiring strings!" demanded Hart Crane. But apparently mere toil did—and does, in a mutual dependency between nature and humanity, stone and sweat, that is as ancient to monuments as it is noble.

21

UNDER THE BRIDGES

ALONG THE RIVERSIDE, BETWEEN THE BROOKLYN AND
MANHATTAN BRIDGES, RUNS A PLEASANT ESPLANADE
(DESIGNED BY CARR, LYNCH AND SANDELL, 1997),
which is the first section of the East River Bikeway and Esplanade. A
plaque informs us that one day it will extend from Pier A in the Battery
up to East 63rd Street, where it will join with the esplanade that runs all
the way to 125th Street. This first stage, with its square gray paving stones,
curved metal benches, separated pedestrian and bike lanes, and attractive
fences, not too high, overlooking the seawall, exists underneath the FDR
Drive, sunless and noisy with the thud of cars going over metal plates and
asbestos seams.

On the Labor Day weekend when I check out the esplanade, it is mostly being used by Asian-Americans who have walked over from nearby Chinatown: a pregnant woman in a pink gingham dress strolling with her friend, a serious, bespectacled young couple holding hands as they roller-skate, an elderly man fishing, a grumpy, middle-aged pair having an irritable discussion on a bench (no point in my eavesdropping, I can't understand a word of Cantonese). A few amateur photographers are snapping the glorious Brooklyn views: a river sunset, the Watchtower buildings, the Brooklyn Bridge, the River Café, the Empire Stores. A plane flies by with a streamer attached: ANDREA I LOVE YOU WILL YOU MARRY ME LENNY. No one near me jumps up and down, so we have to assume Andrea is elsewhere.

A teenage girl, Indian, beckons to a smaller black girl, walking from the opposite direction with her pals: "Hello! How you doing, birthday girl?" She runs up to hug her, while a boy (most likely the celebrated one's brother) mutters, "It's tomorrow."

The Manhattan Bridge, it would appear from this angle underneath, has been newly painted a dark forest green. I approve. It looks almost as good now as the Brooklyn Bridge. I pass a homeless man reclining on a bench under several heavy woolen blankets, though it's seventy degrees outside. As I come up alongside him, I see wide-open eyes staring straight out of a handsome, intensely wary, black male face.

Across the street is the Soviet-style concrete edifice, long unoccupied (though rented out for film shoots), that used to contain the editorial offices and printing presses of the *New York Post*. I delivered press releases and liquor bottles there, one summer between my first and second years of college, when I worked as a mailboy and messenger for a Midtown public relations company. On lucky days I would get sent out of the mailroom, bearing gifts to the city desk editors at the *Post*, the *Journal-American*, and the *World Telegram and Sun* (for some reason I was never sent to the more respectable papers, such as the *Times* or the *Herald Tribune*: either they had a stricter policy about accepting bribes, or else someone higher up was dispatched for those deliveries). I would walk along South Street reading a thick paperback edition of *The Brothers Karamazov*, hoping to impress the receptionists behind the receiving window, as I wordlessly handed over my envelope or bottle of Scotch.

. . .

A BLOCK OR SO NORTH of the Brooklyn Bridge, just behind the old New York Post Building, between Catherine and Market Streets, squats Knickerbocker Village. This unassuming enclave of bare brick apartment towers, privately managed, which might easily be mistaken for one of the nearby government projects, made history as the first major housing development even partially supported by public funds. Though currently in scale with everything around it, it seemed huge when it opened in 1934, "a blockbuster," according to the *AIA Guide to New York City*, which added that "it maintains its reasonably well-kept lower-middle-class air today." The other historical significance of Knickerbocker Village is that it stands on the same site as the notorious Lung Block, which it obliterated.

Whenever we are tempted to bemoan the monotony of these brick high-rise compounds that dominate the riverbanks of the Lower East Side, we might stop for a moment and think about all the Lung Blocks that used to populate the site.

Ernest Poole, the journalist and novelist of *The Harbor* whom I discussed earlier, wrote journalistic exposés about the Lung Block, which had the highest tuberculosis incidence of any street in the city. Poole was part of a circle of idealistic young reformers (including Isaac N. Phelps-Stokes, who later wrote the monumental study *The Iconography of Manhattan Island*) trying to raise a moral outcry about housing conditions in the Lower East Side. In *The Bridge*, his 1940 memoirs, he describes how he went down to the Lower East Side in 1902:

The Lung Block, as I named it then, was far down on the East Side near the river. In early years, when that quarter was a center of fashion in our town, many of the buildings had been great handsome private homes, but long ago they had been turned into grimy rookeries, the spacious rooms divided into little cell-like chambers, many only stifling closets with no outer light or air. I can still smell the odors there. In what had been large yards behind, cheap rear tenements had been built, leaving between front and rear buildings only deep dank filthy courts. Nearly four thousand people lived on the block and, in rooms, halls, on stairways, in courts and out on fire escapes, were scattered some four hundred babies. Homes and people, good and bad, had only thin partitions between them. A thousand families struggled on, while many sank and polluted the others. The Lung Block had eight thriving barrooms and five houses of ill fame. And with drunkenness, foul air, darkness and filth to feed upon, the living germs of the Great White Plague [tuberculosis], coughed up and spat on floors and walls, had done a thriving business for years.

Poole vividly described a young, tubercular Jew, near death, crying out for more air. The paradoxical proximity of the Lung Block to the expansive, world-connecting river was also noted:

There was a huge Danish woman too, on the Lung Block, who became my friend. Sailors came and stayed with her, "deep-water" sailors, by which I mean that they shipped on voyages around the Horn to Singapore and Shanghai and other fascinating ports. As gifts or loans when they sailed away, they had left a lively marmoset, a scarlet parrot, heathen idols, painted shells and other things that pulled my thoughts out of the stinking rooms near by and sent them careering far off over the Seven Seas. I sometimes felt the Wanderlust and, in those lovely days of spring, wandered along the East River piers where lay the last of the ships with sails, listening for "chanteys" of their crews as they heaved on the ropes and slowly, slowly the big ships moved out on the river, bound by the sea. But from such whiffs of the ocean world back I would dive into the Lung Block, all the more bitter that human beings should be choked to death in such foul holes, when there was so much fresh air and health and sunlight so close by.

Poole went to work, writing up the horrors in strong muckraking fashion. A radical friend, scoffing at the notion that the pen was mightier than the sword, told him, "What the Lung Block needs is the ax." (Later, Robert Moses would similarly remark that "when you operate in an overbuilt metropolis, you have to hack your way with a meat ax.") Undaunted, Poole shouldered on: "My report was featured in the press. Reporters came to write up the block. I took them around, with photographers. Hearings were held up at Albany. I gave my testimony there. So we raised hell with the politicians, and at twenty-three I thought that our campaign would succeed. I was wrong. For the landlords on the Lung Block had many influential friends. So came delays, delays, delays, until in the papers the story grew cold. It took thirty-two years to bring the ax. It came at last, under the New Deal. The rotten old block was razed to the ground and in its place you may see today the airy sunny apartment houses of Knickerbocker Village."

Fred C. French, the same developer who had built Tudor City a few years earlier (1925–31), put together Knickerbocker Village, which, completed in 1933, housed 4,000 persons on five acres in twelve-story blocks around inner courts. During the Depression, the federal government had made available a small pot of funds for private developers nationwide to clear slums and construct housing developments in their stead, based on a set of guidelines regarding building standards and occupational density. French had to travel to Washington more than fifty times, hat in hand, to get an $8-million loan from the federal government's Reconstruction Finance Corporation for the housing development. The sticking point was the government's objection that the complex had a density at least double that recommended by federal guidelines, but which the developer argued was needed for a satisfactory investment. In the end, the government agreed. French, who was both public-spirited and profit-minded,* helped offset the costs for buying the land and developing Knickerbocker Village in two ways: first, by raising the density of land use through taller apartment towers; and, second, by replacing low-income tenants with middle-income households. (This same strategy would be followed later by the Metropolitan Life Insurance Company, which tore down another chunk of the Lower East Side along the river to build Stuyvesant Town and Peter Cooper Village).

There is certainly an argument to be made for the state helping middle-class, white-collar workers in urban areas defray housing costs. Less valid was the argument employed that by subsidizing new housing for the

---

*French told some impressed Princeton students in 1934: "Our company, strangely enough, was the first business organization to recognize that profits could be earned negatively as well as positively in New York real estate—not only by constructing new buildings but by destroying, at the same time, whole areas of disgraceful and disgusting sores." (Quoted in Max Page's *The Creative Destruction of Manhattan*.)

middle class, you would then free up thousands of units for rental by low-income tenants. The trickle-down theory, applied to housing, proved as faulty as elsewhere, since rents in the vacated apartments were still beyond the reach of the poor. The effect of slum clearance on its inhabitants was thus to push them into new slums, as Anthony Jackson showed in his study of Manhattan low-cost housing, *A Place Called Home*. "When 386, mostly Italian, families had been forced to leave the old 'Lung Block' . . . to make way for Knickerbocker Village, four-fifths of them moved into other nearby tenements. At Stuyvesant Town, a survey showed that roughly three-quarters of the 3,000 displaced families would move into other slums."

NOT EVERYONE SAW THE SLUMS on the Lower East Side as blight. Jimmy Durante, the entertainer, who grew up in the Lung Block ward, reminisced to Joseph Mitchell about a time "'when the East Side amounted to something'. . . . Sitting there in the dark theater, nursing his hangover, the big-nosed comedian began to talk about his childhood, the days when he used to run wild on Catherine Street, raising hell with the other kids, the days when he liked to go barefooted and they had to run him down and catch him every winter to put shoes on him. . . ." Like most children who were reared in slums, he had a slightly different perspective from that of the housing reformers: "'We kids used to have a good time,' he said. 'They tore down where my home was and where my pop had his [barber] shop. They tore it down to put up this high-class tenement house, this Knickerbocker Village. Most of the old-timers moved out long ago."

There was, it seems, in the insular poverty of the Lower East Side, a yeasty substance breeding ambition along with despair. You have only to read the charged memoirs of Anzia Yezierska's *Red Ribbon on a White Horse* or Mike Gold's *Jews Without Money*, both writers from the Lower East Side, to sense their pride in the ghetto they were so desperate to escape. The emotional glue that bound the tenement dwellers to the Old Country dissolved when the rickety buildings were demolished and replaced by anonymous, modern high-rises. As Alfred Kazin wrote about a similar urban renewal, "despite my pleasure in all the space and light in

Brownsville . . . I miss her old, sly and withered face. I miss all those ratty little wooden tenements, born with the smell of damp in which there grew up so many school teachers, city accountants, rabbis, cancer specialists, functionaries of the revolution, and strong-arm men for Murder, Inc."

Some of the nostalgia of Kazin and Durante for slum-bred ambitions seems in retrospect a disguised ethnic boasting. The ghetto may have proven a launching pad for Jews and Italians to reach the middle class by the second generation, but it did not have the same catapult effect for the Hispanics and African-Americans who took their place. The new, non-white poor were in no position to organize protests at the razing of tenements, nor were they necessarily as attached to them as previous groups had been.

Thus, Robert Moses had a point in scoffing at the notion that "since the slums have bred so many remarkable people, and even geniuses, there must be something very stimulating in being brought up in them." But the more debatable point was Moses' leap from asserting that the "slum is still the chief cause of urban disease and decay" to contending that its "irredeemable rookeries" had to be eradicated. It takes a certain literalism to go from deploring the disease and crime in a poor neighborhood, to indicting the very buildings themselves as criminals. After all, the hovels that constituted the Lung Block had begun their existence in the early nineteenth century as respectable houses for well-off families; only later were they were subdivided and rented to the poor at unspeakable densities. Current medical science suggests that even the Lung Block buildings might have been spared—given a good disinfectant cleaning and spruced up, their rear tenements removed for better light and ventilation—and restored to salubrious respectability. But that is not how it appeared to most social reformers of the day (including those far more committed than Moses to helping the poor): they hated the suffering they witnessed in the tenements so much that they came to blame the very mortar, bricks, staircases, walls. Having invoked so often the metaphors of pathology (slums were described as "cancerous," "pestilential," "abscessed," "a tumor," "pus-filled,"), it seemed the most sensible course to call for their surgical removal.

. . .

AMONG THE LOWER-MIDDLE-CLASS STRIVERS attracted to Knickerbocker Village were Julius and Ethel Rosenberg, who moved into a three-room apartment in the spring of 1942. They paid $45.75 a month for their river-view, eleventh-floor accommodations, and made use of the project's nursery school and playground after they had children, and it was there, the bulk of evidence now suggests, that Julius conspired with Ethel's brother, David Greenglass, to spy for the Soviet Union.

Knickerbocker Village had one of the strongest and most insurgent tenant unions in the city, the Knickerbocker Village Tenants Association (KVTA). In 1947, when the landlord, French, tried to raise the rent 12 percent and evict tenants who exceeded income limits, the KVTA waged a campaign against him in the press and the courts, vowing a rent strike as well. I like to picture Julius going to these meetings and putting in his two cents' worth, though he probably regarded such local efforts as trivial, compared to stealing atomic secrets.

If you grew up in a Jewish ghetto in the 1950s, as I did, you could not escape the Rosenberg case. Newspaper photographs of Ethel in her mouton coat and upswept coif looked strikingly like my mother. In fact, every other woman in our neighborhood looked like Ethel: dark-eyed, pudgy, scared, self-righteous, and exalted with ideals of social justice. We felt personally imperiled by the Rosenbergs' persecution, removed as we were by less than a few degrees of separation. When my mother joined a fight to have a traffic light installed in front of our nursery school, many of her fellow protestors were Communists. She became friends with these Party members, up to a point, but then they bored her by turning every conversation into a political harangue. Never mind the millions of kulaks slain by Stalin, or the Moscow Show Trials; my mother didn't like Communists because they violated the rules of conversation. No one in my family, to my recollection, ever maintained the Rosenbergs' innocence; if anything, we assumed they were guilty, but thought they shouldn't be executed because the secrets they stole were probably small potatoes, and because capital punishment was wrong.

My Aunt Minna was a Communist: when my brother and I stayed one summer with her in California, she would get apoplectic as soon as anyone appeared on television who had named names. Lloyd Bridges in *Sea Hunt?* "He sang. Change the channel!" I thought of Communists as a slightly cracked set of familiars, character actors left over from the Yiddish theater, admirably wanting to make the world a better place, but rigid in their refusal to consider opposing facts. Who knows whether I might have joined the Party had I grown up in the thirties instead of the fifties? By the time I started college, in 1960, JFK was off to the White House, Arthur Schlesinger Jr. was advising him, and the Communist Party no longer counted, except as a joke. My mother told me, "If you're ever on unemployment insurance and they send you to interview for a job you don't want, just bring along a copy of *The Daily Worker*."

In one of the best New York waterfront movies, Samuel Fuller's *Pickup on South Street* (1953), a number of key scenes were set a stone's throw away from the Rosenbergs' apartment, on a South Street pier. Coincidentally, it revolved around a plot by Communist spies to steal government secrets. "If you don't cooperate," the FBI agent tells the cynical hero, "you'll be as guilty as those traitors who gave Stalin the A-bomb." The hero, or anti-hero (played by Richard Widmark), is a pickpocket who hides out in an abandoned bait shack, perched on pilings in the East River, and reached only by a flimsy catwalk. The atmospheric night scenes prove again that the waterfront and film noir make an irresistible combination. Through the shack window we glimpse the Manhattan Bridge, and a dependably passing tugboat or barge (courtesy of rear projection, since the film was really shot, for the most part, in California).

The great supporting actress Thelma Ritter gave the film's most memorable performance as Moe, an aging necktie peddler and stool pigeon in a tired flower-pint dress, who is saving up for a fancy funeral. She tells the threatening Communist agent, Joey, in her weary Brooklyn accent, "Look, mister, I'm so tired, you'd be doing me a big favor, blowing my head off." Moe and the Rosenbergs: both from the same New York working-class milieu, striving to reach the lower middle class; both doomed to a premature, unnatural death by the Cold War.

Apparently Julius and Ethel felt cramped in their small apartment in Knickerbocker Village, after their two children were born. I stare up at the nondescript brick towers, and wonder what they would have thought about the transformation of the Lower East Side in our day. They did not live to see the particular horror of 1960s "urban renewal," with its wholesale destruction of neighborhoods deemed slums, and its displacement of the working poor. Gentrification, which began later, in the 1980s, probably displaced as many poor tenants in the long run as did urban renewal, but it had a gentler effect on the streetscape—indeed, preserving what might otherwise have crumbled into dust. Those surviving parts of the Lower East Side's old tenement environment that survived have seen their housing stock slowly improved and renovated through gentrification for the past twenty years, while playing host to bohemian cultural activities and chic little boutiques: not so bad a fate for the old ghetto, all things considered.

THE ESPLANADE GIVES OUT, and becomes an inhospitable parking area and repair shed for city sanitation and fire department trucks. So I cross over to the inland side. One public housing complex after another: the Rutgers Houses, Laguardia Houses, Two Bridges, Vladeck Houses, Corlear's Hook Houses. The one architectural standout is Gouverneur Court, which used to be the old Gouverneur Hospital. It has those magnificent red brick rounded bays with black wrought-iron balconies that I've often admired in a car from the FDR Drive. Now I'm seeing it at street level and it's quite impressive. A plaque informs me it was built in 1898, and is now on the National Register of Historic Places. Its red sandstone has wonderful carved ornamental detail. Surprisingly, it was not turned into expensive condos, but preserved, under a deal brokered by then-mayor David Dinkins, for lower-income occupants (the management sign says AFFORDABLE HOUSING FOR NYC.)

An affable, proprietary tenant in blue shorts, with incredibly thick glasses, who looks like he hangs out often in front, seeing my curiosity about the building, tells me, "It's all single-room apartments. Section 8." Section 8 is a federal program that provides subsidies for impoverished, often elderly people, or people on disability.

"It's beautiful."

"You should see the courtyard."

"I'd like to," I say. "Can you take me in for a moment?"

"Nah. You can't go into Gouverneur House without photo ID. They're very strict about it."

Just then another tenant, a middle-aged woman in shorts and curlers, comes out of the building. "Hey, Denny, want some coffee?"

"Nah. I never had a taste for it. I get all my caffeine from Coca-Cola."

"It's getting cold."

"September, it's all over. You won't be able to wear shorts no more."

"I went to the doctor, they say it's a heat rash. I was afraid it's diabetes. Everyone I know got diabetes."

"You'll be okay."

"You're a saint, Denny." She waves at him, and walks away. He nods: Saint Denis. He continues to guard the steps, looking out across at the stern Vladeck Houses, angled all different ways. I head back toward the East River, to try to pick up a navigable walking trail along the waterfront.

THIS RAGTAG MILE of East River waterfront, from the Williamsburg Bridge just north of Corlears Hook to about 14th Street, where the Con Edison East River Station power plant now resides, once contained virtually all of the important New York shipyards. Their innovative craftsmanship was on such a high level that, during the transition from sailing ships to steamships, the East River yards led the country in shipbuilding activity, and their only rivals worldwide were the shipbuilders of Clydebank, near Glasgow. In the early 1850s, considered the golden age of American shipbuilding, the East River shipbuilders, mostly Yankees transplanted from Boston, turned out sturdy packet ships, clippers, yachts, steamships, and warships, using the finest white oak imported from Georgia and Florida, the best cedar, locust, and pine from the Chesapeake Bay. Often they would lay out a half-hull on the ground, and build the rest from that template. The yards had their own blacksmith shops and sailmaking establishments. The bulk of ship-repair operations were also situated in the East River Yards.

In *The Rise of New York Port*, Robert Greenhalgh Albion characterized the labor relationship that prevailed in the yards as "a survival of the old craft system, with masters, journeymen, and apprentices. Nearly every one of the prominent East River builders worked up through the various stages." The working day was long, extending in summer from four-thirty in the morning to seven-thirty at night, with breaks for lunch and dinner. The pay was only $1.25 a day, until a series of strikes drove it up to $1.75. "By the time of the clipper boom, when skilled shipwrights were at a premium," wrote Albion, "wages sometimes ran as high as $2.50 a day, which was the main reason that the cost of construction was higher at New York."

Though Manhattan's nineteenth-century harbor continues to be celebrated nostalgically, not a trace remains of its shipbuilding industry in the public's mind. Nor can I make out any shards of that great enterprise, as I trek alongside the FDR Drive.

To GET A TRUE FEELING of New York's nineteenth-century industrial waterfront, in fact, you really have to go out to Brooklyn—specifically Red Hook. There's something soaring about the way the space opens out there, both to the sea and within the streets themselves, the way the 150-year-old warehouses extend all the way to the wharf, and there's no highway to cut you off or pinch you into a concrete walking strip. You breathe in an amazing silence there that, come to think of it, may not be at all like the hurly-burly nineteenth-century waterfront, but is conducive, at any rate, to the peaceful contemplation of history.

I like to start at the very tip of Red Hook, where the magnificent Van Brunt's and Beard Street Stores, arched brick warehouses from 1869, line both sides of the street heading to the water. (In appearance, they're cousins to the Empire Stores, near the Brooklyn Bridge, also built in the post–Civil War era—if anything, more impressive.) The windows of the Van Brunt Stores buildings on the eastern side are mostly boarded up and look possibly derelict, though a sign informs you of their hours of operation. It's a curious thing about old warehouses that even when they're still functioning, they often look abandoned, their mute, underfenestrated concrete or brick façades giving no clue either way. Across the way, at Beard Street, the very same brick façades have been spiffed up and rented out to a variety of businesses, including a woodworking shop and a film sound stage. If you keep on past the warehouses you come to a little public space, a lip of park at the water's edge across the harbor from Liberty Island, that lets you look the Statue of Liberty straight in the eye. For once, you are facing her head-on.

Nearer to shore, there's an odd, crescent-shaped breakwater, the Erie Basin, ugly with parked cars impounded by the police department, though how they drove onto it is a mystery, since from this angle the spit of land seems attached to nothing.

Going back along the Stores to a side street lined with trolley tracks, which bisects the endless warehouses, you will come upon a magical little inlet with police boats and other small craft docked on either side. By the way, somewhere in the Beard Street Stores is, or was, the Trolley Museum; on certain occasions the objects of its collection were wheeled out and set on these selfsame tracks. It makes me feel like Methuseleh to remember that I rode trolleys as a boy, growing up in Brooklyn, and now they are trotted out as exotica, like barouches. There is also, moored nearby, something called the Waterfront Museum and Showboat Barge, painted a deep brick red, open on weekends and rentable for children's parties; it was transported to Red Hook to show twenty-first-century Brooklynites what nineteenth-century barges were like. Verging toward a melancholy realization that everything may someday end up entombed in its own curatorial institution (the Museum of Dental Floss, the Museum of Mid-List Writers), I am distracted from it by the happier thought that the vista before me is remarkably untrammeled. One is privileged to see the little canal, the fishing boats, the warehouses, all as it must have been forever, or at least the past hundred years. The factories and warehouses on the canal have that brilliantly additive, piece-by-piece, higgledy-piggledy look of tropical green stucco alongside corrugated aluminum that Frank Gehry works so hard to achieve.

You can also look out, a block away, toward a most remarkable wreck of factory transformed into melted cheese. This was a suite of buildings connected by chutes, owned by the Philippine dictator Ferdinand Marcos, which had been an immensely profitable enterprise for importing and refining much of the sugar in North America. After his regime collapsed, the whole complex caught fire—some suspect arson, though the watchman assured me the conflagration was started by machinery—leaving the beams and floor structure irretrievably dripping, pendulous, like a modernist sculpture on an apocalyptic theme.

Sometimes I think I can only relax in a site that has not been specifically earmarked for leisure, but where there is still some commercial or industrial activity, or the ghost of same, to contemplate: docks or factories or the like. At least that's my preference. Surrounded by the intermingling currents of river and ocean estuary crisscrossed by tugs and barges, you get an unobstructed view of the Statue of Liberty to your left, the brick officers' quarters of Governor's Island to your right, while across the harbor are the cranes and forklifts of Port Jersey and, beyond this, Newark and Elizabeth, New Jersey, where most of the Port of New York ended up. Just beyond the steel jetty, a bit to the south, you can see that mixture of rotting timbers, tall grass, jagged rocks, and wharfside warehouses which constituted the 1970s–1980s New York waterfront, after it had been given up as a port but before it had begun to be "rehabilitated."

If you go along Beard Street, you pass a walled-in shipyard, with a drydock of skilled Greeks still repairing the bottoms of boats, though now they grumble about the lack of work. (Newport News gets most of the ship-repair business these days.) An Argentine freighter, abandoned by its bankrupt owner, rusts in the harbor, waiting patiently to be rescued by some adventurous entrepreneurs. In this very same shipyard, some years back, a damaged freighter was stashed for six months by its owner, while he tried to raise the money to pay for repairs. Its Central American crew, most of whom spoke no English, was afraid to venture out past the gamy Red Hook projects into the city; and since the owner had stopped paying them, though he still brought them food, they had essentially become slaves pinioned to the ship. (This episode formed the subject of Francisco Goldman's fine novel *The Ordinary Seaman.*) Nowadays they would merely have to venture a few blocks inland and they would come across a soccer park used heavily by Central Americans, with some of the best weekend street food to be had in New York City.

Now back to the Manhattan waterfront.

DISTINCT FROM OTHER GREAT CITIES of the world, Manhattan is almost pathologically averse to letting you wander to the river's edge and get close enough to touch the water. It has erected a prophylactic wall of fences and other physical barriers that overprotectively stave off potential accidents, intentional harm, and, most of all, liability suits. It was not always thus. A sampling of one year's city coroner reports in the early nineteenth century bears out how frequently and casually Death visited the waterfront:

ACKERMAN, CORNELIUS—suicide by drowning, b. New York, age 29 (6 Feb. 1826)

ACKERMAN, DUKE—drowning while going on board sloop *Lowell* (27 Oct. 1835)

BAPTIST, ISAAC—drowning when he fell from the wharf (21 Aug. 1836)

BARCELO, JAMES—suffocation from charcoal fumes on board the brig *Merced,* b. Spain, Age *c.* 33 (6 Feb. 1826)

BERRY, NELSON—hemmorhage of the lungs, b. on the ocean, a rigger by occupation, a sailor all his life, age 35. He has been married to his wife Sarah for 7 years. He has no children. (26 Aug. 1839)

BIRRCKENBECK, BENJAMIN—fall from the gangway of ship *Panthea,* age *c.* 45 (10 Mar. 1841)

BOISE, JACOB—blowing up of flagship *Fulton* at the Navy Yard (4 June 1829)

BUNDY, EDWARD (colored)—accidentally knocked from main deck to the lower hold of the ship *Silver de Grace* by a tierce of rice (12 Jan. 1836)

A simple notation of "drowning" was as frequently entered as any explanation for decease. Wrote Kenneth Scott, in his Introduction to *Coroners' Reports, New York City, 1823–1842:* "Inasmuch as New York was a port, drowning was an extremely common form of death. Many, especially when intoxicated, lost their lives when trying to board a vessel or go ashore." Alcohol blurred the line between accidental and intentional self-destruction. Perhaps it was this pattern of "border crossings" that eventually led the municipal authorities to place the river's edge off limits to its citizens.

There is a scene in Chaplin's *City Lights* (1931) that makes you realize the degree to which access to the water's edge means, in part, the freedom to commit suicide. On a simple river-walk, below a bridge or elevated promenade, a soused millionaire is getting ready to drown himself with a rope and a heavy stone. Charlie the Tramp waddles blithely down the staircase attached to the bridge and takes up a river-walk bench for the night, when he notices the would-be suicide's preparations. He tries to convince the man that life is worth living ("Tomorrow the birds will sing"), in the process entangling himself with the rope and the wealthy, self-destructive sot, so that both keep landing in the drink and having to pull themselves out. A fine bit of physical comedy—but what strikes me is how easy it was in yesterday's cities to do away with oneself by drowning.

A century ago, "the river" had a fateful ring. It connoted suicide, especially for destitute women or prostitutes overtaken by despair. Such women were often said to end up "in the river." Beyond the actual incidence of such tragedies, the realist school had a penchant for drowning denouements, a residual romanticism that popped up in "fallen women" narratives worldwide, from Vienna to Tokyo, around the turn of the twentieth century: the victim of social forces was shown poised on the bridge, ready to jump.

In Stephen Crane's *Maggie: A Girl of the Streets* (1893), the author describes the moments preceding his heroine's death through the invocation of ominous waterfront imagery: "The girl went into the gloomy districts near the river, where the tall black factories shut in the street and only occasional broad beams of light fell across the pavements from saloons. . . . When almost to the river the girl saw a great figure. On going forward she perceived it to be a huge fat man in torn and greasy garments. His grey hair straggled down over his forehead. His small, bleared eyes, sparkling from amidst great rolls of red fat, swept eagerly over the girl's upturned face. . . . Chuckling and leering, he followed the girl of the crimson legions. At their feet the river appeared a deathly black hue."

The customers as well would sometimes end underwater. James McCabe, nineteenth-century chronicler of New York's secrets, wrote of men enticed by "prostitutes, connected with professional thieves and assassins. . . . More than one has found his grave in the Hudson, dragged there in the darkness of the night, after being drugged by poisonous liquors and robbed of his valuables."

The river was also the repository of another sad human cargo. In 1858 a committee established to investigate the treatment of abandoned children reported that "our own Hudson and the East River carry with them to the Atlantic, with the returning tide, the dead bodies of infants cast out by unfeeling mothers."

That New York rivers continue to serve as a mortuary for suicides and homicides may be seen by the bodies fished out each year, around mid-April, by the harbor police, during what has come to be called "Floaters Week." But the river is no longer morbidly connected in the public's mind with the fate of fallen women—not because streetwalkers' lives have so improved, but because narrative tropes exhaust themselves.

CORLEARS HOOK IS A RIVERFRONT AREA on the Lower East Side, near Gouverneur Hospital and below Grand Street. From 1820 to 1850, it had the distinction of being one of three main concentrations of commercial sex in New York. Some even claim Corlears Hook was responsible for the term "hookers" as a synonym for prostitutes, though this may be carrying local pride too far.

On that same Saturday night in early September, I visit Corlears Hook, now a public park bisected by the FDR Drive. On the inland side is a playground with basketball hoops, toddlers' climbing equipment, and tree-lined paths. I cross a highway overpass to get to the river side, where a grassy lawn, on which several black families have set up their own picnic tables and are barbecuing chicken and steaks, slopes down to the water. I feel the heat from their flaming grill carried uphill in a warm night wind. The smell of lighter fluid mixes with the brackish river. The grass is littered with plastic cups. There are no signs of prostitutes or vice; the park has expunged all that. It is a peaceable community scene, but something still tells me it is private. I wander over to a ruined, abandoned amphitheater, marked extensively with graffiti. The amphitheater seats appear to be in still-usable condition, but the roof is a mess, hole-ridden and parts dangling. I wonder when the city will get around to repairing it. It waited so long to fix the Goldman Concert Shell in Central Park that there was no saving it.

On one side of the Corlears Hook Amphitheater stage, I come upon a sign that says:

Waiting for Godot
Aug 9–16   FREE
7:30 PM

Now I don't know what to think. Is the trashed-out condition of the band shell merely a set design, or has some guerrilla theater troupe, bringing classics to inner-city neighborhoods, decided to make witty use of the dilapidated stage for its Beckett production? Farther north begin the playing fields of the East River Park. This generous amenity along the waterfront, with softball fields and tennis courts, extends from Corlears Hook all the way up from the Lower East Side to the East Village. Unfortunately, this part of the waterfront promenade is currently fenced off to the public, because of damage done by marine borers to the seawall, which will cost an estimated $30 million to repair.

On the ballfield, a man and a boy (I presume father and son) are kicking a soccer ball. The bank of lights are on, as though in preparation for a night game, but no one is using the facility except for this one man and boy, and I'm not sure how they even got into the playing area, given the fact that it's so fenced off. Then why are the stadium lights on? Are they turned on automatically, at a certain hour? Walking out of the park, past a lone wino glued to his bench, toward Henry Street, a creepy feeling overcomes me: alone at night, expecting to have come upon a festive atmosphere, and instead finding very few people outside.

I go back to my house to read up on the East River Park. It seems to have been part of Robert Moses' visionary attempt at waterfront improvement, in tandem with building perimeter highways in the late 1930s, shortly after his enlargement of Riverside Park on the West Side. According to the authors of *New York 1930*, Robert A. M. Stern, Gregory Gilmartin, and Thomas Mellins, "Corlear's Hook Park on the Lower East Side was nearly doubled in size through landfill, from 8.6 to 15.5 acres, and constituted the southern section of a fifty-three-acre East River Park. The main portion of the enlarged park ran between the highway and the East River, extending south from the Williamsburg Bridge to Jackson Street and north to Tenth Street, and was accessible via a footbridge at the park's southern end near the Vladeck Houses, a public housing project of 1940. Redesigned by the Park Department, Corlear's Hook Park included sports facilities, playgrounds, a waterfront promenade, an outdoor concert area with a capacity for 2,000 spectators, and tree-shaded lawns intended to serve, as Francis Cormier, a landscape architect for the Park Department, put it, as 'gossip centers.'"

It's curious to compare the benign intentions of planners and the more crusty reality sixty years later. Not that it isn't still a wonderful park—or will be, when the underwater foundations have been repaired. So that derelict band shell really was a big deal once. Two thousand spectators! How many culture-loving, impecunious couples in the forties must have started out there on a first date? Rachmaninoff, Gershwin, Shakespeare, all for free. "Symphony, chamber music, opera and jazz in a small, neighborhood park. A little out of the way, possibly risky, but worth a wary try," wrote the divine Kate Simon in her 1959 guidebook, *New York Places and Pleasures*, about the East River Park Amphitheater. Was that cup-strewn slope with barbecue grills what the planners had in mind as a "gossip center"? If so, they were basically on target. But not even Robert Moses could have seen ahead to the shipworms.

POSTSCRIPT: The East River Amphitheater, whose degraded condition I lamented, was miraculously repaired in a week by volunteer labor, working around the clock, for a television show about civic projects called "Challenge America." The modest concrete band shell has a polished white exterior with blue tiles inside, and two enormous butterfly-wing thingies with strung wires (are these purely decorative, or do they have some acoustic function? If the former, I say get rid of them) extended from its front and back. The trowel job on the band shell looks clumsy and patchy, but this volunteer workmanship is preferable to the decades of bureaucratic delays that might have hindered a professional restoration, had it been bid and haggled over the usual way. The wooden benches are all new and nailed together shipshape, if splintery on the derriere. All in all, it is a fine precedent established for vigilante urbanism by communities that would take repair jobs into their own hands.

22

CON EDISONLAND: FROM ONE POWER PLANT TO ANOTHER

AMONG THOSE OPERATIONS DRAWN TO THE EDGES OF MANHATTAN, WE MUST NOT OMIT THE ELECTRIC COMPANY, CONSOLIDATED EDISON, WHICH BUILT TWO large power stations on this part of the East River: one at 14th Street and one a mile north, between 38th and 41st Streets. Power plants were originally sited on rivers because they burned coal, which was brought in by barge, and because they required huge amounts of water for cooling and other operations. Later they switched to burning oil, also barge-transported, and now are increasingly converting to gas while keeping oil as a backup. Although much of the demand for river water has been reduced by technology, the underutilized waterfront remains a tempting dumping ground for power plants. At present, nearly three-quarters of New York City's electricity is generated by power plants along the East River (many located on the Queens side, in Astoria and Long Island City), which says something either about the lack of respect for, or the touching confidence in, this much-abused waterway. Con Edison, the sole producer of steam for New York City's hospitals and other public buildings, is a key player in the East River's future, one way or another.

It is the customary karma of large, monopolistic utility companies, such as Pacific Gas & Electric or Consolidated Edison, to go unloved. Rather than receiving gratitude from their customers, they seem to inspire mistrust bordering on hatred. Far be it from me to say whether this antipathy is justified, but it is one of the few things that truly unite the people of a metropolitan region. I know I am no different: a native New Yorker, I was raised to hate Con Edison. The blackouts, which we blame on Con Ed without hesitation, are an intrinsic part of New York folklore: anyone who lived through one can tell you where he or she was when the lights went out, and what happened for the next twenty-four hours.

It is hard to put a face on Con Edison; there remains something covert and conspiratorial about its vast, tentacular "power grid," its seeming freedom from accountability, its annual importuning for rate increases, deserved or not, its militantly self-congratulatory corporate image (DIG WE MUST, FOR A GROWING NEW YORK! read the sign placed outside every street-cut for many years, since replaced by the zippy ON IT). The English travel writer Stephen Graham, in his 1927 book of nocturnal perambulations, *New York Nights*, found himself on the East River waterfront, "listening to the ceaseless Edison works. Oh, what is Edison contriving there, are they engines of death or of life?" Experience suggests both.

Four smokestacks painted sober gray and black, emitting white plumes of smoke, with exterior ladders running up their sides, are the most visible landmarks of the East 14th Street power plant. Closer up, you see two massive buildings with brick façades, much wider than tall, connected to each other by corrugated steel chutes, and sprouting stacks of coiled wire like the laboratory headdress of Elsa Lanchester in *The Bride of Frankenstein*. The buildings date from the height of America's distinguished industrial/mill architecture, but somehow these two gigantic brick boxes, holding inside them the power that feeds, or at least takes the edge off, a metropolis's mad, sweet-tooth hunger for energy, are not distinguished, but simply mammoth.

The Con Edison power plant takes up more than three entire square blocks, from Avenue C to the river, and from East 14th Street to East 16th Street. It fills both sides of the Franklin Delano Roosevelt Drive, so that East River walkers are reduced to a narrow concrete path adjacent to the highway, cars whizzing past, while, behind a fence, Con Edison's shacks, minimally used for unloading fuel tankers, continue to hog the riverside.

A gleaming, energy-efficient Con Edison office building of curved green glass, with white lattice roof, at East 16th Street and the FDR Drive, has been added to the utility park. Designed by Richard Dattner (who did the Riverbank State Park), it is as graceful as a MOMA design-shop fruit bowl placed beside a tractor. As you drive by, it gives off an impression of tranquil marine transparency, though, close up, you can't see a damn thing inside.

The plant on East 14th Street, a behemoth to begin with, is slated for considerable expansion, mostly because the Midtown station a mile north is being sold off to real estate developers. Con Edison, realizing it possessed the only large area left undeveloped in Manhattan, saw that the sale of this land near the United Nations would be lucrative enough to pay for the expansion of the downtown plant, with no loss of capacity, and at the same time reap the company a hefty profit. It was, as they say, a "win-win" situation, except perhaps for the poor, largely Latino residents in the Lower East Side who lived downwind from the East 14th Street works: the plant's emissions would impact on them more severely than on communities to the north. According to public health statistics, Puerto Ricans are especially susceptible to asthma; and a disproportionately high number of asthmatics already lived in the housing projects alongside the East 14th Street plant. The anticipated plant expansion would inevitably increase the emission of fine particulate matter (called PM 2.5, because the particles are 2.5 microns or less), which recent medical studies have linked to asthma, lung cancer, and heart disease.

The East River Environmental Coalition, a group of tenants and community organizations, appealed the expansion. This neighborhood group did not take issue with the validity of expanding the plant to meet the city's power needs; nor did it question Con Edison's assertion that improved technologies would make the new power plant much cleaner and more efficient, reducing the level of most pollutants (excluding PM 2.5) emitted overall. The problem was that this state-of the-art plant was going to be tacked onto a dirty, antiquated plant—one of eighteen obsolete plants in New York State that had been "grandfathered" by legislative statute, meaning it did not have to abide by modern clean-air standards. Since its pollution problems arose from burning oil in addition to gas, and from using old equipment, the community board wanted Con Edison to upgrade (or, in current lingo, "repower") the old plant to burn only gas, and to install new equipment. Eventually a settlement was reached, whereby Con Edison agreed to increase its use of natural gas in the old plant, and install a nozzle in a smokestack to reduce the impact of fine particulates, in return for approval of Con Edison's expansion. While this settlement was a victory for the community, the nozzle will not be installed for another five to ten years, nor will it then entirely alleviate the pollution caused by the expanded East 14th Street plants; and so the fight continues.

EVEN BEFORE CON EDISON had bracketed the area with its electric plants, power suppliers dominated this strip of Manhattan waterfront. "In the 1840s, a number of gas tanks were erected near the East River. Because of leaks in the tanks, a foul stench invaded the East Side between 14th and 23rd Streets. Who, but the poor and the disreputable, would live there? And so the city's notorious Gashouse District was born," wrote Edward K. Spann in *The New Metropolis*. A neighborhood populated initially by poor Irish workers and, later, by equally indigent Italians, Germans, and Jews, it had become, by the post–Civil War period, "one of the most turbulent sections of the city, for the celebrated Gas House Gang was just coming into power, and was terrorizing a large area," wrote Herbert Asbury in his juicy popular history, *The Gangs of New York*. "Scarcely a night passed in which gangsters did not loot houses and stores and fight among themselves in the streets and dives, and the police were powerless to stop them."

That is, until the captain of the twenty-first precinct, Alexander S. "Clubber" Williams, introduced the reign of the nightstick. In 1871,

Asbury notes approvingly, Williams "organized a strong arm squad which patrolled the precinct and clubbed the thugs with or without provocation. The district was soon comparatively quiet, and remained so throughout Williams' administration." (A less admiring portrait of Williams can be found in *The Autobiography of Lincoln Steffens*, where he is shown presiding over the beating of Jewish strikers. Eventually the captain, grown rich beyond the reasonable expectation of a uniformed officer's salary, was hauled in during one of those periodic investigations of New York police corruption; his explanation, that he had made the money speculating in Japanese real estate, failed to wash.)

THE SLUMS AND DOCKS are long gone, replaced by that city-within-a-city, stretching from East 14th to East 23rd Street, the giant apartment complex known as Stuyvesant Town and Peter Cooper Village. (The latter is said to be a smidgen roomier and more upscale than the former, though I am never able to detect any of these advantages by comparison of their exteriors.) These middle-income,* rent-stabilized apartments were the city's gift to the war generation. Built by the Metropolitan Life Insurance Company, they are a reminder of a time when New York pioneered the construction of affordable housing in prime locations. When they debuted in 1947, Lewis Mumford deplored their totalitarian demeanor (now considerably softened by trees), and Dorothy Day, the saintly founder of the *Catholic Worker*, lamented in her autobiography that she and her fellow bohemians had to quit their cozy East River cold-water tenements, which were being razed to make way for that perfectly hideous Stuyvesant Town, and relocate to the still-neglected shores of Staten Island. One can sympathize with Mumford's and Day's opposition, or shudder at the thought of any more developments like Stuyvesant Town taking bites out of Manhattan's grid, while still acknowledging its utility and proven success. Though the complex still has little to recommend in the way of architectural charm, being merely a succession of brick high-rise barracks that stretch along the river district as far as the eye can see,

---

*Lately, some of Stuyvesant Town's apartments have been marketed as luxury rentals, undercutting the original intent.

what is amazing is how well it has fulfilled its intended purpose (the provision of safe, decent, reasonably priced housing, and a lot of it), and how well the whole thing has become casually absorbed into the city's texture. It is enough to make one rethink one's notions about what makes for good urbanism.

ACROSS FROM STUYVESANT TOWN, and a few blocks north of the Con Edison plant, at the widest point of the East River, where a natural sandy cove has formed, a lovely new waterfront park has sprung up along the curved shoreline. Small—extending only from East 18th Street to East 21st Street at this point—Stuyvesant Cove Park packs in a botanical garden's worth of exuberant nature. Hundreds of yellow daffodils, grape hyacinths, and other wildflowers, and ten varieties of North American native trees (eastern poplar, ironwood, red mulberry, eastern red cedar, black cherry, butternut, common hackberry, swamp white oak, white oak, and blackberry viburnum) speckle the park with color. All the plantings—trees, perennial shrubs, grasses, and flowers—have been chosen because they are indigenous to the area, and because they tolerate sea spray and New York weather, survive in relative drought, and attract local and migrating birds. So far, cormorants, robins, gulls, ducks, geese, and swans have all been spotted around Stuyvesant Cove.

One reason the cove feels sequestered and cozy is that there is not excessive distraction from the highway, which is raised above ground at this point. Another reason is that the old Marine and Aviation Pier, at the northern end, nests the cove with a crescent-shaped, visually delimited space. A winding serpentine wall does a good job of dividing bike path from esplanade, gives the park a more natural, wavelike flow, and increases your sense of event as you walk the length of the park. Elegantly spare wooden chairs with perforated stainless-steel backs, three to a table, are placed at strategic viewing spots before the river, ready for an impromptu picnic, gin rummy game, or sunset meditation.

Farther inland, several open shelters, made of Alaskan cedar, have been strategically placed to separate the park visually from the highway. This clever, award-winning design is the work of Johanson and Walcavage, the plantings by Ila di Pasquale. Eventually the park simply stops, where the project's budget gave out, and becomes a blacktop lot, from East 21st to East 23rd Streets. Plans are under way to erect here an environmental education center, with classrooms designed in accord with the latest sustainable-architecture principles by a leading "green" architect, Colin Cathcart. The center will sport a light pavilion look, meant to blur the lines between building, water, and landscape. Photovoltaic panels will be installed to trap the sun's energy, and 100 percent of the power will be supplied by sun, water, and wind.

Stuyvesant Cove Park is the fruit of more than twenty years' stubborn struggle on the part of its community. Actually, the effort to build a park here goes back much longer, as Ann Buttenweiser notes in *Manhattan Water Bound:* "In 1835, the Common Council's Committee on Wharves, Piers and Slips touted the benefits 'to health and ornament' that sea and exercise would provide if the city were to reserve thirty acres at Stuyvesant Cove . . . for a park," but the project was abandoned in favor of leasing the land to shipping.

In the 1970s, Community Board 6, concerned that it had the lowest per capita amount of public open space in the city, began to campaign for a park at the cove. In 1990 the community fought off a mega-development called Riverwalk that had been planned as a platform of luxury towers over the cove, and proposed instead a waterfront park. All the land along the cove's edge belonged to the Economic Development Corporation, which had to be persuaded to surrender its plans of adding to the city's tax coffers and accept a waterfront park. The EDC still envisioned installing a restaurant or shopping center to pay for the park's upkeep, but the community association implausibly persuaded the EDC to accept an environmental study center, funded by grants, which would invite local schools to participate, and use the cove as a learning laboratory, studying how to create a habitat for migratory birds and monarch butterflies.

The vision animating the park is so intensely ecological and "natural" that you need to take a step back to grasp just how wonderfully contrived it is, given what used to be on the site. I mean the huge construction dock of the Transit Mix Concrete Corporation, with its detachment of barges and cranes. Transit Mix was one of many concrete plants that dotted the waterfront. William Kornblum, now a CUNY sociology professor, recalls in his genial book about sailing New York harbor, *At Sea in the City*, what it was like when he held a summer job there in 1961:

> The yard and the dock were among the most active ready mixed concrete supply sites in the city. Its silos for construction materials towered four or five stories over the East River Drive. The dock on either side was crowded with barges carrying mountains of sand or gravel or Lelite, a lighter composition aggregate for floors and other interior cement jobs. From this dock on the East River had come a great deal of the concrete for all that good housing along the river, as well as for innumerable commercial sites inside the island. The controversial Pan Am Building (later Met Life) was going up then, to destroy perhaps forever the beautiful expanse of Park Avenue and its silhouette of Grand Central and its lower-rise office building. We were pouring its concrete well into the overtime evenings.

Eventually all these concrete plants, considered unsightly and inappropriately industrial for the new waterfront, were removed. In fact, not a single concrete plant remains in Manhattan—as though its populace had lost sight of how much the island's prosperity rests on new construction, or had forgotten, perhaps, that concrete was usually necessary to said construction. Although the concrete industry has become more mobile, setting up temporary yards and dismantling them when a job is done, many construction sites still rely on the stuff being trucked in. Since wet cement has a transportation life of only sixty to ninety minutes before it over-hardens, many Manhattan construction sites suffer costly shutdowns when cement trucks, coming from the outer boroughs or beyond, are delayed in heavy traffic.

The Transit Mix Concrete Corporation having long since quit the scene, Stuyvesant Cove Park is certainly a miraculous improvement over the vacuum left there by its passing. I can remember visiting the area several years ago and seeing nothing but parked cars, garbage, and the occasional rat.

The Gulf filling station on East 23rd Street, still in operation, is a reminder of the cove's industrial past. The former Marine and Aviation Pier, its art deco lettering faded but visible against the roofed structure extending over the water, has been consigned to parking. Just north of it is a narrow marina, taken up with charter yachts and gaudy showboats rented out for parties, such as the *Paddlewheel Queen*, which seem to have strayed a long way from the Mississippi.

Where the cove completes its parenthesis, and the shoreline juts out once again, there appears the Waterside residential complex, with the United Nations International School tucked into its southern end. It would be nice to follow the river at this point, but the UN School has blocked off all public access for security reasons. The school itself is a graceless, precast-concrete ocher block with a round blue UNIS logo pinned on like a breastplate, which is scarcely enticing enough to merit challenging its off-limits demeanor. If you want to reach Waterside's (theoretically) fine open public space along the waterfront, which is usually closed for repairs, there is no way to cross through at ground level; the gate for that purpose is almost always closed, so you have to take an interminable escalator up, cross the barren, windswept plaza, and then follow a set of stairs down again to the river. By that time you will have been surveilled by any number of security guards, cameras, and wary residents.

Most waterfront housing in Manhattan is built on the inland side of the highway, but Waterside rises on the river side, making it the exception. Built in the early 1970s, the 1,470 units of what were originally subsidized middle-income housing were designed by Davis, Brody & Associates, using the firm's signature Cubist, cut-diamond profile. I always get a guilty feeling when I come upon Waterside; I want to like it more than I do. Its spartan brown towers loom up impressively, the tops of them protruding like giant periscopes, and if modern buildings were judged only as sculpture, they would be entirely satisfying. They have rigor and intelligence and formal consistency. But they are not friendly. Especially at the ground level, the severity of their unvaried, dark brown brick façade is off-putting. Nor can you penetrate them from the ground in any way, the lower floors being all used for garages.

The upper platform is one of those grim, windswept, empty expanses that make you yearn for the lost art of plaza making. A semi-deserted supermarket, restaurant, dry cleaner, liquor shop, card store, hair salon, and ATM together put forth a forlorn attempt at neighborhood retail. Children play ball or ride their scooters on the bleak plaza, imperviously resourceful, as always. A few of the towers seem to stand on stilts, like Le Corbusier's *pilotis*, providing remarkable views through their hollowed-out bases.

Waterside puts me in mind of the Castel Sant'Angelo, the harsh Roman fortress on the Tiber. It feels cut off from the city. The ground level is all garage, and you can't cross the Franklin Delano Roosevelt Drive unless you're suicidal, so the only way of crossing the road on foot is to take an overpass. On the other hand, there are buses and taxis right outside the door; and not every part of the city has to be in the thick of things.

Waterside represents an experimental model of the sort of housing complex that once threatened or promised (depending on your point of view) to cantilever over New York's waterways. Above and beyond the issue of turning over the river's edge to high-rise housing, there are certain cautionary lessons to be derived from Waterside: its façades and foundations have suffered extensive leaks from water damage, which have proven very costly to repair. The owner, Richard Ravitch, naturally wanted to raise rents substantially to pay for repairs and the tenants, whose reasonable rents had been protected by state Mitchell-Lama subsidies, were up in arms about this prospect. In the end, a deal was brokered to limit rent increases, in exchange for a multimillion-dollar tax break extended by the city to the owner. And the Mitchell-Lama tenant subsidies went out with the tide.

NORTH OF WATERSIDE, access to the river turns even dicier. You cross the ever-darkened street beneath the FDR Drive and walk along the inland side, past Bellevue Hospital Center, famous for its psychiatric unit ("Bellevue," once synonymous with the place they sent you when you went nuts), past NYU Medical Center, past the Water Club, a pleasantly retro, upscale restaurant masquerading as a barge, and one of the rare opportunities to have a drink and enjoy the view along the river side of the East River. A bit farther north is the 34th Street Heliport, where those in a hurry can catch a chopper to the airport or the Hamptons, and where, each night, hungry men line up to receive a free meal from the Coalition for the Homeless volunteers.

I witnessed one such meal run on a hot Sunday evening in June; the temperature had reached 93 degrees earlier in the day. The van, one of two that started off at 6:45 P.M. from the side entrance of St. Bartholomew's Church on East 51st Street, held more than three hundred meals as well as three regulars and myself. The driver and leader, Bill Dean, was a very tall, bald lawyer in his mid-sixties who showed up in the sweltering heat wearing a blue blazer, a straw hat, and a tie, looking as though he had just stepped out of a Louis Auchincloss novel. Coincidentally, I knew Dean from another life, when he had coaxed me into organizing a reading series at the New York Society Library. An avid fan of Melville's "Bartleby, the Scrivener," which he presses on everyone, he is one of those quintessentially do-gooder New Yorkers in the best possible sense: he has been distributing meals to the hungry for thirteen years. The other two, also long-term volunteers but more casually dressed, were Stefan, an Austrian-born graphic designer, and Al, a gruff-voiced man with a goatee who worked for a telecommunications company. As we drove to our first stop, the talk was mostly World Cup soccer and gossip about women volunteers.

The van pulled up under the highway ramp beside the heliport (farther upriver loomed the United Nations Secretariat building, catching the end of a sunset); and about thirty men, who had been waiting patiently for us, began to form a single line. An estimated two-thirds of them came from the Bellevue Men's Shelter, a few blocks away; the rest lived "outside." I asked if the men at the shelter did not receive meals there, and was told that they probably did, but were still hungry. Because the weather was so hot and the uptown kitchen, where Coalition for the Homeless meals were prepared, is not air-conditioned, the kitchen staff had decided to go with sandwiches. We handed each person in the line the wax-paper-wrapped sandwich (beef bologna and cheese), an orange, and a small milk carton. One man, a beer-barreled, grizzled oldster, grumbled first that it was only a sandwich and not a cooked meal, and second that he couldn't get two sandwiches. "We've a lot of stops to make tonight," explained Dean, "so only one per person."

"Hey," the oldster said, "if I'm gonna get fucked, I wanna be kissed, too."

He was the only ingrate. The other men, drawn from every race, were uniformly polite, often muttering words of gratitude. I was struck by how clean, presentable, and "normal" (i.e., fit and work-ready) most of them looked. All the races of mankind were represented. Some attempted to lighten the embarrassment by banter. "Do you have any condiments?" said a Hispanic man with a pencil mustache, and we gave him a packet of hot dog mustard. "May I trade this in for some Grey Poupon?" he joked.

OUR NEXT STOP WAS CHINATOWN, at the parking lot in front of the Criminal Court Building on Centre Street. There, a much larger group had assembled in two lines, male and female. The distaff line consisted of Chinese grannies, interested in collecting the bargain of free food. The men, however, looked gaunt and beaten down. One black man gestured angrily at the elderly Chinese women and said, "Hey, give me two sandwiches! I'm *really* homeless, not like them over there." Stefan would occasionally slip the requester another sandwich.

At the third stop, in front of the Battery's Staten Island Ferry Terminal, the group awaiting the Coalition's van looked much more down and out: hair matted, clothes dirty, expressions addled. Many slept in the park, some camped out in the ferry terminal, others hid in doorways of the Financial District. Here the rule of one food item per customer went by the boards, and we handed out as many sandwiches or milk cartons (for some reason, oranges were disdained by this crowd) as requested. Those who could not bring themselves to ask for two at a time lined up patiently again for seconds or thirds. Among these was a young woman of movie-star beauty, with an angelic smile—I assume she was a crack addict, though I might have been completely wrong. Next, boxes of clothing were distributed. A slight, nervous man, dodging around the edges, blurted, "I'm living outside. Can you give me two shirts?"

All around us, the people we had served sprawled on benches, munching sandwiches, chatting with each other, and looking momentarily assuaged. Bill Dean took me by the arm and showed me—half a block from where the homeless had gathered—a bust of the author of "Bartleby" embedded into the façade of a new building on Pearl Street, and a plaque announcing that here Herman Melville was born.

SEVERAL BLOCKS NORTH OF THE HELIPORT, you will come to the Con Edison Waterside power station. This site stretches from East 38th to East 41st Streets, and from First Avenue to the Franklin Delano Roosevelt

Drive. The power station projects very different impressions depending on which side of it you encounter. The façades along First Avenue are for the most part handsome, early-twentieth-century buildings, with arched windows that go up four stories, lots of curved ornamental stonework, and the words THE N.Y. EDISON Co. carved quaintly above the door. Looking at the backside of the Con Edison Waterside Station, overlooking the river, you get much more the sense of a powerful dynamo. Here, corrugated steel sheds, fat connecting pipes, catwalks, and ladders rule: it's an impressive, if daunting, display of old-fashioned industrial might, haunted, idled, and about to be torn down.

After federal legislation deregulated the power industry in the 1990s, Con Edison decided to phase itself out of the energy-production business, while continuing to deliver electricity. (It would also remain a producer of steam, which is still a moneymaker in Manhattan, where the closeness of skyscrapers makes it sensible to heat buildings that way.) The utility company, seeking to convert valuable Midtown property into cash, put its Waterside plant on the market. Originally Con Edison was only going to dispose of its non-generating buildings, but the real estate community advised the utility that the site would fetch much more money if the new properties did not have to sit cheek-by-jowl with generating plants. Con Edison may have also gotten a little greedy in soliciting bids for the property, driving the price up so much that only a very large, dense, luxury residential project could turn a sufficient profit. Several capable developers dropped out, sensing that such density would enmesh them in long, fruitless fights with the community planning board. The winning bidder was FSM East River Associates, a partnership of two New York developers, Fisher Brothers and Sheldon Solow, and Morgan Stanley, the financial firm. The final sale price for the property will depend on the size of the development rights approved by the city, which will consider input from the community planning board in making its decision. Some members of Community Board 6 are indeed worried that a development as large as this one is anticipated to be will entail very tall buildings, blocking the views of neighbors and casting extensive shadows over the surrounding blocks, while increasing the area's volume of traffic to unconscionable levels. Other members feel that the streets can handle the additional vehicles, and that there is nothing wrong with allowing a few more tall buildings in

Midtown, but worry that the urban design will be too prosaic. Beyond that, what will it do for the waterfront?

One of the first acts of the developer, FSM, was to hold an architectural competition soliciting world-renowned, cutting-edge architects such as Rem Koolhaas, Peter Eisenman, Richard Meier, and Frank Gehry, along with a few more-staid firms, such as Skidmore, Owings & Merrill, and Pei Cobb Fried and Partners, who had considerable local experience building in New York. This competition inspired much drooling and dreaming in the architectural community. It also whetted the market's and the public's appetite for the project: If something truly futuristic or original could arise where the generating station had been, it would almost justify the demolition of the power plant and the sale of Manhattan's waterfront to the wealthy. A jury, headed by knowledgeable, esteemed ex-university president Bill Lacey, was appointed, and the various architectural schemes published in the newspaper. It was assumed that the jury would pair one of the visionary architects with one of the more pragmatic local firms. Imagine the chagrin when the winning pair was announced as the two pragmatic local firms: Marilyn Jordan Taylor of Skidmore, Owings & Merrill, and Henry Cobb of Pei Cobb Freed! These results pleased nobody.

A part of me had to be amused at the way the New York real estate lobby felt it could stand up to the avant-garde mafia without blinking, and say, in effect, "Sorry, we're not interested in your cockamamie deconstructivist schemes, we think we can make more money with the usual boring, buttoned-down designs." On the other hand, I was disappointed, discouraged, left, like everyone else, with a cynical, bitter feeling, as when a backroom deal has been struck. I no longer looked forward to whatever they might build at the Con Edison site, if it was only going to be more of the same.

Months after, I heard talk that at least one of the old Con Edison buildings might be salvaged. Granted, the idea of turning power stations into cultural institutions was already becoming something of a cliché; but if clever adaptive reuse had converted a London turbine plant into the Tate Modern, or a Paris railroad station into the Musée d'Orsay, why not turn a Con Edison generating building into a museum or school? While neither old building on First Avenue was an out-and-out historical masterpiece, their façades had character. They possessed "wonderful soaring interiors," I was told.

In Europe there is a growing movement, known as Industrial Archaeology, intended to preserve pieces of the industrial past, sometimes by keeping them as ruins, or as monuments to their past use, and sometimes by saving the shell and putting the interior to an entirely different function. In the United States, too, conferences are held in which hobbyist scholars of old factories and turbines and float-bridges deliver papers on the poetry of mechanical solutions. New York City has thus far done precious little to preserve its industrial heritage. Consider that the heroes and philosopher-kings of nineteenth-century America were for the most part its engineers and inventors—and that it is still possible that the greatest achievements of American civilization will turn out to be its engineering genius. True, at the moment this genius no longer excites the cultural imagination of many educated Americans, or, worse, inspires resentful ambivalence. Who knows, though, if someday our descendants will revere the technical innovations and study the works of Consolidated Edison?

I am not sure myself that it is worth going to the mat to preserve either of these old Con Edison buildings. But I think one reason the community board and civic groups such as the Municipal Art Society have remain fixated on adaptive reuse is that they think it might promote a better urban design, a better street-wall, than the suburban banalities of a tower-in-the-park enclave. At the moment, the chances of retaining any fragment of the Waterside power station are slim, while the odds of the resulting project looking similar to banal Trump Place, on the West Side, are very strong.

WHAT ABOUT THE PROJECT'S WATERFRONT ACCESS? Just south of the site, there already exists a two-block fragment of waterfront esplanade, from East 36th to East 38th Streets, called the East River Esplanade Park. Designed by the landscape architect Thomas Balsley (who also did the Queens West Gantry Park, the Chelsea Waterside Park, and Riverside Park South), this particular esplanade is pleasant and popular; it has a formal, Jardin Luxembourg quality; the best part of its design is the separation of levels between the benches overlooking the river and a raised portion underneath the trees. At the southern entrance, East 36th Street, a "fitness cluster" offers instructions for stretching exercises and an inclined gymnastic bench. You can also enter the esplanade at 37th Street through an elegant granite underpass (though it often has a urine smell.) The East River Esplanade's ordered lines, geometric symmetries, and round stone planters are very different in feeling from Stuyvesant Cove's wilder rambles, but both have their virtues. This piecemeal, budget-starved way that the overall East River Esplanade is coming into existence may not be a bad thing: it makes for some variety reflecting differences in adjacent neighborhoods, more so than the monolithic strip that the Hudson River Park threatens to become.

In any case, you could extend the Balsley esplanade up to 42nd Street (and beyond, if only the United Nations would permit pedestrian access to its edge). The main obstacle to reaching the waterfront from the Con Edison site is the obtrusive northern ramp of the FDR Drive. Were it to be torn down, you would still have to traverse the highway at grade (with the aid of a traffic light), but visual access to the river would be much better. You might also decide to deck over the FDR Drive at this point: imagine a large deck from 38th Street to 42nd Street, which would extend from the ground floor of whatever new buildings arose on the Con Edison site, down to the river. The question is, who would pay for such a deck: the developer, the city, both?

On First Avenue, between East 41st and East 42nd Streets, wedged in as an afterthought between Con Edison's Waterside Station and the United Nations, is the Robert Moses Playground. An asphalt punch-ball field corralled by a chain-link fence, next to a ventilating building for the Queens-Midtown Tunnel, it is as bare and bleak a tribute to the man who created more elegant parks, swimming pools, and beaches than anyone else in New York history, as the harshest critic of Moses might wish for.

23

EXCURSUS

ROBERT MOSES,
A REVISIONIST TAKE

I AM STRUCK BY THE FACT THAT WHENEVER PEOPLE FROM ALL WALKS OF LIFE—STOCKBROKERS, ENGLISH PROFESSORS, ARTISTS, HOUSEWIVES, CARPENTERS—TALK TO ME ABOUT New York City, they knowingly trace its problems back to Robert Moses. There exists a startling consensus that Moses was a monster, the enemy of the good. This Manichaean tale—how Robert Moses ruined, or tried to ruin, New York—has indeed become the city's postwar master-narrative, its Romulus-and-Remus myth. It has proven extraordinarily useful, as master narratives often are, and has only two drawbacks: (1) it may not be true—or true anywhere approaching the extent that people now believe; (2) it prevents our interpreting New York's history with greater accuracy and nuance, not to mention developing more-sophisticated narratives that might better suit our planning for the city's future.

The genesis of the "satanic majesty" version of Robert Moses is of course Robert Caro's magnificently readable and researched biography, *The Power Broker*, which appeared in 1974. That it is a great work of investigative reporting and urban history, no one can deny. The summer I read it, I gobbled it down like a detective novel, to find out the answers to a lurid crime. I felt I had stumbled upon a Rosetta Stone that explained for the first time the city around me, its physical mysteries and flaws.

I placed it alongside Jane Jacobs's *Death and Life of Great American Cities*, both working together to support the informal, pedestrian culture I loved about old cities, as against the modern planners' sterile, street-killing interventions. Both books, in a sense, formed me; they became part of the molecular structure of my brain; I thought *through* their premises' scrims, as did many in my generation. The quarreling Moses and Jacobs became in my mind Uncle Rob, the prosperous blowhard who tells you at a family gathering that you don't understand the first thing about power and money, or the way the real world operates, and Aunt Jane, the retired English teacher who is always carping and trying to get you to sign a liberal petition. The fact that they were both Jewish (I know, he converted to Christianity, but still . . .) made it seem even more as though they were my arguing relatives.

Over the years I began to experience little voices of inner doubt, which made me entertain timidly pro-Moses thoughts. Some arose from overhearing architects and planners mutter, "What I'd give for a Robert Moses to cut through the bureaucratic crap." As this seemed the equivalent of "Mussolini made the trains run on time," I was inclined to dismiss it. But the more I witnessed New York City's paralysis in tackling any new public works or large civic improvements, the more I suspected that maybe Moses had a point. However delightful Jane Jacobs's vision of the choreography of Greenwich Village street life may have been, it seemed static, frozen in time, like a stage set of gingerbread houses where the same charming operetta takes place every day. Her preference for the ad hoc and community control left no room for planning regionally, much less executing great urban schemes such as Central Park or the reservoir system.

Then I came across a book by Moses himself, *Public Works: A Dangerous Trade*, and discovered a mind far more playful and subtle than the caricatured villain we had made of him, and a literary style (founded on Samuel Johnson, his favorite writer in college) better than that of most of his critics.

Here he is on a subject dear to my heart, the treatment of New York in literature:

> New York is just too big, too complex to be covered by any one writer. At best he can only offer his little tribute to something he loves, but which is beyond him. . . . The finest short piece on New York in recent years was done by E. B. White. It is the tribute of a kindly, observant aficionado recording the immensely kaleidoscopic and other outward manifestations of the city rather than its subtleties, inner moods and deeper implications and meanings. . . . Most New York pieces, contemporary or prophetic, wallow in staggering statistics, like an up-to-date Baedeker guide. A big city lends itself peculiarly to exaggeration, distortion, superlatives and hyperbole. . . . We are told that there are more Neapolitans in Gotham than in Ischia, more Hebrews than in Haifa, more Irish than in Connemara, more Monégasques than in Monaco, more Down-easters than in Mount Desert, more Lapps than in Lapland, more Swedes than in Gothenburg, more Scots than on Loch Lomond, more Eskimos than in the Aleutians and more French Canadians than on the Restigouche River. They give us *ad nauseum* the exact total of nickels and dimes deposited during the rush hour in the subways, and of quarters snatched by toll collectors at tunnels and bridges, of yards of spaghetti unfurled and red ink guzzled daily on Mulberry Street.

Not bad, eh? But let me try to make the case for Robert Moses on other than literary grounds. My first argument is that he accomplished much more good than harm. He built Riverside Park and Jones Beach and dozens of neighborhood playgrounds and swimming pools, added 20,000 acres to the city's parkland, and 40,000 acres to Long Island's parkland, built seven major bridges (the Triborough, the Throgs Neck, the Bronx-

Whitestone, the Henry Hudson, the Verrazano, the Cross-Bay, the Marine Parkway) and almost all the highways and parkways in Greater New York, 627 miles total, without which the city would have become completely immobilized and stagnant. The fact that Caro spent hundreds of pages diligently and judiciously chronicling the magnificent things Moses did matters little, partly because most people who summarize *The Power Broker* never actually read that massive work, and partly because the public loves contemplating Moses more as its vampire than as its benefactor.

My second argument is that Moses is unfairly held accountable for many questionable urban policies that were national, even global, at the time. It was not Moses who chose the automobile as the preferred mode of transportation in the twentieth century, or passed the federal highway construction act that unloosed billions of dollars for suburbanization, or decided that highways ought to be placed along the waterfront (that was done everywhere, alas), or decreed that public housing should be sited according to neighborhood racial patterns (that was standard governmental "wisdom" at the time), or mandated millions for slum clearance. He merely implemented those policies; yet somehow he has become their personification. Caro's perception is that because he carried out those policies so forcefully and skillfully, everyone else copied him. I would argue that those policies were going through, Moses or no Moses. What Moses did was to follow the flow of dollars, wherever it happened to be at the moment, and siphon off a sizable chunk, creating and maintaining control of his own revenue stream, for what he deemed the betterment of New York.

Even regarding his questionable policies, his record is sufficiently a mixture of good and bad that how we choose to evaluate Moses, case by case, depends largely on our initial predisposition for or against him. Yes, he placed highways on the river, cutting off the populace from waterfront access, but he also tucked them under beautifully in places (such as the Brooklyn Promenade, Carl Schurz Park, and the Battery). Did he fail to tuck them under throughout because he was evil, or because the budget did not permit more? Yes, he rammed through thousands of low-income public housing units that were grim, depressing, and monotonous; but the city, in its chronic housing shortage, would today be desperate without them. Yes, he tricked Staten Island into letting the municipality use Fresh Kills as a garbage dump by claiming it would only be temporary; but as it happens, it served that function beautifully, and now that it is closed, New York faces a major waste-disposal crisis, costing the city a billion dollars a year. Yes, he engaged in slum clearance that cruelly displaced thousands of poor people; he replaced it with housing for the middle and upper class, but also with facilities that helped consolidate New York's status as world capital: the United Nations headquarters, Lincoln Center, the Coliseum, and the Fordham, Pratt, and Long Island University campuses. I have to say that cities are not obliged to maintain slums as slums, and when a market for higher-end uses exists, it may make fiscal sense to go for it, taking into consideration the greater good. Of course, you hope that in upgrading these neighborhoods, a commensurate effort is made to provide decent low-income housing elsewhere for those displaced—a hope often disabused. Moses often seemed cheerfully indifferent to the plight of those dislocated by his constructions. On the other hand, Moses built more public housing than anyone else did.

My third argument is that too much of the anti-Moses sentiment derives from his character (at least as it has come down to us from Caro), and that we are far too petty, too limited by our culture of resentment and political correctness, in assessing it. *The Power Broker* paints an indelible portrait of the man as an elitist, a racist, and a wannabe WASP patrician, an early champion of meritocracy whose later arrogance and intellectual contempt led to the autocratic refusal to listen to others, and (horrors!) a builder of highways who never drove a car himself. Some of these judgments seem the work of a hanging jury. We are told that, having failed as a politician because he lacked the common touch, he amassed uncommon power behind the scenes. Well, what is wrong with an able person seeking to accomplish things as an appointed official, if he cannot get elected to public office? Must we act naïvely shocked that, in a capitalist democracy, considerable clout may rest in the hands of non-elected individuals? Perhaps the time has also come to forgive Moses for roughly taking people by the arm when he wished to make a point. Of course the man was arrogant. He was the greatest city builder in history, as Caro himself acknowledges. He made Baron Haussmann look like a subcontractor.

A better title for Robert Moses' life story might have been *The Master*

Builder; but by calling his huge study *The Power Broker,* Caro fixed a label on Moses that would throw him more into the company of Boss Tweed and Mayor Daley than of Daniel Burnham and Edwin Lutyens. Not that it didn't make good dramatic sense; by doing so, he could transform his biographical subject into a Shakespearean tragic protagonist, a Richard III or Macbeth, grasping for more and more power. Caro's argument that power is an addictive drug, or "the more you have it, the more you want," rests on the unspoken assumption that power itself and the desire for it are intrinsically evil. To place that argument in context, we must remember that *The Power Broker* came out of a particular historical moment, dominated by Vietnam antiwar politics. The legacy of that moment—the lingering prejudice, or should I say intellectual consensus, against the exercise of power and the pursuit of glory—is so in tune with our age that it requires taking a step back to grasp just how peculiar it would have seemed to the ancient Greeks, say, or to the makers of the Italian Renaissance. While what motivated Moses, to Caro, was the sheer abstraction, Power, to my way of thinking it was the chance to use his gifts effectively, to accomplish his vision. For instance, when Moses took over the public housing authority, an unsympathetic observer could see this as a naked grab for more power: his need to control every facet of New York City's operation. But Moses himself, given his very justified confidence in his abilities as a builder of public works, and his awareness that no one else around was even remotely as capable, might have felt that if those units were going to get built, it would have to be by him.

Moses was also a pragmatic politician. He knew how the levers of society operated, and his dislike of planning critics and do-gooders rose largely from his sense that they did not. He defended the Metropolitan Life Insurance's building of Stuyvesant Town, even if it meant splitting off an uptown counterpart, Riverton, for blacks, because to turn down the offer would have, Moses felt, discouraged any private builders in the future from touching moderate-income housing in New York. Acknowledging in a letter that the Metropolitan Life's chairman, Fred Ecker Sr., was "hard-boiled and conservative" and had surrounded himself with some "very poor advisors," Moses went on to say: "The only constructive suggestion I can offer is to get Fred senior to take more Negro tenants at Stuyvesant and Cooper, get himself a *new* housing vice-president with more milk of human kindness and less ice water in his veins, and keep abreast of the times. . . ." Did Moses have racist tendencies? Very, very likely. But as we can see from this letter, it was not the entire story; being a pragmatist, he also understood that integration was a sign of the times.

Another example of this pragmatic approach: Moses wanted to place the United Nations headquarters in Flushing Meadows, the old World's Fair site, where he thought the organization would have more room to grow than in Midtown Manhattan. But when the United Nations hierarchy, cool to the Flushing Meadows site, started leaning toward another city, Moses got on the phone and, with Nelson Rockefeller, helped broker the deal by which the Rockefeller family bought the East Forties property from William Zeckendorf and donated it to the city. For a man lambasted as rigid, Moses showed remarkable flexibility when it mattered. Not that his ability to compromise earned him any points with purists, but the secretary general of the UN, Trygve Lie, who favored a Manhattan site, certainly appreciated it.

In keeping with the Shakespearean tragedy scheme, Caro breaks down Robert Moses' life into discrete segments: Moses the Good, Moses the Bad, with 1954 being the fault line. When he built parks for kids and fought the Long Island barons to put a parkway through to the shore, so that the public could bathe at Jones Beach, he was a populist and a good guy. When he put a highway through a working-class quarter of the Bronx, he was an autocrat and a bad guy. This *All the King's Men* scenario of a fall from virtue distorts his basic unitary nature. He saw himself as consistently operating the same way, following the same broader regional vision.

Unarguably, the destruction of city's fabric by the Cross-Bronx Expressway and other Moses highway projects was deplorable. But the dice seem unfairly loaded when Caro, recounting the Cross-Bronx Expressway saga, pits King Robert against the little people, such as Sam and Lillian Edelstein, and lo and behold, the reader chooses Sam and Lillian. The sad fact is that even when no highways went through those old Jewish working-class neighborhoods, they were doomed to change and wither, gone the way of the two-cent seltzer glass, the egg cream, the well-made knish, and all those other nostalgic memories. There is only so much you can blame on highway construction.

I might add that some of the worst sins for which he is held accountable are projects that never got made, such as the Lower Manhattan Expressway. Awful they undoubtedly would have been; but it seems topsy-turvy to minimize all the wonderful deeds he did, while fixating on his unbuilt plans. We Lilliputians can no longer take the measure of Robert Moses. We have problems with great men in general. From my own, ant's, perspective, he was one of the greatest Americans of the twentieth century, a maker and a *macher* who changed the shape of our lives, on a par with Thomas Alva Edison and D. W. Griffith and W. E. B. Du Bois and Frank Lloyd Wright. I await the day when he gets his own postage stamp, or at least an avenue named after him in his beloved New York.

24

TUDOR CITY,
THE UNITED NATIONS,
AND
THE UPPER EAST SIDE

A T THE END OF 42ND STREET—AFTER ALL THE BRIGHT
LIGHTS AND NEON AND BACKSTAGE DRAMA WITH RUBY
KEELER COMING TO THE RESCUE, AND RUNAWAYS
turning tricks and sex shops and gamblers that earned it its raffish nickname, "the Deuce"—as far east as you can go without falling in the river,
that notorious thoroughfare reforms and culminates in tranquil,
respectable Tudor City and the United Nations, the hope of the world.

Tudor City consists of twelve buildings (with 3,000 apartments and
600 hotel rooms) extending from East 40th Street to East 43rd Street,
between First and Second Avenues. It is a harmonious, serenely planned

private kingdom, like nothing else in Midtown, and I have always been intrigued by it, wishing I could live in so protected an environment right in the middle of the city, yet mistrusting its stage set air of self-satisfaction.

Designed and built by the Fred C. French Company in 1925–32, it was begun in the boom years of the twenties, ran smack into the Great Depression, and continued on course during those dark days, finishing around the same time as the Empire State Building and Rockefeller Center. Fred C. French was a bold developer, responsible for the elegant skyscraper at 551 Fifth Avenue (with massive bronze doors, polychromed faience panels, and Ishtar-inspired Babylonianism) that today bears his name, and for Knickerbocker Village, the decent, moderate-income housing project in the Lower East Side, among other New York properties. His vision regarding Tudor City was to provide better living conditions for white-collar workers in the new office towers ascending around Grand Central Station. "Men could walk to work in the morning. Children could play in the community gardens, out in the open air," French told *New Yorker* reporter Robert M. Coates in 1929. Influenced by the garden-city ideas of Patrick Geddes and Lewis Mumford, the Tudor City plan called for a ribbon of high-rise, high-density residential towers encircling a green open space. French assembled a five-acre parcel on Prospect Hill that had held some smaller brownstones and townhouses (a few of which still stand), but was otherwise sparsely populated, and built his three-sided fortress around a landscaped forecourt, open to the west.

I enter the park at the center of the complex. The sign says TUDOR GREENS, and there are actually two parks, like mirror images of each other, on either side of the ramps leading to 42nd Street. Well kept, with obvious pride, the greens are spacious, containing gravel paths and benches, tree-lined, wonderfully shady on a summer's day. A few new saplings are being planted. The gardener, a longhair moving briskly and purposefully about, has his own toolshed at the end of the park. I share a bench with a squirrel, who looks unintimidated. Two workmen in construction uniforms are catching a rest: one, lying down on his bench, is looking up at the sky; the other, sitting near, talks to him in Spanish. An old woman with a walker enters the park and takes hesitant steps, her daily constitutional. A thin, scholarly woman in her forties, with grayish-blonde ponytail and sweat pants, is reading a book and underlining it intently, on a bench far removed from everyone. Everyone gives off an air—unusual for a big city—of feeling utterly safe.

And indeed, Tudor City is nothing if not an enclave, niched into various cul-de-sacs. Straight ahead of me is a fence with a DEAD END sign, on an abutment that overlooks the United Nations, First Avenue and the FDR Drive below; at the southern end is another DEAD END sign marking a pleasant overlook. All the buildings face in, toward the greens, away from the surrounding metropolis. When the complex was originally built, slaughterhouses and a coaling station occupied the land where the United Nations now sits, which explains why the three river towers along Tudor City Place turn their backs so resolutely on the water: the smell must have been unbearable, and, without air-conditioning, people would have had no other option but to open their windows. (If you stand below Tudor City, on First Avenue, and look up, you will see the merest scattering of windows over otherwise unbroken brick walls.)

Tudor City perches on a promontory overlooking the East River—the same promontory, in effect, that shelters those other tony residential enclaves to the north, Beekman Place and Sutton Place. Tudor City was never quite as ritzy; most of the units were designed as start-up apartments for single people and young married couples without children, who were expected to move away when they raised a family or grew prosperous. The three easternmost towers, each twenty-two stories, were crammed with studios and one-bedroom apartments, and no one had a full kitchen, just a kitchenette. (This is still true today, though now all the units are cooperatively owned.) The only exceptions to this sardine arrangement were the apartments at the tops—duplexes and such that were truly baronial—and the shorter buildings on the north and south ends of the landscaped greens, which had more multiple-bedroom, family units.

James Sanders, an architect friend who grew up in Tudor City, told me, "The complex was a functioning example of mixing income groups, since the best apartments were probably five times more expensive than the cheapest ones." James remembers Tudor City as the perfect accommodation for his parents. His mother wanted to be near the bright lights of Broadway, his father, enamored of garden cities, wanted a home overlooking green space. He recalls a strong community feeling: everyone knew and watched out for each other; the Tudor City kids played together in the greens and, on snowy days, pulled their sleds across the turnaround. Partly because it stood on the water's edge, the complex got plenty of light and air—more so, in fact, than the luxury apartment houses on Park Avenue, with their gloomy inner rooms, reserved for the maid or the second child. Still, Tudor City seemed to be mimicking those broad, bulky Park Avenue apartment houses, especially in the way that service shops—a dry cleaner, a pharmacy, a grocery, a café—were discreetly tucked into the street level.

At the base of one tower is a storefront with toy dollhouse furniture and plastic fruit: "Lovelia Enterprise Showroom." Somehow this business, with its trifling yet exclusive air, epitomizes the tweedy atmosphere of Tudor City. Like the London Terrace Apartments (1929) on West 23rd Street, or the Tudor-style Hudson View Gardens (1924) in Washington Heights, Tudor City looked to England for its aesthetic pedigree, at a time when most other Manhattan apartment courts were attempting a Parisian flair.

What strikes me most now about the design, done by H. Douglas Ives, French's in-house architect, is the studied ornamentation, which reinforces a solid impression of quality. The Tudor decorations on the façade make the massing of these very massive buildings less oppressive, as they work their way up from the stone at street level, to the brick in the middle floors, relieved by a variety of indentations, to the more-fantastic treatments of the roof apartments. There are allusions to the ecclesiastical (one building is called The Cloister), or feudal (turrets that recall a medieval castle) or academic (a lobby with leaded colored-glass windows and a reading nook, that suggests the parlor of an Oxford dormitory). All this is done, in retrospect, very lovingly, and seems poignant in its plea for dignity. One could never get away with it today, because modernist aesthetics wouldn't stand for that level of historicist ornamentation, nor are there enough poor, skilled Italian stone carvers around, willing to work for peanuts. Of course, there is something faintly fatuous about pumping up a Tudor three-story chalet to the skies, and running all those brown ornamental lines over their façades; it was architecturally reactionary even in its day. But no more so than those faux-Tudor high-rise apartment blocks in London, from the same era, which appear so graceful to the American visitor's eye. All in all, Tudor City remains one of the most distinctly civilized, urbane places in New York. Even its flashy Tudor City rooftop sign, which clashes with the restrained architecture, works, by injecting some necessary vulgarity into the picture.

The trees sigh in the breeze, and I think of closing my eyes and going to sleep here. Maybe if I were a resident of Tudor City I would, but being merely a visitor I sense they would shoo me out of the park if I started snoozing. Something else keeps me on edge. Across the park from me, at the base of one of the towers, is the Tudor Grill, and I'm vividly recalling with a knot in my stomach a birthday party I attended there one winter for a little boy: the child of my friends, a lovely couple, who had just turned three. The restaurant was closed for the private affair, with balloons and party favors and plenty of food. Waiters circulated with hors d'oeuvres, meat-carvers stood by. Since then, the boy has had to battle a chronic illness; the couple's marriage has collapsed and shattered under the strain. I can't see the innocent Tudor Grill sign without thinking of a charming, beautiful boy at three. So we fill out even the most benign spaces of the city with personal tragedy.

STANDING ON THE OVERLOOK, where Tudor City ends in a cul-de-sac, I gaze down at the United Nations headquarters, at the familiarly elegant, green-mirror-glassed facade of the Secretariat towering over the low-slung, saddle-shaped, off-white General Assembly Building. There is something not quite Manhattan about the UN complex, something more reminiscent of the 1939 World's Fair, with its trylon and sphere, out in Queens. "Blood Alley," that old congeries of slaughterhouses and rendering plants which used to occupy the site, has been more than expunged; it has given way to a marvelously iconic, abstract composition of vertical forms balanced against horizontals, made all the more postcard-flat because you can only view it (unless you are on a boat) from the direction of the streets that look east toward the river. Because of its security fears, the United Nations has never permitted any pedestrian access to its water frontage in the rear (though it seems to me that a terrorist might do as much damage, lobbing a shell from a motorboat or from a passing car, as on foot). From time to time, the city has approached the United Nations with offers to cantilever an esplanade over the water, even one walled off from the complex, but the UN has always rejected the idea.

The 572-foot Secretariat Building looks better with each passing year. I have come to love that shimmering, book-shaped rectangle with two spacious glass sides facing the water and two thin stone sides at the edges, and those intriguing grillwork strips punctuating the façade every twelve or so floors—though part of what makes it moving is that it has the poignant fragility of many early modernist masterworks, as if the panes were getting tired of shouldering their stoic purity. (It has 5,400 windows that actually open and close, and its energy consumption is enormously wasteful, by today's standards). Neglected for decades because of the UN's budget constraints, it now needs a major overhaul, especially the interiors, which still have their original fixtures, obsolete telephone switchboards and wiring, and leaking air-conditioning vents.*

When the Secretariat was completed in 1950, it was the first postwar glass skyscraper done in the International Style, and fulfilled the fondest dreams of New York modernists. A committee of international architects, led by New York's own Wallace K. Harrison, who had worked on Rockefeller Center, had conferred regularly, while the lone genius Le Corbusier went off and developed the essential design. Later, Le Corbusier fulminated that he was not allowed to supervise the construction of "his" building; but in truth, he lacked the engineering skills to accomplish in hard materials the innovative free-hanging glass-and-metal curtain wall he had sketched with pencil; those practical refinements fell to Harrison, whom Le Corbusier disdained as a local hack, to figure out.

Harrison admittedly did not have Le Corbusier's rigorously elegant flair, which shows in the hodgepodge General Assembly Building *he* designed. Completed in 1952, its exterior is a mundane version of that spacecraft-landing architecture popular in the 1950s, further compromised by the absurd, dinky dome that a United States senator insisted be added to the top, to get Congress to pass its share of the construction costs. Its interior, dominated by the lobby, is a mélange of boomerang-shaped bal-

---

*The whole United Nations headquarters complex requires an estimated $1-billion refurbishment to overhaul its aging buildings and deal with its intensifying space needs. One option under discussion would be to add ten stories to the Secretariat Building, a terrible idea. Another would be to erect several smaller structures on the seventeen-acre site. (Of course, the most logical course would be to expand south onto the Con Edison site, but it would bring in less profit for the landowners than private high-rise residences.) Though a billion dollars will be difficult to raise from member nations, such renovation makes more sense than the estimated $1.2 billion in maintenance costs, including emergency repairs and excessive energy bills, which would be required over the next twenty-five years.

conies and ramps that suggest an airport terminal. One day I decided to take the tour of the General Assembly and Conference Buildings (the Secretariat, alas, is closed to the public). After several security checks, I joined a group and was led past hallways chock-full of donated national arts and folk crafts, most of it of the peace-kitsch variety, into a succession of delegate chambers done in variations of fifties Swedish Modern, and invited to imagine the United Nations at work—uplifting, in an anachronistic, One World sort of way.

A replica of the General Assembly's lobby was used in Alfred Hitchcock's *North by Northwest,* when the advertising executive played by Cary Grant, mistaken for a murderer, is forced to flee the United Nations building. Hitchcock told Truffaut in their interview: "The place where the man is stabbed in the back is in the delegates' lounge, but to maintain the prestige of the United Nations, we called it the 'public lounge' in the picture, and this also explains how the man in the knife could get in there." If the United Nations could seem so logical a crime scene to the makers of thrillers, one can understand the UN's reluctance to let ordinary citizens wander along its waterfront side. Still, that this organization, dedicated to open, democratic debate in the resolution of conflicts, should have so averse a response to the public's presence speaks to the strange lack of presence that the world's government has exerted on its host city. Anywhere else, such an institution would dominate the city's cultural life and cocktail gossip—but not in New York. The occasional tabloid outcries over driving accidents or illegal parking by UN personnel who enjoy diplomatic immunity only underscore this shadowy relationship.

The lack of engagement, or standoff, between New York and the United Nations finds embodiment in the curiously muffled way the city's streets meet the UN complex. First, there is the utter absence of ceremonial entrance: visitors come in through a side door. Second, along this particular stretch of First Avenue bordering the United Nations, the main car traffic has been diverted through an underground tunnel (an inspiration of Robert Moses when he was City Construction Coordinator), which makes sound security sense and promotes the dignity of the ensemble, but also gives the front of the complex the stiff, deserted air of a suburban corporate headquarters.

When the United Nations was first being built, there were calls for an entire city-within-a-city to be constructed for the organization's personnel. These ambitious plans never got off the ground, partly because any expansions would have encountered already-functioning city neighborhoods. One particularly dense public-private residential high-rise project, proposed in the 1960s, was resisted by populists such as columnist Pete Hamill, who objected to "the assumption that . . . somehow these free-loading diplomats assigned to the UN have some blessed right to live across the street from their job, while the rest of us have to come screaming into Manhattan on the subway cages." So the decision—or non-decision—was made to leave the development of a UN district to the marketplace's impulses. Piecemeal, a mysteriously self-reflexive zone of glass-and-steel office towers and apartment houses arose north of the United Nations complex along First Avenue, which one might call "UNville." It lay just south of the exclusive residential addresses of Beekman Place and Sutton Place, and partook of their prestige by proximity, attracting as residents not only UN people but high-society and entertainment types, though it remains repellent for walking purposes to the casual stroller who comes in on it from elsewhere.

The twin luxury high-rises of 860–870 United Nations Plaza, designed by Harrison & Abramovitz in 1966, seem to pay homage to the Secretariat by quoting its slab glass form. Here, too, in the heart of UNville, at 845 United Nations Plaza (otherwise known at First Avenue between 47th and 48th Streets), the developer Donald J. Trump chose to erect in 2001 what he claimed to be the tallest residential tower in the world, the seventy-two-story Trump World Tower. It was steadfastly fought by goo-goo associations and by its well-heeled neighbors, such as Walter Cronkite, whose views it threatened to obstruct, but went ahead and got built anyway; and the Mies-influenced glass box design, by New York architect Costas Kondylis, has since garnered the praise of several architectural critics. I neither love it nor hate it, but feel proud of the city for absorbing this once monstrous-seeming intrusion with the merest shrug.

I remember one summer evening going to a fancy book party in this neighborhood, thrown by a wealthy magnate for a writer friend of mine. The penthouse suite, located in an expensive but architecturally undistinguished luxury tower, was furnished in that impersonal, Ritz-Carlton Hotel style amid which multimillionaires, to my shock and disappointment, are often content to live; then again, the owner lived elsewhere and only used the place to house his art collection and host his parties, and it had spectacular views overlooking the East River. I wandered over to the windows as twilight was coming on, and stared out at the ruins of the old Smallpox Hospital, which lies at the southern end of Roosevelt Island, and which was once part of a suite of nineteenth-century institutions that included an almshouse, a prison, and a lunatic asylum, and tried to savor the social ironies for as long as I could, before diving into the chitchat.

The Smallpox Hospital (or what remains of it) is an 1856 Gothic Revival structure designed by James Renwick, the architect of Grace Church and St. Patrick's Cathedral. Gray and crenellated, benign in daylight, it is a haunted, spectral sight after dark. How many times have I been mesmerized, on the FDR Drive at night, by its gap-toothed, jack-o'-lantern façade, lit up seemingly from within, like an X-ray, or like a black-and-white negative. Preservationists on Roosevelt Island, realizing it would take millions of dollars to restore the building, wisely decided to let it crumble before our eyes—every society needs ruins to contemplate, just as every Hamlet needs a skull. They were more protective of their lunatic asylum, or, as it is sometimes gently called, the Octagon Building, putting a new roof on the mid-island structure to "stabilize it as a ruin." (Is this a contradiction in terms?) The madhouse, erected in 1839, which once crammed together 1,700 patients, is not as impressive from the outside as the Smallpox Hospital, but recent photographs of its interior, by Stanley Greenberg, suggest a giddy, Piranesian architecture.

An unsigned article in *America Illustrated,* 1883, described the institution in the language of its day: "In the Lunatic Asylum the patients are mainly from the poorer classes, and are particularly women. Mania afflicts more than four-fifths of them, the disease of the remaining fifth being dementia, general paralysis or idiocy. . . . The building has no rooms stronger than the usual sleeping apartments of a hotel, and the only attempt at security is in the cast-iron sashes of the windows; and these may be easily broken. The building is well-adapted for the more harmless forms of insanity, but is too insecure for cases where there are dangerous propensities; while to convicts who feign mental derangement in the hope of escape, the greatest facilities to that end are afforded."

THIS WHOLE EDGE OF THE EAST SIDE, just north of the United Nations, used to be a ghetto filled with tenements. You can read about it in Sholem Asch's 1946 novel, *East River*. Asch (1880–1957) was born in Poland and immigrated to this country, where he became a best-selling American author who wrote in Yiddish (hard to picture this happening now) and had his books translated into English, most notably a trilogy on the life of Christ, *The Nazarene, The Apostle,* and *Mary,* which attempted to reconcile Judaism and Christianity. My parents used to own his books. Anyway, his one New York novel was called *East River,* and was set in the half-Irish, half-Jewish waterfront tenement neighborhood around First Avenue and East 48th Street, in the early decades of the twentieth century. The novel is one of those ghetto sagas about two brothers: one, Irving, eager for money and power, who grows up to be a ruthless garment manufacturer, exploiting the workers; the other, the scholarly, polio-afflicted Nathan, who becomes a socialist organizer, confronting the bosses. Both are in love, naturally, with an Irish *shiksa* named Mary. The novel's style glops together naturalism and melodrama in a conscientious, repetitive prose that is both dated and remarkably consonant with today's potboilers. Yet its incidental detail gives a sharp picture of the way people lived along the city's waterfront around 1920, as in this description of a stifling New York summer, before air-conditioning, when everyone crowded onto the fire escapes:

> Most of all they sought relief in the cool winds that came once in a while over the East River. But direct approach was blocked to them. The streets ended in "dead ends" hemmed in by fences erected by the owners of the feed storehouses and stables. In a couple of places, however, there was an old unused dock, the planks water-soaked and rotted. From these docks one could hear the splashing of children swimming close to the shore, driven to find relief from the overpowering heat, disregarding the perils of the holes and falling timbers of the dock.
>
> Other entrances to the waterfront were provided by the stables on the

river shore. By climbing over fences and scrambling over the stable roofs it was possible to get down to the water's edge. But 48th Street had two yards that opened on the river, and of these the people of the adjoining blocks were properly jealous.

The two yards were private; one, controlled by Tammany, issued tickets to those loyal to the local political machine.

The yard was full of people; men, women, and children in the neighborhood. They had brought with them mattresses, blankets, pillows, cans of cold tea or beer or ice water, ready to spend half the night there, until the tenement rooms got cool enough to return to.

From such passages, we can see how long public access to this stretch of waterfront has been coveted, and how long it has been selectively controlled. Near the end of the novel, which is set in the 1940s, gentrification comes to the neighborhood, and, while it means improvement for some, it also makes the river even more inaccessible for others.

"They've blocked off the river!" Moshe Wolf said in astonishment. "The road to the river is blocked."

"Yes, Pa. They're going to build a big apartment house there. The river will belong to the people who live in the house now."

"And I thought the river was free, that it belonged to everybody."

"The river is still free, Pa. It's only the entrance to it that's blocked."

Actually, the river did not "belong" to the people who moved into the big apartment houses, either, except in a visual sense. They could look at it as spectacle, like a permanent video installation installed in their picture windows, but they had even less opportunity to enjoy its immediate smell and touch than did the ghetto-dwellers who had previously sweltered on these blocks.

For a decade or so, the old ghetto and the new, deluxe apartment houses coexisted dissonantly by the East River's edge. This strange, albeit temporary, commingling of classes and neighborhood types served as the main dramatic situation for *Dead End,* the 1937 film directed by William Wyler.

As he demonstrated in other movies from that period (*Dodsworth*, *These Three*, *The Heiress*, *The Little Foxes*), Wyler was a stickler for long takes linking characters to their environments, and he used the noted deep-focus cameraman, Gregg Toland, to make the most of these foreground/background spatial relationships—in this case, highlighting the economic clashes within a single shot.

As a descending crane shot takes us from the crowned row of luxury towers, looking very much like Sutton Place, to the more stubby, rundown houses below, its opening crawl, written by Lillian Hellman, declares: "Every street in New York ends in a river. For many years the dirty banks of the East River were lined with the tenements of the poor. Then the rich, discovering that the river traffic was picturesque, moved their houses eastward. And now the terraces of the great apartment houses look down into the windows of the tenement poor." In another movie of that period, the screwball comedy *My Man Godfrey*, high and low intermix again, as socialite Carole Lombard retrieves hobo William Powell from a tramp village situated on the East River and Sutton Place. Little does she know that he is actually a millionaire's son, disillusioned with wealth! At the movie's end, he turns the tramps' ash heap into a swanky nightclub called The Dump.

AT THE QUEENSBOROUGH–59TH STREET BRIDGE, the lofty, Guastavino-tiled spaces inside the anchorage have been redeveloped as Bridgemarket, a complex that consists of a Conran's design store, a Food Emporium supermarket, and a chichi, loud restaurant with river views, called Guastavino. To my mind it is an uninspired use of a magnificent space, not unique enough to serve as a true "destination." Its exact replica could be found on waterfronts all around the globe. Still, at least it is inhabited, after decades of inactivity. Henri Langlois, the great, cetacean-shaped founder of the Cinémathèque Française in Paris, once planned to establish a New York branch in these very same vaulted spaces, and how wonderful that would have been. But he could not raise the necessary funds, and anyway, I must stop thinking of these lost opportunities. . . .

Climbing the staircase to the little park, with its dog run and Alice Aycock sculpture, left over from FDR Drive highway ramps, I stare across the East River at Queens and Roosevelt Island. I have to admit I find this industrial view across the East River from Manhattan, with its factories and chimneys and Con Edison's "Big Allis" smokestacks, much more stimulating and comforting than the part of the Manhattan shoreline I am surrounded by, which is nothing but highway, hospitals, and deluxe apartment buildings. "The other bank of the river, because it is the other bank, is never the bank we are standing on: that is the intimate reason for all my suffering," wrote the Portuguese poet Fernando Pessoa. I don't know that I can trace my suffering to the same root cause; in fact, I have no particular desire to exchange places in order to stand on the shore of Long Island City looking back at Manhattan. But I know what he means.

Contrary to Saul Bellow's pungent line in *Humboldt's Gift,* "His face was dead gray, East River gray," the East River usually looks green to me, very rarely gray, except on those clouded, foggy days when it mirrors the sky. Today, with the sun half in, half out, the East River is a somber green with black flecks, choppy, swelling, mucoid, not a Martha Stewart shade, more squid-inky, like broccoli rabe in oil.

In the beautiful final stanza of a poem called "The River That Is East" (the title a quotation from Hart Crane), Galway Kinnell writes:

What is this river but the one
Which drags the things we love,
Processions of debris like floating lamps,
Toward the radiance in which they go out?
No, it is the River that is East, known once
From a high window in Brooklyn, in agony—river
On which a door locked to the water floats,
A window sash paned with brown water, a whiskey crate.
Barrel staves, sun spokes, feathers of the birds,
A breadcrust, a rat, spittle, butts, and peels,
The immaculate stream, heavy, and swinging home again.

The East River has its fans; some have championed it, like Kinnell, in this backhanded way, as the repository of all our flotsam and jetsam. "Another reason [why the East River is more interesting than the Hudson River], perhaps," wrote a journalist named Jesse Lynch Williams in

Scribner's Magazine, October 1899, "is that the East River is not a river at all, but an arm of the ocean which makes Long Island, and true to its nature in spite of man's error it holds the charm of the sea." Still, the East River has never had the positive identity, the constituency, or the foundation support possessed by the Hudson. Is it because it is only 15½ miles in length, or because it has such a history of being polluted, or because it is a tidal strait, not a true river? A tidal strait changes its direction completely with each tidal flow. There are two high tides and two low tides daily; this gives the East River a pulse, a rhythm. But its distinctive tidal pattern also leaves the river dirty. "The tidal excursion (the maximum distance a particle would travel during either flooding or ebbing tides) is about 70 percent of the length of the river itself, which explains why the East River is never completely flushed of contaminants by the tides," writes Malcolm J. Bowman, a marine scientist.

Bowman points out that the oscillating tidal flow of the East River also contributes to the worsening hypoxia problems of Long Island Sound, into which it empties. Hypoxia is a condition of oxygen deficiency resulting from overfertilization by nitrogen, and it can seriously harm the functioning ecosystem, even lead to fish kills. Ironically, part of these nitrogen deposits come from effluents released by sewage treatment plants along the East River, built to improve water quality in the harbor.

Bowman advocates a visionary solution called the East River Tidal Barrage, which would entail constructing a set of tide gates on piers that span the river. He explains the plan this way: "During ebbing tides, Long Island Sound water would flow into New York Harbor (as it does now, except that with gates the water would now be much cleaner) and out into the New York Bight. During rising tide in New York Harbor, flow through the East River would be blocked." The drawbacks of the scheme, besides its cost, are that it would obviously impede river navigation and that it would interfere with the marine habitat. "Lots of fish and other aquatic life-forms don't care about the pollution," noted marine biologist Mike Ludwig, "but they use the East River to get to Long Island Sound. Striped bass in particular use the river as a corridor to the habitat of Long Island Sound." Even if there were agreement among scientists for the Tidal Barrage plan, the funds would be lacking. So, for the moment at least, the East River will remain gateless.

. . .

SINCE ANY ATTEMPT to walk or bicycle northward along the East River waterfront runs into frustrating barriers, I decided to explore that part of the shoreline from the water—more precisely, the Circle Line, which circumnavigates Manhattan. I caught that venerable ark at its pier on West 42nd Street, meeting up with my friend Wilbur Woods, who is the city government's waterfront expert. For the last few decades he has spearheaded the study of the underused waterfront, preparing maps, surveys, and position papers for various mayors and planning commissions. Wilbur, or Bill, as he prefers to be called, is a tall, rangy, baldheaded architect turned planner, whose soft-spoken, reserved manner gives way in conversation to a grinning appreciation for the lunatic machinations of New York development.

As the Circle Line heads south along the Hudson to the island's tip, then turns and begins puttering north up the East River, Bill explains to me the "deal" behind various waterfront parcels. For the most part we successfully tune out the Circle Line announcer's commentary with our own conversation, though, from the bits I listen to, the guide sounds fairly well informed—not as obnoxious as I had feared. One young couple is smooching through the entire boat ride, their lips and limbs locked without pause to take in the shoreline. The other passengers—whether tourists or locals, I have no idea—seem glad for the river breeze, on this sweltering, muggy late afternoon between rainstorms.

Bill Woods's singleminded passion is to provide New Yorkers in all five boroughs with public access to their waterfront, by filling in the patchwork of promenades, vest-pocket parks, and bikeways to make one uninterrupted greenbelt of open space. "If I could just get them to give us a strip of fifty to a hundred feet . . ." he will exclaim, whenever we pass a site blocked from access. At present there are twenty-two gaps in the continuous linear esplanade around Manhattan, he informed me. The largest is probably the one that extends from the United Nations through East 47th Street, all the way up to East 60th Street, where the FDR Drive has been built so close to the river's edge as to make any future esplanade iffy. Around Sutton Place, a private riverfront garden, best seen from the water, has been allowed to deck the highway for three blocks, like a green blanket thrown over the back of a horse: a favor to some extremely well-heeled residents.

Another example of the privileges of the well connected occurs in the East Sixties and Seventies, where several hospitals have been permitted in the last forty years to build so close to the waterfront as to seize the land that had originally been devoted to a public esplanade. "We really let the hospitals get away with murder," Bill comments, "letting them close off the land like that."

"Why *did* you?" I ask him, and then amend the question, knowing he was probably not the one responsible. "I mean, why did the city allow it?"

"That whole lineup—Cornell Medical Center, New York Presbyterian, Rockefeller University, Memorial Sloan-Kettering—is a powerhouse. It's one of the richest and most influential health-care complexes in the country. The people on their boards have clout; one phone call is sometimes all it takes."

When we get to the East Eighties, where that beautiful overhanging esplanade, built under Robert Moses' direction, decks over the highway at Carl Schurz Park and alongside the apartment buildings just south of the park on Gracie Terrace, so that you can gaze out at the river without ever seeing cars, I ask Bill something I have been dying to know: Why couldn't such an elegant solution have been carried all the way down the East River? Why did it have to stop around East 78th Street? I am thinking it must have been a combination of stupidity, snobbery, shortsightedness, and so on, when Bill sets me straight. He points to the cliffs along the Carl Schurz Park esplanade: "The land rose up there, so you *could* put a deck over the highway without much trouble. Also, the apartment buildings on Gracie Terrace were new, which meant they could be built from the start with their foundations raised high. Farther south, the older fashionable apartment buildings had already been built with their foundations set low, and if you were to deck the highway there, you'd be cutting off the lower floors from light and running the traffic outside those people's windows, which they never would have agreed to." That explains everything. Geography rules.

· · ·

MY FIRST SIGNIFICANT EXPERIENCES with the Carl Schurz Park esplanade occurred in the early 1970s, when I moved into a studio apartment on East 81st Street and York Avenue, on the Upper East Side. Newly divorced, back from a year's self-exile in California, I was trying to adjust to single life in New York, and where better to start again than in that frivolous poodle of a neighborhood? French bakeries on nearly every block, glassed-in windows of bistros that offered Sunday brunches of eggs Benedict and sangria, a young crowd, the men in blazers and turtlenecks, the women with Cacherel shirts and decorator scarves—an epicurean avant-garde who took their weekend relaxations very seriously. The neighborhood had the reputation at the time of being a kind of dude ranch for stewardesses, masseuses, or financial trainees who roomed together. Though I never spoke to my neighbors, at least I was in no danger of meeting too many bookworms like myself, and could cultivate my solitude to my heart's content.

My favorite walk was down by the river, near the mayor's house, Gracie Mansion. Along the curved, wrought-iron fence of the Carl Schurz Park esplanade, European fathers with long overcoats bent over their children solicitously, amateur photographers took amateur photographs, tennis couples in spanking white uniforms looked court-bound, a woman sat in lotus position with her face arched toward the sun, a Sunday *Times* next to her on the stone parapet.

From the promenade I would look out to Queens, to a factory across the water with a scarlet neon sign that kept blinking, *Pearl Wick Hampers . . . Bathroom Hampers . . . Pearl Wick Hampers . . . Bathroom Hampers.* It was like a secret code meant to tell me something, or a Zen koan never to be cracked. Downriver were the three Con Edison smokestacks, a comforting triptych painted white, red, and gray, with their spires narrowing to flat, pudgy tops. Antique industrial totems, they stood in the blue-gray light surrounded by storm clouds that had earlier unleashed rains, or were now about to. Across the East River to their left was the old Steinway piano factory, with its grimy black façade and Parisian green cupola. Sometimes a tugboat would start out from the basin a few blocks north, thoughtfully smoking its pipe; would round the bend, pulling three barges capped with dirt like funeral mounds strapped end to end; and then there was nothing else to do but follow it for as long as it passed. Its white spume started the dark green waves slapping against the bulkhead; and, leaning over, one could see pads of black tar jimmied loose and floating along. It was a real city river, like Broadway, cutting a channel between concrete shores.

I never really clicked with that neighborhood, never got used to its chalky luxury apartment tower with fountains and doormen, and left it after three years; but the one part I regretted giving up was Carl Schurz Park, with its serene promenade.

GRACIE MANSION, the official residence of New York City's mayors, is set in a heavily wooded, particularly lush area of Carl Schurz Park. Much as I would like to tell about the time the mayor asked me there for drinks and some advice, the truth is that the public may tour the house every Wednesday, which is how I managed to get inside. As you walk up the steps of the two-story yellow clapboard building with its white porch, surrounded by shady trees and lawn, it almost seems like a country house in Connecticut or upstate New York. No surprise, then, that it was built in the 1770s as a rural retreat by the businessman Jacob Walton, who longed to escape Brooklyn's harried pace. General George Washington commandeered the house in the early stages of the Revolutionary War, thinking to use its strategic overlook by the river, just below tricky Hellgate, to fire on British ships. But the British navy had less trouble maneuvering its vessels through the treacherous channel than expected, and reversed the strategy by firing on the house and leveling it.

After the war ended, Walton sold the property for about $5,000 to Archibald Gracie, a parvenu shipping magnate, who built the present house for entertaining local country squires in the grand manner. It was Gracie who established the Federal-period bones of the house: the munificent entry hall with its circular staircase, and the parlor and library directly off the hall; the dining room, with its French wallpaper covering of bewigged figures, 1830, titled "The Gardens of Paris;" the porch that beckons at the edge of every room to come outside and enjoy the air. (The decor is a combination of history and conjecture: sideboards and lighting fixtures that once belonged to the house, furniture left to the city by the owners' descendants, and antiques loaned by cultural institutions to the

Gracie Mansion Conservancy.) But Gracie suffered the same jinx of financial reversal that seems to have afflicted all of the house's early owners; and in time he needed to sell it to the merchant Joseph Foulke, whose heirs had to sell it to the builder, Noah Wheaton . . . until it passed into the hands of the city, some say in remission for unpaid property taxes. (I love the idea of Gracie Mansion as another *in rem* property that fell into the city's real estate portfolio, like those torched tenements in the South Bronx more recently.) The city assigned it to the Parks Department, who had no idea what to do with it, and for a while used it as a glorified restroom for Carl Schurz Park. It fell into neglect. Then it became the home of the Museum of the City of New-York, from 1923 to 1932; but, needing more space, that institution moved to its present quarters on upper Fifth Avenue, and soon the old house began to deteriorate badly. At this point it was saved by none other than Robert Moses, then commissioner of parks, who had the inspiration of turning it into a permanent mayor's residence. He persuaded his boss, Fiorello La Guardia, to be its first official occupant. La Guardia was very reluctant to relocate to this Colonial mansion, which was hardly his style; but he grew to love living there, and did his famous reading-the-funnies broadcast from its porch.

During the administration of Robert Wagner Jr., the mayor's wife, Susan, found her family too pinched for space by Gracie Mansion's official hospitality uses, and argued that a new wing should be attached to the old house, specifically for parties and other state functions. In 1966 the new wing opened: an architecturally banal extension, with oversized rooms done in slavish imitation of the old Federal-era quarters, but it did have an assembly hall that could seat 150 at dinner, or stand 300 in a cocktail party. It also had an expanded, professionally equipped kitchen, a gift shop with a few meager vitrines of exhibit space, and a sitting room that the elderly volunteer docent who took us around liked to call "Susan's Room," because it held a large portrait of Wagner's somber-looking blond wife, who unfortunately died before the new wing was finished.

When Ed Koch became mayor, it was decided that the old wing had gotten tattered and needed to be restored. Koch hired some interior decorators, who painted the old wood-planked entry hall floor in a faux-marble manner. The tour of Gracie Mansion gives you much more information about French Directoire vs. Federal-style mirrors than it does about the different municipal personalities.* Aside from the portrait of Mrs. Wagner, Ed Koch's interior decorator touches, and a few Lindsay children who etched their names on a window, almost no traces remain of the individual mayors who lived there, which is curious for a building whose whole significance derives from their tenure.

Let us sound, then, ourselves the roll call of those mayors who have inhabited the mansion: Fiorello La Guardia, William O'Dwyer, Vincent Impelleteri, Robert Wagner Jr., John V. Lindsay, Abraham Beame, Edward Koch, David Dinkins, and Rudolph Giuliani. (The present millionaire mayor, Michael Bloomberg, has broken with tradition and remained in his comfortable apartment, though he uses Gracie Mansion for official functions.) I can recite the list with my eyes closed. Some people divide their adult lives vocationally, by the successive jobs they've held, or romantically, by the reign of this lover or that spouse; I distinguish my historical eras by New York mayors. The Man in the White House has always seemed too remote and executive to excite my imagination, whereas the occupant of Gracie Mansion is closer, more like a harassed high school principal or a family relative who might turn up at any function.

It would seem that New York mayoral politicians intentionally style themselves as recognizable family members or neighborhood figures who speak the local patois—so successfully, I might add, that they condemn themselves to the lower rungs of electoral ambition. No New York mayor has ever gone on to become United States President, or even Vice President. More characteristically, they expand their reach through decades of ward politics, with its oscillations of reform and flimflam, to attain a maximum capacity for governance as potentate of the five boroughs.

Of course, larger external forces may reduce them to figureheads. In 1975 New York was embroiled in a fiscal crisis of such magnitude that the city's finances had to be put into receivership, and Mayor Abraham Beame, the little accountant with raccoon eyes beyond dark-frame glasses, was humiliated and his authority eroded by a watchdog agency, the

---

*No mention was made, of course, of the Giulianis' acrimonious domestic situation, as husband Rudy, who had taken a mistress, and wife Donna, who refused to quit Gracie Mansion, became so estranged they stopped speaking to each other, while continuing to live under the same roof.

Municipal Assistance Corporation. The fiscal crisis of the mid-1970s left a dividing line on the cranium of New Yorkers, somewhat the way Vietnam had on the national psyche. Before, the city enjoyed a conviction of centrality, invincibility, expansion; afterwards, self-doubt, contraction, twinges of mortality. Never again would that belief in New York's inexorable advantage, stemming from the days of the Erie Canal, be recaptured—for better or worse.

During the 1980s, an apocalyptic glut of pessimistic scenarios abounded, as many experts predicted the demise of New York. Somehow the city managed to outlive its own death. Then, on September 11, 2001, a fireball literally struck it: confirmation of the tremors we had been experiencing at least since 1975. The Chinese writer Lu Hsun once said that the surest way to understand life is to fall from wealth to poverty. Since the mid-1970s fiscal crisis, I have watched New York City catapult from the edge of bankruptcy to the most gaudy affluence imaginable, to a market "correction" in the early 1990s, which again led to severe cutbacks, to a return of Good Times and enormous budget surpluses under Mayor Giuliani, which disappeared almost overnight, thanks to the current recession. Such reversals of fortune cannot help but make you adopt skepticism as your civic faith.

STANDING ON THE PORCH of Gracie Mansion, looking out across the well-kept lawn, with its Anthony Caro, Louise Bourgeois, Ellsworth Kelly, and other contemporary sculpture on loan from the Museum of Modern Art, to the East River, you get a perfect framed view of the beautifully arched Hell Gate Bridge, with its bowstring trusses engineered by the distinguished bridge builder Gustav Lindenthal. (You can also see the workmanlike Triborough Bridge just in front of the Hell Gate, but that is not as inspiring.) The Hellgate was the longest and heaviest steel bridge in the world when it was completed in 1917, in order to link railroad lines from New York to New England. It was named for the famously turbulent channel that runs outside Gracie Mansion and Carl Schurz Park.

In fact, the second strongest tidal current in the world (the Bay of Fundy off New Brunswick ranks first) occurs in the East River at Hell Gate, where the Harlem River meets the water from the Long Island

Sound around East 90th Street. It was named *Hellegat*, or "hell channel," by the seventeenth-century Dutch navigator Adriaen Block, by virtue of its treacherousness. Hundreds of vessels a year were either lost or seriously damaged by crashing into its rocks. Washington Irving described the Hell Gate in his colorful style as follows: "Being at the best of times a very violent and impetuous current, it takes these impediments in mighty dudgeon; boiling in whirlpools; brawling and fretting in ripples and breakers; and, in short, indulging in all sorts of wrong-headed paroxysms. At such times, woe to any unlucky vessel that ventures within its clutches." Enumerating its dangers more soberly, the government surveyer of the Council on the Hell Gate Passage wrote: "To navigate a vessel through these intricate passages in which the water runs with such speed, breaks noisily even in the calmest times upon the rocky shores and islands, and whirls in a thousand dizzying eddies, requires, even with the superior help of steam, a cool head and a steady hand. But in a sailing vessel, the greatest skill and self-possession will prove, without a commanding wind, insufficient to guard against disaster."

Still, the Hell Gate continued to be used, because it offered a fifty-mile shortcut from the Atlantic through Long Island Sound, and an alternative to Sandy Hook, whose sand bar limited larger ships from crossing, except at high tide. If only the obstructing rocks around Hell Gate could be removed, it would allow bigger ships a safe passage at any time, irrespective of the tides. Local merchants in the early nineteenth century raised money through subscription to blow up the rocks, but the French engineering company they hired made little progress, partly because it was content to lay the gunpowder on top of the rocks, which did little damage below. After the Civil War ended, Congress appropriated funds for the Hell Gate problem, and the capable Lieutenant Colonel John Newton, of the Army Corps of Engineers, was put in charge of the operation in 1866. Newton had the bright idea of drilling holes in the rocks, planting the explosives within the holes, and then removing the debris. Many difficulties still had to be overcome first, as Newton described in his December 19, 1868, report: "The removal of rocks in Hell Gate is attended with peculiar difficulty. The current is extremely rapid, so that divers could not be sent down, in most places, to regulate and set the drills, except at slack water. This fact requires that the drill should act independently of manual assistance, and therefore peculiar and ingenious devices are required." As no such machine existed to drill holes in submerged rocks, he was obliged to invent one. A steam-drilling scow rotated from rock to rock, dodging tugboats and patiently placing charges. This method, which proved effective, nevertheless took twenty years' steady labor to accomplish, from 1866 to 1886.

For the biggest reefs, Hallet's Point, off Astoria, and Flood Rock, near Roosevelt Island, it became necessary to sink a shaft from the shore, dig underwater tunnels that would weaken the structures first, and then blow them up with the largest detonations in history up to that time. Hallet's Point was exploded in 1876, and Flood Rock in 1885. Of the latter event, an *Engineering News* reporter wrote, awestruck: "Mere word painting will give but a meager idea of the spectacular effect of the explosion; for ourselves, we can only compare it to an iceberg with many sharp, glittering pinnacles suddenly raising out to the dark waters of the East River and then slowly settling down again. . . . The highest peaks, we should say, rose about 250 feet above the surface."

The blast succeeded in breaking the reef into large blocks, after which the slow work of removing the debris, to a desired depth of twenty-six feet, could proceed. Thus the Hell Gate was tamed, ending one of the most heroic, arduous endeavors in the city's history. It should take nothing away from that magnificent effort to observe that the Long Island–Hell Gate corridor subsequently became less and less preferred for navigational purposes.

25

EAST HARLEM
AND POINTS NORTH

ABOVE GRACIE MANSION AND CARL SCHURZ PARK,
WHERE THE EAST RIVER FLOWS INTO THE HARLEM,
YOU CAN FOLLOW THE BOBBY WAGNER WALK FOR A
DOZEN blocks: it is a reassuring waterfront esplanade in the familiar
Olmstedian vocabulary of octagonal pavings, bishop's-crook streetlamps,
and overlook benches placed before curved wrought-iron fences. But after
that, the entire East Side shoreline from 102nd Street to the northern tip
of the island is in a state of unimaginable wildness. To attempt to walk it
is to encounter one obstacle after another, to come upon vegetation so high
and neglected that it suggests an Amazon jungle, to be forced to cross and
recross highways at great risk. That this glittering Manhattan, supposed
capital of advanced Western civilization, should have let so large a segment

of its riverside edge collapse into desuetude is cause for, well, puzzlement. One does not know whether to be appalled or elated at finding so much ragged, unkempt, undiscovered, and unidentified territory existing still on the world's most intensely cultivated island. In the main, I have to say I was thrilled to explore this secret waterfront. But I could do it only for several hours at a time, my heart in my mouth, and always in the company of a friend or a group.

My first crack at it occurred as a participant of the Great Saunter, an annual trek around the coast of Manhattan, which is sponsored by Shorewalkers on the first Saturday in May, rain or shine. Shorewalkers is an organization dedicated to hiking the water's edge anywhere in the Greater New York area. It was started by a man named Cy Adler, who is the most challenging sort of crank, namely, one with some good ideas along with the more debatable ones. Adler, a short, bearded man, was a scientist before he retired and became a professional gadfly, suing city agencies and sending out press releases and newsletters on crummy paper stock. Recently he has been trumpeting the construction of underground vehicle tunnels (VUTTS) underneath Central Park, and damming up the Harlem River to make it a lake with parkland on either shore. Originally he wanted to name it Lake Sarah after his mother, but received so much derisive scorn that he backed away from that filial nomenclature, though not from the larger scheme. In any event, the annual thirty-two-mile hikes around Manhattan's circumference, which Cy Adler established over ten years ago, continue with his benign blessing.

I have attempted it three years in a row. This past year, though I thought myself in pretty good condition from the shorter waterfront explorations I had undertaken, I knew this marathon would be the real test. The Shorewalkers congregated, as usual, at Fulton and Water Streets, by the foot of the South Street Seaport. Approximately two hundred people set out on that cloudy, sixty-degree day: an ethnically diverse mixture of young and old, locals and out-of-towners, who came each year from as far away as Georgia and Florida, backpack-wearers and those with tummy packs around their waists, and a solid cadre of veterans with bowed calves, stocky thighs, and stout walking sticks, carrying bottled water in their hands. Knowing no one, eavesdropping on those behind me who made bonding conversation about other hikes and their nine-to-five jobs, while barely remarking on the waterfront they were passing through, I let my mind go blank.

Around 135th Street my calves started getting very tired. We rested at the Little Red Lighthouse, though it was the briefest of respites for slow-pokes like me, since the hardier hikers were already raring to go when I arrived at the lighthouse, panting. As the group took a steep inclined path that diverged from the shore and baby-sat the Henry Hudson Highway, I fell in with a cute, long-legged brunette in shorts named Selena who had been scampering ahead and looking back, taking photographs of us for a documentary video her boyfriend was making about Shorewalkers, and I amused myself by flirting with her, or at least learning various facts about her life, for instance that she had gone to Catholic school and then studied photography at NYU, meanwhile noting the curious way she had of responding to whatever I said with an intake of breath, "Yeees?," all of which momentarily took my mind off the pain of walking uphill.

At Inwood Park, near the Isham Street and Seaman Avenue entrance, we were allowed to stop for lunch. Here Selena said good-bye and scampered off to rejoin her boyfriend, and I collapsed. On the benches across from me, experienced Shorewalkers were applying bandages and moleskin pads to their feet. I sat next to a tall, glowing young man in a muscle tee shirt, about six feet five, and eyed his trail mix covetously.

"You think I could trouble you for some of your peanuts?" I asked, looking up at him.

"Why, didn't you bring *snacks?*" he asked sternly.

"I—I brought a sandwich, but I already ate it," I explained, sounding lamely, fecklessly, spinelessly apologetic, while thinking to myself, *Just gimme the damn peanuts.* With mild disgust, he turned the bag over to me and I gobbled down a few nuts, raisins, and M&Ms. Later he offered me the bag a second time, before rising to go to the men's room. (Actually the park toilet said BOYS.) I bought a hot sausage bun with fried onions from the refreshment stand, sure that my health-minded Shorewalker companions would disapprove. By now I felt alienated from their outdoor group spirit: my right thigh muscle was in considerable pain, my calves ached, my busted knee throbbed, and I could barely manage to keep my legs moving forward. The group marched through Inwood's Dominican neighborhood, looking like a peaceful protest in favor of bottled water, and joined up with the Harlem River Drive at 202nd Street, where a walking path next to the waterfront offered itself.

This walking path, mostly wild grass and tar and gum wrappers, was nevertheless surprisingly ample near its mouth, about thirty feet at this stretch. It seemed as though it must once have been a respectable esplanade, or at least had the makings of an esplanade.* To the left, as we wandered south, was part of the Harlem River that Cy Adler wanted to transform into a six-mile-long saltwater lake and national park. I tried to imagine it, with gates on either end, permitting occasional boats to pass through. It was not high on my priority list. A middle-aged woman, one of the Shorewalkers monitors, came alongside me and encouraged, with a Caribbean accent, "One step at a time."

"Next time I'll bring my litter bearers," I growled, but she misheard me, thinking I'd said "Next time I'll bring my little girls."

"How old are they?" she asked.

"What?"

"How old are your little girls?"

By the time I explained that I'd said "litter bearers," she must have decided I was weird, and moved on ahead to chat with the next group. I brooded that I might have offended her (litter bearers/Hollywood African movies/racial stereotypes). Oh well. I knew I was not making good time when elderly couples started passing me. By now the pathway along the Harlem River had dwindled to a narrow strip covered with broken glass, which permitted only two walkers abreast. Stumbling over broken glass, as cars zoomed by me in the opposite direction, was not exactly my idea of fun; but even this tiny path gave out around 170th Street, and the group had to cross over, clinging to a ramp that held only a foot of walk-space, to the inland, street side of the highway.

At 155th Street I knew from the much sharper pain in my right thigh that I could go no farther, and I started looking for taxis or car service limousines, with their T–C license plates, but it was the middle of Harlem and they were in short supply. An elderly Shorewalkers monitor, waiting for me to bring up the rear, asked me in a German accent if I was all right. I said I was in pain. He told me gently that it was perfectly acceptable if I

---

*The city and state have recently announced their intentions to fix it up as an esplanade.

dropped out. "Anozzer lady just vent for ze bus." On the eighth hour of a twelve-hour hike, I got off the Great Saunter and took the IND subway home. I was never more grateful for the subway system.

As SOON AS THE PAIN in my right thigh had abated, a few weeks later, I resolved to tackle again the Harlem River shoreline, at the same point where I had left off. Perhaps because the Great Saunter had already set the pattern for me of walking south, I decided to start at about East 160th Street and end up around East 90th Street and Gracie Mansion. But unlike the Shorewalkers, who had been forced to hike a good part of that distance on the inland side of the highway, I wanted to explore the very narrow, strange, overgrown waterfront path between the fence and the river, where no one ever seemed to go.

I took along the writer Tom Beller, my ex-student, now friend, and master of that difficult genre, the narcissistic-young-man story. Tom is in his early thirties, very tall, bicycles everywhere, and plays basketball on the playgrounds of New York. The point is, he looks intimidatingly fit, and I feel safe in his company, going into the wilds of the East Harlem water-front—safe enough, anyway, to be free of the persistent looking-over-my-shoulder fear I would feel going through these parts alone.

At the Harlem River Drive, a six-lane highway, we decided to break our attempt into two parts: first attaining the median, and then aiming for a specific pole on the other side to break our run. We waited for a gap in the traffic and dashed across (not recommended), and climbed over a low fence, finding ourselves on a trash-strewn stretch of paved road between the highway and the river. On the Bronx side, we saw a billboard, with white letters against a black background, which said, KEEP USING MY NAME IN VAIN. I'LL MAKE RUSH HOUR LONGER. GOD. In truth, the traffic on the Major Deegan Expressway looked slow-moving enough to suggest that some major blaspheming had transpired.

The narrow lip of land next to the river ended, and we had to hop over the fence again and walk single-file along the highway, following a nar-row, two-foot-wide, raised curb against the oncoming traffic. Given my preferences, I would rather not walk into traffic (should my foot slip, I would fall into a speeding car), but I cherished the sanguine expectation that the Department of Transportation had at least provided this curb all the way to 96th Street, a hope soon to be disabused. Meanwhile, we were having less of a river experience than an encounter with the modern highway. Tom and I couldn't even pursue a conversation, as we had to walk single-file with the noise of traffic around us. He stopped several feet ahead, and I wondered what to make of the enigmatic set of his body. When I caught up, I saw that the raised curb had given out. Were we to continue walking south, we would have had to hug the edge, facing traffic, without any protection.

We looked over at the water. There was no land alongside it, or even any riprap or rocks to cling to. Tom said it might be possible to "shimmy" for about fifty feet, holding on to the ledge while dangling over the river, until we got to some rocks or pilings. This seemed pointless to me; it hardly qualified as walking the waterfront. Maybe if there were some prize money or a medal waiting for us at the end, I would have attempted it; but this way would be a merely private daredevil stunt.

Across the river loomed Yankee Stadium. "We could swim across," said Tom.

"I don't know. The East River current can be pretty strong."

We backtracked to a crossing and dashed over the highway again, near the 155th Street on-ramp, to the inland side. There we found ourselves beside one of the innumerable housing projects that dot the Harlem River: the Colonial Park Houses. Just south of Public School 46, we came upon a rather nice city playground with handball and tennis courts. No one was playing handball that day, but the tennis courts were in full swing: I watched a couple gamely smacking the ball back and forth. The parked vehicles of Highway Department workers took up the last tennis court.

We looked longingly through the playground's chain-link fence toward the river. The highway rose aboveground at this point, and it seemed from our vantage-point that it should be possible to walk underneath the highway and alongside the river, if only we could get over the fence that stood in our way. I asked a middle-aged black man, sunning himself by the handball courts, if there was any opening in the fence, farther on. He seemed appalled at the implied illegality of my question and said, "No, there isn't." Tom and I walked on a few feet, and spotted a hole in the fencing, the kind that kids or vagrants make. As we were trying to measure whether it would be big enough for adults like ourselves to crawl through, Tom said excitedly, "Look at this!" He thrust his arm though the hole and fished out a pair of wire cutters. It seemed to have been left there expressly for the purpose of snipping a few more notches out of the fence. We were both vastly enthralled by this fortuitous find. One of us, I won't say who, clipped the fence wire twice, making a hole suitable for us to corkscrew our bodies through.

Tom thought about taking the wire cutters with us, but I convinced him it was better karma to leave it there for others.

We were now in a dirt enclosure underneath the highway. Seeing small, Y-shaped footprints in the earth, Tom surmised that the place was used for cockfights. I instantly began envisioning the heat and excitement of these illegal activities, men speaking Spanish, smoking cigars and betting large bills, when he shamefacedly offered, "But they could be pigeon tracks as well." On all sides of us, we came up against double fences with razor-wire circles at the top, to discourage climbing farther. It dawned on us that we had backed ourselves into the equivalent of a holding pen in a prison. Even if we were to squeeze our way through a narrow gap in the east-facing fence, we would still be facing a sheer seawall drop over the river, with nothing to hold on to.

"We would do it if we had to," Tom said, regretfully forgoing the challenge.

"Yes, if we were fleeing from the Nazis."

"Precisely."

On the southern end, we saw, through the fence, a train yard with Number 3 subway cars, there to be either repaired or turned around. I found this herd of subway cars mysterious and tantalizing. We could have climbed the fence, which was about ten feet high, to investigate them further, but to what ultimate purpose? I was reluctant to test my luck with the third rail again. And so, after the elation of finding the wire cutters, we realized we had no choice but to leave the holding pen, retrace our steps, and go back to the tennis courts.

At the edge of the playground we came into a middle-class, high-rise complex with balconies, most likely private. The grounds looked well kept, and it had that level of comfort and elegance, including a swimming pool with the sounds of happy children rising as we passed, that you don't usu-

ally find in public housing. East Harlem was proving to be more economically variable a neighborhood than I had thought.

Our objective being to return at the first possible opportunity to the
river's edge, we luckily happened upon another narrow patch on the waterfront side. A low fence separated it from the highway—the best possible
circumstance. This spit of land was quite wild, overgrown with shoulder-
high grass. I suddenly remembered the pleasure I'd had as a kid, hiding in
the bushes between a street and a fence, and pretending to be an Indian.
Of course I was much shorter then, making it easier to conceal myself.

Tom and I plunged through pathless reeds that seemed to require a
machete, passing on the way at least a hundred automobile tires that had
been dumped there, for Lord knows what reason. Some looked in pretty
good condition, new or almost new. Were they surplus stolen goods? Or
damaged tires too tedious to dispose of in the normal recycling way? How
did they end up here? I thought they must have been tossed over the fence
from cars that parked on the highway in the middle of the night, while
Tom conjectured that they had been brought over by boats. I did not see
how or where the boats could tie up. There were also banged-up car parts
strewn about, bottles, and occasionally a pair of underwear. For the most
part I was wordlessly engrossed, a kid again on a hike through new and
fascinating countryside that could turn up anything.

As we pushed south along the water's edge, we came upon fence after
fence in which earlier pathfinders had thoughtfully cut holes for us to
squeeze through. We passed an esplanade that had collapsed, many of its
octagonal paving stones missing, the supporting structure having caved in
from, I assume, shipworm damage. In these gaping holes of the esplanade
you could see down to the black, eddying river.

Our attention was drawn to a large sign: THE CONSTRUCTION OF A POR-
TION OF HARLEM RIVER PRK BIKEWAY BOUNDED BY THE HARLEM RIVER
AND HARLEM RIVER DRIVE BETWEEN EAST 135TH ST AND EAST 139TH ST.
After listing the proposed park's features and the names of the politicians
responsible, it stated: CONTRACTOR PROMISES TO COMPLETE THIS PROJECT
BY JUNE 4, 2002. The deadline had already passed.

At around 130th Street, the land suddenly enlarged, or rather, the highway veered to the west, leaving a free, unimpeded walking space. I was
overjoyed to be able to saunter forward unimpeded, to stroll without inter-

ruption, flapping my arms in the afternoon sun, after hours of scratching our way through thorns, fences, and highway crossings. This promontory, delightfully spacious as it was, also looked like a wasteland, with an enormous mound of road salt, the rusting tower of an abandoned concrete batching plant, tons of asphalt chunks, and the twisted remnants of a barge gantry. It felt sinister, blasted, end-of-the-world. A homeless black couple had built an elaborate shanty out of canvas and driftwood, of the sort one might see in Soweto. I remarked to Tom that this desolate cove could be developed into a beautiful beach—it expressed the city's shameful contempt for the residents of Harlem and people of color, to have allowed their waterfront access to deteriorate into a dump, essentially. At the same time, I was unavoidably drawn to this poetic collage of industrial detritus, excited by my discovery of it, and wished there was some way of preserving these picturesque ruins, just as they were. (I later learned that this stretch of waterfront is slated by city and state officials to be transformed into a recreational area, with fishing and boating piers, an esplanade, and a small private building with a restaurant, shops, and a visitors' or education center.)

We came upon some workmen for a private contractor, who had set up tents to handle asbestos. The tents all bore signs warning about toxicity within. The workmen, in orange vest-jackets, seemed nervous about our traversing their area, but lacked the authority to boot us out. One said, "I just want to warn you that last week someone was stabbed to death right around here."

"That's why I brought my friend," I said.

Below 125th Street, we came upon the Bobby Wagner Jr. Esplanade, which wound past one public housing project after another, followed by the old parabola-shaped asphalt plant, the Richard Dattner–designed aquacenter, and Gracie Mansion. There we caught the subway downtown.

26

EXCURSUS

ODE TO THE PROJECTS

It is all falling indelibly into the past.

— DON DELILLO, *Underworld*

I T IS REMARKABLE HOW MUCH OF THE EAST RIVER WATER-
FRONT IS GIVEN OVER TO PUBLIC HOUSING. WHEN FIRST
APPROACHING THE ISLAND FROM THE BROOKLYN, MAN-
hattan, or Williamsburg Bridge, the shoreline of the Lower East Side
looks like a solid medieval fortification wall of brick projects. Just past the
South Street Seaport starts the succession: the Al Smith Houses, the
Rutgers Houses, the La Guardia Houses, the Vladeck Houses, the
Corlears Hook Houses, the Bernard Baruch Houses, the Lillian Wald
Houses, the Jacob Riis Houses, up to the Con Edison power plant on East
14th Street. There follows a jump of eighty blocks, given over to hospital

complexes, the United Nations, the Gold Coast of luxury apartment towers, and Gracie Mansion, the mayor's residence. Then the parade of public housing picks up again across 96th Street and continues unabated along East Harlem's waterfront: the Stanley M. Isaacs Houses, the East River Houses, the Woodrow Wilson Houses, the Senator Robert F. Wagner Houses, the Abraham Lincoln Houses, the Harlem River Houses, the Polo Ground Houses, the Ralph J. Rangel Houses. Then a forty-block hiatus occurs for Highbridge Park, only to resume at the northern tip of the island, with the Dyckman Houses.

The sight all this concentrated public housing on the East River polarizes me: it makes me sad, because the projects are grim-looking, penitentiary in their massive sameness, the antithesis of visual invitation, a severe welcome-mat to place on the waterfront; yet it also makes me pleased to think that there was a time when our government built thousands of units to shelter those in need, and that it continues to operate the buildings at reasonable rents for low-income occupants. I am a little in love with them—with their romantic, quixotic idealism, at least—and the fact that they still make me quiver in uneasiness whenever I brush against their perimeters does not in any way dilute my determination to love them.

At some point, public housing came to be known simply as "the projects," a term with dementedly futuristic, monumental overtones. One thinks of a mad conceptual architect, covering page after page with drawings of columns and Piranesian spirals. Since the 1980s, there has been a bureaucratic tendency to suppress this term in favor of the more neutral "housing developments." But proof that it still has legitimacy is that my current telephone book lists the separate estates of the New York City Housing Authority (NYCHA) under the subheading "The Projects." Let us hold on to this suggestive label awhile longer; it conveys the grandiose idealism present at their conception. They have since become so stigmatized as medinas of despair, that it will take all our imagination to wrench free of that summation and dream our way back to their original promise, before we can assess their current functioning properly.

WHY *DID* SO MUCH PUBLIC HOUSING end up on the East Side's waterfront and not the West Side's? For one thing, the East River gave up its port functions earlier than the Hudson River, leaving it open to such transformation. With shipping firms and other maritime businesses gone, these deserted, brownfield industrial sites became relatively cheap to acquire—certainly cheaper than slum property further inland. As the urban historian Peter Marcuse told me, "The general picture is, when waterfront property was rundown, stinking, or abandoned, it was considered suitable for public housing. Now the developers of the world would love to get their hands on it."

Another reason was that the city's two most notorious ghettos, the Lower East Side and Harlem, happened to border on the East River and its tributary, the Harlem River, buttressing the arguments of reformers to clear the slums and place housing projects there. The Lower East Side was particularly ripe for renewal, because it had been thinning out. At one time the most overcrowded spot on earth (450 persons per acre in 1870), largely populated by European immigrants, their children began quitting the ghetto as fast as they could, and immigrant restriction acts cut off the supply of new arrivals. During the 1920s, the Lower East Side's population dropped by 40 percent.

Stimulated by the imminent riverfront roadway (later known as the FDR Drive), several proposals were circulated by the Regional Plan Association, the Manhattan Borough President, and the Lower East Side Chamber of Commerce, to raze the slums and rebuild the Lower East Side for luxury housing, along the lines of Chicago's Lakefront Drive. But the coming of the Great Depression put an end to those fantasies. What limited market remained for luxury housing located to the less image-tarnished Upper East Side: Sutton Place, Beekman Place, and River House. So the new dream became to raze the slums of the Lower East Side and replace them with better low-cost housing, more in keeping with the neighborhood's history and its current residents. There was an unquestionable need for decent low-cost housing in the Lower East Side: despite declining population, it had remained the second-densest part of the city, except for Harlem. Since many old-law tenements (cramped, squalid, dark) were too dilapidated to inhabit, and Depression-era jobs were scarce, poor families were obliged to double up in the cheap-rent lodgings available. However, the conclusion that the remedy would have to be *public* housing, built by the government, had been reached only after considerable resistance.

Ever since Jacob Riis began agitating to do something about the squalid tenements in which "the other half" lived, the city had been employing a series of tax abatements and other incentives to encourage private developers to build decent low-income housing, and the developers had, by and large, failed to take up the offer, preferring instead to service better-off clients. Though a few limited-dividend companies, such as those of Alfred T. White (whose slogan was "philanthropy plus five percent") or the City and Suburban Corporation, showed it was at least theoretically possible to build quality low-income housing that turned a profit, most developers wanted more than a five-to-seven-percent return. Riis had put the issue as starkly as possible: "It is just a question whether a man would take seven percent and save his soul, or twenty-five and lose it." To which developers might in fairness respond that they were under no obligation to be social benefactors. Their predecessors had built the slums because old-law tenements had made a lucrative profit. Ironically, the reformist housing standards that were passed for new-law tenements, coupled with rising expectations (hot and cold running water, a toilet in each apartment, light and air, adequate fire protection), had raised construction costs to a point that put rents out of the reach of the poor.

If low-income citizens were to be housed, the government would have to step in and make up the difference in rents between what poor tenants could afford and what the rooms cost to build, or else it would itself have to construct new housing. In short—and here a radical mental leap took place—the government would have to view housing as a basic right, a service owed to all its citizens, like drinking water or garbage collection.

Not only did conservatives view the prospect of the government's constructing housing units as "creeping socialism"; even certain staunch housing reformers, such as Lawrence Veiller, found it anathema. The predisposition of Americans to rely on the private sector and eschew state intervention in such matters ran so deep that only a crisis as immense as the Great Depression could have drawn federal, state, and municipal governments into the role of housing provider. It may help to remember that in the 1930s, shanties were erected in Central Park and Riverside Park, and massive evictions occurred. "One hundred eighty-six thousand families were served dispossess notices during the eight months ending in June 1932 in New York City," wrote Peter Marcuse. "Sometimes small bands used strong-arm tactics to prevent marshals from putting furniture on the street; more often crowds spontaneously gathered to interfere with evictions."

The threat of these protests taking a Bolshevik turn was used as an argument by public housing advocates. "Let us face facts squarely," said Langdon Post, the first director of the New York State Housing Authority. "All revolutions are germinated in the slums; every riot is a slum riot. Housing is one of the many ways in which to forestall the bitter lessons which history has in store for us if we continue to be blind and stiff-necked." Thus, public housing should be seen in the larger perspective, as part of the New Deal's tactical circumventing of revolution through ameliorative social reforms.

Even so, public housing had to be sold initially as a jobs program (the first projects were funded by the Public Works Administration) rather than a shelter-providing one. With 70 percent of building trade workers on relief by 1933, something had to be done to stimulate employment. Helping to put across the public housing agenda was a critical mass of housing reformers, which had been gaining in numbers and political sophistication over the years. Let us recall their praiseworthy names once more, before they sink into oblivion: Catherine Bauer and Mary Simkhovitch, Charles Abrams and Carol Aronovici, Frederick Ackerman and Charney Vladeck, Langdon Post and Helen Alfred, Ira S. Robbins and Dorothy Rosenman, Nathan Straus and Senator Robert Wagner, Clarence Stein and Stanley Isaacs, Talbot Hamlin, Lillian Wald and Edith Elmer Wood. Some came from the settlement-house movement; others were planners, architects, developers, writers, and politicians. Together they fought to introduce legislation that established the New York City Housing Authority in 1934, and the Federal Housing Bill in 1937.

The first municipal public housing effort in New York City was appropriately named First Houses, and it was located at Avenue A and East 3rd Street on the Lower East Side. The city acquired most of the land from Vincent Astor, the civic-minded millionaire who, embarrassed to be holding title to this shabby row of tenements, was looking to unload it. The remaining two parcels had to be wrenched by the courts from a recalcitrant landlord named Muller, establishing an important precedent: the right of the state to condemn slums and replace them with low-cost housing. The project was completed in 1936. A more modest, streetwise beginning could hardly be imagined. It aimed to rehabilitate (with indoor plumbing and fortified walls) a series of old-law tenement buildings, demolishing every third building in the row to leave a sawtooth effect that would permit more light and air, while also creating a combined yard in the rear for the occupants' enjoyment. Some original buildings proved too fragile to undergo rehabilitation, and were replaced by new five-story ones, which mimicked the same humble, Lower East Side tenement façades. Nine connected storefronts occupied the ground floor, to let the project blend inconspicuously into the surrounding neighborhood.

In fact, if you visit it today, you would be hard-pressed to detect the ensemble as public housing, were it not for the wall plaque. First Houses is protected by landmark preservation status, and the sweetly designed inner courtyard has a frozen-in-time WPA air, displaying the same children's ceramic ponies, their colors much faded, and the same uneven, buckling, charcoal-gray octagonal paving stones that testify to the eager but untutored relief labor used. (Union members protested, and afterwards only members of the building trades could be employed on public housing construction jobs.) In its small-scale, artisanal quality and its streetscape-preservationist strategy, First Houses represents the road not taken. Would that it had become the dominant model; but it ran enough over budget (costing three times more than starting from scratch) to deter replication.

The quality design work that went into all three of the city's earliest projects—First Houses, the Williamsburg Houses, and the Harlem River Houses—had been greatly influenced by European public housing (or, as it was called on the Continent, "social housing"). These worker housing-block experiments of the 1920s, particularly in Germany, Holland, Great Britain, and Austria, had attracted some of the finest talents in progressive architecture, whose solutions were human-scaled, fine-grained, and attentive to nature. Operating from a similar sensibility, the Swiss-born architect William Lescaze gave the Williamsburg Houses, which opened in Brooklyn in 1937, a distinctive look by angling all the buildings artily at fifteen degrees to the city grid—a design the Museum of Modern Art honored in its tenth-anniversary show in 1939.

But the most urbanely impressive of the new public housing, which opened a few months after the Williamsburg Houses, was the Harlem River Houses. As a direct result of the Harlem Riots of 1935, the black uptown community had been promised its own public housing development. What made that commitment more urgent was that the Williamsburg Houses had been already pledged to whites. In the beginning, the government assumed that projects should reflect the racial makeup of the surrounding neighborhoods, so that no white project would be placed in a black neighborhood, or vice versa. Ultimately this policy meant that public housing reinforced racial segregation patterns. But in the 1930s, black leaders agitated for public housing in their areas, and seemed pleased with the "separate but equal" results, calling it "a godsend for Negro Americans . . . a new high ground for racial policy" (Robert Weaver, *The Negro Ghetto*).

The Harlem River Houses was the first housing project in the nation built wholly by the federal government. The Public Works Administration paid for it, partly as a work relief effort. As with First Houses, a certain amount of arm-twisting by the courts had been necessary for the city to acquire the land, this time from the Rockefeller family. It covered eleven acres from 151st to 153rd Streets, between MacCombs Place and Seventh Avenue (now Adam Clayton Powell Boulevard).

Because the scale of its buildings resembled the typical tenement walkup, the Harlem River Houses today looks like the neighborhood around it—only better. The façades—a Hudson Valley brick, the same as was used in Federal-era townhouses, and other traditional New York buildings—have been cleaned recently, and shine a brilliant orange-red. As the brick facing approaches the ground, the pattern changes slightly and protrudes, for a corbelled effect. Such subtleties would later become unthinkable in public housing construction. The apartments were built with large, generous windows and hard oak floors. The diverse design team (which included Archibald Manning Brown, a patrician architect and classmate of FDR; Horace Ginsbern, a master of middle-class garden apartment complexes; and John Louis Wilson, the first black architect to graduate from Columbia) was determined to prove by this demonstration project that public housing could work well in the inner city.

The project featured the classic social-housing arrangement of four-story walk-ups surrounding a courtyard. Most noteworthy were the meticulous treatment of the public spaces. Writing about them fifty years later in an *Architectural Forum* appreciation, "The Harlem River Houses," Roy

Strickland and James Sanders singled out the housing development's "tightly framed" landscape design, which gives the courts the quality of "outdoor rooms," and the block-through pedestrian mall, benches, and sculptures. "Nowhere in New York has the social activity of the street been so successfully transferred to and reshaped for the special conditions of the center-block court."

An effort was even made—perhaps the only such by any riverfront housing project—to connect the Harlem River Houses to the water. Originally, lawns and pedestrian paths stepped down to the water's edge. Photographs of the day capture this progression from street to treetop, urban to nature, with the river restrained by a graceful, Gaudi-like serpentine wall. All that disappeared in 1957 to make way for the Harlem River Drive. Today the project's tenants are as cut off from the waterfront as every other uptown community.

Still, the Harlem River Houses remains a shining achievement. "Here, in short," enthused Lewis Mumford when it opened, "is the equipment for decent living that every modern neighborhood needs: sunlight, air, safety, play space, meeting space, and living space. The families in the Harlem River Houses have higher standards of housing, measured in tangible benefits, than most of those on Park Avenue."

VERY LITTLE PUBLIC HOUSING got built during World War II, resources and materials being requisitioned for the military effort. When the war ended, however, the returning veterans found a nationwide housing shortage, and again the government was prodded into action. At first it built only transitional housing for veterans. But then the Housing Act of 1949 allocated federal money for public housing, reopening the argument about how to do it right.

Part of the debate revolved around site selection: whether to place public housing in the heart of the slums, or at the city's outskirts. Anthony Jackson summarized the debate in his book, *A Place Called Home*: "Specialists such as Clarence Stein and Catherine Bauer argued that well-designed neighborhoods with lower densities could be built only on cheap peripheral land and that as the demolition of slums inevitably displaced their occupants, they might as well move away to better conditions. Other specialists contended that central sites were already intensely developed with services, that these huge costs would have to be duplicated in new suburbs, and that rehoused families naturally wished to remain near their social and business connections."

Those advocating peripheral development countered that slum property, however decrepit, could be costly: slum dwellers are often charged comparatively higher rents for wretched accommodations, and pay because they have no choice. Some housing reformers evinced distaste for building in the slums because it would mean bailing out slumlords by purchasing their property at market value. Others felt that the influence of the surrounding slum would corrupt these isolated islands of quality and pull down the new public housing to its level. The attraction of outlying areas, to these reformers, was that you could start on vacant land with a clean slate, and place the buildings sufficiently apart from each other to ensure plenty of light and air, lower densities, and lower coverage. Land or lot coverage (the amount of ground that buildings take up, relative to the space surrounding them) could be held to 30 percent or below, which seemed at the time fabulously desirable. Nirvana was thought to be 20 percent.

Today the obsession of these housing reformers with low land coverage seems poignantly wrongheaded, bespeaking an innocent faith that open space could itself heal and protect the poor. This open-space ideal dovetailed with the Corbusian tower-in-the-park model, then the hottest idea in city planning. Le Corbusier had declared that "sun, vegetation, and space are the three raw materials of urbanism"; his tower-in-the-park solution reflected a fundamental hostility to the traditional city street. Many reformers and settlement workers shared this dislike for the street: the New York grid system of blocks, sliced into small twenty-five-foot properties or fifty-foot double lots, seemed too adaptable to the slum tenement. A continuous street wall, with stoops and gutters, was like a theatrical stage that highlighted everyone's comings and goings and threatened, they felt, to expose children prematurely to the sexual facts of life. Congested quarters, too, spread tuberculosis and other communicable illnesses. Because the worst New York slums had been notoriously congested, density itself came to be seen, simplistically, as evil.

Actually, cities often thrive on density: fashionable Park Avenue has one of the highest residential densities per block in the country. In working-class neighborhoods, mixed-use, day-and-night street life can make a place feel safer, by adding more "eyes on the street," whereas amorphous, deserted open space—often the result of low coverage—can easily fall victim to misuse. Jane Jacobs, in her 1961 book, *The Death and Life of Great American Cities,* brilliantly articulated these insights. Under her influence, city planners have come around to replenishing the holes and dead spots in the urban fabric (the positive term for which is "infill"). But at that time the trend of progressive planning flowed in the opposite direction. The Regional Planning Association, following the intellectual lead of Mumford and Stein, advocated thinning out the dense metropolis through decentralization: building garden cities in the outlying boroughs (such as Sunnyside, Queens) or in then-agricultural regions (such as Radburn, Maryland). If big cities were bad, it followed that public housing should be cordoned off from the contaminating influences of congested neighborhoods nearby. Streets running through the projects would have to be closed off, creating superblocks along the perimeter. Formerly the New York grid had been almost sacrosanct, but the federal government had the power to block off the streets in its projects, if it wanted to (and it wanted to).

For all their refinements, both the Williamsburg Houses and the Harlem River Houses had established the problematic precedent of the superblock. The Museum of Modern Art exhibition catalog explicitly singled out Lescaze's Williamsburg Houses design with this praise: "The regular gridiron of the city street system has been modified to triple-size superblocks. . . . This reduces the dangerous through-streets and permits a more advantageous arrangement of the buildings." The use of the adjective "dangerous" as modifier tells us much about the anti-street prejudice of American architectural modernism in its utopian mode. Among urban visionaries, such as the illustrator Hugh Ferriss, much thought was given at the time to separating pedestrian and vehicular traffic. The irony is that the elimination of through-streets actually added to the danger of most projects, by isolating them and removing a potential stream of casual passersby.

Retail, which had been present at street level in all the early projects— Harlem River Houses even had a liquor store and several restaurants— began to be phased out as "not appropriate" for the dignity and nonprofit status of public housing. Social service agencies serving the projects were happy to step in and take over these ground-floor spaces. The buildings themselves were often positioned in such a way as to turn their backs to the street, making it necessary for residents seeking their entrances to take long, winding paths into the project grounds. So a moat went up. Step by step, through a combination of misguided good intentions and budgetary considerations, the isolated, high-rise tower enclosures that we associate today with public housing came into being.

High-rise towers undoubtedly offered certain economies: compared with building two or three times as many low-rise walk-ups, the costs would be lessened for roofing, foundations (one of the high-ticket items in construction) and laying underground pipes. Since the most expensive part of a high-rise was its elevator core, the builders and architects of these massive housing towers were preoccupied with maximizing a core's efficiency. Hence the bow-tie configurations and "letter" layouts (H, X, L, Y, or U) of much public housing, which allowed several wings to share the same elevator core.

During the 1950s, Robert Moses took over the city's slum clearance program and construction of public housing, and rammed through thousands of units, most of them boxes of relentless banality, angled more or less arbitrarily—no feng shui here—onto a cleared field. In defense of these stark, Stalinist projects, such no-frills construction may have been the only way to get quantities built for the budget allotted. The logic was: the more we lower costs, the more units of low-cost housing we can build overall. It was true. Far fewer units would have resulted by pursuing a refined, low-rise model based on Harlem River Houses, much less a tenement rehabilitation model, such as First Houses.

It was only in the 1980s, under Ed Koch's second mayoral term, that the city relinquished its policy of high-rise public housing construction for the neighborhood preservation strategy of gut rehabilitation, keeping the trusted shell of old six-story walk-ups or brownstones, while replacing the interiors with wooden floors, clean white walls, and new plumbing. Even so, that vast housing effort, the equivalent of a small city rising in the Bronx without violating the existing urban fabric—one of the great untold stories of modern town planning—was made possible only by the city's inheriting a large stock of buildings, via arson and landlord abandonment, in remission of unpaid taxes.

. . .

THE STIGMA THAT CAME TO BE ATTACHED to low-income projects issued partly from their unadorned dreariness, a point borne home by comparing them with dozens of tonier complexes built around the same time for the middle class, under a New York State subsidy program for limited-profit housing companies, known as the Mitchell-Lama Act. However subliminally the differences registered, you could instantly tell whether a set of brick high-rises was Mitchell-Lama by the presence of *any* design elements, such as limestone roof trim, pretty window treatments, string courses running around a building's façade, a canopy or bit of stonework at the entrance; balconies were a dead giveaway.

Unfortunately, the lack of architectural adornment in public housing issued not merely from budgetary constraints, but from mean-spiritedness. Project tenants were allowed only one closet with a door in each apartment; curtains were installed on the remaining closets to save money and encourage tidiness. No doors were permitted between the kitchen and the living room: an "open plan" meant fewer wall partitions. The floors were now an unforgiving concrete. In some projects, elevator service stops skipped every other floor. The use of cheap brick and aluminum sash windows, institutional tiles, and the most durable, vandal-resistant materials, usually reserved for prisons or hospitals, sent a message to project residents that they were not to be trusted with anything nicer.

It was presumed that the average American taxpayer would be deeply offended at seeing those benefiting from government housing receive something beyond the bare minimum. Many Americans were loath to spend any sums on the poor, regarding welfare assistance or food supplements as "handouts," while not at all averse to accepting the government's vastly larger handouts in the form of corporate or mortgage tax breaks. In a Brookings Institution study, Henry Aaron calculated that "for a typical year (1966), the government subsidy provided to the poor by public housing programs was $500 million, while the subsidy provided primarily to middle-class home owners through the income tax law was almost $7 billion." (Richard Plunz, *A History of Housing in New York City*).

In any event, because of this parsimonious approach, the Housing Authority had to spend massive amounts later for maintenance against vandalism, graffiti, and other acts of hostility directed at a dour physical plant, not to mention the social costs occasioned by more-serious crimes of burglary and rape as well as other violence.

PUBLIC HOUSING'S IMAGE PROBLEMS went far beyond questions of design. The projects were stigmatized mainly for warehousing the poor, the nonwhite, the failures of an affluent society. Initially, public housing had been meant to serve families of the so-called working poor and lower middle-class, who were reeling from the acute shortage of low-cost housing, first in the Depression, then immediately after World War II. These units were not even imagined as permanent residences, but as stepping-stones for upwardly mobile workers to escape the slums, on their way to something better.

The first tenants of public housing, reportedly "ecstatic" with their new apartments, had been screened carefully, according to a point system that included employment, housekeeping skills, and morals. After a family was accepted, a social worker would visit the tenants once a week to collect rents and offer assistance, while casually checking that all apartments were being properly maintained. This system of "friendly visits" may strike us today as offensive paternalism. Yet the housing projects with the tightest screening and scrutiny procedures remained safer and better run, while those that left tenants to their own devices tended to deteriorate.

During the 1930s and 1940s, the left helped organize citywide tenant unions, which demanded more resident control of the projects, including tenant selection, and less management snooping. By the 1950s, the tenant unions began finding it hard to enlist the new nonwhite residents of the projects, who, according to the historian Joel Schwartz, "never did share the sense of project citizenship that their predecessors had enjoyed in the 1930s. They took up their tenancy as successors rather than hardy pioneers, at a time when public housing was no longer heralded but widely maligned."

A change in our notions of poverty had also transpired. As long as the have-nots were white, poverty was seen not as a chronic condition but as an unfortunate rite of passage, to be overcome in an individual's lifetime, or certainly by the second generation. It was only when nonwhites proliferated in public housing, from the mid-1950s on, that poverty came to be regarded as a self-perpetuating "cycle," and the projects as last-ditch hotels for the neediest. This perceptual shift may be tied partly to racism and partly to the worsening economic situation for nonwhite blue-collar workers. During the 1950s, for instance, Puerto Ricans arrived en masse in New York at precisely the moment when the manufacturing and port sectors, which traditionally had provided entry-jobs for unskilled labor, started to leave the city.

Meanwhile, the destruction of miles of ghetto neighborhoods uprooted many more poor people from their homes than could be counterbalanced by the number of new public housing units built. By the mid-1950s, more than 50,000 households had been displaced by slum clearance, and the $100 maximum compensation allowed under law for their pains did not go far. Slum clearance and the construction of low-income housing, often lumped together, were in fact two different phenomena with separate agendas. A section of the 1949 Housing Act called Title 1 had provided $1.5 billion for slum clearance and redevelopment, or what came to be known as "urban renewal," a euphemism for the razing of poor neighborhoods and their replacement with middle- or upper-class districts. Robert Moses summed the matter up with his usual brusqueness: "Title 1 was never designed to produce housing for people of low income. The critics failed to understand that Title 1 aimed solely at the elimination of slums and substandard areas. It did not prescribe the pattern of redevelopment, leaving this to local initiative."

In New York City, both results occurred: tenement housing was replaced with redevelopments such as Lincoln Center, the Coliseum, college campuses, parks, and highways, while substantial units of low-income projects were also built, many on the same blocks where older tenements, bars, and bodegas had been razed. In this manner, approximately one-third of East Harlem came to be covered with postwar subsidized housing, much of it resented and despised.

WE CAN DATE THE POINT when the projects began to seem hell on earth from this famous passage in a James Baldwin essay, which appeared in 1960:

The projects in Harlem are hated. They are hated almost as much as policemen, and this is saying a great deal. And they are hated for the same reason: both reveal, unbearably, the real attitude of the white world, no matter how many liberal speeches are made, no matter how many lofty editorials are written, no matter how many civil rights commissions are set up.

The projects are hideous, of course, there being a law, apparently respected throughout the world, that popular housing shall be as cheerless as a prison. They are lumped all over Harlem, colorless, bleak, high, and revolting. . . . Even if the administration of the projects were not so insanely humiliating (for example: one must report raises in salary to the management, which will then eat up the profit by raising one's rent; the management has the right to know who is staying in your apartment; the management can ask you to leave, at their discretion), the projects would still be hated because they are an insult to the meanest intelligence. . . . A ghetto can be improved in one way only: out of existence.

For Baldwin, the culprit was the ghetto. Curiously, this was what the housing reformers and the slum clearance lobby had been saying all along: you have to tear down the ghettos. Baldwin, with his characteristic blend of brilliant laser acuity and apocalyptic generalization, had hit on a truth: public housing had become, in effect, the New Ghetto, as segregated and harsh as the old ghetto had been.

This same argument was later advanced by Douglas S. Massey and Nancy A. Denton in their hard-hitting 1993 polemic, *American Apartheid:* "By 1970, after two decades of urban renewal, public housing projects in most large cities had become black reservations, highly segregated from the rest of society and characterized by extreme social isolation. The replacement of low-density slums with high-density towers of poor families also reduced the class diversity of the ghetto and brought about a geographical concentration of poverty that was previously unimaginable."

So was this all that public housing had accomplished: to give hideous permanence to an ugly system of American apartheid? Twist the kaleidoscope another quarter-turn, and the picture becomes more complicated.

AFTER ALL AGREED the projects were a very bad idea, time went by and they remained standing and we were left with a more ambiguous understanding. We had to rethink our position: faced with the city's chronic housing shortage, its inflated rents and homeless problem, the projects, which domicile three-quarters of a million people, began to seem not necessarily so bad, maybe even useful, certainly something we were grateful to have around. I shudder to think how New York would have coped without them.

In city after city, the federal government has torn down high-rise public housing, imploding the buildings with dynamite, as at Pruitt-Igoe Houses in St. Louis, and replacing them wherever possible with scatter-shot low-rise houses, under a special Housing and Urban Development (HUD) program called Project Hope 6. But not a single public housing building in New York City has been torn down. In fact, there are still long waiting lists, several hundred thousand people waiting to get into the city's public housing, and the turnover rate is lower than normal because the tenant population stays put longer. Whether they do so because they are happy with their accommodations or just resigned, given the even worse alternatives awaiting them, the fact remains that they are being sheltered adequately and sometimes more than adequately.

Whatever its aesthetic shortcomings or social stigmas, public housing in New York has proven to be, on the whole, a success. Why has the program worked better here than elsewhere? First, there already exists a culture of apartment towers in the city, so that less opprobrium attaches to high-rise projects. True, one might say the same for Chicago, which has a more troubled public housing record, but that leads to the second reason. New York has managed to keep the percentage of its tenants on public assistance down to 33 percent, largely because of its low turnover rate. (In Chicago the welfare figure is closer to 90 percent). The Housing Authority has striven to maintain balanced demographics of one-third low-income workers (the "working poor"), one-third lower middle class (the latest rulings have lifted income ceilings, making it more possible for strivers to remain, if they so desire), and one-third welfare recipients. Advocacy groups for the homeless and the welfare poor have compassionately lobbied to open the public housing gates wider for these neediest cases. But there would be a downside were this to occur: those on welfare come with many more social problems—higher rates of drug addiction, criminal records, school truancy—so that you would not only be hurting the other housing tenants by allowing the projects to be overrun by families on public assistance, you would not necessarily be doing a favor to those presently on welfare who have been allowed entry.

The third reason, I am told, is that the New York City Housing Authority is a much more capably run agency than the typical housing authority, offering not only better support services for its tenants, but a more sophisticated, enlightened viewpoint regarding its urban mission. I decided to test this hypothesis by talking to some officials at NYCHA, and getting their perspective on how the projects are functioning.

LEN HOPPER IS IN HIS LATE FIFTIES, of average height, paunchy and very friendly, with a snow-white mustache and beard. A native of Bayside, New York, where he still lives, he was trained as an architect and then fell in love with landscape design; he has spent most of his professional career at the New York City Housing Authority. A former president of the American Society of Landscape Architects, he is highly respected in his field, and is frequently asked to speak at conferences.

Hopper first has me see a slide show of recent NYCHA housing developments that have undergone improvements, then takes me around to the projects on the East River. We inspect the grounds, but do not go into any apartments, which would be an intrusion on the tenants' privacy. I am well aware that I am being given a guided tour slanted toward the positive, but this is precisely what I want.

At our first project, the Jacob Riis Houses, which runs along the river from East 6th to East 13th Streets, I feel I am trespassing. This reluctance to enter is partly brought on by the project's indefinite border, which refuses to behave like a normal street, so that crossing onto its grounds is like violating an invisible gate. In an odd way, it's like entering a college campus in an urban setting for the first time: buildings are strewn about, you're not sure you know how to navigate the public space, or, indeed, if it is public space. With the projects, an added caution arises from fear. But I don't show that to Hopper, I act gung-ho, laughing at the anecdote he tells me about out-of-town visitors who could not believe he was asking them to get out of the car and venture forth on foot. Sure enough, once inside the project's grounds I relax, and begin to see the housing development through Hopper's eyes, as a series of site-design problems.

In the Jacob Riis Houses, what had been a large, undifferentiated space at the heart of the projects, he tells me, has been subdivided into a number of areas with specific functions: playground, garden, lawn. "This space used to be so large and unbroken you could land a 747 jet on it," Hopper remarks. During the mid-1970s, when New York was going through its fiscal crisis, the city had no money for maintenance or landscaping, and simply paved over everything with asphalt. All this anonymous, asphalted open space invited antisocial loitering and criminal behavior, such as drug deals, robberies, and violent assaults, which peaked during the crack cocaine epidemic of the 1980s. Since then, the projects have become much safer overall. Not only have they benefited from the abatement of crack and a nationwide decrease in crime, but the housing authority has altered its thinking about how to make the spaces under its care more secure.

Spurring that transformation in thinking was a slender book that came out in 1972, Oscar Newman's *Defensible Space: Crime Prevention Through Urban Design.* Newman, a sociologist and a disciple of Jane Jacobs (hence his advocacy of informal surveillance by residents, and his distrust of undifferentiated open space), based his study of crime on the New York City Housing Authority projects, because their variety of spatial arrangements and building types made comparisons easier. Also, NYCHA wisely kept data tracking crime to specific locations: whenever a cluster of criminal incidents appeared at one site, it became possible to analyze the problem from a spatial standpoint, and ultimately, if possible, correct the situation through physical design adjustments. In a famous example, Newman showed how two projects only a few blocks apart, almost identical in acreage, density, and population characteristics, had strikingly different crime rates. The one with the lower crime rate was, for the most part, low-rise, like the Harlem River Houses, with its overall space divided into "smaller, more manageable zones," and with its activity areas (including benches) located closer to the buildings, so that they could be placed more under the scrutiny of neighboring residents. Its building lobbies led to only a few apartments at a time, and everyone in a wing knew each other, making it easier to spot an unwanted intruder. By contrast, the project with greater crime rates was composed of high-rise slabs and "had the appearance of a large, monolithic project." High-rises were more subject to elevator crimes, particularly frightening for the defenseless victim, and inviting easy escapes by perpetrators through fire stairs.

Newman made many commonsense observations about sight lines, such as that circuitous paths and shrubs positioned at turns in the paths created visual barriers, giving criminals places to lie in wait. Such empirical observations led to a new specialty called CPTED (Crime Prevention Through Environmental Design), which has come to dominate the field—so much so, alas, that landscaping and architecture for public housing can sound at times like a subdivision of criminology. The good part about CPTED is that it gives a ready-made, pragmatic rationale for funding aesthetic improvements in a project and enhancing the residents' quality of life, through new gardens, playgrounds, child-care centers, and so on. Len Hopper came to work at NYCHA during a time when "defensible space" was the watchword, and he has sagaciously used that vocabulary to justify expenditures on amenities, while departing from Oscar Newman's recommendations when he disagrees.

For instance, he does not share Newman's fondness for fences, because their ubiquity promotes a police-state atmosphere. In the Jacob Riis Houses, Hopper shows me a green lawn cordoned off by a dauntingly high fence, imprisoning the grass, which only affords visual pleasure from between bars. He had tried to persuade the residents at least to install a fence five feet or lower, so that people could look over it and enjoy the view; but they chose the higher one, as residents often do, because it made them feel safer.

In Hopper's view, the best way to ensure that the grounds of a housing development will be safe is to get the residents involved, by giving them decision-making power and a hand in the renovations, to the point where they can take pride in their immediate environment. He tells me about vegetable and flower gardens tended lovingly by project dwellers; about community meetings on design issues that draw more than a hundred residents, where building models are moved about to offer various options; about teenagers paid to learn elementary drafting and construction work; and about volunteer mothers who take turns sitting in the lobby of a high-rise project tower, from where they can chat with incoming residents while keeping an eye out for strangers entering the grounds.

At the Riis Houses, he shows me an amphitheater that was built by

Paul Friedberg, a celebrated recreational architect, with funds from the Brook Astor Foundation. Amphitheaters were all the rage a few decades ago, promising a renaissance of Greek tragedy and guerrilla theater troupes and community meetings in low-income neighborhoods; but these bare, concrete circles descending into a pit turned out to be awkward, dead spaces, used only a half-dozen times a year, if that, for performances. Relatively secluded in a lower quadrangle, the Riis Houses' amphitheater became a hangout for drug dealers, drawing rough customers from the surrounding slum and intimidating the project's residents, who were terrified of getting mugged if they came within fifty feet. The benches suffered physical damage and defacement with graffiti, and when funds became available to restore the amphitheater, it was also decided to rethink the site. A spray shower was added to the amphitheater's base, so that little kids could use it during the summer months; the steps and surrounding paths were modified to connect it more directly to the housing development, and trees, landscaping, and colored pavers were employed to soften the initial impression of concrete minimalism.

Quality-of-life improvements in the projects also issue from new technology. In the past, for instance, garbage was often stored in brown bags in the open, near where children played, and sanitation trucks would drive right into the playground areas to collect it. Worse, the garbage would draw foraging rats that ripped open the bags between collection days. The solution was to set up an enclosed area, with a row of garbage compactors that would keep the refuse contained inside and compress it eight times more. At another Lower East Side project, Hopper showed me one such operation: The city's sanitation truck hooked up to the garbage compactor and extracted the debris cleanly. These compacting machines did not come cheap: each cost $25,000, the set of four totaled $100,000, and the area had to be laid out properly, an additional $100,000. But the results—no more mountains of garbage, no more rats, and, given the compression, much less bulk to be transported by truck and added to dumps—made for an ecologically sound practice that private apartment houses would do well to emulate.

There is something profoundly moving to me about this patient effort to assess, inch by inch, the space of a housing development and put it to active, positive use, while at the same time redressing the misuses that have cropped up through past mistakes. Until you actually see the gorgeous flower bushes and lush lanes of shade trees and tactfully placed outdoor seating in some of these projects, you might be forgiven for thinking that "public housing landscaping" was an oxymoron.

WE MAKE A TOUR of some public housing in Harlem, along the river, starting with the Harlem River Houses. By now I am attuned to certain grace notes I might not otherwise see: the beautiful glass brick staircase in the Rangel Houses, or the popular basketball courts of the East River Houses. Most intriguing of all are the Polo Ground Houses, around 157th Street and Harlem River Drive, which I had explored on my own, some months back, and found too drab to see as anything but the archetypal high-rise project (as well as a desecration of the old Polo Grounds baseball stadium). This time Hopper shows me the central court, another amphitheater, surrounded by stadium seating. The space looks complexly and convivially broken up, inviting you to wander each section. A metal trellis painted bright blue, red, and yellow, fabricated from elements similar to those of the play equipment, makes an exuberant, sporty logo for the project. Shade trees ("for vertical definition") and lampposts hover over the more intimate benches and seats placed in the outer ring; brick-shaped concrete pavers ("for color and texture") line the ground at an angle, like the brick path of an English garden; a spray shower anchors the amphitheater's base, ensuring summer use, and much has been done to enliven the open area ("to disperse forms"), to give it "a more human scale," to lessen "the overbearing feeling of the tall towers," and keep it from being "just an empty bowl." (Not only am I seeing it through Hopper's eyes, I am processing it through his language.)

Down the hill, a new community center is being constructed to serve the Polo Grounds Houses and its immediate neighbor to the north, the Rangel Houses. Hopper is happy with the results, saying, "We almost got it right this time. These towers-in-the parks that everyone hates give us some of the nicest opportunities." I look around at the Polo Grounds towers, designed (if you could call it that) by Ballard Todd Associates, architects, in 1968. At thirty-one stories apiece, the four towers are the tallest in the NYCHA domain, serving an estimated population of 4,200. In spite of their utter lack of distinction, I am not sure what, if anything, distinguishes them from a more desirable, middle-to-upper-middle-class downtown housing enclave such as Stuyvesant Town. When you walk around Stuyvesant Town, you see the same unrelieved façades of cheap brown brick, the same flat roofs, the same shadows cast by one high-rise on another in late afternoon. In fact, according to Hopper, Stuyvesant Town, Riverton, and other postwar private housing developments were actually built by NYCHA, which was subcontracted for the construction because of the agency's greater experience with these types of buildings. The main differences between Stuyvesant Town and a project such as the Polo Grounds Houses are not physical so much as tactical: the former has a much more elaborate security system (with a panopticon-like sentry hut perched in the middle), twice the rent, and more-stringent entry requirements than the latter.

Then what explains the stigma of public housing? How much of it can be assigned to the brick alone? Brick, after all, is a prestige material. True, I have seen white-brick housing projects that looked more benign than the dreary brown-brick ones, but can color alone be such a deciding factor? Structurally—if one were to make an X-ray of building types, their steel frames and ducts, their double-loaded corridors (i.e., apartments lining both sides of a central hallway) and even their floor plans—very little difference exists between project housing and subsidized middle-class housing. For that matter, there is very little structural difference between a project building and a luxury apartment tower. All New Yorkers who live in high-rises occupy roughly the same building, regardless of the price they pay. Different materials, you say? Only at an ornamental level, such as lobby marble. Space? Many costly studios and one-bedroom apartments are no roomier than those in the projects. So the main difference becomes service: doorman, concierge, elevator operator, housekeeping staff. If anything, the projects, constructed by strict government regulations, have been built better and have lasted longer than many luxury high-rises, with their thirty-year planned obsolescence.

The prevailing sociological wisdom has been that the low-income minority population that ended up in the projects had largely rural roots, so that they did not possess the background to adapt to high-rise housing, and therefore were especially hard on these buildings. I wonder. My suspicion is that if the twelve-to-thirty-story projects had come equipped with doormen, concierges, swimming pools, and elevator men, the poor, even those on welfare, would have adapted smartly to their new circumstances. In any case, just as tenements were once demonized as being in themselves responsible for crime, prostitution, and a culture of poverty, so now high-rise projects are seen as the culprit. The tower-in-the-park projects were deemed enough of a failure nationwide that the 1968 Federal Housing Act even made it illegal for families with children to be placed any longer in high-rise project buildings, unless there were no other options available.

THE PERIOD THAT SAW the federal government's greatest investment in New York City's public housing began in 1965, under the administration of Lyndon B. Johnson, and lasted ten years. After 1975 the federal government started to disengage from the construction of public housing. No funding has been available to build new public housing since the 1980s, when the last of the projects already in the federal pipeline were completed. But Congress, having defunded new public housing, has never managed to bring itself to delete from its budget the maintenance of preexisting projects. Inside that operating subsidy there exists some wiggle-room for improvements.

Len Hopper recommended that I speak to David Burney, the architectural director of NYCHA, to get his thoughts on upgrading the projects. Burney, thin, trim, good haircut and tie, looks like a wireless radio operator in a British World War II movie—unflappable and incurably decent. He grew up in London, and came over to the United States to work at Davis, Brody and Associates, but eventually became disenchanted with private-sector housing, and decided to work for NYCHA. Like Len Hopper, Burney appreciates the agency because it allows him to practice his profession while accomplishing some social good. (The Hasids say it takes only thirty-six good people to keep the world in balance. Sometimes I wonder why a place as accident-prone as New York does not simply fall apart, and then I meet these able idealists, and understand why.)

Burney maintains that the high-rise factor has been overplayed in accounting for public housing's image problems: "Above a certain height, ten stories or so, New Yorkers aren't conscious anyway of how high the building they've just walked past goes up." The continuity of the street-wall may be more critical than a building's height. If you had high-rise public housing that met the surrounding neighborhood in a typical street configuration, with adjoined buildings and ground-floor retail, it would help to remove the gawkiness of the projects. You might start by filling in some of that amorphous, empty space between towers with low-rise apartment buildings or "incubator" workshop spaces for residents to start small businesses.

Burney shows me architectural plans to put in more infill housing along the sidewalk perimeter of the Baruch Houses, in the Lower East Side. "We've got something of a street-wall here already," he says, pointing to the drawing, "but the space leaks out. We want to put in townhouses there." He envisions running streets through some superblocks. He is also eager to place more retail in housing developments. "Before, there was no incentive for NYCHA to do retail, because the agency couldn't keep the rentals. Every dollar had to go back to Washington. Now, as a result of recent deregulation, the high-performing housing authorities have more freedom to install retail. It's a way of generating revenue, so the agency has become interested." You could invite in supermarkets and cineplexes, even a fancy bistro that could capitalize on the reverse-chic ambiance of a Projects address. Placing more retail in the projects would also lead inevitably to upgrading the areas around the shops, he says, because the storekeepers would expect a higher level of service and street design.

He would like to see NYCHA go into partnership with private developers, who could keep the income stream from the retail and help defray the costs for building more housing units. All that open space left standing in public housing developments represents "a fair amount of undeveloped land in pretty desirable neighborhoods."

Burney is most enthusiastic about an ambitious five-year program he has been directing, to build community centers in housing developments. They offer the first opportunity in a while to enhance the architectural quality of the projects: budgeted around $59 million apiece, they break dramatically with the past's brick-box monotony, and are boldly handsome, gleaming with high-tech, shaped-steel curves. These award-winning recreation centers, featuring gyms and swimming pools, were made necessary by a spike in the teenager population. The elderly, the next anticipated demographic bulge, will be served by construction of senior citizens' centers. There is also a ten-year plan to clean the brick façades of the projects, which may remove some of the stigmatizing grime.

But all these cosmetic improvements are, in a sense, a stopgap in lieu of what should take precedence: the construction of new public housing. In 2001 alone, the number of homeless people sleeping in shelters leapt 23 percent, the largest one-year increase since the city started keeping records in the 1970s. As the homeless problem has revived, it is also time we revived the dream of public housing. Whether it will occur again in our lifetime is the question: the federal government seems to have opted out of new public housing construction for good. But the political climate could change, and there is also the possibility that the city and state could undertake additional public housing, even without the Federal Government's involvement.

As it happens, the need for new public housing and for old housing developments to be more fully integrated into the city fabric have a common solution: infill on the Housing Authority's open land. David Burney points out that nobody else but NYCHA is doing low-income housing in the city at this moment, and NYCHA actually has the resources within its operating budget to build some new housing. All that has been lacking is political will—the leadership that can only start with the mayor and work its way down through his appointees. Meanwhile, Burney draws up his excellent plans.

When I look ahead at public housing's future in New York, I am staggered by the possibilities. If mistakes were made in the projects' design and execution—as everyone is so quick to agree—why couldn't these flaws one day be corrected? During the 1980s, the façades of many mundane, glass-box office buildings were given postmodernist makeovers to render them more attractive to the rental market. A dubious aesthetic practice, perhaps; but why couldn't the projects, too, be retrofitted someday? The Projects. Their promise never stops beckoning. If New York, in the twenty-first century, can imagine its waterfront as a single zone, tantalizingly unfinished and therefore ripe for some master plan, why can it not also conceive of its public housing as an invaluable, decentralized galaxy comprising thousands of acres, each piece waiting to be polished and reset to shine within its larger Milky Way?

27

NORTH BROTHER ISLAND

WE THINK OF NEW YORK CITY AS A FIVE-BOROUGH AMALGAM, BUT IT IS REALLY AN ARCHIPELAGO, MOST OF WHOSE ISLANDS ARE UNKNOWN EVEN TO the native New Yorker who has lived here all his life. Some, for instance Rikers Island and Wards Island, house city and state facilities; others, Liberty and Ellis Islands, have become national monuments; still others, such as Governors Island in New York Harbor, the privately owned Gardiner's Island, and the many nameless, mucky mounds in Jamaica Bay, hover in a continuous state of tantalizing potential, fantasy, and neglect, oddly unexploited by a metropolis otherwise so ruthlessly opportunistic in its land use.

In the nineteenth century these islands were often pressed into service as sites of exile and/or charity, *cordons sanitaires* where the criminal, the insane, the syphilitic, the tubercular, the orphaned, the destitute, the immigrant awaiting decision, were quarantined. Hart Island became a potter's field for the unknown dead. Rikers Island remains a prison.

To say that these unfortunates were tucked away like lepers, out of sight of polite society, would be inaccurate. Rather, the public charity institutions were often proudly displayed in the nineteenth century as the utopian arm of a mercantile metropolis, and even became part of the standard tour on the agenda for distinguished visitors passing through the city, such as Charles Dickens. Margaret Fuller, early feminist and member of the Transcendentalist circle, wrote an account in the *New-York Herald Tribune* about her visit to Bellevue Alms House, the Farm School, the Asylum for the Insane, and the Penitentiary on Blackwell's Island (later renamed Welfare Island, now Roosevelt Island). Deploring the lack of either employment or instruction for the paupers, the wholesale supervision of the insane, the scrimped water and lack of hygiene in the penitentiary and farm school, Fuller concluded that "we longed and hoped for that genius, who shall teach how to make, of these establishments, places of rest and instruction, not degradation." That genius never materialized, but the islands, for the most part, forfeited their social mission, as they were abandoned in turn.

WHEN JOHN WALDMAN, an ichthyologist with the Hudson River Foundation, invited me to join him and several others on an expedition to the deserted North and South Brother Islands, in the vicinity of Hell Gate, I leapt at the chance, not sure quite what to expect. I had come to know Waldman through his excellent book, *Heartbeats in the Muck,* about the reviving environment of New York Harbor. He is a good-looking man in his forties, with silky, prematurely silvered hair, a scientist most at home in the outdoors. We gathered at the Chelsea Piers, by West 23rd Street and the Hudson, where two motorboats, one belonging to the Parks Department, one to the Hudson River Park Trust, were docked, waiting to transport our group.

The expedition's leader was Dr. Paul Kerlinger, an ornithologist and consultant hired by the New York City Audubon Society to conduct population surveys of the birdlife in the harbor islands. The other three members worked for the Parks Department and the Urban Park Rangers. Now that the abandoned North Brother Island has come under the jurisdiction of the city's Parks Department, along with four other islands that constitute a Harbor Heron complex (South Brother, Shooter's, Prall's, and Island of Meadows), and declared a bird sanctuary, that agency is obliged to check on it from time to time. But Paul Kerlinger's bird count was the one serious bit of business that had to be accomplished on the day's expedition.

I got on the Parks Department speedboat with Waldman and Kerlinger; the two outdoorsmen knew each other, and were happy to swap fishing stories, while I fiddled with my life jacket and glimpsed the Hudson River, New Jersey, and the bay flashing by at noon. It was exhilarating to be on the water on a warm spring day in a fast boat that rocked and bucked each time a nearby craft's wake hit us. Say what you will about the need for shoreline views to contemplate the rivers: the glory of New York Harbor is being out on it. We turned up the East River and streamed past U Thant (formerly Belmont) Island, a sprig of rock barely longer than a king-sized sofa, parked in the water in front of the United Nations. It held a wire-sculpture peace arch, intended as a tribute to U Thant, the late UN secretary general, and a tree with a dozen birds nesting.

Our boat, which was manned by two Parks Department employees, headed north alongside Roosevelt Island. I had never seen Roosevelt Island's eastern shore. The balconies of the mixed-income housing made an attractive impression. These days I feel much more warmly disposed to Roosevelt Island, as a modest but effective "New Town in Town" achievement.

Past the Triborough Bridge, our boat headed along the Bronx side of the East River, and, just west of Rikers Island, reached our first destination, North Brother Island. As there was no longer a functioning pier to tie up at, the boat drew as close as possible to the rocky beach, and we jumped out and waded the last ten or twenty feet. From the boat I had hurled my sneakers, with the socks bunched inside, onto the beach, which was a mistake because the socks fell out and landed in the water. I then remembered my earlier, sensible vow to pack a second pair of socks for the trip, and wondered what had distracted me from it.

Not knowing how to prepare for such an excursion, I had ended up bringing very little. John Waldman had remarked that I certainly traveled light; he had expected I'd come with cameras, food, provisions. He himself brought two saddlebags; but since the trip was supposed to last no longer than three or four hours, I felt justified in my restraint.

Along the beach were a rusted iron gantry and the twisted remains of a wooden pier. Planks of lumber and shards of pottery and glass were strewn about the sand, Robinson Crusoe–like. I wondered if the pottery and glass indicated past landfill, as these materials were commonly used for that purpose.

We split up into two groups for the bird count, Paul Kerlinger, John and I going inland, straight into the bush, and the other three hugging the shore. Kerlinger was a rangy, scraggly-mustached, weatherbeaten, independent type in his fifties, wearing khaki shirt, blue jeans, and wading boots, and a cap that read SMITH & WESSON (though later he explained he hated guns, just wore it so that the birds would shit on the logo). He told me to watch out for poison ivy, which seemed to be the island's favorite invasive species. I decided to put on my socks, wet or no, to protect my ankles from contact.

North Brother is a twenty-acre island: standing on the shore, you can't see it all in one gulp, but you can easily see Rikers Island and the Bronx, under whose jurisdiction it falls. Queens, oddly enough, administers South Brother Island, about a third of a mile to the east. The Dutch called the two Brother Islands the Gezellen (companions).

South Brother Island once belonged to the brewer Jacob Ruppert, who also owned the New York Yankees. Ruppert built a fancy summer house on the island, and I was told by one of our group that he would invite Lou Gehrig and other prominent Yankees to parties there, sending taxi boats to fetch them; but since the house burned to the ground in 1904, the part about Lou Gehrig is clearly impossible, as Gehrig was not born until 1903-unless, that is, Ruppert had presciently invited the one-year-old Gehrig to his parties, knowing that he would someday figure importantly in the Yankee scheme of things. Anyhow, South Brother Island is now completely overgrown, "reclaimed by nature," as they say, with no sign of human intervention upon it.

By contrast, North Brother Island, also overgrown with heavy vegetation, still contains many abandoned institutional buildings. First, the Sisters of Charity ran a tuberculosis hospital there; it closed when the city took over the island and built Riverside Hospital in 1885 for the treatment of communicable diseases. It had 332 beds, and its best-known resident was Typhoid Mary (Mary Mallon), an Irish immigrant who, as a food handler, was responsible for starting several typhoid epidemics.

Typhoid Mary's story is a fascinating one. At its crux is the anomaly that typhoid can be transmitted by healthy carriers, who show no sign of the disease themselves. Such was Mallon, who worked as a cook for a number of wealthy Park Avenue and Long Island families; when the epidemiologist Dr. George A. Soper tracked the spread of many 1906 typhoid cases to her, and explained his desire to take her blood, feces, and urine samples, she understandably denied her involvement, pointing to her evident health. Soper described her as about forty years of age, "five feet six inches tall, a blond with clear blue eyes, a healthy color and a somewhat determined mouth and jaw." So determined was she, in fact, that she came at him with a carving fork. Eventually, with the assistance of several police officers, they were able to subdue her, and, having established beyond any doubt that her excreta tested positive for *Bacillus typhosus,* they sent her to North Brother Island, where she was permitted to live and cook for herself in a small bungalow. There she might have languished undetected, had it not been for William Randolph Hearst's newspapers, which picked up the story in 1909 and made her into a sensationalistic folk hero/ogre. The irony of her situation, that she was not ill, but had to be incarcerated indefinitely in a hospital nonetheless, struck her as supremely unjust, and provoked the compassion of New York Health Commissioner Dr. Ernest J. Lederle, who freed her with the understanding that she would change her employment. At this point the erstwhile immigrant victim Mallon begins to tax our sympathies, by changing her name (not her employment) and working as a cook in several establishments, perhaps because it was the only trade she knew, perhaps because she cared not a fig about others and wanted to wreak her revenge on society—in any event, causing new typhoid outbreaks in New Jersey and Massachusetts, before exercising extreme chutzpah by taking a job at New York's Sloane Hospital for Women, beneath "the very noses of New York health authorities under the alias Mary Brown," wrote Alan M. Kraut, in his book *Silent Travelers.*

"The forty-eight-year-old woman was captured and remained in detention on North Brother's Island for the rest of her life. At first she had periodic rages described by one journalist as like 'a moody, caged, jungle cat.' However, with age came resignation and calm. She worked in a laboratory at the hospital and led a quiet life." Suffering a stroke, she spent the last six years of her life as a paralytic in Riverside Hospital, and died on the island in 1938.

After the end of World War II, at the height of one of New York's periodic housing shortages, the city rented out the hospital and some Quonset huts to returning veterans. Later still, the hospital was used as a drug rehabilitation center (imagine how removed from the streets the junkies must have felt there), before closing in 1963.

We can see the brick hospital chimney from the shore. We pass by a supply shed whose roof has utterly caved in, panes broken, rotting lumber, black-on-black shadows, the sun a reluctant visitor: John and I look inside it and wonder why it's so beautiful, we can barely pull ourselves away from this gravity-composed shambles, this perfect Walker Evans photograph. With the beach nearby, it suggests an ideal location for the scene in a film noir where the robbers meet to divide up the loot and perhaps pull a double-cross.

Kerlinger stalks ahead, carrying a long pole with a rearview mirror attached at one end. Every time he sees what looks to be a potential nest, he thrusts the mirror up in its direction so that he can count the eggs or avian occupants. He calls out the results to John, whose job it is to write them down in his notebook. "Two e" means two eggs, "three y" means "three young," and so on. Unless otherwise specified, all the numbers refer to the black-crowned night heron, the main species left on the island. (That is, except for gulls, which own the island and wheel constantly overhead with Hitchcockian menace, and which there is no pressing need to count.) Black-crowned night herons are wading birds that leave their nests at night and dive for fish. These wading birds come annually to breed among the island's heavy vegetation and to feed on the fish and mice in the vicinity. There may also be a few yellow-crowned night herons left, though we are not finding any. Many more bird species used to roost here, but the inhospitable tree cover pattern drove them away.

Much of the island is now covered in Norway maple, a tall, overbearing tree that allows for little undercover growth. In ensemble, the Norway maples compose shady canopies that might be fine for campfires or satanic rituals, but that provide no protection for birds' nests. "If it were up to me," says Kerlinger, "I'd bring in a chainsaw and cut these down and plant black cherry." He throws off impromptu lessons in birding: the way you tell an active nest is that it has white shit underneath. Black-crowned night herons build their nests out of any flimsy material, snowy egrets use fatter twigs, and ibises prefer grass. Kerlinger cocks his head and hears an ibis cry, a sort of warble caught in the throat; I hear mostly a riveter from the mainland.

We find many nests, some in vine-tangled trees, others right on the ground, invariably with three speckled brown eggs. After they hatch, one may kill off the other two—"sibicide," Kerlinger explains—not that they eat their siblings for food, but it increases their own chances of survival. The little herons with peach-fuzz heads that squawk at us as we pass look so cute, it's hard to imagine them natural-born killers.

We come across no animals—no squirrels or rats or raccoons—even though there must be a few, perhaps at night. But the place seems abandoned by mammals, period.

What makes the island eeriest, though, are the remnants of urban living that sprout up amid jungle profusion. A lamppost without its globe stands in waist-high catbrier, a fire hydrant sticks its snub nose out of bittersweet, a fence marks off the woods that had once been a tennis court; along a crude dirt road you suddenly notice it has a reinforced iron edge, like many older sidewalks.

Strangest of all are the large hospital buildings, still displaying their turn-of-the-century ornamental detail, their copper roofs and stone carvings and princely brick façades, though the panes are shattered and the window shutters all askew, and perpendicularity undermined at every turn, and ivy vines twined pythonlike around each orifice. The solid, handsome architecture of another day confronts us in all its defenselessness. "What does it say about me," I ask John, "that I'm more moved by the buildings than the birds?"

The island itself seems an undiscovered treasure, a place for future generations to picnic and disport themselves with Watteau-like *fêtes galantes*. How profligate is New York, or how far the city has still to go to reach its maximum built-up condition, for it to have ignored such delectable nearby morsels of land. I am enchanted by this place.

Nevertheless, after an hour and a half I have had all the nest sightings and bird counting I can take. The novelty of a sunny afternoon spent on a deserted island within sight of the Empire State Building, which none of my friends has ever heard of, much less set foot on, has yielded to weariness and a desire for flight, now that rain clouds are scudding overhead. The temperature has suddenly dropped.

The two groups meet up at the beach and wait for our boats to return and pick us up and take us to our next destination, South Brother Island. Kerlinger assures us that it is a much smaller island and the counting won't take as long.

Bob from the Bronx, a Parks Department employee with the perennially embarrassed grin of a superior Nietzschean being trapped in an ingratiating bureaucrat role, offers slices of Italian bread from the loaf he has wisely brought along. I decline, thinking I will be home soon and can eat more interestingly than plain dry bread. John shares his potato chips and water with me. We are wondering what is keeping the boats.

When the Parks Department speedboat arrives, it manages to get stuck in mud, about twenty yards from the beach. The tide is very low, and the crew decides to wait until the tide rises sufficiently to lift the boat. A half hour passes, and John observes, "I don't think the tide's coming in, I think it's going the other way, out." All agree with his pessimistic assessment. I wonder aloud why the second boat, which is hanging back across the water, closer to the Bronx, cannot come in and take us off this godforsaken place. No, that is not the protocol: for one thing, the second boat is even less equipped to approach the shore and not get stuck than the first; for another, it wouldn't dream of leaving its companion boat in immovable straits. Why, then, can't the second boat try to pry the first boat loose by means of a rope? I demand. Everyone agrees this is worth trying, and after about an hour the second boat heaves alongside the first and is trying to play catch with the rope. When several attempts to toss the rope from one boat to the other end in failure, we begin to suspect that we are in inept hands. These are not your crafty old salts, your artisans of the sea; these are landlubber civil servants, ex-limousine drivers out of their depth.

"Tie it to your stern!" John keeps calling out to the boat. "You'll get more leverage that way!" Sotto voce, he tells me, "They're clueless." Tied to stern or aft, the rope makes no difference, the boat refuses to budge. I suggest that several of us go into the water and push the boat as you would a stuck car (I seem to be full of proposals; as the least handy person on the expedition, I have no sense of shame about offering suggestions that will be shot down). This time I am told the river bottom is too mucky; like quicksand, it would swallow you up. As proof they offer the sight of the stuck boat's crew member trying to push off with a metal rod of some sort, and the rod sinking farther and farther into the bottom.

We are "beached." Now I know the meaning of that term in a personal way I never did before. There are *Survivor* jokes aplenty. Everyone is sitting down on the sand, conserving energy. It has begun to drizzle. John puts on a poncho, and I eye an old blue sweater in his pouch. He is kind enough to let me borrow it, saving me from hypothermia.

Gazing at the becalmed inlet, I think about the other catastrophic history, besides Typhoid Mary, for which North Brother Island is noted: it was here that the burning excursion boat *General Slocum* was beached. On June 15, 1904, 1,358 passengers, mostly women and children, German-born or of German descent, parishioners of St. Mark's Lutheran Church on the Lower East Side, boarded the *General Slocum* at the pier on East Third Street for their annual Sunday-school outing. The steamboat headed up the East River as the band played the Lutheran hymn "Ein Feste Burg Ist Unser Gott." Ten minutes after the boat had left the dock, fire broke out in the storeroom. There followed a succession of errors, which turned what should have been a minor problem into a grisly massacre of the innocents. A drunken deckhand poured a bag of charcoal onto the fire to arrest it; the crew panicked; the skipper, Captain William Van Schaick, inexplicably ordered the boat to continue north, instead of docking it at 125th Street. Meanwhile, harbor barges and tugboats, seeing that roaring furnace on the water, offered to help, but the captain ignored them all, pounding the boat upriver. A port rail gave way, sending hundreds to a drowning death; children burst into flame; mothers sacrificed their lives; and still the ship continued on its course, until finally it came to a stop at North Brother Island.

According to a contemporary account in *Munsey's Magazine* by Herbert N. Casson, "North Brother Island is used as a place for the city's sick, but it now became a place for the dead. The limp, charred bodies were laid out in long rows on the grass. . . . By midnight six hundred and eleven lay on the lawn and four hundred more were still in the river. . . . The doomed ship had scattered its living freight over two miles of the river's length, and for days the bodies were picked up and brought to the island of sorrow."

In all, there were 1,031 casualties, making it the greatest nautical disaster up to that point in history, and the outcry would undoubtedly have provoked much reform legislation, had it not been for the fact that laws already existed on the books to prevent just such a debacle. In the investigations that followed the disaster, it was learned that every possible safety measure had been compromised by the steamship company's penny-pinching management: the life preservers were ancient and rotten, and filled with cork dust; the cheap water hose burst apart in three sections; the life-rings had been reinforced with iron, condemning those who used them to sink instantly; the lifeboats and rafts were wired to the deck; the ship carried barrels of hay and oil, against regulations; the requisite steam valve in the storeroom was missing. The inspectors of New York Harbor had been corrupt and negligent. The crew, consisting of underpaid, unskilled landsmen who had never been given a fire drill, had, instead of assisting the passengers, dived overboard, saving their own skins. It is some comfort to know that the captain later did ten years' hard labor in Sing Sing, though the Knickerbocker Steamship Company escaped punishment.

Kerlinger makes a call on his cell phone, and learns that the tide will not come in again until 11:00 P.M. I imagine the effect of phoning my wife on his borrowed cell phone and telling her not to wait up, I will not be taking her out to dinner or helping move things out of the basement for tomorrow's stoop sale, as planned, because I am moored on an island off the Bronx. That should go over well.

"Don't worry," Kerlinger says, "we don't have to spend more than a half hour on South Brother Island. I can do estimates from a few samplings, as long as I set foot on the place."

I am less and less interested in seeing South Brother Island. It appears I have been bitten by something, and I look down at my ankle to see if it

---

*The next day my ankle swelled up. The doctor diagnosed an infection from insect bite, for which I had to take a two-weeks' treatment of antibiotics.

is a mosquito bite or the ringlike formation that is an initial symptom of Lyme disease. The itch is ferocious.*

Bob and Kerlinger get into a discussion about birders, of which there are more than sixty million in the United States. Kerlinger thinks they ought to organize more effectively and sponsor a strong lobby in Congress. Bob says, "Birders are not good collective types, they're loners," with that apologetic grin of his.

John suddenly whips off his pants, revealing a pair of swimming trunks underneath, and decides to wade in the water regardless of how squishy it is. "Just call me Muck Boy," he says. The tide is so low that he can walk all the way out to the boat with the water no higher than his waist. He returns, and gets two volunteers (not me) to join him in trying to push the boat out of the mud. Though they again fail to budge the Parks Department boat, they think that the combination of their pushing from the front and the other boat towing with a rope from the back will dislodge it. After another half hour of coordination, the second boat approaches, and the maneuver works.

Now both boats stream off to the other side of the river. We wait. A half hour passes, during which we speculate what might be happening, and why they do not try to rescue us. The boats seem fused, mated involuntarily, like dogs copulating. Kerlinger takes out his cell phone and calls the Parks Department boat, which notifies him there is a problem with the cooling system. They are trying to repair it.

Another hour passes. Cancel the *fêtes galantes;* I see why there are no plans to develop any public access to North Brother Island. Not that they couldn't overcome the problems—build sturdy piers, use more powerful boats—but at the moment I am feeling bested by nature. "New Yorkers were right to turn their backs on nature," I tell John. "See how these tides screw you up?"

"It's true, Baltimore Harbor and Boston have tides that are much gentler."

I cadge a slice of Italian bread from Bob. We have moved up the shore to a slightly deeper anchoring point, from which we watch the maneuvers of the two boats, tacking back and forth across the river to no discernible purpose. There is no longer any question of stopping at South Brother Island, Kerlinger has long ago given up that plan.

We have been waiting three hours to be delivered, when the Parks Department boat returns, the crew telling us that we are all to climb aboard this one craft (exceeding its capacity, according to earlier warnings). The second boat will follow us in case something bad happens. The Stranded Six wade into the water and belly-flop onto the boat in seconds flat, so passionately do we want off the island. On the boat we decide it has been an "adventure"—a word applied to experiences that end in rescue.

28

HIGHBRIDGE PARK

HIGHBRIDGE PARK RUNS TWO AND HALF MILES, FROM THE POLO GROUNDS HOUSES AT EAST 155TH STREET ALL THE WAY UP TO DYCKMAN STREET (THE EQUIVALENT of 200th Street). For most of that length, it faces the Harlem River. Next to the water there is a tiny strip of all-but-unwalkable "esplanade," then comes the Harlem River Drive, then, looming above the roadway, the precipitous Highbridge Park. Aside from the housing projects, it is *the* dominant presence on the Upper East Side waterfront, north of 96th Street. Almost as long as Central Park, it constitutes a major chunk of

Manhattan's parkland acreage, yet remains unknown—hidden in plain sight, you might say. Mention Highbridge Park to most knowledgeable New Yorkers and you draw a blank. (Had you asked me before I began studying the Manhattan waterfront, I would have been similarly ignorant.)

Despite abutting a dense barrio, it is the most underutilized major park in the city. One reason is its rugged topography: on the edge of a bluff, the Manhattan Palisades, it slopes steeply downward, which affords wonderful views of the Harlem River Valley but few opportunities for picnicking. In the nineteenth century its vistas included the last remaining farms in Manhattan. Highbridge Park was designed by Calvert Vaux (Olmsted's partner in Central Park and Prospect Park) and Samuel Parsons Jr., and initially, when it opened in 1888, it boasted many of the features in Vaux's previous parks, such as elegant wrought-iron railings and fieldstone walls. Polite society would watch from semicircular overlooks the horseraces down below, on the Harlem River Speedway, before it was motorized.

Over the twentieth century, however, it fell into neglect. As the neighborhood around it grew poorer, it began to suffer from budgetary inattention; and it had no recourse to the private philanthropic assistance that propped up Central Park and Riverside Park, which were adjacent to wealthier areas. It became, according to ex–Parks Commissioner Henry Stern, the city's "most damaged, most cluttered" major park—a repository for stolen, stripped cars and illegally dumped garbage. The guardrails were vandalized, the stone walls broken, the paths overgrown, the park signs stolen, the weedy flora allowed to grow as it might with little landscaping attention, until it turned into a near-deserted, formidably impassable wilderness.

Then, in 1997, the New York Restoration Project, which was founded by the entertainer Bette Midler, began to clean up Highbridge Park, working with the Parks Department to clear away the auto wrecks and the hundred of tons of debris, and planting flower bushes in their place. The park was tentatively declared suitable for visiting.

I began frequenting Highbridge Park over a period of several months. Each time I entered it I got lost. There seemed to be no discernible pattern of stone staircases leading to clearly marked gravel paths, as in other city parks; or rather the pattern had become interrupted, overgrown, and unless you memorized your progression through the scruffy vegetation, you would be just as lost the next time. The stairs that existed were so crumbling that footing became precarious, and you had to take them very slowly. For the most part there was no clearly marked path downward, which left no choice but to crawl through the steeply sloping woods. Not that it wasn't fun to inch my way down through the thicket, gauging footfalls rock by rock so as not to twist an ankle, holding on to sturdier tree branches for balance. Whenever I reached a high rock, with signs of recent campfires, I would look down to ascertain what would be the least treacherous direction; some of the drops looked like sheer vertical cliffs.

One time when I was exploring Highbridge Park, I was amazed to find myself in a grove of highway columns, in the middle of a forest. It was like coming upon Stonehenge. I stood there listening to the clatter of trucks hitting uneven metal plates. It was in these lower, densely wooded slopes of the park that I always got lost. Still, there is something to be said for getting lost, particularly in a lucidly laid-out, gridded city like New York, where it has the charm of novelty. You can imagine yourself one of James Fenimore Cooper's heroes, picking up cues from a bent twig.

The top part of Highbridge Park, near the entrance at 174th Street, was much more intelligible. Coming from the subway, I would walk along Amsterdam Avenue past the Dominican men fiddling with their cars, past the local bodega, and into the park itself, where a spacious lawn sloped upward to the community swimming pool and the water tower. As long as I penetrated no farther into the park, everything made sense.

At East 174th Street, Highbridge Park holds two historically important engineering works, whose construction preceded it, and with which its identity will always be entwined: the High Bridge, and Highbridge Water Tower. The 1,400-foot High Bridge began life as a spectacular, Roman-style, fifteen-arched aqueduct that crossed the Harlem River. Taking ten years (1838–1848) to construct, it was part of a network of tunnels and aqueducts built to transport water from the Croton reservoirs in upper Westchester County south to Manhattan. This "Croton water" proved a great necessity, not only because New York's population was growing dramatically during these years, but because the city's frequent, devastating fires and cholera epidemics could only be fought with large amounts of clean, dependable water.

In his book *Water for Gotham,* Gerard T. Koeppel tells the story of the conflict between low-bridge and high-bridge advocates. The latter solution, which won out in the end, was costlier but more architecturally refined.* Indeed, the High Bridge not only served as an aqueduct, it quickly became a treasured scenic landmark. Painters and sketchers of the day recorded its rhythmic arches at every opportunity; strollers adored it (Edgar Allan Poe used to cross over it regularly from his Fordham home in the Bronx); and pleasure steamers in the summer conveyed passengers every hour through the length of Harlem River, via the High Bridge, depositing them at riverside cafés within clear sight of it. One picture magazine enthused, "The glimpse of the High Bridge from 'Florence's,' with the agreeable foreground of soft-shell crabs, oysters, and miscellaneous vials, suggested by our sketch, is an enjoyment which has been, and may, we trust, long be."

So much for predictions. Today, dwarfed by bigger, more-modern bridges on both sides of it, the High Bridge looks somewhat dinky and hybrid; many of its supporting arched masonry piers were removed in 1923 (because they blocked navigation), and replaced by a central steel span, which cost it much of its historical charm. It is still the only original aqueduct structure left in Manhattan, and the oldest remaining bridge linking Manhattan to the mainland. Regrettably, its fine pedestrian walkway has been closed for decades. Actually, it was reopened for a brief spell several years ago, and then almost immediately shut down—officially for "structural repairs," though the real reason was that someone had dropped a brick from it onto a passing Circle Line boat. This is how temporary decisions evolve into permanent ones in municipal government. Were I put in charge, I would open the bridge to strollers for three hours each Sunday,

---

*Koeppel quotes the skeptical response of one of the engineers, Fayette Tower, in a letter to his younger brother: the low bridge presented "decided advantages of economy and utility—yet the citizens of N.Y. have suffered the load of some 8 or 10 millions for construction of the Aqueduct to be increased by the addition of half a million just for Architectural beauty in a place where there is little necessity for it."

as a start, and hire a guard or else erect side-fences tall enough to prevent the launching of projectiles.

At the Manhattan end of the High Bridge stands the Highbridge Water Tower, a 200-foot-high landmark that can be seen for miles. This octagonal, gracefully tapering structure with slender slit windows looks almost like a medieval campanile. It was built in 1866–72, shortly after the Civil War, and was designed by John B. Jervis, the same chief engineer of the Croton Water System who supervised the construction of the High Bridge. The water tower's purpose was to increase hydraulic pressure by employing two pipes, one thinner than the other, and capitalizing on the effects of gravity; a pumping station and a reservoir, which held 11 million gallons of water, crouched next to the tower. (After the city replaced the Croton water system, Robert Moses transformed this reservoir into a public swimming pool, still in popular use.) At the height of its operation, the water tower helped move 80 million gallons of water a day into Manhattan. Now it sits idle, like the minaret of some forgotten religion.

Though originally constructed for practical purposes, not public visits, it was so well built, inside and out, that it has since been restored and given landmark status. I have been inside it, during the one day a year when the public is invited. The Urban Park Rangers give an annual tour, for which I signed up. Most of the tour-takers seemed ancient (is this how I will spend my retirement years?); but there were a few younger couples and some college-age, athletic-looking single guys, who charged to the front of the ascent. You took a spiral staircase, beautiful cast-iron steps with diamond-shaped dropouts; the landings had spare, wood-planked floors; the walls in the tower were solid granite; the views phenomenal. On one landing I paused to catch my breath, and heard an old man climbing the steps sigh to his wife, "I forgot to take my pill."

When I got to the top, a tense man with a serious-looking camera shooed me aside, saying apologetically, "I don't like people in my pictures." I wandered over to the Urban Park Ranger, who was explaining that the water tank that used to be at the top had been vandalized and burned. But that fire was a good thing, maybe, he said, because it paved the way for a complete restoration. I thought it grand, too, that the city had polished the water tower's interior to jeweled perfection, but strange that it should have spent so much money on a facility almost never open to the public.

. . .

IN ORDER TO MAKE SENSE of Highbridge Park, I decided I needed to ask the New York Restoration Project for its perspective on the park, and the whole North Manhattan waterfront. Fortunately, I had an inside contact: the NYRP's assistant director, Amy Gavaras, was an old acquaintance of mine.

I meet Amy at Starbuck's on Second Avenue and Ninth: her boss, Joseph Pupello, is parked in his SUV outside, ready to start the tour. When I step into the car he is on the phone to his little boy, about one year old, and his mother, who is baby-sitting. He rolls his eyes impatiently and long-suffering at his mother's conversation, trying to get off the phone so he can say hello to me. Finally he does, shaking my hand and explaining, "It's the first time my mom has had the kid overnight. She knows what to do, she's raised half a dozen children, but she's a little—you know, she had to have both hips replaced—"

"Frail?" I offer.

"No, she's not *frail*. You should see my mother!" he says. An intense ex-dancer-choreographer, now obsessed with gardens and parks, he works for Bette Midler, who started the New York Restoration Project with her own money; so he's either caught Bette's brassy, campy, putdown style, or has always possessed it. He has a bit of the standup comic in him, including the mournful downside between jokes.

I ask him about the NYRP. He starts in with his corporate rap. "Our purpose is to make the private sector feel comfortable, to give them a 'scenario' for a site that they can see themselves fitting into."

"Plus, we have to make the public sector feel comfortable, too," Amy reminds him from the backseat.

"Yeah, like we want to be partners with government. This means having to change the way government operates, because they don't know how to be partners. As soon as they see someone's interested in a problem, they retreat, they get very passive. And with the community, we want to offer ourselves as a long-term partner. They keep thinking we're going to go away. We're not going to go away. That's why we say, 'Give us a contract. Then you know we'll do what we say we will.'" He's already aggravated and bored thinking about it, talking this nonprofit brochure lingo.

We're off to Highbridge Park. I tell him my initial impressions from recent explorations: "That park has a schizoid nature, one part of it is wilder than any other park in Manhattan, less landscaped, closer to its aboriginal form, maybe—"

"But you gotta understand that most of the vegetation is invasive species. Japanese knotweed, ailanthus, all those weeds."

"Right. Anyway, one part is wild, the other part is anchoring this transportation node, all these columns from highway ramps in the middle of the park."

"Yeah." He gets it immediately. "That Mayan ruin thing. Like there had been a civilization and then nature had overrun it."

"One of Robert Moses' engineers said that they'd turned the area into the biggest bowl of concrete spaghetti he'd ever seen," Amy contributes.

"We call Highbridge Park Robert Moses' roadkill," says Pupello.

Moses and his engineers had to find a way to link up the Major Deegan Expressway and the Harlem River Drive and the Cross-Bronx Expressway, the new Alexander Hamilton Bridge and the old Washington Bridge and the Highbridge Aqueduct, by putting in "twenty-two separate ramps and eighteen separate viaduct structures," reported Robert Caro in *The Power Broker,* all in an incredibly narrow, steep embankment. They had to fabricate individual slender concrete columns to make it fit; the result was a tour-de-force of engineering, but a heckuva strange use of park space. I am wondering to what degree Highbridge Park had been invaded with such a cat's cradle of infrastructure because its surrounding neighborhood was poor and politically powerless, and to what degree that construction was unavoidable or maybe even necessary. Is there a way to make the best of it—to celebrate this commingling of wild nature and concrete spaghetti?

"Highbridge Park is so complicated, such a mixture of problem and potential," I say, breaking the silence. "You could spend your life on it."

"Please," he says sardonically. Not a happy thought.

We pass by an underpass, unremarkable-looking but tidy. "This used to be Tire Alley. We cleaned out 10,000 tires in there." He tells me that the NYRP cleaned up every illegal garbage dump in northern Manhattan, on the east and west sides: an essential precondition to further improvements. I am sensing a mixture of pride and frustration in his voice, because much

of what his organization has accomplished remains invisible to the unin-
formed eye: to the degree it worked, it looks normal now.

He is driving slowly, very slowly north along the Harlem River Drive,
inspecting the landscaping, the paint jobs, telling Amy to make a note of
this or that. He is either incredibly picky or totally focused on housekeep-
ing-type details. Rarely is he satisfied. Whenever he sees signs of other
work crews he asks Amy, "Are those our people?" She'll say, "No, I think
it's the DOT, they started repairing the outer fence last week." Or, "That's
DEP; they're supposed to have re-landscaped that lower part when they
went in and fixed the sewer."

"They'd better," he grumbles.

Now we arrive at his current pride and joy, Swindler's Cove. At Tenth
Avenue and Dyckman (the equivalent of 200th Street), we drive past a
newish public school, P.S. 5, which has red-frame windows and cheerful
chromatic details. We pass, on the left, a fenced-in pond that Pupello says
has been cleaned up only recently by the city, thanks to a community
activist named Ted Bocacas, editor of a local handout paper named the
Uptown Dispatch, who complained to the authorities that the garbage-
laden Sherman Creek could become a breeding-ground for West Nile
virus–carrying mosquitoes.

The driveway beside the school is clogged with teachers' cars parked
on both sides of the narrow road, with just enough room for a vehicle to
pass between. Pupello wants to clear up who has jurisdiction over this driveway, to make sure fire trucks can get back there in an emergency.
Although it looks like school property, Pupello insists it's been mapped as
an official street. If it's a street, then the Department of Transportation has
responsibility for it; if not, then the Board of Education. Both agencies
refuse to claim it at the moment.

At the end of the driveway is a chain-link fence, which stopped me the
first time I began poking around there alone. This time, with the NYRP's
assistance, I am ushered into the enchanted Swindler's Cove.* First you
see a vegetable garden and a round tent like an inverted hogan. "There's
God," says Pupello, pointing to a gardener, serenely solitary, self-

---

*This raffish-sounding name has nothing to do with past swashbuckling, smuggling activities in the
area, but was the name of one of Bette Midler's employees, who died young.

motivated, and self-sufficient in appearance, named Edwards Santos, who has been working for the NYRP for several years. Having begun as an intern, he has been given more and more responsibility, to the point that this garden and much of the adjoining land can be considered his baby. He also helps oversee the construction, by high school students, of rowing gigs (two of which are parked in the tent). The vegetable garden—zucchini, squash, peas, and onions—is largely the effort, overseen by Santos, of students from the adjoining public school and from a nearby junior high. Santos shows us a bunch of redbud trees he is about to plant, donated to the project from Chelsea Gardens.

Sloping away from the garden down to the water is what will someday soon, I think, be an amazing new wetlands park. It allows you to go right down to the riverbank: no promenades cantilevered above a highway, no highway to cross. I know of only a few spots in Manhattan, one at the farthermost end of Inwood Park, one in Fort Washington Park near the George Washington Bridge, and one in Riverside Park near Columbia, that have similar access to the water. Knowing how paranoid the city government usually is about accidents or suicide, I ask Joseph how he gets around that insurance problem.

"You can't be paralyzed by 'liability fear,'" he says. "I don't see it as a problem. You're not going to stop people from killing themselves no matter what you do. They can jump off an esplanade. They can drown themselves in the bathtub."

I agree. "You can't 'protect' people from the natural world."

He points to an area near the balustrade where they plan to build a boathouse, which they will use to train high school students in rowing—especially young women, through a federal program called Title 9 who can then become champion rowers and get college scholarships. Pupello subscribes to the fait-accompli principle: establish facts on the ground. "First you figure out what service they need, then you develop it and offer it to them. Don't wait for them to approve it first. The Board of Education refused to let students row during school hours, for fear of accident, but they said the students could work on building the boats during the school day as vocational training. So we made the rowing an after-school activity."

Pupello points out some egrets and cormorants that have settled at the water's edge: proof that wildlife is returning. They are sunning themselves on pilings near the spartina grass, which was planted by the Department of Transportation as part of a million-dollar "mitigation" project. By law, in return for every square foot of landfill, the offending party is supposed to help mitigate the loss of natural wildlife by restoring another section of the waterfront to wetlands. Sometimes this wetlands mitigation process becomes a futile, expensive exercise in deflecting guilt; but here it seems to have worked beautifully. A family of mallards is already wallowing in the mud. As we walk along the newly "aboriginal" wetlands, Pupello indicates the concrete foundation where a boathouse stood, and the remains of a shuffleboard court. This lot used to be part of a functioning boating culture, like the marina directly across the island at Dyckman Street; now it will be turned into something wild.

Once we leave their fenced-in park, I am shown the two adjoining plots of Sherman's Creek. The first, padlocked, belongs to a boat club. I peek in and see some rusty hulls and a very decrepit boathouse close to disintegration, the ensemble looking basically like a junkyard. The edges of the creek are choked with garbage. The club members are mostly *goombah* old-timers who hang around the boatyard drinking beer. It's a seedy scene, but the city, which has been leasing to the boat club for forty years, is loath to kick out a taxpaying business that alone has shown interest in previously abandoned property.

Pupello envisions his own Swindler's Cove, the boat club plot and the adjacent Sherman's Creek lot (which was cleaned up after the West Nile scare) as all one unit: he has even offered to negotiate for the city with the boat club, when the time comes, so that a continuous waterfront edge can be created for recreational use.

We enter the third plot of land, into which washes Sherman's Creek. It's not nearly as polished, as worked, as Swindler's Cove, and it's covered with phragmites. (This tall swamp grass, another invasive species, thrives in ecologically distressed areas all over the world.)

"Can't we start cutting this stuff down?" whines Pupello.

"Sure," says Amy. Her role is the calm one.

"How do we get rid of it?" he demands. "If you cut 'em down, they'll just come back twice as strong, won't they?"

"The theory is that you need to dig a trench and have the saltwater infiltrate."

He laughs. "Okay, let's do it!"

Looking at the ragged landscape in front of me, I muse that it's hard to know how much to alter, how much to keep.

"Yeah, well, there's a charm in decay," Pupello allows.

Across the street from P.S. 5 and Sherman's Creek is a public housing project, the Dyckman Houses. "Were people in the projects consulted or brought into the planning process for the park?" I ask, as we get into the car.

"Yeah, sure . . . a little," says Pupello, uncomfortably. How little is little? I don't press him. They'll benefit from the park, in any case.

As we drive north up Tenth Avenue, we pass a lively Hispanic supermarket with stalls in front, a Con Edison substation, a Manhattan Bible Church. All these separate establishments, which mean nothing to me except as visual filler, Pupello understands in a deeper, more political way. And he keeps up a running commentary: "Con Ed has lots of parcels of land up here that they don't know what to do with. Manhattan Bible Church owns a lot. See that road?" he points to an alleyway, strewn with garbage, which runs along the side of the 207th Street overpass. "We agreed to take care of the roads on both sides of that bridge. The guy next door who owns the scrap-metal plant put up a fence, which he shouldn't have, because it's a public thoroughfare, and now we can't get to it. We offered to buy out his business, but he was asking too much. It's remnants of the old industrial waterfront. My God, the chickens are back!" Pupello mutters this last to himself, and I see black, scrawny fowl pecking away on the road. You could view it as a colorful village folkway transported to the city, or as a bad omen that chaos has returned. From his facial expression, I suspect he is tending toward the latter.

Now he picks up his head and notices something across the street. This time he is furious as he drives into the offending area. Along the river's edge, on the northern side of the 207th Street overpass, is a large fenced-in lot, where some sort of carnival or pop concert has taken place. There's a big sign in front that says SUMMER FAIR. EVERY WEEKEND TO THE END OF JUNE, followed by a list of Latin bands. Inside, another sign says FUTURE HOME OF USED CAR LOT. The lot is festooned with overflowing black trash bags, left from the weekend's events. But that isn't what bothers him.

"Those bastards! They fenced off the city street and paved it over! They're gonna be in big trouble. I'm writing a letter."

He is hopping mad, fuming as he struts, hands on hips. Amy is taking photographs. "Did you get one with the 'No Trespassing' sign?" he asks. She nods. Now he catches the eye of a bearded longhair in a Grateful Dead T-shirt, standing by a motorcycle, in front of a factory building with the sign: NYC TRANSIT AUTHORITY 9TH AVE UNIT SHOP. The man looks like an aging Hell's Angels biker, but is in fact the manager of the mass transit repair shop. He seems to know Pupello, and is agreeing with him, nodding his head.

"See what they did?" demands Pupello.

"Not only that," says the Deadhead. "They put asphalt over landfill, without any further support, which you ain't supposed to, and they put a ferris wheel on top of *that*. The whole thing could have crashed with kids getting hurt. Then they brought in these king-sized trucks that could have easily put a hole in the pavement."

"Bette brought the mayor here one time, to show Giuliani."

"I remember. I got a real Bette Midler fan working for me. We have a signal we use for whenever she comes around, so he could hear it even if he's in the can—run out and see her."

Now everything is Bette, Bette, Bette. Bette, and the asshole that owns the future used-car lot across the way. I'm staring at the elevated train tracks that run right by the factory, and at the factory sign's acronym: MABSTOA. I know it has something to do with mass transit workers, but it makes me think of "mastodon." The manager, whose name is Lou Centi, invites us into his shop.

He explains that the shop is mostly given over to bus repairs: AC compressors, electric motors, stuff like that. But there are also workers from the other union, rapid transit, who service subway train parts. It's what they call a "commingle" shop. He is obviously very proud of the place, which seems to be humming along, the crew made up of skilled workmen in their forties or fifties, even older, gray-haired veterans. Centi volunteers the information that some have been working at the job between twenty-six and forty-three years. Even after they retire, they keep working. Why not? There are only eighteen workmen in the place, so it's not too large, everyone can help each other out. For years they couldn't get the bosses to spring for a cleaning person, but now they even have that, "though she's four months pregnant and can't do the heavy stuff," says Centi. "The big problem is it's not air-conditioned, and the worst thing for AC compressors is to get water in them. So the repairmen are sweating and their sweat is dripping into the AC compressors. It gets real hot in here in summer. You got these big electrical fans with vents. It wouldn't be hard to install an air-conditioning system on the roof, but they don't wanna, 'cause they're planning on opening up a big shop on Zerega Avenue in the Bronx.

"They're always talking about Zerega Avenue, Zerega Avenue," says Centi, resentfully and histrionically, as if we too, Amy, Pupello, and I, go around spicing our conversation with references to Zerega. We are all in such a rage to get to Zerega Avenue. "But it's gonna be so big that the departments will be too far away from each other. There'll be no cooperation, no communication, and in the meantime no one will be working hard. Here, everybody works hard because I make 'em. They know if they come work for me, they gotta put in a full day. My father was a tough little Italian guy, ran a private bus company, and he didn't stand for no laziness. I remember once I had a hundred-and-four fever, I phoned him and said, 'Dad, I got a hundred-and-four.' 'So?' 'I don't feel well.' 'Yeah? So?' 'I don't know, Dad.' 'The thing about a bus is,' my dad says, 'it needs a driver to pick up the passengers. You can rest between runs.' That's the way he taught me. That's the way I am with my guys. The work gets done here. This would be a real shame, to close this down." I hear doo-wop music in the background, either a radio or—could this be? Are the workers really harmonizing as they sit at their stations hammering and testing parts? I see in Centi's eyes that, all things considered, this repair shop is utopia. It doesn't get any better than this. It's not too big, not too small, you've got a good, experienced crew of hard-working guys. Sure, it could be air-conditioned, but aside from that, it's the Platonic model of mass transit repair shops. And now they're going to shut it down. Just because of Zerega Avenue.

"What's going to happen to this place?" I ask.

"The rapid will take it over," he explains, meaning the subway system.

"But I'm not going to Zerega. I'm not staying here, either, when the rapid moves in."

"So what will you do?" asks Amy.

"I'll go back to Dispatch. My skills are always in demand." So saith Lou Centi, the bearded Grateful Dead fan/shop supervisor, having delivered himself of his aria of lament. Pupello quizzes him about how he disposes of his toxic wastes, but everything seems kosher.

As we leave, I contemplate this working remnant of the old industrial waterfront. Can't we keep utopia humming a little while longer? Must we all move to Zerega?

A STONE'S THROW AWAY from the MABSTOA factory, one of the most important archaeological finds about New York City's Native American past was made. In January 1895, an engineer and archaeological hobbyist named William L. Calver was walking along the Harlem River looking for artifacts. At Ninth Avenue and 209th Street, where workmen were digging up the area to put in new streets and subway lines, "Calver spotted bones in the dirt the workmen had dug up and, with his cane, began poking around a shell pocket in the embankment looking for the bones' source," wrote the authors of *Unearthing Gotham*, Ann-Marie Cantwell and Diana diZerega Wall. "What he uncovered was the burial of a fully articulated dog. Shortly thereafter he found a second dog burial, covered like the first with oyster shells and pottery sherds. Calver was elated with his discoveries. . . . Soon after Calver discovered these dog burials, he and [his fellow hobbyist Reginald] Bolton began exploring an adjoining area where construction crews were exposing what we now know to be a Late Woodland settlement. Over the next few years, Bolton and Calver excavated a number of human burials (both primary and secondary), many large storage and trash pits, midden material, hearths, and a total of eleven dog burials, each curled up, as Bolton described it, 'nose to tail.'" Cantwell and Wall speculate that dogs may have been a special, reverential significance for these Late Woodland peoples, though they do not rule out Bolton's suggestion that "the Indian dog shared the meal, but sometimes he was the meal itself."

What to make of this whole ragtag neighborhood, a jumble of Native

American artifacts, Latino food markets, car lots and factories and revival missions along the Harlem River waterfront, on the northeast tip of the island? I love it; it's so funky and unselfconscious. Still, I have to admit I cannot get to the river easily; street after street terminates in fenced-in railroad yards and semi-abandoned electric plants. At the very least, it cries out for an overall waterfront access plan.

The New York Restoration Project commissioned such a preliminary report from the Project for Public Spaces in 1998. Among its sensible observations were that Highbridge Park needed a new vision—one with enough public attractions to compensate for the difficult hillside site that keeps people away. Pupello himself had the crazy idea of operating a bungee-jumping concession off the bluff. Ultimately, people would have to have a reason to descend that steep hill: most notably, to get to the river. The major obstacle to waterfront access at present is the Harlem River Drive. The report recommended that the highway be reclassified, or demoted, to a "Park Drive," which would also mean a reduction, north of the George Washington Bridge entrance ramp, from four lanes to two lanes, with regular signalized crossings introduced for pedestrians. It also suggested that Tenth Avenue be tamed by "traffic calming" procedures, and that the present hardscrabble/broken-bottle shore path be outfitted with a fully designed esplanade, complete with benches, toilets, trees, lampposts, and so on.

None of these proposals is especially radical. They are commonsense approaches to a more balanced waterfront, which could accommodate walkers and bicyclists as well as cars. All are waiting in the wings indefinitely for the proper combination of political leadership and economic upturn. In that respect, they are typical of the superabundance of good policy and design ideas for improving the Manhattan waterfront, which have been appearing in official studies, professional journals, and unpublished reports, and which currently sit in drawers and files collecting dust. Meanwhile, Highbridge Park and its environs remain an enticing urban puzzle.

29

THE DILEMMA
OF WATERFRONT
DEVELOPMENT

WE CAN EXPECT THE WATERFRONT TO REMAIN FOR DECADES AN UNRESOLVED ZONE, IN WHICH POLISHED SECTIONS AND DECREPIT SHARDS OF THE OLD industrial port coexist in an unsettling or perversely pleasing disharmony. What used to be said of New York—"it would be a great city if they ever finished it"—can now be said of its waterfront. It is the nature of dynamic cities to remain incomplete, in flux, torn down and rebuilt; that is one aspect of their ability to grow. And perhaps it is for the best that waterfront development takes so long to transpire, because it keeps open at least the possibility of a more incremental, mixed-use, historically sensitive approach to the river's edge. Still, a part of me wishes they would wave a magic wand and let me see, once and for all, this brave new waterfront we are promised. I want to be disappointed all in one gulp.

What to do with the New York waterfront? The art of waterfront design is not a secret; there already exists a body of highly evolved thinking that represents the collective wisdom of architects, landscape designers, and city planners on that subject. And yet the empty harbor presents a most recalcitrant challenge.

The hardest thing for cities now is to replace their vibrant old ports with lively, casual urban texture. Different as they are, the three most important recent projects that have begun to transform the Manhattan waterfront—Battery Park City (a new town), the South Street Seaport (adaptive reuse of an old historic quarter) and the Hudson River Park (a "green necklace" of public access)—all have in common a certain antiseptic, deadened quality, as though the theoretical air of the original prospectus renderings clung to them even after they were translated into physical realities. All three have made wonderful additions to the open public space of New York. Yet all three resist integration into the nitty-gritty, everyday city, partly from failure for the skin graft to take, partly from explicit intent. The original marketing of Battery Park City as a residential zone depended in part on its being perceived as separated from the city, safely insulated from the "undesirable aspects" of urban life. "This combination of a unique location and an air of isolation was exactly what determined the commercial success of the project," wrote Han Meyer in his useful book, *City and Port.* Meyer further noted that South Street Seaport, with its comfortably suburban retail, "has become an enclave, which may be a successful tourist attraction" but which "remains an isolated phenomenon in the context of contemporary New York and a rewarding target for sarcasm and irony."

Urban design today seems at odds with the spontaneous uses people make of the city, in their casual daily routines. The discipline of city planning has become tentative, guilt-ridden, and uncertain of its mission; and new construction technologies foster a monotonous gigantism that impedes the flow of street life. While acknowledging that "the city of daily life is simply difficult to incorporate into the built work, given the means and concepts that architects typically use," planner John Kaliski nevertheless insists: "As urban environments continue to evolve, designers must find new ways of incorporating the elements that remain elusive: ephemerality, cacophony, multiplicity, and simultaneity." These are the very elements ingrained in New York culture, from Duke Ellington to Frank O'Hara, from Weegee to Merce Cunningham to Martin Scorsese. Is there some way of incorporating the city's everyday syncopation and aesthetic spirit into a design for the new waterfront? Or is the discipline itself so programmed to work against the city's flux, by pinning space down into single-use, static forms, that it would be hopeless to try?

ANY REDESIGN ON THE WATERFRONT must start from the premise of public access. A venerable legal principle, known as the Public Trust Doctrine, dating from the Roman era, assures the citizenry the right to public waterfront access. This noble principle has been sometimes honored more in the breach than in the observance, but recent lawsuits by citizens' groups have helped to reestablish the precedent. Because it took such a battle just to ensure that right, and because New Yorkers have so often been faced with threats of massive luxury housing taking over the river's edge in boom times, there is an understandable fear of allowing any private use to contaminate the shore. I think this is a mistake. By all means, the public should be able to get to the water's edge, to walk along the riverfront and enjoy sea breezes. But that does not mean that the entire waterfront needs to protected by a prophylactic greenbelt. That would be a very monotonous and antiurban strategy. We ought to remember that people do not relocate to New York only to commune with nature: the pleasures of living in a big city derive partly from surrounding oneself with the street's retail enticements. This horror against allowing commerce to invade the new waterfront derives from a fundamental misconception that confuses public access with open public space, untouched by the private sector. Many of the great "people magnets" in the world—think of the Piazza Navona in Rome, or the Piazza San Marco in Venice—are a mixture of public and private.

If the only way to ensure public access to the waterfront is to keep the whole area around it commercial-free public space (a dubious proposition at best), then let's put architecturally prominent public buildings at the periphery, as other great cities have done. The waterfront could house schools, libraries, courthouses, post offices, police stations, transit stations, firehouses—could be a destination point for ordinary citizens in the course of their daily routines, not just when they are in a leisure-seeking, park mood.

Parks are splendid; and surely quiet, contemplative places have a crucial role in the daily life of cities. But they can also be an overdone solution, from lack of imagination if nothing else. In trying to ensure that the public would have waterfront access, many communities have regarded the safest strategy as demanding that all vacant areas be turned into parkland. As James Howard Kunstler wrote, in his book *The City in Mind,* about Boston's decision to turn over to green space the land liberated from burying the Fitzgerald Expressway (the "Big Dig"): "In the context of contemporary cultural confusion, 'green space' or 'open space' essentially means build nothing. It is a rhetorical device for putting city land in cold storage *in the only currently acceptable form,* that is covered by grass and shrubs, aka *nature. . . .* To make matters worse, 'green space' and 'open space' in this context are always presented as abstractions—and if you ask for an abstraction, that is exactly what you'll get. You'll get a . . . berm! But a berm is not a park. A bark mulch bed has no civic meaning. This is 'nature' in cartoon form."

Another reason for this omnipresent park solution to the waterfront problem is a rarely discussed collision between the values of environmentalism and those of urbanism. Over the last twenty-five years, much of the energy and organizational acumen fueling waterfront revitalization has come from environmentalist groups. They were the first ones to have understood that nothing salubrious could happen to the waterfront until the Hudson River began to be cleaned up; they lobbied for it, made it happen, and deserve all the credit for the happy results. They continue to be understandably suspicious of any large-scale development on the waterfront, knowing how it might tax the existing infrastructure, sewage or otherwise, and lead to more pollution.

Most urbanists have an environmentalist side; it's part of the liberal package, and if you love your city enough, you don't want to see it destroyed or degraded by pollution. Many environmentalists, however, are not similarly predisposed toward the urban; their idea of heaven is not New York City but the wilderness. Now, it would seem to me that the hope of the world is for urbanists and environmentalists to join hands, realizing that their common enemy is suburban sprawl, which removes thousands of natural acres every week, and which drains the fiscal and civic energies of big cities. Given that the most energy-conserving environment in America is probably a Manhattan street, a truly progressive environmental activist might lobby for *greater* density in cities, as well as against office parks or shopping malls in the hinterlands. But I do not see Environmental Liberation Front radicals spray-painting graffiti in support of infill; congestion goes against their whole moral sensibility. And congestion at the waterfront now seems doubly objectionable—even though the historical pattern of many older cities, such as London, has been to grow outward from the docks, with highest densities achieved closest to the river's edge.

What I would like to see in some of the waterfront is a compromise: low-rise density that will not overtax the sewage treatment plants, but will begin to invite the activity of a human hive, or casbah.

THE DILEMMA OF waterfront development is global. Everywhere—London, Glasgow, Buenos Aires, Honolulu—cities are faced with converting their industrial waterfronts to other uses. A Washington-based organization called the Waterfront Center puts out glossy, upbeat coffee-table books such as *The New Waterfront,* celebrating what it calls "A Worldwide Urban Success Story." The authors, Ann Breen and Dick Rigby, write: "We like to think that the popular success of many new waterfronts is a tangible sign of the vitality of cities, even in a world increasingly dominated by suburbs. That the inherent magic of water will draw people together at certain places or for special events is proof that the growing sense of isolation in our cities does not have to be."

Others, such as the geographer Brian Hoyle, in a magazine given over to waterfront concerns, called *Aquapolis,* find the departure of the port from the city more problematic. "In urban terms the result is a vacuum, an abandoned doorstep, a problematic planning zone often in or very close to the traditional heart of a port city, a zone of dereliction and decay where once all was bustle, interchange and activity."

In city after city, the same monotonous ideas for recycling the old waterfront are put forward: (1) an aquarium; (2) a festival marketplace; (3) a convention center; (4) a museum; (5) a sports stadium; (6) a residential enclave, or "town within a town," à la Battery Park City. "You will see a surprising similarity in projects constructed in every part of and in every climate of the globe," observed planner Richard Bender in *Aquapolis*. "This is because projects more often express the processes of organization, finance, and management that create them rather than the lives and conditions of the communities where we find them. Too often, this development creates a kind of citadel, walled off from, raised above, or turning its back on the adjacent community."

The economics of waterfront redevelopment lead again and again to the monolithic. Those developers who have the initial start-up capital and teams of lawyers tenacious enough to work through years of regulatory approval, tend to want the highest return on their investment, by squeezing the maximum number of million-dollar co-op apartments or high-rental offices out of their property. If the developer is the regional government, it will usually want some massive cultural or theme-park project it can exploit as a logo. Even small interventions in the waterfront's fabric require a momentum that can carry the developer into much larger schemes than originally foreseen; and the waterfront becomes a dumping ground for gigantic, hollow spectacle.

IT SHOULD BE POSSIBLE to have a relationship to the water that is more day-to-day, functional, less contrived/aesthetic or compensatory/spiritual. Those who use the river regularly understand the language of its tidal changes, its placid moods and rages, where it is shoring up dangerously, when it is rising. If you speak to ferryboat captains, professional and amateur fishermen, divers, coast guardsmen, harbor police, canoeists, swimmers, and marine biologists, you find they have quite specific, quirky things to say about the waters surrounding a city. Such was the technical lore possessed by Joseph Mitchell's harbor monologuists, and he listened to them all, patiently and with fascination, as I to my regret cannot. But I can at least see that if the waterfront is to come alive again, it must regain a sense of purpose, and not just become a theatrical backdrop.

In short, we need a true water policy. So far, almost all the planning attention around New York's waterfront has gone into land-use policy, with very little thought, beyond lip service, given to what should take place on or with the water. Intrepid kayakers, canoeists, swimmers, sailboat enthusiasts, and anglers have made forays into the Hudson River (the East River is more treacherous) to establish that it can be done, but there is still very little supporting infrastructure for them along the shore: places to tie up small craft, sandy beaches, electrical outlets for motor-powered boats in or near the bulkhead, fishing piers. South Cove in Battery Park is lovely, but its timbers are for show. No boat can dock there, as we learned after the attack on the World Trade Center.

September 11 taught us how unbalanced our waterfront policy had become. Carter Craft, the director of Metropolitan Waterfront Alliance, analyzed the problem as follows: "The fight to create waterfront access was won by the aesthetes. Decades of decay and encroaching blight had to be beaten back. Flowers replacing corrugated steel. Grassy lawns where working piers once stood. Come September 11 this limited design palette was a recipe for disaster. 'We didn't have anywhere north of Battery Park where a tugboat could pull up,' said Capt. Andrew McGovern of the Sandy Hook Pilots. 'The bulkheads in Battery Park City weren't strong enough, and even if they were, there is nothing to tie up to. The first couple of days of the disaster we were bringing everything by water—food, firemen, body bags, acetylene—all of it was brought over to Manhattan from a pier in Jersey City, a condemned pier.' The region finally realized that the water is more than just a quiet vista."

After having eliminated all those "unsightly" waste transfer stations on the Manhattan waterfront, interim transfer stations had to be installed along the Hudson and the East River to receive equipment and to discharge waste materials excavated from Ground Zero. The World Trade Center attack, which destroyed several subway stations, also caused ferry service to be reactivated between Brooklyn and Lower Manhattan, showing how much more could be done with water transportation in the city. An expanded ferry service, such as existed at the turn of the twentieth century, could, in future, link Manhattan not only with the other boroughs, New Jersey, and Westchester, but circumnavigate the island perimeter, connecting various waterfront amenities. The New York Olympics 2012 Committee has a water-based vision of ferrying athletes to the main sports arenas and facilities, most of which happen to be on the water, thereby guaranteeing the athletes won't get stuck in traffic on the Long Island Expressway; afterward, the city could inherit a fine ferry network and conceivably integrate it into its own mass transit system. Most major New York hospitals are also located near the water, and water ambulances could transport patients for emergency surgery.

Finally, the waterways could be used again for shipping goods into the city. Granted, Manhattan will never have enough backup space for containerized shipping; but once the shipments have been broken down in Newark, why can't they be placed on barges and brought up the Hudson or the East River and distributed from there? You could again have working docks all along the waterfront. Where is it written that trucks alone must deliver goods to the metropolis? For that matter, you could reconnect a rail freight system to the waterfront, and build a rail freight tunnel out of Red Hook in Brooklyn. You could continue to restore and expand pieces of the port on the Brooklyn shore, which has more upland space than Manhattan and a deeper channel than New Jersey. Of the four modes of moving goods—water, rail, truck, and air—the first two have been largely dismantled in the past century to benefit the newer ones: a big mistake, since boats and trains are less polluting and, in the long run, more economical.

Parenthetically, an increase in the river craft using the New York harbor would also make the waterfront more stimulating for passive contemplation, since any gazing at the water is immeasurably improved by the sight of a vessel moving steadily through it.

I AM TEMPTED TO END with a few more-concrete suggestions about what I think should be done. Perhaps I am too much under the influence of those critics who say: "Mr. So-and-So has failed to recommend solutions for the problems he calls to our attention, and therefore risks leaving the reader in a state of despair." I would not for anything want to leave you in despair. On the other hand, I am not a professional architect or planner, and would hate to have to bluff the part.

As it happens, recently I came across a report titled "A Better Edge" that the architect James Sanders had prepared for the Parks Council in

1990. Reading through it, I was heartened to see many of the viewpoints I have stumbled on, through my own halting reasoning processes, corroborated by the report's author, even as I was edified to see how much further Sanders's thinking went, with fresh proposals and imaginative refinements I could not have figured out by myself. The summary I now offer is a blend of my ideas and those (the majority) that I have purloined from him.

Now that everyone recognizes that "waterfront access" is good, this concept needs to be made workable. Especially in a city such as New York, where there exist major physical impediments to reaching the rivers, such as highways, power plants, superblocks, railyards, housing projects, brownfields, factories, sanitation department parking lots, private development enclaves, and other barriers, as well as psychological ones, such as the tradition of non–public access, it becomes necessary to reach farther inland and develop a clear and inviting procession, from several blocks away, that will lead would-be waterfront enjoyers toward their goal. Thought will have to be given to drawing pedestrians from streets and avenues near inland subway and bus stations, with a wide choice of routes down to the water. Strategies may involve extending the street grid farther to the river's edge, redesigning the main approach street to the water as a tree-lined, handsome thoroughfare, displaying signage or pennants to alert pedestrians to follow the water-bound route, improving sightlines to the water, and erecting some culmination—a gateway, column, flagpole, or mast—that can be seen from a distance, lit with strings of lights at night, to welcome people to the waterfront.

To help the public across the physical barriers encountered at the edge, it will be necessary to "breach the wall" wherever possible with creative solutions. For instance, an elevated highway structure can have its underside and column supports reconfigured as arches or vaults, using inviting materials at key entrance points. A farmers' market can nest under the elevated structure, receiving protection from rain and snow year-round. Where the highway is not elevated but at grade, pedestrian bridges and overpasses should be erected, designed much more appealingly and imaginatively than they have been in the past, so as to overcome the New York public's fear of using them.

Once the public reaches the water, there should be wide paths to accommodate pedestrian circulation. A promenade as continuous as possible is desirable, with shade trees, benches, well-designed lampposts, and high-quality paving materials; but it must have the variety, incident, and urbanity of a popular boulevard for it to be truly pleasurable. There can be cantilevered lookouts, pushing out over the bulkheads, to relieve the circulation of walkers, joggers, and bicyclists at densest points. There should certainly be some central civic public feature—a square with a fountain, artwork, café, or bookstall—built into the promenade every so often. Where it is impossible for the city to acquire land from private owners to make a continuous promenade, these public plazas can still occur, where the street ends at the waterfront.

There is no end to pleasurable activities that can draw people to the waterfront. Fishing piers, with basins and tables for cleaning fish, a bait shop, and handrails notched with rests for fishing poles, represents one possibility. You can reintroduce pleasure piers, those semi-enclosed, public recreation structures popular in days gone by, and offer court games such as handball and racquetball, shuffleboard, miniature golf, concerts, dances, public lectures, classes, carousels, carnival rides. Offshore, you can have floating swimming pools, with clean, chlorinated water and changing rooms—and even a floating beach, using a barge vessel filled with sand. Water theaters with live performances or floating movie screens can bring a dramatic flair to the riverfront; view towers can offer panoramic vistas; water clubs and restaurants can come equipped with retractable glazed doors, open in the summer months, shut in the winter.

Ultimately, however, the edge must become something more vital and necessary than a place just for pleasure strolling, looking out, and imbibing: it must draw people as a site of routine, day-to-day activity.

For this to happen, the water itself must be restored as a circulation system, and the waterfront as a place of transfer. That means a combined, integrated system of ferries that cross the rivers and bays, connecting opposite shores; water jitneys that travel along a shoreline and connect with the ferries; and water taxis that take individual customers or small groups to destinations on demand. Such a network will bring people to the waterfront, and counteract the isolationist tendencies of waterfront redevelopers.

In addition to this boat transportation system, there can be excursion boats and pleasure craft, including motorboats, kayaks, canoes, and sail-boats. All these boats will need new docks. While ferries require substantial docking facilities, those for water jitneys and water taxis can be slighter. As for pleasure craft, what are needed are not necessarily more full-sized marinas for stationary yachts, but many small-boat launches up and down the waterfront. There can also be seasonal mooring docks, floating and movable, designed for small boats to tie up, and canoe and kayak launches. Boathouses, lighthouses, windmills, and water shops, selling oysters from barges, could add color to the waterfront edge.

In general, to achieve a better balance in waterfront planning, the emphasis should shift from very large projects, which have garnered most of the attention up to now, to small-scale and moderate-scale projects. The city should help small entrepreneurs to operate on the waterfront, realizing that often it is the smaller businesses or nonprofits (such as the River Café, BargeMusic, and the River Project) that have ignited a vital spark at the river's edge. In line with that thinking, structures built on the waterfront should, whenever possible, employ a light, transparent architecture so that they do not themselves turn into new visual barriers.

Where the public enters at a higher elevation than sea level, such as the bluff at Highbridge Park, a cascading edge can be effected, though flights of stairs or ramps that curve intriguingly, and are frequently interrupted by landings equipped with seats for overlooks. At the seawall, there can be steps leading down to the water, with rising tides covering the bottom steps and retreating tides uncovering them. There can also be "stepdowns," or platforms reached by ramps or steps, that are carved into the bulkhead or project out from it. The bulkhead itself may be decorated, so that different sections acquire a neighborhood identity.

Not everything needs to be bustling and crowd-attracting. Sites of intimacy or discovery, little gardens and coves almost hidden away, make for a restorative change of tone, and a waterfront that will reward recurrent exploration.

A softer edge can be achieved, in places, by nurturing wetlands and grassy lawns sloping down to the water. Wetlands environments can be protected from the public by wooden boardwalks. Lagoons could be introduced, with artificial lakes and paddle boats rented by the hour, and smaller basins notched out of the shore, designed for model boats. One could take a playful attitude toward the shoreline. Much as Olmsted and Vaux artificially composed wild, Edenic landscapes in Central Park and Prospect Park, so the island's edge might be sculpted to give it a more varied, dramatic, and "naturalistic" coast.

Lest all this sound an impossible fantasy, please consider that many of these strategies existed as part of the everyday reality of nineteenth- and early-twentieth-century cities. They are drawn from New York's own traditions and practices—largely forgotten, I realize, but by no means impossible to put into practice once again. The quickening of the urban pulse at the waterfront will go a long way toward improving the city's morale.

IN PROMOTIONAL MATERIALS and slide-show lectures for waterfront projects, there is always a sentence thrown in about "the magic of water," accompanied by assertions that "people have a remarkable tendency to be drawn to the water." No real estate or recreational development can go forth without appeal to the spiritual properties of H^2O. That water is life-giving and life-sustaining, no one would dispute. I merely wonder why, if this substance is so universally mesmerizing, its magnetic qualities need to be reiterated. We do not, for instance, feel obligated to make claims in a stock prospectus that money has great attractions, or, in a handbill for phone sex, that erotic pleasure has a strong, undeniable appeal. Could it be that the case is not so clear-cut?

The mystical longing to get to the edge; the impossibility of doing so. Prevented by highways, railroad yards, fences, gradient problems, environmental laws against reaching the water, there is yet another issue that is never discussed, namely, you get there finally and there is—nothing, an emptiness, the river flowing interminably by, now nearly devoid of ships or other human presence. Granted, there is something soothing in itself about watching moving water, for thirty minutes at the maximum, and there is something beautiful about the sunlight or clouds rippling on water, about the natural landscape intruding on the cityscape, good for shall we say another fifteen minutes, but this play of water and light that is supposed to be unquenchably rewarding soon becomes a sterile delight for the urbanite raised on spectacle and shopping. The empty harbor becomes, paradoxically, the zone revealing to us our own shallow impatience, alienation from nature, unattainable sexual desires, professional pettiness, the substance of our nattering inner monologue. We *say* all we want is access to the water; we *mean* access to inner peace, to meaning, to purity, to a mature acceptance of our place on earth, and other such improbables. The water's edge is the infinitely beckoning, infinitely receding mirage of our consumerist society: the place that will finally tell us we have arrived.

ACKNOWLEDGMENTS

IN RESEARCHING THIS BOOK, I was aided by many specialists who took pity on me. Sometimes I tried my hunches out on them, to see if I was not completely off-base; more often, I simply "appropriated" their knowledge. While there must be *some* original ideas in this book, I would be hard-pressed to point to them, so indebted am I to the warp and woof of other people's thinking.

I would especially like to thank three professionals who so generously offered their insights and expertise: Carter Craft of the Metropolitan Waterfront Alliance and Kent Barwick of the Municipal Art Society made themselves unfailingly available, as did Wilbur Woods, of the New York City Department of Planning. I also learned much from conversations with the architects David Burney, Richard Dattner, Stanton Eckstut, Laurie Kerr, and Craig Whitaker; with the city planners Paul Levy, Laurie Beckelman, Peter Marcuse, Deren Rieff, and Harry Schwartz; with architectural writers Dolores Hayden and Ada Louise Huxtable; with marine biologists Mike Ludwig (National Oceanographic and Atmospheric Administration), John Waldman and Dennis Suszkowski (Hudson River Foundation); with nonprofit administrators Cathy Drew (the River Project), Joseph Pupello (New York Restoration Project), Cy Adler (Shorewalkers), Raymond Gastil (Van Alen Institute), Mary Brosnahan Sullivan (Coalition for the Homeless), and Andrew Darrell (Environmental Defense); with activists Marci Benstock and Albert Butzel; with photographers Barbara Mensch, Stephen Scheer, Margaret Morton, and Stanley Greenberg; with officials Robert Gill (Port Authority of New York and New Jersey) and Heather Sporn (New York State Department of Transportation); with landscape architects Maggie Ruddick and Len Hopper; with journalists David White and Thomas R. Flagg; with Professors William Kornblum (CUNY Graduate Center) and Elaine Savory (New School); with Eric Washington of the Manhattanville Historical Society; with Judy Berdy (Roosevelt Island Historical Society) and John Pettit West III (Community Board 6).

I want to thank the friends who accompanied me on waterfront jaunts: Tom Beller, Leon Falk, Vivian Gornick, Larry Joseph, Elizabeth Mitchell, Ann Patty, James Sanders, David Shapiro, Jack Stevens, and Lee Zimmerman. I would also like to thank those friends of mine, such as Lynn Freed, Ann Snitow, Ben Taylor, and Sharon Thompson, whose enthusiastic good wishes and advice helped me more than I can say. I received tremendous support from the faculty and administration of Hofstra University, my employer. I also got much valuable input from the other research fellows at the Center for Scholars and Writers (especially Ileen DeVaux, Ann Mendelsohn, Francisco Goldman, Claudia Roth Pierrepont, Joseph Cady, Steve Fraser, Rachel Hadas, Eiko Ikegami, and Jonathan Bush), and the staff and incomparable librarians of the New York Public Library. Barbara Hirschmann was a sage support throughout. I am very indebted to Vijay Seshadri and Kent Jones for reading the first draft and offering suggestions. I thank my editor at Crown, Doug Pepper, both for his enthusiasm and for trying to save me from my worst self, not always successfully.

Finally, it pleases me to thank two most important, lovely, and helpful individuals: my wife, Cheryl, who listened patiently to more waterfront harangues than anyone should have to, smoothing the way meanwhile for my preoccupation; and my daughter, Lily, whose sparkle and strength inspired me always—the new waterfront, if and when it is ever completed, will be hers to inherit, embrace, or dismiss, as she sees fit.

INDEX